THE ENGLISH NOVEL

WALTER ALLEN *has written:*

THE ENGLISH NOVEL

A SHORT CRITICAL HISTORY

by

WALTER ALLEN

A Dutton **dep** *Paperback*

NEW YORK

E. P. DUTTON

To

L. P. HARTLEY

in friendship and admiration

WALTER ALLEN was born in Birmingham, England, and is a graduate in English of Birmingham University. He is a novelist and critic and has contributed articles and reviews to most of the leading English literary journals. For the past few years he has been closely associated with the *New Statesman* and has broadcast frequently on books for the B.B.C.

THE ENGLISH NOVEL was first published in 1954.

CONTENTS

ACKNOWLEDGMENTS

THE AUTHOR AND PUBLISHERS are grateful to the following for permission to quote copyright passages from the books named:

E. M. Forster and Edward Arnold, Ltd., for *Howard's End, A Passage to India, A Room with a View,* and *Aspects of the Novel;* Mrs. Frieda Lawrence and William Heinemann, Ltd., for *Sons and Lovers, Aaron's Rod,* and *The Letters of D. H. Lawrence;* Wyndham Lewis and Methuen & Co., Ltd., for *The Writer and the Absolute;* W. Somerset Maugham and William Heinemann, Ltd., for *Of Human Bondage;* Leonard Woolf for *The Common Reader* and *Mrs. Dalloway* by Virginia Woolf; the Trustees of the James Joyce Estate and Jonathan Cape, Ltd., for *Portrait of the Artist as a Young Man,* and John Lane The Bodley Head, Ltd., for *Ulysses* by James Joyce; the Trustees of the Hardy Estate and Macmillan & Co., Ltd., for *The Return of the Native, Far from the Madding Crowd, The Mayor of Caster-bridge,* and *Jude the Obscure;* the Owners of the Copyright and Methuen & Co. for *Anna of the Five Towns,* and Cassell & Co., Ltd., for Arnold Bennett's *Journals;* John Farquharson on behalf of the Estate of the late Henry James for *Partial Portraits, The Portrait of a Lady,* and *The Wings of the Dove,* and John Lehmann, Ltd., for *The Princess Casamassima* (Chiltern Library); the author's executors for *The First Men in the Moon* by H. G. Wells.

Constable & Co., Ltd., for *Soliloquies in England* by George Santayana; J. M. Dent & Sons, Ltd., for *Lord Jim* and *Nostromo* by Joseph Conrad; Victor Gollancz, Ltd., for *Return to Yesterday* by Ford Madox Ford; William

Heinemann, Ltd., for *The Forsyte Saga* by John Galsworthy; John Lane The Bodley Head, Ltd., for *The Good Soldier* by Ford Madox Ford; MacGibbon & Kee, Ltd., for *Portraits* by Desmond MacCarthy; John Murray, Ltd., for *Landscape into Art* by Kenneth Clark; The Oxford University Press for *The Dickens World* by Humphry House, and *The Autobiography of Mark Rutherford* and *The Revolution in Tanner's Lane* by Mark Rutherford; Charles Scribner's Sons, Ltd., for *The Art of the Novel* by Richard P. Blackmur; and Martin Secker & Warburg, Ltd., for *The Liberal Imagination* by Lionel Trilling.

AUTHOR'S PREFACE

IT WAS SIR WALTER RALEIGH, in his little book on the English novel, who noted that novelists had commonly been great readers of novels. No doubt it would be surprising if this were not so, and certainly novelists have not changed in this respect since Raleigh wrote his book sixty years ago. For my own part, when I look back, it seems that the main concern of my life since I was a schoolboy has been reading novels, discussing novels with friends, writing about novels, and trying to write novels myself, and all these activities exist in my mind as a single activity. This book, then, which has been written over a period of years spent also in reviewing contemporary fiction and writing fiction of my own, is primarily an account of what the history of the novel in England looks like to someone who follows the craft of fiction himself.

Even so, it is not the book I originally planned to write. That was to have taken the story down to our own times, to the novels of—to mention some obvious names—Miss Elizabeth Bowen, Mr. Joyce Cary, Mr. Greene, Mr. Waugh, Mr. Hanley, Mr. Hartley, Mr. Henry Green, and even beyond. But I was then faced with the twin problems of length and scale. If in a book on the novel of 150,000 words there is room only for 6,000 words on Dickens, the greatest genius among our novelists, how much space is one to give Mr. Cary or Mr. Greene? As put, of course, the question admits of no real answer. Our relation to Mr. Cary and Mr. Greene is different from that to Dickens. Our immediate interest in Mr. Cary and Mr. Greene is that they are our contemporaries, the material of their art our world, our lives. Because of this, we cannot hope to be able to judge them as we can novelists of the past. The critical approach to our contemporaries must differ from the critical approach to writers of the past, if only because we are too near our contemporaries and share too much with them the situation of our own time.

The obvious novelists with which to end my study seemed therefore to be Joyce and Lawrence, emerging as they did round about 1914, the year which marks a break in so many other things beside fiction. Joyce and Lawrence, with their lesser coevals, represent something like a watershed between the novel of the past and the contemporary novel. The contemporary novel has its own problems, its own excellencies, and, I would say, its own masters, masters for us however different they may appear to our grandchildren. These are to be the subject of a later book.

My indebtednesses. Innumerable of course, and to a whole host of people and books and reviews; to friends with whom I have talked for years, and long before this present work was even dreamed of; to how many articles in periodicals and reviews of new fiction, those of Edwin Muir during his long spell on *The Listener,* for example, published during the past twenty-five years; to books on subjects formally quite unrelated to fiction. The critics who have shaped or influenced both my general view of the novel as a literary form and my opinions on individual novelists will, I imagine, be obvious enough to those familiar with the field. Wherever possible, I have given specific references in the text. Here, there is room only for a list of the books which I know have influenced me. I hope it may be useful to any who, having read this work, wish to consider the subject more widely and more deeply.

First, the classics of criticism of the novel. The introductory chapters to the eighteen books of *Tom Jones*; Sir Walter Scott's *Lives of the Novelists*; Hazlitt's *The English Comic Writers*; Trollope's *Autobiography*; the relevant essays in Walter Bagehot's *Literary Studies* and Leslie Stephen's *Hours in a Library*; Henry James's prefaces collected in *The Art of the Novel*, with R. P. Blackmur's introduction; the relevant essays in James's *Partial Portraits* and *Notes on Novelists*; and the correspondence on fiction between James and Stevenson edited by Janet Adam Smith under the title *Henry James and Robert Louis Stevenson*.

Then the books on what may be called the theory of the novel. *The Craft of Fiction*, by Percy Lubbock; *Aspects of the Novel*, by E. M. Forster; *The Structure of the Novel*, by Edwin Muir; Elizabeth Bowen's "Notes on Writing a Novel" in *Collected Impressions*; *A Treatise on the Novel* and *Some Principles of Fiction*, both by Robert Liddell.

A few collections of essays on novelists or various aspects of fiction have been especially valuable because of the attitudes towards fiction that subsume them. *The Common Reader*, by Virginia Woolf; *Early Victorian Novelists*, by David Cecil; *In My Good Books*, *The Living Novel*, and *Books in General*, all by V. S. Pritchett; *The Great Tradition*, by F. R. Leavis; *The Liberal Imagination*, by Lionel Trilling; *Axel's Castle* and *The Wound and the Bow*, by Edmund Wilson; and *An Introduction to the English Novel*, by Arnold Kettle.

Some passages in this book have appeared, generally in a rather different form, in *The Times Literary Supplement*, *The New Statesman and Nation*, and *New Writing*. To the editors of these I make, gratefully, the usual acknowledgments.

WALTER ALLEN

INTRODUCTION

LITERARY HISTORIANS, horrified it seems by the newness of the form, have commonly thought it necessary to provide the novel with a respectable antiquity, much as the genealogist fits out the parvenu with an impeccable family tree. In their own way they have been very successful; at any rate they have succeeded admirably in confusing categories. They have managed to write, for instance, of the *Chanson de Roland* and *Euphues* as though these works really had some connection with the novels of Richardson and Dickens. They have devised such labels as the "Elizabethan Novel," the "Jacobean Novel," terms whose only fault is that they imply a relationship between the works so described and novels as we know them that does not exist. In their eagerness to supply the novel with a dignified ancestry they have behaved rather like a man who, setting out to write a history of the motorcar, should think it proper to begin by devoting a third of his space to the evolution of the oxcart.

The historians have been guilty of a confusion: they have assumed that the words *fiction* and *novel* are synonymous and interchangeable. They are not. At the heart of the confusion is the fact that the story is common to both. So long as men have told stories there has been fiction, whether in verse or prose, and only to this extent is it true to say that any work of fiction written before about 1670 in England is in some sense an ancestor of the novel. But the novel itself is something new. True, it has never been found easy to define, but this does not prevent us from knowing a great deal about novels. How could we fail to, when for the past two centuries the novel has been the major prose literary form in England, France, and Russia? And we can date with complete accuracy the earliest books in English that today we habitually read as novels, books, that is, that we judge by the same terms of reference as we do the works of Jane Austen, Balzac, Turgenev, and E. M. Forster. In 1678, a tinker and itinerant preacher, in jail for his religious convictions, wrote *The Pilgrim's Progress*; in 1719, a failed haberdasher who had turned journalist and government spy wrote *Robinson Crusoe,* and, three years later, *Moll Flanders*; in 1740, a middle-aged master printer wrote *Pamela.*

Even if we cannot define it, we know what to expect when we read a novel:

> We find there a close imitation of man and manners; we see the very web and texture of society as it really exists, and as we meet it when we come into the world. If poetry has "something more divine" in it, this savours more of humanity. We are brought acquainted with the motives and characters of mankind, imbibe our notions of virtue and vice from practical examples, and are taught a knowledge of the world through the airy medium of romance.

Thus Hazlitt, writing before the greater part of the world's major novels had appeared. With every major novel as it appears our interpretation of the novel as a literary form must to some extent alter; yet Hazlitt's statement of our expectations of a novel remains substantially true, as may be seen if we set beside it a statement from a modern critic, Lionel Trilling, in *The Liberal Imagination*:

> For our time the most effective agent of the moral imagination has been the novel of the last two hundred years. It was never, either aesthetically or morally, a perfect form and its faults and failures can be quickly enumerated. But its greatness and its practical usefulness lay in its unremitting work of involving the reader himself in the moral life, inviting him to put his own motives under examination, suggesting that reality is not as his conventional education has led him

to see it. It taught us, as no other genre ever did, the extent
of human variety and the value of this variety. It was the
literary form to which the emotions of understanding and
forgiveness were indigenous, as if by the definition of the
form itself.

We know, too, what the novelist sets out to do when he
writes a novel. Like any other artist the novelist is a maker.
He is making an imitation, an imitation of the life of man
on earth. He is making, it might be said, a working model
of life as he sees and feels it, his conclusions about it being
expressed in the characters he invents, the situations in
which he places them, and in the very words he chooses
for those purposes. The word "conclusion" is inescapable,
though it does not follow that the conclusions are consciously arrived at. They may indeed be at odds with the
novelist's avowed intentions. Novelists have given many
reasons for writing novels: Richardson believed he did so
to inculcate right conduct, Fielding to reform the manners
of the age, Dickens to expose social evils, Trollope to make
money by providing acceptable entertainment. The reasons
were genuine enough but rationalizations after the event.
Part of the impulse that drives the novelist to make his
imitation world must always be sheer delight in his own
skill in making; part of the time he is, as it were, taking
the observed universe to pieces and assembling it again for
the simple and naive pleasure of doing so. He can no more
help playing than a child can. And there is this further
to be noted. The child cannot help but play, but how he
plays is not under his conscious control, a fact made use of
by psychiatrists in the psychological analysis of children.
In play the child symbolizes, by the way he arranges his
toys and so on, his emotional relation to the universe. In
play he expresses a personal myth. The novelist does much
the same through his "choice" of characters and the actions
they undergo. A partial proof of this may be seen in the
fact that of all the enormous range of human types and

their relationships to one another, to society, and to God theoretically available to any novelist, only a relatively infinitesimal number find their way into the work of even the greatest. It is, too, a matter of common observation that even the greatest seem to be exploring similar types and situations from novel to novel, exploring more deeply, doubtless, in each successive book, almost as though the exploration was the product of an obsession. This indeed is so. The novelist is free to choose his material only in a limited sense, and his choice is governed by the deepest compulsions of his personality. It is these that dictate both the nature of his novels and the conclusions about life he expresses through them. This is why in judging a novel we are faced with the task of assessing not only the author's ability to create characters, for instance, but also the values inherent in the characters and their behavior. It is this latter which enables us to say that Jane Austen or Conrad is a greater novelist than such writers of the second rank as Trollope and Bennett, for all their generosity, breadth of canvas, or fidelity to the surface of observed life.

I have referred to "characters and their behavior." To some critics the words would be illegitimate. "This assumption," writes L. C. Knights in his ironically titled "How Many Children Had Lady Macbeth?" in his essays *Explorations,* "that it is the main business of the writer—other than the lyric poet—to create characters . . . long ago invaded criticism of the novel." Character, it is contended, is the creation of the reader, not the writer. Doubtless it is no argument to say that novelists themselves have commonly believed that it was an important part of their function to create characters. A novel is a totality, made up of all the words in it, and it must be judged as a totality. Of this totality characterization is only a part, yet it is plainly an essential one and the first in order of importance since, so far as the reader is concerned, without it the most profound apprehensions of man's fate count for nothing. Only through character can the novelist's apprehensions of man's fate be uttered at all.

When Mrs. Leavis, in *Fiction and the Reading Public*, says that "all a novelist need do is to provide bold outlines, and the reader will cooperate to persuade himself that he is in contact with 'real people,'" she is describing what goes on only in the reading of fiction of a low order of ambition and attainment. The more highly a novelist has organized his characters the less they can be reduced to "bold outlines." And the organization of a character is conditioned by everything in the novel. Hardy's characters, for instance, are simple enough; there is nothing particularly subtle about Gabriel Oak, Bathsheba Everdene, and Sergeant Troy, but the way we are made to see them depends not only on Hardy's rendering of them but on his execution of the novel as a whole. John Holloway has shown in *The Victorian Sage* how Hardy plants his vision of the nature of things, of which his characters are at once testimony and victims, and subdues his reader to it not by delineation of characters and action alone but also by every detail of natural description he uses, every comment he makes, and every metaphor or image he employs. Hardy's view of life, which dictates the way in which we react to his characters, is implicit in every sentence he writes. The reader is simply not free, as Mrs. Leavis seems to imply, to fill the outlines of the characters as he pleases.

This is true of the characters of all good novelists. Part of the novelist's art is to mediate between his characters and the reader; and he does so with every word he puts to paper, for every word he chooses furthers his expression of his attitude towards his characters and the total situation he is rendering. This is plainly so with novelists like Fielding, Thackeray, and Meredith, who speak in their own persons, interpreting character and action, during the course of their novels; it is just as much so with novelists like Defoe, Richardson, Flaubert, and James Joyce in *Ulysses*, who appear studiously to keep themselves out of the actions they narrate. We say they are objective; actually, they betray their opinions on their characters and situations and —inasmuch as every novel is an extended metaphor of the author's view of life—on life itself. They do so by their very choice of the characters they write about, the thoughts and feelings they give them, and the behavior and motives they attribute to them, and they cannot do otherwise.

Every novelist, then, gives us in his novels his own personal, idiosyncratic vision of the world. The vision is acted out by images of men and women. It is, so to speak, populated; and this is why we may quite legitimately talk about a novelist's "world." We mean by it the whole realm of his imagination as he has put it down on paper, and we mean further that this realm, fictitious though it is, is yet somehow a self-contained entity consistent in itself and conforming to the psychological laws which govern its creator and his response to life. To create such a world is not the highest achievement of a novelist, but unless he does so he will never reach the highest.

Since a novel is a unity consisting of every word in it, to isolate—as in practice we have to—milieu, plot, characters, dialogue, style, is to commit an act of abstraction; all these, together with what other components a novel may have, condition and qualify one another. But a consideration of one of these elements may often show where the novelist has gone wrong in his rendering of the others, and if we are deprived of the right to make these abstractions we suffer, critically, an enormous loss. Of these abstractions the most important is character. Ultimately, it is only through his characters that the novelist can succeed in what is his main social—as opposed to aesthetic—function, which is to awaken, as Graham Greene, echoing Lawrence in *Lady Chatterley's Lover* and paralleling Trilling in *The Liberal Imagination,* has said, "sympathetic comprehension in our readers. . . . The novelist's task is to draw his own like-

ness to any human being, the guilty as much as the innocent."

It is a sign of the relative newness of the form that in
England no popular novelist a hundred years ago could
have written of his aims as Graham Greene does. The novel
emerged from the underworld of taste and its development
has been conditioned by this. Until quite recently, the only
men who have taken the novel seriously have been novelists, and, often relatively uneducated men, they have frequently brought little to the study of it but their own
experience as novelists, novelists, moreover, who interpreted
their craft in no very exalted way.

The notion of the novel as a literary form having something to do with art in the sense of being consciously made
and shaped to an aesthetic end is quite new. Though there
have been few more consummate artists in the novel than
Fielding and Jane Austen, for the greater part of its course
in England the novel has been naive, the product of men of
genius modest enough to believe they were fulfilling their
duty as long as they were pleasing an unexacting public.

Among novelists themselves this view of the novel has
largely disappeared. Rightly or wrongly, the novelist has
come to see himself as an artist; wrongly, Sir Desmond Mac-
Carthy would seem to say. He writes in an essay on Trollope, in *Portraits*:

> It is tenable that one of the mistakes of late nineteenth-
> century and early twentieth-century criticism has been to
> regard the novel as "a work of art" in the same sense that a
> sonata, a picture, or a poem is a work of art. It is extremely
> doubtful whether the aim of the novel is to make an aes-
> thetic appeal. Passages in it may do so; but it aims also at
> satisfying our curiosity about life as much as satisfying the
> aesthetic sense. . . . I am inclined myself to regard it as a
> bastard form of art, rightly concerned with many human in-
> terests which the maker of beautiful things must eschew.
> (*Vide* Jane Austen.)

It may be admitted that the impulses that move men to write novels are many and obscure, and not all of them are aesthetic. Yet the opposition Sir Desmond makes between the aesthetic appeal and the satisfaction of our curiosity about life is surely false; it need not exist at all; the two may be fused. This is evident if we consider a poem, Wordsworth's Immortality Ode, for instance. Wordsworth's aim there was certainly not solely to create beauty; he was concerned just as much with making statements about a number of things of great importance to himself; about growing old, about growing up, and about immortality. These statements exist in the form they do, move us as they do, because they are made poetically. The poem is an entity, a thing in itself, an end in itself. The pleasure we get from it comes from the fact that it is as it is; if it were something else our pleasure would be different. And we do not "understand" the poem by paraphrasing it, by "translating" it into prose. The meaning of the poem cannot be separated out from the form of the poem or the way of expression; the meaning, in fact, is the poem and the poem is the meaning. Something has been made, and our curiosity about life, in this instance our curiosity about Wordsworth's beliefs, has been satisfied *because* our aesthetic sense, if that is the term we decide to use, has been satisfied. If our aesthetic sense were not satisfied we should feel the poet had not succeeded wholly in telling the truth—*his* truth—and our feeling of curiosity about the truth he is trying to express would to that extent have been thwarted.

There are few novels we can discuss as we can the Immortality Ode, and one reason for this is the much greater compactness of poetry as compared with prose, the much greater degree of crystallization which takes place in a poem. We can hold even so complex a work as the Immortality Ode whole in our mind, as we cannot often a novel. Sir Desmond MacCarthy cites Jane Austen's, which are ideal for our purpose because of the limits she deliberately chose to work within. But I cannot agree that her concern with beauty led her to eschew "many human interests." She satisfies our curiosity about life completely—about the life she is prepared to describe for us, which is as much as we may ask of any novelist.

We should be silly to blame Trollope, who certainly satisfies our curiosity about a great many things, for failing to satisfy also our sense of design, of beauty. If a novelist can do both we are entitled to say he is greater—other things being equal—than one who does not.

But Sir Desmond MacCarthy is at least right in this: if our notions of what a novel ought to be prevent us from seeing the virtues of a work which does not fit into them, so much the worse for our notions of the novel. In art we have to put up with what we are given, and it is the artist who is the dictator, not the critic. The critic who attempts to survey the course of English fiction during its two hundred and fifty years of life cannot take up a rigid position, if he hopes to say anything to the point on the individual works that make up his subject. He must rejoice in formal beauty where he finds it but not overestimate the consequences of the lack of it. Where he must not fail is in understanding why works that seem secondary to us were important in their own day, both in their own right and as transmitting genes of development to the future, and, where major works are concerned, in responding to the quality of life in them that makes them living forces not only for modern readers but also for modern writers. Above all, perhaps, he must put out of his mind any notion of evolution in the form of the novel that can be equated with improvement. There is nothing in the development of art analogous with material progress. Art does not get better and better. Its manifestations merely change, and Richardson is as perfect in his way as Henry James in his. And they exist side by side, with Fielding and Conrad, and Dickens and Jane Austen and Scott and all the rest, in a continuous present. Somehow their value for their own times and their value for us now must be held in the mind simultaneously.

THE ENGLISH NOVEL

THE BEGINNINGS

THE COMPARATIVELY sudden appearance at the turn of the seventeenth century of the novel as we know it was a manifestation of a marked change in the direction of men's interest. Comparable and related changes, sometimes resulting in new forms in art and literature, had of course occurred in the arts before. Until about the fifteenth century, for instance, there was no such thing as portrait painting as we know it. It began as representations of the Virgin or the Holy Family. Then, as the Renaissance advanced, the painter's attitude to his subject changed; he went on painting Virgins, but more and more his model is obviously a flesh-and-blood and not at all virginal peasant girl or great lady. After a space of years the pretext disappeared entirely; to paint a woman it was no longer necessary for the painter to pretend that he was painting the image of the Mother of God.

Similarly a change occurred in English literature round about the years 1580-90, a change so radical as to appear a new mutation in literature: the sudden irruption of Elizabethan drama. Before 1580 nothing existed in the form of a play in English from which anyone could possibly have prophesied the magnificent outburst of Marlowe and Kyd and the still greater dramatists who followed them. Elizabethan drama has its prehistory, but its beginnings in Marlowe and the University Wits are simply not explicable in terms of medieval mystery plays and miracle plays or the

Senecan tragedies of Sir Thomas Sackville. The change from the mystery play to Marlowe was a qualitative change; it represented a change in men's interests, in their attitudes to themselves, to one another, and to the world about them.

So with the appearance of the novel round about 1700. Nothing that preceded it in the way of prose fiction can explain it. There were no classical models for it. It is true that today we can read the account of Trimalchio's feast in the *Satyricon* of Petronius as a wonderful piece of realistic fiction, and no doubt it was known to some of the English eighteenth-century novelists; but if it influenced our novel at all it did not do so until the novel was already an invented and accepted form. In any case, influences from the past can only operate when there are minds receptive to them. There can scarcely have been any one book that has more profoundly shaped the novel as a whole than Cervantes' *Don Quixote*. It was translated into English in 1612, but we have to wait another one hundred and thirty years, until Fielding's *Joseph Andrews* in 1742, before we see the influence of the great Spaniard truly at work in our literature; and then, by becoming part of Fielding, Cervantes became part of the English novel.

The drama apart, the only works in English before Bunyan that have the quality of novels as we know them today, though they do not have their form, are some things in Chaucer, the prologue to *The Canterbury Tales* perhaps, the *Wife of Bath's Tale* and *Troilus and Criseyde*, together with his Scottish disciple Henryson's *Testament of Cresseid*. In these works of Chaucer's there is a warm delight in character for its own sake and a compassionate realism in the observation of behavior comparable to what we find in the novels of Fielding, while the grimness and relentlessness of Henryson's *Testament* may well suggest to the modern reader the Naturalistic novelists of the later nineteenth century. Yet while we almost automatically read *Troilus and Criseyde* and the *Testament of Cresseid* as though they were novels in verse, we have to remember that readers of the fourteenth and fifteenth centuries saw them very differently and found in them qualities lost to us almost entirely. They were works of their world and time. It happens that they transcended both. Perhaps they might have bridged the gulf between the medieval metrical romance and something like the novel we know today, but Chaucer and Henryson were an end, not a beginning. Chaucer's death in 1400 coincided with a change in the structure of the language, and after him the art of poetry was more or less lost for a hundred and fifty years. When it was rediscovered it flowered marvelously in Elizabethan drama.

And the dominance of the drama from about 1580 to 1640 is in itself one reason why one could not expect great prose novels during the Elizabethan and Jacobean periods. Every age has its major literary form, to which the most able and ambitious spirits of the age are irresistibly attracted whether it suits their especial talents or not. It is a commonplace that the great periods of the novel have not also been great periods in drama, and it was in the drama that the most vital impulses of Elizabethan literature found their expression. The drama was the form that fiction took. But it was not a fiction of a kind similar to that which we find later in the novel. The Elizabethans were interested in quite other things than those that have fascinated the novelists. From its very nature the novel demands a greater or lesser degree of realism, of fidelity to the facts of the world as men commonly see them. The Elizabethans, Jonson apart, cared practically nothing for realism; theirs was not a drama of manners, and their theme was not man in society. Their notion of character was quite different from ours, and for them theatrical effectiveness was much more important than plausibility. Nor did coherence and probability of story mean much to them. Their audiences asked not for a mirroring of life as they knew it—though they were sometimes given it—or for convincing renderings of lifelike characters in a lifelike world, but poetry, language in every way heightened and, in a sense, extreme, with characters that could utter such language. In essence Elizabethan drama is probably nearer to opera than to the novel, though this does not mean that the Elizabethan dramatists were incapable of creating the kind of characters we find in the later drama and in the novel; Shakespeare is full of them, but they move in worlds that are largely nonrealistic.

Probably the most important difference between us and the Elizabethans, the one that subsumes all the others, is their attitude towards history. History, as we understand it, for them scarcely existed. They do not seem to have thought of the past as something unlike the present; such a notion as the spirit of an age was alien to them. *King Lear,* for instance, is set in pre-Saxon Britain, *Henry IV* in fourteenth-century England, *Hamlet* in eighth-century Denmark, but these plays are not "historical" in our meaning. They are not plays about ancient Britain, Denmark in the Dark Ages, or medieval England; they exist and are played out at one and the same period, and the period is outside history in our sense. For the Elizabethans, it seems, time was an element through which the successive generations of men moved; it was not something that changed men and made one generation of men unlike another.

But the novelist must deal with men in a specific place at a specific time, and the novelists, especially the greatest, have normally been acutely conscious of their time and the qualities in it that appear to distinguish it from other times. This idea of history, of society as a constantly changing structure, is not apparent until after the Great Civil War (1642-52). Dryden, for instance, particularly in his criticism, sounds a strikingly modern note as compared with the Elizabethans.

Yet the effect of the Elizabethan drama, and of Shakespeare above all, on the novel in England can scarcely be overestimated. It was immeasurably greater than that of the fiction of the period. To read the great Elizabethan plays as novels is no doubt to find them unsatisfactory as novels, but as soon as they were printed this is how they must have been read. During the seventeenth century they were widely read, and one obvious effect on the early novels is seen in the typographical layout of Bunyan's *Life and Death of Mr. Badman* and Richardson's *Pamela:* Bunyan sets out his dialogue as though it were the texts of a printed play; Richardson precedes his novel with a dramatis personae. These are perhaps trivial instances; the real influence was elsewhere, all-pervasive and so more easily felt than defined. It shows itself, however, in the mixed form of the traditional English novel, in the intermingling of tragedy and comedy. The very fact that Shakespeare wrote in English made the novel as it was written in nineteenth-century France, for example, impossible in England except as an occasional sport. Since Shakespeare has always been the ultimate standard of comparison for imaginative writing in our language, the novel was bound to approximate to the mixed form he followed. Ways of looking at life original in him have become ingrained habits of mind in his successors. The English novelists are Shakespearean often without knowing it. Behind the shrewd, humorous peasants of Scott, George Eliot, and Hardy, for instance, who are always subsidiary to the main action, lie Shakespeare's rustic characters. In the same way we see his heroines, those of the romantic comedies especially, behind Fielding's and Meredith's. And so long as Shakespeare is performed and read in England his influence on the novel will continue, simply because for us his work is the final standard of imaginative writing.

The most important work of prose fiction in English before *The Pilgrim's Progress* was written more than a century before the rise of Elizabethan drama. This was Mallory's *Morte d'Arthur*. Great work of prose though it is, it is by no stretch of imagination a novel. If we take it as such, we might as well accept *The Faërie Queene* as a novel too. It is the final gathering together, expressed more beautifully than ever before, of the legends of Arthur and the search for the Grail which so obsessed the medieval mind. When we come to what is called the Elizabethan novel we may all the more marvel at the achievement of Elizabethan poetry and drama. It would be wrong to imply that the only interest in the prose fiction of that age is now academic; many of these works may still be read with pleasure, but scarcely ever with that we derive from novels. Lyly's *Euphues*, published in 1579, has a story of a kind, but that is not its main interest either for its author or for us. Lyly uses his sketchy story in order, in the first part of his book, to lament the frailty of woman, the folly of youth, and the illusions of love, and in the second part, *Euphues and His England*, to celebrate the glories of England and her queen. What particularly attracted attention to *Euphues* and still gives it more than a curiosity value is Lyly's style. Parodied in his lifetime by Shakespeare among others, and often derided since, it was enormously influential in its day, on no one more than Shakespeare himself as a young man. It was a wholehearted attempt to give to prose the formal order and complexity of structure we find in much Elizabethan poetry. It is, in fact, pattern writing, self-conscious, highly artificial, rhetorical. Witty and often pointed, it appeared ridiculous in the eyes of its contemporaries and of later generations because of what was least important in it, the constant use of analogies from a fantastic natural history. Strip it of these ornamentations and what is left is a prose fundamentally not very dissimilar from that of Dr. Johnson.

Since *Euphues* was written in the form of letters it has been seen as a precursor of Richardson's novels. This seems to me so absurd as to be no more worth arguing about than the theory that because *Arcadia,* published in 1590, contains a character named Pamela, Richardson therefore borrowed the name of his first heroine from Sidney. As a work of literature *Arcadia* is of a greater stature than *Euphues,* but it is no more a novel. Sidney, too, aimed at giving prose something of the formal pattern of verse, but, a better poet than Lyly, he was able to do something else, to give his prose, on occasion at any rate, the beauty of poetry. It is for these incidental felicities that we read *Arcadia* today. As a pastoral romance it is a superb example of the Elizabethan lack of the historical sense. Arcadia is, in fact, a dream world compounded of Sidney's knowledge of Christianity and classical antiquity, medieval chivalry, and Renaissance luxury. Almost intolerably prolix, it expresses, through a long tale in which nymphs and shepherds live side by side with princesses and kings, Sidney's conception of the knightly code.

So far as England is concerned, *Arcadia* was the first of many prose romances which, pastoral or otherwise, are of a kind. Young men of noble birth are shipwrecked among shepherds and shepherdesses in a vaguely ancient-Greek landscape; the course of the action always includes mistaken identity and love which, however hopeless it may seem, is always true. Such works include Robert Greene's *Menaphon* and *The Carde of Fancie,* Thomas Lodge's *Rosalynde,* and Emanuel Ford's *Ornatus and Artesia.* They contain nothing of reality, which is no criticism of them, because the impression of reality was not what their authors were after. If the stories of, say, *As You Like It, The Winter's Tale,* and *The Faithful Shepherdess* had been written as simple prose narratives, with none of the attempts at characterization that are essential to drama of any kind, if only as a rough guide to the players, the results would have been much like these. What they still have, and what has kept them fresh and sweet, is a quality of lyricism which makes them the prose equivalent of the Elizabethan song and the limpid pastoral verses of Robert Greene himself.

The romantic and pastoral, however, is only one part of Elizabethan prose fiction. Something akin to the realistic drama, the splendid plays of Jonson, Massinger's *A New Way to Pay Old Debts,* and Beaumont and Fletcher's *The Knight of the Burning Pestle,* exists in prose fiction, in a cruder and less sophisticated form. The importance of these works is that they were *popular;* they were what the people read, as distinct from the fashionable society which read the pastorals. They had, therefore, little or no literary dignity or status; often they were, in more senses than one, "underworld" literature, the counterpart of the pulps, crime stories, tabloids, and "true confessions" of our own day. They were not always put out as fiction; in Greene's *Groatsworth of Wit, bought with a Million of Repentance* and the later *Repentance of Robert Greene,* the author of *Menaphon,* taking his own dissolute life as his theme, preached in a much more direct prose than any he used in his pastorals powerful sermons on the text "Man's time is not of itself so short, but it is more shortened by sin." In his "coney-catching" pamphlets, he exposed with gusto and moral aplomb the common swindles and rogueries of the time. Ten years later he was followed by Dekker, with such pamphlets as *The Wonderful Year, 1603,* an account of the plague that swept London and its consequences, *The Seven Deadly Sinnes of London* and *The Guls Horn-Book,* all of which were "exposures" of the practices of crooks, chiselers, and confidence tricksters not very different, except in the degree of artistry brought to bear on them, from Ben Jonson's exposures of metropolitan life in *The Alchemist* and *Bartholomew Fair.* These pamphlets were not written as fiction, but they have much more life in them than most Elizabethan fiction, and they reveal that insatiable interest in the affairs of the everyday world which had to be absorbed into prose fiction before it could become the novel.

Something like this interest had already appeared in Thomas Deloney, in whom the London tradesmen found their spokesman. Before turning prose writer he had been a silk weaver and peddler, and the author of many ballads on the wrongs of the day. In his stories *Jack of Newbury* (1597), *The Gentle Craft* (1598), and *Thomas of Reading* (1600), he celebrated the exploits of clothiers and shoemakers for the benefit of clothiers and shoemakers themselves. His characters, Jack of Newbury, Thomas of Reading, and the rest seem to have been actual historic personages, though this is the least important thing about them. They appear as the heroes of semicomic or semi-heroic incidents, never subtle and often pretty slapstick, and behind them we feel a whole tradition of humble popular tales. In Deloney Shakespeare's groundlings assert themselves and discover their sense of native dignity, and we find nothing like this anywhere else in the literature of the time.

Deloney's work is pure homespun; the realism is rough and ready, the writing naive, unaffected, and direct. His genuine dramatic power is shown by the fact that, reading the account in *Thomas of Reading* of the murder of Thomas Cole and of the behavior of the murderers afterwards, an innkeeper and his wife, one immediately thinks of the murder of Duncan and the recriminations of Macbeth and Lady Macbeth. *Macbeth* was written later than Deloney's story. It is not known whether Shakespeare knew it, but the parallels are striking. This in itself is tribute enough to Deloney's force of imagination and expression.

Today, the most widely read work of Elizabethan fiction is Thomas Nash's *The Unfortunate Traveller, or The Life of Jack Wilton*, published in 1594. In content, if not in atmosphere, it looks back to Marlowe's *The Jew of Malta* and forward to Webster's great tragedies. It is, in other words, a powerful expression of that mingling of horror and fascination which the Italy of the time, with its unrivaled luxury and its glittering vices and corruption, held for Elizabethan Englishmen. As a novel, or as novel *in posse,* it has commonly been overrated, because critics have fallen under the spell of Nash's prose. Understandably, for as a writer of imaginative prose he was unequaled in his age by any except Shakespeare, Jonson, and Webster. And his prose is still a living thing; in our own time it has influenced both James Joyce and Wyndham Lewis. The following description of a scholar of Wittenberg conveys something of its quality:

> A bursten-belly inkhorn orator called Vanderhulke, they picked out to present him [the Duke of Saxony] with an oration, one that had a sulphurous big swollen large face, like a Saracen, eyes like two Kentish oysters, a mouth that opened as wide every time he spake, as one of those old knit trap doors, a beard as though it had been made of a bird's nests plucked in pieces, which consisteth of straw, hair, and dirt mixed together.

Structurally, Nash's prose is primitive, a piling up of simple sentences that go on and on breathlessly. But within its limits, nothing more racy, graphic, and energetic has ever been written. In its immediacy of effect, its arresting, galvanizing imagery from everyday life, it is the complete antithesis of the kinds of prose Lyly and Sidney wrote. It is rooted in an enormous zest for the physical attributes of life, for the hurly-burly and confusion of living. It enlarges and exaggerates whatever it touches into the comic and the grotesque; and it renders incomparably the external of things. It is very much a satirist's prose, the counterpart in many respects of Ben Jonson's dramatic blank verse, and in Nash, as in Jonson, we encounter a way of rendering life—from the outside, so that the figures that move through it appear almost as monstrous puppets who are yet vibrantly alive because of their creators' vitality and inordinate zest for whatever captures the eye—that we meet throughout the course of the English novel, in Smollett, Marryat, Dickens, Wells, Joyce, and Wyndham Lewis especially.

The Unfortunate Traveller remains the most sheerly *enjoyable* of all Elizabethan prose fictions. But it is not in any modern sense a novel. It is a rogue or picaresque story given a measure of actuality because pegged down to a definite series of historic events. It opens with a scene in the English camp before Tournay, which was besieged by Henry VIII in 1513, and ends with the Field of the Cloth of Gold. Real happenings and real persons, the siege of Leyden, Erasmus and Thomas More, Luther and Cornelius Agrippa, are introduced to suggest literal truth, the impression of which is also aimed at by the narration of the story by Jack Wilton himself, the page of the Earl of Surrey, whom he accompanies on his travels through Germany and Italy. Plot scarcely exists; the story is merely a string of incidents and intrigues of which Wilton is the hero, and the incidents described are pure sensationalism, an "exposure" of the wickedness of Renaissance Italy as the Elizabethan loved to imagine it. At one point in the story, for example, Jack and his Italian wife, Diamente, are arrested through the machinations of an evil Jew, to whom Jack is given as a slave. The Jew sells him to a physician as subject for dissection; he escapes, and passes into the power of the Pope's mistress, who wants him as a lover. To her the Jew sends Diamente as a present, with orders to poison her secretly. Jack and Diamente reveal the plot, and the Jew is arrested and tortured to death, in one of Nash's most brilliant passages of description. But while the Pope's mistress goes to visit the Pope, Jack and his wife decamp with her jewels. The whole is a series of improvisations calculated to horrify and thrill the stay-at-home Englishman. What gives it its value is Nash's attitude towards the events related; he is humorous, satirical, antiromantic, possessed of insatiable gusto, and these qualities combine to knit the sinews of his prose.

It was during this period that the English began to acquire the habit of reading, in the absence of which the writing of novels is scarcely conceivable. *The Cambridge Bibliography of English Literature* lists one hundred and fifty prose tales written in English and published between 1500 and 1660, the great majority of them later than 1580; and there are almost as many translations from the French, Italian, and Spanish. To these may be added the published scripts of plays, which must have been read as stories.

There is, however, a reason besides the dominance of the drama which explains why novels as we know them were impossible during the sixteenth century and the first half of the seventeenth: it is one of language. In the blank verse line, the Elizabethans and Jacobeans had created one of the supplest and most subtle instruments of expression ever devised. But their prose, for the ordinary purposes of prose, was clumsy. It could be noble in eloquence, as in Taylor's and Donne's sermons, that is to say where speech was heightened to oratory, and when it followed the spoken language of the people, as in Deloney and some of the playwrights, it could achieve an admirable rough-and-ready directness. But it was not until the later years of the seventeenth century that an English prose came into general use flexible enough, articulated enough, for the task of analyzing character and the ordering and arranging of significant detail.

Here, as in so much else, the watershed between the old and the new was the Civil War (1642-52) and the years that led to the restoration of Charles II. The new prevailed, even though the Stuarts were brought back to the throne, but as we try to define the shifts in mental climate and habits of thought which ultimately produced an atmosphere in which novels could be written, we are faced with confusion and contradiction. During the greater part of the seventeenth century what prose fiction there was was merely a pale imitation of French originals, which in translation were highly popular in court circles. The many-volumed *Astrée* of Honoré d'Urfé portrayed a world of Arcadian innocence which had no more to do with real life than Sidney's *Arcadia,* and yet the landscape described was that of an actual country, the scenes of the author's childhood and youth. There is a similar contradiction in the interminable, high-flown romances of Mme. de Scudéry, the *Grand Cyrus* (1649-53) and *Clélie* (1656-60). Absurd to the modern reader as these books are—Sir Walter Scott calculated that the hero of the *Grand Cyrus* slew a hundred thousand men with his own hand—the characters, for all their exaggeration, were recognizable portraits of men and women of fashionable Paris, and the amusements the author attributed to her Persians and Romans were the amusements of French society of the day. It was from such works that, after the Restoration, the dramatists got the inspiration for and the spirit of their "heroic" plays, which appear now to have been written, as Dr. Johnson said, "with a seeming determination to glut the public with dramatic wonders, to exhibit in its highest elevation a theatrical meteor of incredible love and impossible valor, and to leave no room for a wilder flight to the extravagance of posterity."

The fact is, what we should now call the scientific spirit operated only intermittently. The scientific and the magical still existed side by side, and despite the absurdities of the romances and the heroic drama, one can see, right at the beginning of the century, examples not quite of scientific interest in character but at least of attempts to define fairly precisely human types. An English edition of the *Characters* of the late Greek writer Theophrastus had appeared in 1592, and its influence, probably reinforced by that of Bacon's essays, with their trenchancy and succinctness of analysis, led during succeeding years to a crop of books in which the nature and behavior of such types as the coward and the hypocrite, the good merchant and the happy milkmaid, were diagnosed and described. Perhaps charactery was never anything more than a literary exercise, but its relation to the novel is obvious. The first magnificent fruit of its marriage with reality, however, is seen in works of history, especially in the great portrait gallery of Clarendon's *History of the Rebellion*. This was inevitable. Before the novel, which must to a greater or less degree be an imitation of the actual world, could be born, there had to be works already in existence which were not imitations, that is not fiction, but faithful descriptions of the actual world. So, among the strongest influences on what was becoming the novel were works of history like Clarendon's and soberly careful accounts of real life adventure, distant countries, and strange peoples like Dampier's *A New Voyage Round the World*.

Such books supplied the corrective to the undisciplined fantasies of the writers of fiction. For a period of about seventy years before the publication of *Pamela* in 1740 we are, as it were, in frontier territory, in a sort of Alsace-Lorraine of literature. The blood of the inhabitants is mixed; some are obviously, whatever they conceived themselves to be, pure novelists; in others, other strains predominate. During the greater part of this period what we look for in the novel today, observation of manners and the rendering of the changing panorama of actual life, we find not so much in the writers of fiction as in diarists like Pepys and Evelyn, for the arts of autobiography and memoir writing were a twin birth with that of the novel. In France and Spain romances of real life had already appeared in the form of works written in reaction against the high-flown artificiality and Arcadianism of writers like D'Urfé and Mme. de Scudéry, works that celebrated, generally in a vein of swaggering cynicism, the exploits of rogues. These romances were translated and imitated but produced nothing of literary value; the most famous of the English versions, Head's *The English Rogue* (1665), is a dreary, ill-written compilation, describing the life of "Meriton Latroon, a witty extravagant," from his boyhood, through prison, to his departure for the East Indies. There is no attempt at characterization, and the story is merely the stringing together of facetious and sensational incidents.

When at this time reality did enter English fiction it came from the least expected of quarters and in the least expected of forms. Bunyan was fifty when he published *The Pilgrim's Progress* in 1678. He had of course no thought of writing a novel; indeed, we read it as a novel today simply because of the amount of felt and observed reality that it contains. It was written as a religious allegory, as a tract or a sermon. Scholars have tracked down works that may have influenced Bunyan and he may conceivably have read. They do not matter in the least: Bunyan was a transcendent genius, the first to appear in English prose fiction of any kind, and his work is as original as anything in literature can be. The kind of work he wrote was completely unheralded and, it has been said, had no influence on any fiction that came after it, but of that I am not so sure. It is possible to interpret "influence" altogether too narrowly. Within a comparatively short time after its appearance *The Pilgrim's Progress* became the peculiar possession of the English people, of all classes, to an extent beyond any other work except the Bible. Its influence, like the Bible's, is therefore strictly incalculable. One can only say that if it had not been written the English people would be different from what they are. At the lowest, it set a standard in storytelling, vivid characterization, and natural dialogue which must have influenced, however little they may have realized it, a host of later novelists.

An allegory of the Christian in search of salvation; even

so, if the word "picaresque" is now stretched, as it commonly is, to mean any novel in which the hero takes a journey whose course plunges him into all sorts, conditions, and classes of men, *The Pilgrim's Progress* is not so different in form from the conventional picaresque novel. Christian's progress is nothing if not a journey through the world, and though the characters encountered on the way have only moral tags for names they are unerringly characterized by the words Bunyan puts into their mouths. They come alive in their speech, and come alive immediately:

> *Obstinate:* What are the things you seek, since you leave all the world to find them?
> *Christian:* I seek an inheritance incorruptible, undefiled, and that fadeth not away, and it is laid up in heaven, and safe there, to be bestowed, at the time appointed, on them that diligently seek it. Read it so, if you will, in my book.
> *Obstinate:* Tush! away with your book. Will you go back with us or no?
> *Christian:* No, not I, because I have laid my hand to the plough.
> *Obstinate:* Come then, neighbour Pliable, let us turn again, and go home without him; there is a company of these crazy-headed coxcombs, that, when they take a fancy by the end, are wiser in their own eyes than seven men that can render a reason.
> *Pliable:* Don't revile; if what the good Christian says is true, the things he looks after are better than ours: my heart inclines to go with my neighbour.
> *Obstinate:* What! more fools still? Be ruled by me, and go back. Who knows whither such a brain-sick fellow will lead you? Go back, go back, and be wise.

No dialogue of such easy and homely naturalness had been heard in English fiction, which means that Bunyan's allegory is deeply rooted in the actual. It is of this world in its most familiar aspects; its concreteness is startling in its vividness if we compare it, say, with an allegory like *The Faërie Queene*. And when we come to the scenes of Vanity Fair and the trial of Christian and Faithful, it is scarcely an exaggeration to say that we are in the presence of a work that already fulfills Smollett's definition of a novel, as "a large, diffused picture, comprehending the characters of life, disposed in different groups and exhibited in various attitudes, for the purposes of a uniform plan." To the making of *The Pilgrim's Progress* went a lifetime of passionate observation of men and women.

This is even more clearly apparent in *The Life and Death of Mr. Badman,* which appeared in 1680. Again a moral tract, its purpose is to describe "the life and death of the ungodly, and of their travel from this world to hell." But this time there is no allegory; instead, we have a familiar dialogue between Mr. Wiseman and Mr. Attentive on the subject of their neighbor Mr. Badman. Doubtless the form is clumsy, but it is "carried" by the raciness and the absolute fidelity of the dialogue so that the impression Mr. Badman makes on his godly neighbors could hardly come through more strongly. Mr. Badman is a bad man, but his badness, as Bunyan presents it, is accurately observed, the badness we find in life; he is not an abstract moral monster.

No doubt Bunyan was an unwitting artist, but he was one all the same, and in nothing more than in the account of Mr. Badman's death.

Attentive: Pray, of what disease did Mr. Badman die?—for now I perceive that we are come to his death.
Wiseman: I cannot so properly say that he died of one disease; for there were many that had consented and laid their heads together to bring him to his end. He was dropsical, he was consumptive, he was surfeited, he was gouty, and (as some say) he had a tang of pox in his bowels. Yet the captain of all these men of death that came against him to take him away, was the consumption, for it was that that brought him down to the grave.
Attentive: Pray, how was he when he drew to his end—how was he when he was (as we say) at the grave's mouth?
Wiseman: Why, there was not any other alteration in him than was made by his disease upon his body. His mind was

the same, his heart was the same. He was the selfsame Mr. Badman still.

Attentive: Pray, how was he in his death? Was death strong upon him, or did he die with ease, quietly?

Wiseman: As quietly as a lamb. There seemed not to be in it, to standers by, so much as a strong struggle of nature. And as for his mind, it seemed to be wholly at quiet. . . .

Bunyan's unerring sense of and appetite for the real is all the more striking when we set beside him the professional fiction writers who were his contemporaries. The best of them was Mrs. Aphra Behn. Her most famous prose fiction, *Oroonoko: or, The Royal Slave,* represents the first appearance of the idea of the noble savage—some seventy years before Rousseau; and it could be interpreted as the forerunner of all anti-imperialist or anticolonial literature. But its main interest for us here is in Mrs. Behn's attempt to engraft verisimilitude onto a conventional story of romance. Mrs. Behn came to prose fiction from the heroic drama, and in essence the story of *Oroonoko* is that of heroic drama, the story of ill-fated lovers ever-faithful maintaining themselves even in death on a plane of almost impossible nobility. Mrs. Behn, however, showed her originality in two ways. First, Oroonoko is presented as the grandson of an African king, "a man of an hundred and odd years old." Oroonoko is young, handsome, and virtuous, and a great warrior; he loves Imoinda, the daughter of a great native general; she returns his love, but the old king falls in love with her and she is taken into his harem. The two lovers come together in slavery in Surinam. And this is the second part of Mrs. Behn's originality: she claimed to have been brought up in Surinam by a kinsman who was governor of that colony, and for two centuries her claim was accepted on the strength of what seemed the first-hand knowledge of the West Indian colonies shown in *Oroonoko.* It now appears unlikely that she was ever in Surinam, and the source of background material was probably George Warren's *Impartial Description of Surinam*, published in 1667.

Oroonoko is a compendium in himself of all the virtues, an educated as well as a noble savage since even in his native Africa he has learned French and English and acquired a touching admiration for the ancient Romans. It is, to put it at its mildest, implausible, yet Mrs. Behn sustains our interest in her hero in spite of his incredibility. She does so partly because of the impassioned speech she puts into his mouth, speeches traditional enough in heroic drama but here, against a more or less realistic background, having something of the effect of aria in opera; we find ourselves accepting a convention. And there is something else: a device old by the time Mrs. Behn used it but still remarkably successful. On the title page of her fiction, *Oroonoko* is called "A True History," and the first paragraph opens with its solemn assurance that what we are about to read is not fiction: "I was myself an Eye-witness to a great part of what you will find here set down; and what I cou'd not be Witness of, I receiv'd from the Mouth of the chief Actor in this History, the Hero himself." And Mrs. Behn, speaking in her own person, narrates the story with a combination of sobriety and passionate indignation at the behavior of the white settlers of Surinam towards their slaves and Oroonoko especially that still makes a genuine impact on the reader. Mrs. Behn uses Oroonoko and his virtues as a rod with which to scourge her fellow Christians. What now invalidates *Oroonoko* is not so much its author's failure in art as our greatly increased knowledge. She did not fill up the uncharted map of central Africa with "Here be monsters" or "The Anthropophagi live here"; she merely asserted Africa was inhabited by the noble characters of the heroic drama. And this was not implausible, for if the characters of the heroic drama were never met with in London streets, at least they were very familiar to London playgoers.

Oroonoko was, in fact, a cunning adaptation of romance as Congreve describes it in his prefatory letter to his own work of prose fiction *Incognita*. "Romances," he says, "are generally composed of the Constant Loves and invincible Courages of Hero's, Heroins, Kings and Queens, Mortals of the first Rank, and so forth; where lofty Language, miraculous Contingencies and impossible Performances, elevate and surprise the Reader into a giddy Delight, which leaves him flat upon the Ground whenever he gives of . . . when he is forced to be very well convinced that 'tis all a lye." Novels, he goes on to say, are of a more familiar nature. They "come near us, and represent to us Intrigues in Practice, delight us with Accidents and odd Events, but not such as are wholly unusual or unpresidented, such which not being so distant from our Belief bring also the Pleasure nearer to us." It is exactly this kind of work Congreve proposes to write in *Incognita*.

It is not yet a novel in our sense, and perhaps it is no more than a very brilliant trifle; Congreve cannot have been more than twenty-one when he wrote it and may have been only seventeen. It was his one attempt at prose fiction; after it, he turned his great talents to the drama, and *The Way of the World* and *Love for Love* must seem to us now to contain far more both of reality and of realism than we find in *Incognita*. But the trifle fascinates, apart from its intrinsic qualities of wit and lightheartedness, because of what it promises for the future. I think it had no influence on the course of the novel; our fiction would have been unaffected if it had not been written. And yet it is difficult not to see *Incognita* as a seed in which the mature flower potentially exists.

Incognita is a story of confusion of identity: two young men, close friends, go to a masked ball in Florence, exchange names, and fall each in love, thus setting up a chain of consequences developed with the skill of a great master of artificial comedy. Had Congreve written his squib when he was older he would undoubtedly have set it in London, with a much greater gain in reality. But what is interesting now is Congreve's avowed intention in this story "to imitate Dramatick Writing, namely, in the Design, Contexture and Result of the Plot. I have not observed it before in a Novel." He was right: before *Incognita* prose fiction had been artless in form; indeed, form can hardly be said to have existed at all. In *Incognita,* we glimpse in miniature the formal aspects of the kind of fiction we associate particularly with the names of Jane Austen, Henry James, and Ivy Compton-Burnett.

Then there is Congreve's style, a style of witty, conversational ease that allows him to comment on the action and characters he is describing, indeed, to keep up a running commentary on them, even at times burlesque them, without in any way flawing the surface texture of the work. This civilized speaking voice, polished, skeptical, and humorous, knits the work together and gives it its texture. Here the young Congreve looks forward to Fielding and Thackeray and again to Jane Austen.

Congreve could probably have been as fine a novelist as he was a dramatist. He took more pride in being a gentleman than in being a writer of genius, but the writing of plays was at least compatible with being a gentleman. It was not yet so with fiction writing. Its public was "low," its status that of a commodity for the masses which bore, in the eyes of men of letters, no relation to literature. In other words, it was not yet an accepted form, much less an inevitable one even for writers whose interest in character was strongly developed. The characters of Addison's *Spectator* papers, Sir Roger de Coverley, Sir Andrew Freeport, Will Wimble and the rest, are famous in the same way as characters in the novel are; they have the autonomy of great fictitious personages; we feel them living beyond the confines of the essays that describe them.

Born fifty years later, Addison could hardly have failed to be a great novelist, but when he began to write the *Spectator* papers in 1711 it was still not inevitable that a concern for character on the part of an author should take the form of writing novels, and Sir Roger and the others exist on the threshold of a novel that was never written.

When, in the second decade of the eighteenth century, the novel really emerged, it did so from a man to whom art and literary theory meant nothing, from a writer who was not a gentleman but a tradesman dealing in commodities. In a sense, the relation Defoe bears to the artist is that of the forger, but he was forging not works of art but transcripts of actual experience. We see him as a novelist after the event, as it were. A novelist was the last thing he wished to appear as, and, by a paradox, it is exactly this that makes him the archetypal novelist.

When he wrote the first part of *The Life and Strange Surprising Adventures of Robinson Crusoe, of York, Mariner,* by far the best known of the three hundred and seventy-five works with which he is authoritatively credited, Defoe was fifty-nine. By any standard he was one of the most remarkable men who ever lived. Yet while it would be absurd to maintain that his genius has not received its due, one does notice quite commonly in his critics a certain meanness of spirit towards him; praise tends to be grudging; and one can only see in this the vestigial remains of the contempt, which is one of class, expressed in Swift's reference to him as "the fellow that was pilloried, I have forgot his name." In fact, Defoe was almost the prototype of a kind of Englishman increasingly prominent during the eighteenth century and reaching its apotheosis in the nineteenth: the man from the lower classes, whose bias was essentially practical and whose success in life, whether in trade or industry, was intimately connected with his Protestant religious beliefs and the notion of personal responsibility they inculcated. It was men of this kind who made the industrial revolution, first as scientists and technologists, like Joseph Priestley and Watt, and then as industrialists, like the Lancashire and Yorkshire textile manufacturers.

Defoe stands to these in the relation of a prosaic Leonardo. Without benefit of a university, he was a man of wide learning, speaking half a dozen languages and reading seven. His interests and activities were many; he was in turn shopkeeper, manufacturer, journalist, and government spy, and his title to be considered the founder of English journalism is as great as his claim to be father of the novel. His curiosity was endless; he was a man, as his *Essay on Projects* and *A Tour Through Great Britain* show, who had only to look for his mind to be filled with ideas, ideas concerned always with the practical, with man as trader, manufacturer, agriculturalist.

This new type of Englishman, empirical, self-reliant, energetic, and with the sense of a direct relation with a God made in his own image, he expresses in the character of Crusoe. The sources of the book have been hunted down by scholars, but his indebtedness to earlier writers cannot take away from Defoe's originality. In writing *Crusoe* he was not, of course, consciously writing a novel; he was writing a spoof autobiography which was to be taken by his readers as fact. *Crusoe* sums up, as it were, within itself all the travel books that had gone before it from the time of Hakluyt on. It is in its way a highly scientific work; its facts, geographical and otherwise, are as accurate as the knowledge of his day could make them. This was of the nature of the man. The secret of the uncanny verisimilitude he achieves has often been analyzed. He was the master of the literal; he produces his illusion of complete reality by employing a mass of circumstantial detail of a kind no one, we think as we read, would bother to invent. In *Robinson Crusoe,* for example, the shipwreck and the hero's sojourn on his island, though the most important parts of the book, are still only parts. Before he reaches the point of being cast away, Crusoe passes through a whole gamut of adventures, including a period in slavery to the Barbary corsairs. By the time we reach the shipwreck it has already become in our mind something that would inevitably happen to a man like him; it is, in other words, in character. The smaller lies have conditioned us to accept the bigger one. It is certainly incredible enough: Crusoe is on his island twenty-eight years, two months, and nineteen days. The exactitude is characteristic; it is partly because we can follow Crusoe's experiences at times from day to day and always from year to year, with the dates given, that we swallow the impossible. In a way, the impossible has been caged by the calendar and tamed. But we accept Crusoe's story even more readily because Defoe puts the stress all the time not on the island or on the dangers surrounding his hero but on Crusoe the man himself. It is Crusoe who fills the picture, and he does so as a truly heroic figure, a man dominating nature. Crusoe is the first great individualist, but he convinces as such by his ordinariness; having assumed his large impossibility, Defoe henceforward is scrupulous in keeping within the bounds of the possible. As Coleridge pointed out, in what he does Crusoe "arrives at no excellence . . . the carpentering, tailoring, pottery, etc., are all just what will answer his purpose . . . Crusoe rises only to the point to which all men may be made to feel that they might."

It was Coleridge's contention that Crusoe was "the universal representative, the person, for whom every reader could substitute himself." If this is so, it is because of the fidelity and the thoroughness with which Defoe has drawn Crusoe's likeness. Here, in his excursion into imaginary autobiography, Defoe had nothing to guide him but his own genius. Indeed, the phrase "imaginary autobiography" is itself misleading if it suggests that there were autobiographies extant that Defoe could use as models. Apart from a few works from remote periods, such as the *Confessions* of St. Augustine, the prose literature of self-revelation scarcely existed in Defoe's day; the diaries of Pepys and Evelyn, written during his boyhood, were not made public until the nineteenth century. Yet Crusoe is a strikingly complete character; though there are whole areas of human experience on which he has nothing to say, this does not make his completeness and roundness the less, for those he does report on are rendered so fully that we can work out for ourselves his attitude to the others. At first sight the clue to Crusoe's character may seem to be his: "It was in vain to sit still and wish for what was not to be had, and this extremity rouz'd my application"; together with his powers of observation and deduction, as shown for instance in his account of his first encounter with the goats on the island:

> I observ'd if they saw me in the valleys, tho' they were upon the rocks, they would run away as in a terrible fright; but if they were feeding in the valleys, and I was upon the rocks, they took no notice of me, from when I concluded that by the position of their opticks, their sight was so directed downward, that they did not readily see objects that were above them; so afterward I took this method, I always clim'd the rocks first to get above them, and then had frequently a fair mark.

But there is also the other side to Crusoe, the religious side, his preoccupation with theology, his moralizing. It comes out especially in such a passage as this:

> This renew'd a contemplation which had often come to my thoughts in former time, when first I began to see the merciful dispositions of Heaven in the dangers we run through in this life; how wonderfully we are delivered when we know nothing of it; how when we are in a quandary, as we call it, a doubt or hesitation, whether to go this way or that way, a secret hint shall direct us this way, when we intended to go that way; nay, when sense, our own inclination, and perhaps business has call'd us to go the other way, yet a

strange impression upon the mind, from we know not what springs, and by we know not what power, shall overrule us to go this way; and it shall afterwards appear that had we gone the way we should have gone, and even to our imagination ought to have gone, we should have been ruin'd and lost. Upon these and many like reflections, I afterwards made it a certain rule with me, that whenever I found those secret hints or pressings of my mind, to doing or not doing any thing that presented, or to going this way or that way, I never fail'd to obey the secret dictate; though I knew no other reason for it than that such a pressure or such a hint hung upon my mind.

As much as Milton, Crusoe is God's Englishman, and God helps those who help themselves. The sense of partnership between God and man is with Crusoe all the time.

The two sides of Crusoe, the practical and the religious —and it is none the less religious because so often expressed in moralistic terms—come together in such a passage, which Coleridge acclaimed as "worthy of Shakespeare," as:

> I smil'd to myself at the sight of this money: "O drug!" said I aloud. . . . However, upon second thoughts, I took it away; and wrapping all this in a piece of canvas . . .

Within a year of the publication of *Crusoe* a parody of it had appeared, ending with the point-blank assertion that Defoe was a liar. He retorted that the book was in fact allegorical, every important passage in it corresponding to an event in his own life. However disingenuous Defoe's defense may be in detail, in a sense it is obviously and profoundly true. No doubt Defoe began with no other intention than to write a fake autobiography of a sailor like Selkirk or Dampier, but the reader who returns to it today as an adult cannot fail to see in it more than the adventures of the castaway on an uninhabited island. Indeed, simply by describing those adventures, Defoe had done more: he had dramatized as sharply as possible the inescapable solitariness of each man in his relation to

God and the universe, and it is the index of his triumph with his hero that Crusoe still remains adequate as a representation of the human being in this timeless situation.

Defoe's achievement is even more remarkable when we add to *Robinson Crusoe* his other fictions. They show how generally applicable were the methods of producing the effect of reality he had devised in that book. Of his other fictions the two most outstanding now are *A Journal of the Plague Year,* perhaps the most convincing recreation of an historical event ever written, and *Moll Flanders.* Here, he holds and delights us with a character in a perfectly ordinary setting; the advantages, as far as keeping the reader's attention goes, of the exotic and the strange are foregone. He has to depend entirely on the impression he makes of telling the simple truth, and at no point in the novel can there be any doubt of his success:

> The child had a little necklace on of gold beads, and I had my eyes upon that, and in the dark of the alley I stooped, pretending to mend the child's clog that was loose, and took off her necklace, and the child never felt it, and so led the child on again. Here, I say, the devil put me upon killing the child in the dark alley, that it might not cry, but the very thought frighted me so that I was ready to drop down; but I turned the child about and bade it go back again, for that was not its way home. . . . As I did the child no harm, I only said to myself, I have given the parents a just reproof in leaving the poor little lamb to come home by itself, and it would teach them to take more care of it another time.

Today, we might call *Moll Flanders* a sociological novel dealing with the making of a criminal, for the emphasis throughout is on the effect of environment on character. But the greater interest is that, written in the first person as a "true confession" with the moral tag at the end that "true confessions" in any age must have, it is further evidence of the protean nature of Defoe's imagination. It was one thing to create Crusoe, quite another to create

Moll, and one scarcely knows which feat to admire the more. Moll exists completely in the round; so perfect is Defoe's assumption of her character that her personality is fully exposed. In *Moll Flanders* more than any other of his fictions Defoe is revealed as the first wholly unambiguous instance in our literature of that interest in character in itself, that obsession to impart character, which Virginia Woolf found the distinguishing mark of the novelist. In this respect, if in no other, Defoe is the archetypal novelist.

To talk of his influence is to plunge into imponderables. It would be as easy to discuss and weigh the influence on our novel of the English weather or the English climate. One can only say, as of Bunyan, that without him we should all be different from what we are. One great contemporary he certainly influenced, Swift, who, though possessing many of the attributes of a novelist, cannot be called one. *Gulliver's Travels* is a work of fiction but not a novel, though in it Swift uses circumstantial detail after the manner of Defoe in order to persuade us of the truth of his Lilliputians and Brobdingnagians. And great as his genius was, one feels that Swift could never have been a novelist. Satire can only be part of the novelist's make-up; in Swift's it was everything.

THE EIGHTEENTH CENTURY

1

THE FIRST GREAT flowering of the English novel began in 1740, with Richardson's *Pamela,* and ended thirty-one years later with Smollett's *Humphry Clinker.* Of the four great novelists of the century the first, Richardson and Fielding, are the greatest. No two great writers have ever existed in one period in sharper contrast with each other. They embody the two extremes of the creative impulse. Coleridge wrote in the *Biographia Literaria*: "While Shakespeare darts himself forth, and passes into all forms of human character and passion, the one Proteus of the fire and flood; Milton attracts all forms and things to himself. All things and modes of action shape themselves anew in the being of Milton; while Shakespeare becomes all things, yet for ever remaining himself." In this contrast Coleridge is isolating two permanent and opposed kinds of creative imagination in their purest and most comprehensive expressions. If Coleridge's distinction is applied to eighteenth-century novelists, then Fielding approximates to Shakespeare and Richardson to Milton.

Samuel Richardson was born in Derbyshire in 1689. His school nickname, "Serious and Gravity," would have fitted him throughout his life. He was intended for the church, but since the family means did not allow this he was sent to London at the age of seventeen to be apprenticed to a printer. The very pattern of the industrious apprentice, even to the point of marrying his master's daughter, he became, as industrious apprentices should, a successful businessman, printer of the journals of the House of Commons, Master of the Stationer's Company, and Law Printer to the King. He turned novelist at the age of fifty, by accident. In 1739 he was commissioned by two London booksellers to compile a volume of *Familiar Letters* which should not only serve as models for the uneducated in their correspondence but also demonstrate "how to think and act justly and prudently in the common Concerns of Human Life." Among them were to be included a number "to instruct handsome girls, who were obliged to go out to service, as they phrase it, how to avoid the snares that might be laid against their virtue." He remembered a true story he had been told twenty-five years earlier, while staying in the country, of the way in which the local landowner had come to marry his wife. A child of humble parents, reared in the strictest principles of morality, she had been engaged as a maid by the landowner's mother. After his mother's death the squire tried, in Richardson's words, "by all manner of temptations, to seduce her. . . . She had recourse to as many innocent stratagems to escape the snares laid for her virtue: once, however, in despair, having been near drowning. . . . At last, her noble resistance, watchfulness, and excellent qualities, subdued him, and he thought fit to make her his wife," in which station "she behaved herself with so much dignity, sweetness, and humility, that she made herself beloved of everybody, and even by his relations, who at first despised her; and now had the blessings both of rich and poor, and the love of her husband." The result was, Richardson put aside the *Familiar Letters* for a future occasion and, retaining only the letter form for his narrative, wrote *Pamela, or Virtue Rewarded*.

It was immediately and overwhelmingly successful. Richardson became the center of a circle of adoring women who found in him a sage, a prophet, and a lawgiver. We, however, come to Richardson with two centuries of novels behind us; it is scarcely possible for us to imagine the intense shock of novelty that *Pamela* must have had for its first readers. There had been nothing like it before. In addition, Richardson had discovered one of the most potent formulas of the best-selling novel, what has been called "the principle of procrastinated rape." There is Pamela, there is Mr. B. hot in pursuit of her virginity. Will she lose it? Will she? Won't she? The suspense is everything, and the screw is turned to the uttermost. Pamela loves Mr. B. and she holds out for marriage, and she has been accused, along with her creator, of preaching a merely prudential morality, of confusing morality indeed with respectability. There is truth in this, and yet, when we are considering the impact of the novel on its first readers, it is beside the point. Richardson as sexual moralist is not, perhaps, a very endearing person, but he was not simply a sexual moralist. What Richardson's readers were so ardently responding to was his treatment of the situation of their time, and what that situation was is as plain in his work as in Fielding's. Fielding, it has often been said, saw it as his task to reform the manners of the age; Richardson, by delineating models of virtue, sought to improve its morals. All this is true, so far as it goes, but the real problem facing them and their contemporaries was not crudity of manners, barbarity, or defective morals as such but the existence at all levels of inordinate, arbitrary, and irresponsible power against which the ordinary private citizen was helpless. It is not by chance that the would-be seducer of Pamela, Mr. B., is a Justice of the Peace, for in *Pamela* Richardson was tackling the situation of the age in the most intensely dramatic manner possible. Against an almost omnipotent authority Richardson pitted helplessness combined with virtue—and despite all hazards helplessness combined with virtue triumphed, simply because it was virtue, and what is more, forced authority to accept it on its own terms. It was this that the age applauded; Richardson was the spokesman of justice, and when he makes his Pamela write to her parents in such words as:

> . . . one may see how poor people are despised by the proud and the rich! yet we were all on a footing originally: and many of these gentry, who brag of their ancient blood, would be glad to have it as wholesome and as *really* untainted as ours!—Surely these proud people never think what a short stage life is; and that, with all their vanity, a time is coming, when they must submit to be on a level with us. The philosopher said true, when he looked upon the skull of a king, and that of a poor man, that he saw no difference between them. Besides, do they not know, that the richest of princes, and the poorest of beggars, are to have one great and tremendous Judge, at the last day; who will not distinguish between them, according to their circumstances in life; on the contrary, may make their condemnations the greater, as their neglected opportunities were greater! Poor souls! how do I pity their pride!—O keep me, heaven, from *their* high condition, if my mind shall ever be tempted with *their* vice, or polluted with so cruel and inconsiderate a contempt of that humble estate they behold with so much scorn!

justice could hardly have had a better spokesman.

Richardson did not conceive of justice in anything like political terms. A resolute Tory, he was no critic of the class structure of his day. His protest was in the name of religion and morality; but, by making his central characters in his first two novels women, and opposing them to the libertinage of men, he did much to elevate the position of women, not least in their own eyes. And though *Pamela* may seem to us now a study in crude black-and-white morality, with a strong vein of concupiscence running through it, and though the details of the plot may not stand much inspection, his age was right to applaud it as it did, for all its ethical code needed the corrective of Fielding's satire.

As a novel, *Pamela* is today of historical rather than of intrinsic interest. This is not in the least true of *Clarissa*, published in 1748. The longest novel in English, its very bulk probably prevents its being much read now; yet it remains by any standard a very great novel indeed. Its theme is much the same as that of *Pamela*: conscious virtue (female) pursued by unrelenting viciousness (masculine); but just as it is much more subtle, much more richly orchestrated than the earlier novel, so the theme is raised to an altogether higher level, treated on the tragic plane. Clarissa Harlowe, the model of her sex in every conceivable respect, accomplishments, virtue, filial obedience, beauty, is the youngest child of a wealthy, purse-proud, land-hungry family. The rich, handsome, brilliant rake Lovelace falls in love with her; he has already paid his addresses to her sister and has quarreled mortally with her family. Another suitor, whose estates are conveniently adjacent to those of the Harlowes, is found for her; Clarissa cannot love him and refuses to marry him; she is made a prisoner in her parents' house, subjected to the conceivable utmost of family pressure, still refuses, even promising to remain single all her life so long as she is not compelled to marry the egregious Mr. Solmes, and then, just before a final attempt at compulsion is to be made on her, is abducted by Lovelace. She loves him, or would love him if only he were penitent and virtuous. He conducts her to a brothel, where, always pleading his love for her, always promising marriage and yet delaying the necessary preliminary formalities, he makes several attempts on her chastity, which she indignantly repulses. At last, he rapes her while drugged. After that, despite all his pleading and the pleading of his family and friends, she will not marry him. She wastes away until she dies, and Lovelace himself is killed in a duel by one of her kinsmen. As her friend Miss Howe writes to her, Clarissa's "only crime is her merit"; she is persecuted and driven to her death by her family and by the libertine who loves her, who loves her, indeed, almost to the point of madness.

Thus baldly synopsized, *Clarissa* may seem to be no more capable of rational scrutiny than *Pamela*. But this is to ignore altogether the intensity of its author's imagination and the masterly nature of its composition. Like the earlier novel, *Clarissa* is told entirely in letters, in letters often of enormous length between Clarissa and her family, Lovelace, and her friend Miss Howe, and between Lovelace and his friends and tools. The technique has often been ridiculed: Sir Leslie Stephen computed that one of the correspondents in Richardson's third novel, *Sir Charles Grandison*, must, to have composed the letters she is supposed to have done during a period of three days, have been writing steadily for eight hours a day. We have to accept a fictitious world whose inhabitants live, as it were, for the pen, who are constantly sitting down, as soon as anything has happened to them, to write detailed descriptions of the events and long analyses of their reactions to them, in the form of letters to their friends; letters replied to, with equally lengthy observations on the events described, and often transmitted to a third character who in turn adds his or her comments to the initial event. As a convention—and every novelist must expect the reader to accept the convention he has chosen for his way of narration—it is no more absurd than that of the omniscient first-person narrator in a novel like *David Copperfield*, or the assumption that we must make when reading Virginia Woolf's *The Waves* that we are overhearing half a dozen people talking to themselves in interior monologue at key moments in their lives. Once it is accepted it breaks down only when Richardson doubts its rationality himself and thinks it necessary to make his characters justify or explain their inordinate pleasure in the art of letter writing. Then, for the moment, the illusion is wrecked.

The positive virtues of Richardson's technique for the purposes he had in mind were enormous. One of them he describes in his preface to the novel:

All the letters are written while the hearts of the writers must be supposed to be wholly engaged in their subjects (the events at the time dubious): so that they abound not only with critical situations, but with what may be called *instantaneous* descriptions and reflections (proper to be brought home to the breast of the youthful reader); as also with affecting conversations; many of them written in the dialogue or dramatic way. . . . Much more lively and affecting must be the style of those who write in the height of a *present* distress; the mind tortured by the pangs of uncertainty (the events then hidden in the womb of fate); than the dry, narrative, unanimated style of a person relating difficulties and dangers surmounted, can be . . .

Richardson's is a dramatic technique; the letters the characters write to one another are the equivalent of dramatic speeches; and while we read *Clarissa* or *Sir Charles Grandison* we exist, as we do when watching a play or a film, in a continuous present, always at the cutting edge of the character's suffering, analyzing, experiencing mind. And we not only have the character as he sees and presents himself; through the letters of the other characters we see him as others see him. The result is a much greater immediacy and intensity in the rendering of character in itself than we find in almost any English fiction until we approach the present age. Yet though his novels could have been written by no other man, though they are impregnated with his values, though all things and modes of being shape themselves anew in him, Richardson himself, while telling his story, is quite outside the action; he never intervenes, he never speaks in his own voice. The most subjective of writers in that the world he created was an acutely personal one, specialized to himself, no man could have been more objective in his presentation of it.

Richardson owes much of his success to the very length at which he writes. In *Clarissa*, for instance, he takes more than a million words to relate the events of eleven months. He writes as it were in slow motion; his characters scrutinize themselves as though they were their own subjects under a microscope. We know as we read that Richardson's is not quite the real world—Hazlitt called it, in a brilliant phrase, "artificial reality"; we are not convinced that Richardson knows at first hand the wealthy and fashionable world that is his background, yet the illusion of reality is none the less strong, so intensely imagined is the world he is depicting. He was not, we may assume, a man much given to frequenting brothels and consorting with prostitutes and procuresses; yet his great brothel scene and the description of the lingering death of the bawd Mrs. Sinclair have a detailed vividness and a compulsion that suggest Zola, and are indeed as horrifying as anything in that writer, as is seen in the description of the prostitutes round the dying woman's bed:

> The other seven seemed to have been just up, risen perhaps from their customers in the fore house, and their nocturnal orgies, with faces, three or four of them, that had run, the paint lying in streaky seams not half blowzed off, discovering coarse wrinkled skins: the hair of some of them of divers colours, obliged to the blacklead comb where black was affected; the artificial jet, however, yielding place to the natural brindle: that of others plastered with oil and powder; the oil predominating: but every one's hanging about her ears and neck in broken curls or ragged ends; and each at my entrance taken with one motion, stroking their matted locks with both hands under their coifs, mobs, or pinners, every one of which was awry. They were all slip-shoed; stockingless some; only under-petticoated all; their gowns, made to cover straddling hoops, hanging trollopy, and tangling about their heels; but hastily wrapped round them as soon as I came in. And half of them (unpadded, shoulder-bent, pallid-lipped, limber-jointed wretches) appearing, from a blooming nineteen or twenty perhaps over night, haggard well-worn strumpets of thirty-eight or forty.

The passage is taken from a letter to Lovelace by his friend and former accomplice Belford, a rake reformed by the contemplation of Clarissa's unconquerable virtue and her resolution under persecution. Richardson's genius is such that every character in turn, no matter how small his part in the action, is perfectly individualized in the letters he writes; open the book anywhere at random and the letter picked upon will unfailingly proclaim its writer. The number of characters is not large; the convention Richardson worked in prevented that; but all are triumphantly alive, from Clarissa's malignant brother, an ogre of rancorous envy and diseased, ingrown pride, to the ludicrously conceited Rev. Mr. Brand, a magnificent example—one day to emerge as Mr. Collins in *Pride and Prejudice*—of what Richardson could do in comedy when he wanted to.

But the two great characters of *Clarissa* are the heroine and Lovelace. V. S. Pritchett has said that Richardson was mad—mad about sex, and I doubt whether it is possible for the critic who comes to *Clarissa* after reading Freud to deny that the novel must have been written by a man who was, even though unconsciously, a sadist in the technical sense; the loving, lingering, horrified, gloating descriptions of Clarissa's long-drawn-out sexual humiliation at the hands of Lovelace, the rape that is constantly threatened and constantly deferred until, when it occurs, it has an additional horror simply because of its long postponement, provide an element of quite inescapable pornography compared with which the obscenity of Smollett and the indecency of Sterne, so often rebuked by the righteous, appear innocent. The remarkable thing is, the tragedy would be impossible without it. *Clarissa* is a tragedy of sex. It seems impossible, in the early stages of the novel, that Clarissa herself, a creature almost inhuman in her perfections, can ever become a tragic heroine; yet she does, for it is not her virtue as such, but her sufferings and her intransigence under suffering, that make her human. She comes to life as a tragic heroine precisely at the point when, having endured the ultimate sexual humiliation from Lovelace, she refuses to marry him.

The character of Robert Lovelace, her ravisher, is one of

the greatest in literature; he stands out in Richardson's pages with the daemonic magnetism of a figure of myth. He comes straight out of the depths of his creator's unconscious and yet, at the same time, is one of the most convincing renderings of a man of intellect that exists in fiction. His letters bear continually the imprint of intellectual vivacity and curiosity, and he has a gaiety and wildness— a wildness of the mind—that are incomparable. He is a most subtle creation, who, restless analyst of his own actions though he is, scarcely knows any more than his creator does the true motives for his behavior. He is a man for whom woman is the eternal enemy, whose generosity can be appealed to but whose pride—and for Lovelace pride is sexual pride—must never be slighted. "Caesar was not a prouder man than Lovelace," he writes to Belford, and, on the sex war, "I love, when I dig a pit, to have my prey tumble in with secure feet and open eyes; then a man can look down upon her, with an *O-ho, charmer, how came you there?*" The real lure of Clarissa for him consists in the very intransigence of her chastity; he is as much her victim as she is his. In the end, he wants her so fiercely that to have her he will even consent to marry her, but even that would have represented a kind of defeat for him, for it is he, and he alone, who of his own free will must confer favors on his victims, and in Clarissa he has met an adversary whose pride as a woman is as great as his pride as a man. It is the necessity of his existence, therefore, that Clarissa must be violated in her deepest instincts, be broken and humbled, and the dream is the sweeter because, by so doing, he will at the same time revenge himself on the despised and hated Harlowes:

> It would be a miracle, as thou sayest, if this lady can save herself—and having gone so far, how can I recede? Then my revenge upon the Harlowes! To have run away with a daughter of theirs, to make her a Lovelace—to make one of her family so superior to her own—what a triumph, as I have

heretofore observed, to *them*! But to run away with her, and to bring her to my lure in the *other* light, what a mortification of their pride! What a gratification of my own!

Lovelace is the one character in Anglo-Saxon fiction comparable with the original Don Juan, the Don Juan who, like the characters of Hamlet and Don Quixote, still fascinates successive generations of human beings because he expresses in symbolic form, and thus retains its mystery as he does so, one abiding aspect of human nature. It is improbable that Richardson knew the original Don Juan at first hand, though he may well have read Molière's comedy and the Restoration dramatist Shadwell's not quite absurd play *The Libertine*, to the incidental action of which *Clarissa* has a few small similarities. If he did know them, his debt was trifling enough; we have to read them in the light of *Clarissa* to see how successfully he transmuted his libertine hero into an English setting and English terms. Lovelace is one of the great originals of fiction.

Clarissa is easily the best of Richardson's novels. *Pamela* was an excessively brilliant trial run, executed in the crude contrasts of a moral tract, and *Sir Charles Grandison* is too much of its time. The hero represents Richardson's ideal of manly virtue as Pamela his ideal of female virtue. It was a deliberate attempt to redress the balance, since both Mr. B., of *Pamela*, and Lovelace had been villains. Perhaps Sir Charles is the author's dream picture of himself, a man of lofty birth, great riches, perfect breeding, endowed with every gift, accomplishment, and virtue, the very embodiment of *noblessse oblige*—and surrounded always, like his creator, with a chorus of adoring women, from among whom he must choose the one most worthy to be his consort. Grandison is indeed Richardson's "just man made perfect," and for all the excellences of the novel, its admirable dramatic passages, he is in the end no more convincing than the virtuous in fiction usually are. He is, in fact, too much of a good thing; he scatters the largesse of his benevolence on all sides, but neither his principles nor his virtues are submitted to any very searching test; he remains always in command of every situation. In Sir Charles, Richardson exposes his own ideas of what constitutes human goodness; he is, perhaps, Meredith's Sir Willoughby Patterne taken with dead seriousness, at his face value, without any of the satire Meredith brought to bear on him. He is, in other words, a most devasting prig, the greatest in fiction, and since he is perfect from the beginning, all that the action can represent is a series of variations on the theme of his goodness.

Faced with so formidable a literary innovator as Richardson, scholars have naturally sought to estimate his indebtedness to other writers. They have not found the task easy. Did he owe anything to the novel *La Vie de Marianne*, by the French novelist Marivaux, which had been published ten years earlier and had begun to appear in an English version before Richardson wrote *Pamela*? The two works have qualities in common, yet the theory that Richardson was influenced by Marivaux is far from generally accepted. The whole question of literary influence, the indebtedness of one writer to others, is much more difficult and complex than some literary historians seem to think. The apparent influence of an older novelist on a later may, in fact, be no influence at all, in the sense that the later writer's work would have been in some way different had he not known his forebear's, but rather a relation between affinities. In the physical sciences it has become a commonplace that discoveries are frequently made simultaneously by two or more minds working quite independently of one another. It is as though the discovery itself has come into existence of its own accord, as the result of the development of knowledge leading up to it, and is as it were waiting to be discovered. Likewise, two or more writers living at more or less the same time may show similar modes of seeing the world and of rendering it in the novel. By 1740, both in France and England, the novel was, as it were, in the air, already in existence potentially; all that was needed was someone to write it; and Richardson and Marivaux have much in common because the forces that shaped them were common to both.

The influence of Richardson himself on later novelists has been so huge as to be incalculable. For the first generation of the novel no writer of fiction could escape him, even if, like Fielding and Smollett, he was writing consciously in reaction against him. When Johnson said that he "had enlarged the knowledge of human nature," he was speaking simple truth. Richardson had altered men's awareness of themselves even without their knowing it. What he had introduced into fiction, and therefore into the modes of thinking and feeling of countless readers, were the analysis of emotion and motive, introspection in the widest sense, and ultimately the belief in the value of emotion and of feeling for their own sakes. When a felt emotion is valued simply because it is felt, then if we have not already reached sentimentality we shall find it waiting for us just round the corner. It is from *Pamela, Clarissa,* and *Sir Charles Grandison,* powerfully abetted by Sterne's *Tristram Shandy,* that modern sentimentality derives, along with the masters of the sentimental, writers like Rousseau, Dickens, and Thackeray.

What was not taken over by later novelists was Richardson's technique and the reason for his technique, his impulse to show characters as personalities, thinking and feeling for themselves with the author himself absent from the stage, refusing, almost as a point of honor, to intervene in the action. Other novelists were to use the letter form as a vehicle for fiction, but never for Richardson's reasons. And for anything like his direct rendering of the minds of his characters in the very moment of thinking and feeling, we have to wait for more than a century, for the appearance of Henry James, who had many affinities with him, James Joyce, Dorothy Richardson, and Virginia Woolf.

2

The main tradition of the English novel, as it was commonly written until well into the second half of the nineteenth century, derives from Henry Fielding (1707-54). His first novel, *Joseph Andrews,* was at first conceived as a satire on *Pamela,* its situations and values. Fielding decided that Pamela should have a brother, a virtuous footman named Joseph, who would repulse the advances of Lady Booby as his sister had done those of Lady Booby's nephew, Richardson's Mr. B. It was, as it turned out, a false start, for, having discovered the form of the novel, Fielding went on to do something quite different from merely poking fun at Richardson.

Fielding shared with his half-brother, Sir John Fielding, who succeeded him at Bow Street, the distinction of being the best magistrate London had during the eighteenth century, and the qualities and experience of life that he brought to his office would have been remarkable in any epoch. His cousin Lady Mary Wortley Montagu wrote of him:

> I am sorry for H. Fielding's death, not only as I shall read no more of his writings, but I believe he lost more than others, as no man enjoyed life more than he did, though few had less reason to do so, the highest of his preferment being raking in the lowest sinks of vice and misery. . . . His happy constitution (even when he had, with great pains, half demolished it) made him forget everything when he was before a venison pasty, or over a flask of champagne, and I am persuaded he has known more happy moments than any prince upon the earth.

Our first impression of Fielding, then, is of a man with an enormous zest for living, spendthrift both of his money and his health. Despite his aristocratic origins, Fielding had experienced at first hand the appalling economic and social insecurity of an age that still retained an almost Elizabethan brutality and lack of inhibition. But his bodily vigor and appetite for life were allied with an intellectual energy and a generosity of spirit no less strong. Keats's famous phrase, "the holiness of the heart's affections," might have sounded strange on his lips, but his belief in it was passionate, as his life and his books alike show. And he knew, from his own experience as well as from observation, what the real canker of the age was: the prevalence, at all levels of society, of unconditioned and therefore tyrannical power.

Like Richardson, he became a novelist almost by accident. The passing of the Licensing Act of 1737, that curious censorship of the stage which is still with us and which Fielding's own dramatic satires on Sir Robert Walpole had brought into being, had put an end to his not unsuccessful career as a playwright. Driven out of the theater, he had become a barrister practicing on the Western Circuit and then a political journalist until he was appointed Justice of the Peace for Westminster and Middlesex. It was not regarded as an especially honorable office, but he was indefatigable in the course of his duties, was the instigator of many reforms in the administration of justice and prevention of crime, and wore himself out in the public service. His novels may in a sense be seen as by-products of a busy career, but the immediate end he proposed for them was not so very different from the ends for which he worked as the most fearless and honest magistrate of his day, the reform of the manners of the age. In this respect, *Tom Jones* and *An Inquiry into the Cause of the late increase of Robbers* are as one.

Fielding's work was, with that of his friend Hogarth, the most powerful artistic expression of the social conscience of the age. It is not easy to overrate the brutality and squalor of much of eighteenth-century life, which may be summed up in public executions on a vast scale ("Many cartloads of our fellow creatures"—the words are Fielding's —"are once in six weeks . . . carried to slaughter") and gin ("drunk for a penny, dead-drunk for twopence"); but we do well to remember the reforming zeal which was already active. J. H. Plumb, in his *England in the Eighteenth Century*, has reminded us that in 1735 "there were 99,380 actions taken out by the Society for the Reformation of Manners in the London area alone." Fielding, both as novelist and magistrate, was a society for the reform of manners in himself, and it was only natural that, when writing *Joseph Andrews*, he should not long be content with reforming Samuel Richardson's manners alone.

Like most of the greater eighteenth-century writers he saw himself as a moralist and satirist, but he was much more besides. What he was besides was, as it were, the fine flower of his didactic purpose. The first English theorist of the novel, his criticism falls short of his creative achievement; he did more than he knew. This is plain from his preface to *Joseph Andrews*. He knew that he was doing something new in English prose fiction. He was writing, as he says, the comic epic, a form differing from comedy as the serious epic from tragedy; "its action being more extended and comprehensive; containing a much larger circle of incidents, and introducing a greater variety of characters. It differs from the serious romance in its fable and action, in this; that as in the one these are grave and solemn, so in the other they are light and ridiculous: it differs in its characters, by introducing persons of inferior rank, and consequently of inferior manners . . . lastly, in its sentiments and diction, by preserving the ludicrous instead of the sublime." At one level, the level at which it has worn least well, *Joseph Andrews*, with its burlesque of the similes of classical epic, was an exercise in the mock heroic, like Swift's *The Battle of the Books* and Pope's *The Rape of the Lock*. But as he points out, the mock heroic, what he calls burlesque, is admitted in his style and diction only; it is carefully excluded from the characters. The characters are modeled from the life: "Life everywhere furnishes an accurate observer with the ridiculous."

But he felt, it seems now, that he must justify his creation of ridiculous, we should say comic, characters. "The only source of the true ridiculous, as it appears to me," he writes, "is affectation. . . . From the discovery of this affectation arises the ridiculous, which always strikes the reader with surprise and pleasure." He was putting forward the classical theory of comedy, a view later restated by Meredith in his famous essay. Yet he was doing his own creations less than justice. He points out, rightly enough, that the great master in English of the kind of comedy he thought he was writing was Ben Jonson, but if we approach Fielding's novels with him in mind we shall find an art very different in its whole nature from Jonson's. We shall find an art much more akin in spirit to Shakespeare's.

The springs of Fielding's comedy are sometimes affectation, which according to Fielding arises either out of vanity or out of hypocrisy. Yet the most splendid character in *Joseph Andrews,* indeed, in all Fielding, is Parson Adams, and he is a creation of pure humor. Perhaps he owes something to Don Quixote, but he is in every sense an original character, one of the archetypal characters in English fiction, and the secret of the pleasure he gives us can no more be reduced to a critical formula than Falstaff's can. Adams, with his absent-mindedness, his small pedantries and vanities, his naive trust in human goodness, which is always being betrayed, is the heart of the novel. Fielding —and the reader—laugh at his innocence, which is constantly getting him into one series after another of misunderstandings and imbroglios; yet it is Adams, with his simple belief that Christianity is to be practiced as well as preached, who is the measuring rod for all the other characters; he is the reagent submission to which exposes the true nature and composition of the rest of the *dramatis personae.* He is, in fact, largely the source of the satire in the book:

> "I suppose, sir," said the bookseller, "your sermons are of a different kind."—"Ay, sir," said Adams: "the contrary, I thank Heaven, is inculcated in almost every page, or I should belie my own opinion, which has always been, that virtuous and good Turks, or heathen, are more acceptable to the sight of their Creator, than a vicious and wicked Christian, though his faith was as perfectly orthodox as St. Paul's himself."—"I wish you success," says the bookseller, "but must beg to be excused, as my hands are so very full at present; and, indeed, I am afraid you will find a backwardness in the trade to engage in a book which the clergy would be certain to cry down."

That is a simple instance. A better one would be the whole wonderful scene between Adams and Parson Trulliber, who is more concerned with his pigs than the cure of souls, and who believes, at first, that Adams too must be a pig dealer.

"Written in Imitation of the Manner of Cervantes, Author of Don Quixote," says the title page of the novel, an important piece of information often omitted from modern editions. The Quixote figure is Adams, but the structure of the book also follows Cervantes. *Joseph Andrews* is a novel of adventures met while traveling on the road. Joseph, thrown out of his footman's employment in Lady Booby's service in London, for showing himself adamant against seduction either by her ladyship or by her woman Mrs. Slipslop, sets out to walk home to his sweetheart Fanny. He meets Parson Adams, whose teaching has so fortified his virtue, walking to London in the hope of getting his sermons published, but Adams has characteristically forgotten to bring his sermons with him and so returns with Joseph. They run the gantlet of dishonest innkeepers, irresponsible and brutish country gentlemen, pompous, sycophantic, and sometimes equally brutish clergymen. It would be foolish to attempt to synopsize the plot, which is a parody of romantic plots in general, with missing heirs, babies stolen and exchanged at birth, and birthmarks to be discovered and foundlings restored to their heritage in the last chapters. The plot, though well handled, is not important. What matters is Fielding's endless fertility of comic invention. According to Fielding, Homer had written a comic epic which, had it not been lost, would have been a model of its kind as his epics are in tragedy. Elizabeth Jenkins, in her admirable study of the novelist, comments on this: "The scene in Lady Booby's house . . . where Beau Didapper steals to Mrs. Slipslop's bed in mistake for Fanny's, and Parson Adams, hearing a scream, rushes in the dark to the bedside, where, misled by the feel of the beau's delicate skin and of Mrs. Slipslop's beard, he starts punching the latter unmercifully, is a scene on what one might venture to call a Homeric scale." And it could be paralleled elsewhere in the novel. Fielding had the gift which is the prerogative of great comic writers of being able to cap absurdity of situation on absurdity of situation in a single scene, and to go on doing it beyond what we expect to be the climax.

Joseph and Fanny, his sweetheart, are not much more than lay figures or are meant to be. But the other characters, though not drawn so completely in the round as Adams, are terrifically and often terrifyingly alive; they have the distinctive individuality of the figures in Hogarth's prints, of the half-naked drunken virago sprawled on the steps, with her baby falling from her arms, in the "Gin Lane" plate, for instance.

At first sight, Fielding's fierce eye for externals appears to be that of the caricaturist. We should, therefore, expect his characters to be "flat," in E. M. Forster's sense of the word. But this is not so at all. Flat characters are representations of *idées fixes*; typical flat characters are Smollett's

Hawser Trunnion and Dickens's Mrs. Micawber. They are characters incapable of surprising us. Now, most of Fielding's personages in *Joseph Andrews* are episodic; they appear only once, met and passed in the course of Joseph's and Adam's peregrinations. But we feel, of Mrs. Towwouse, Parson Trulliber (the finest of them all, after Adams himself), Mrs. Slipslop, and the rest, that they would be capable of surprising us if they were given the opportunity. "I describe," said Fielding, "not men, but manners; not an individual but a species." But he always describes the species in terms of the individual. Trulliber may stand for every boorish, semi-illiterate parson of the day who was more farmer than priest, but in the first instance he is Trulliber. He appears in one chapter only, but he is rendered with such fierce intensity that we feel that he, and the type he represents, have been caught and pinned down for ever and for good. We do not need to know more of him, but we are persuaded that if we wished to we could.

Another source of the vitality of Fielding's characters is the element in which they live, Fielding's mind and style. Like the style of Thackeray, who learned much from him but not enough, Fielding's is that of a man talking to us at his ease. It is direct, unaffected, the product of a mind stored with knowledge of men and of books—he is always driving a point home with an apt quotation, from the classics or from Shakespeare. He is telling a story, the action of which has been long over. Action and characters, therefore, exist not only in the context of the story but also in the context of the author's mind, a mind decisive in quality, with firm views on human nature and behavior. We feel that Fielding knows everything there is to know about his characters even though he does not tell us all. They are so real to him that, even though he may give us no more than a glimpse of them, they become real for us. Behind every simple statement of Fielding's we feel the force of a deep and varied experience of life, an experience that, however bitter it may have been, has not darkened the essential humanity of his nature.

This wholehearted acceptance of life is nowhere more apparent than in the irony with which his mind is pervaded. It gives his every word tremendous authority, because we feel nothing can escape it. It is his great weapon against pretense, vanity, hypocrisy, inhumanity; his great weapon in defense of generous feeling. It cuts all ways, as the following passage shows. Joseph has been robbed, beaten up, stripped, and left unconscious by the roadside. A coach comes by. Joseph is unwilling to enter until he is "furnished with sufficient covering to prevent giving the least offence to decency: so perfectly modest was this young man; such mighty effects had the spotless example of the amiable Pamela, and the excellent sermons of Mr. Adams, wrought upon him":

> Though there were several great-coats about the coach, it was not easy to get over this difficulty which Joseph had started. The two gentlemen complained they were cold, and could not spare a rag; the man of wit saying, with a laugh, that charity began at home; and the coachman, who had two great-coats spread under him, refused to lend either, lest they should be made bloody: the lady's footman desired to be excused for the same reason, which the lady herself, notwithstanding her abhorrence of a naked man, approved; and it is more than probable that Joseph, who obstinately adhered to his modest resolution, must have perished, unless the postillion (a lad who has since been transported for robbing a hen-roost) had voluntarily stripped off a great-coat, his only garment; at the same time swearing a great oath, for which he was rebuked by the passengers, that he would rather ride in his shirt all his life, than suffer a fellow passenger to lie in so miserable a condition.

Irony is implicit in Fielding's view of life. In *The History of the Life of the late Mr. Jonathan Wild the Great* (1743) it is explicit, single-minded, and sustained. Some pages of Swift apart, it is the grimmest and most brilliant prose satire that we have; and perhaps it is even more

effective than Swift's because it is not the work of a mis-
anthrope.

Its theme is greatness as conventionally interpreted, the
cult of success for its own sake. Whether it was intended
as an attack on Walpole is now of merely academic interest; *Jonathan Wild* can never in all its history have had
more point than it has acquired during the past twenty-
five years of dictators and totalitarian politics. The great
man whose career Fielding relates was a thief and organ-
izer of robberies, a racketeer in crime itself, who had been
hanged at Tyburn in 1725. He is presented throughout in
terms of the utmost admiration: he is great, not good: "No
two things can possibly be more distinct from each other,
for greatness consists in bringing all manner of mischief
on mankind, and goodness in removing it from them."

Wild is, as it were, the superman of crime, beyond good
and evil; Fielding is constantly showing us how his greatness might have been compromised had he allowed himself to be swayed by merely human considerations of generosity or pity, but Wild never succumbs. To the last, his
progress through the underworld of London is triumphant.
Against him is set his old school friend, the shopkeeper
Heartfree, whom he swindles and robs and whose wife he
abducts, a man so pusillanimous as not even to dare commit murder in order to escape from prison. His "low and
pitiful behavior" in loving his family and trusting his
friends rightly earns him the contempt of the whole jail.

Apart from the interlude describing Mrs. Heartfree's
return from Africa, a flaw in the construction of the novel
but fascinating as a glimpse of Fielding's idea of utopia,
the intransigent grimness of the comedy never relaxes.
It is as continuous when Wild is off the scene as when he
is on; one may instance the behavior of the prison officer
who charges Heartfree, at the moment when he is to be
led out to execution, five guineas to spend ten minutes

with his wife, and then twenty to make it an hour, and, having accepted the money, discloses when the time is up that a reprieve has already arrived.

What gives *Jonathan Wild* its enduring power is the single-mindedness with which the theme is treated, the unrelenting way in which Wild, the gangster, is made to stand for greatness at all levels. In his other novels Fielding attacks unbridled power and its attendant evils incidentally and in their local manifestations: corrupt magistrates, prison officers, noblemen who are a law to themselves, and so on; in *Jonathan Wild* he shows it, by implication, as a principle operating throughout society, and he does so in terms of a comedy which, however remorseless, is still comedy.

Yet fine as *Joseph Andrews* and *Jonathan Wild* are, they scarcely prepare us for so great an achievement as *The History of Tom Jones*, which, after two centuries, remains among the handful of supreme novels. The new element in *Tom Jones* is Fielding's architectonic quality; no plot has ever been carried through with more consummate skill, and the skill can be truly appreciated only after the book has been closed. In reading, one is delighted with the swiftness of the narration, the economy, the nimble and inexhaustible invention. Fielding had learned much from his experience in the theater, especially how to break up the narrative, set his scene in a minimum of words, and carry on the action in short, swift passages of dialogue. But it is only after reading that we realize how every detail has its place in the action, is a preparation for what is to come, the full significance of which cannot be apparent until the novel has reached its end; then, what seemed at first glance a happy stroke of invention reveals itself as part of the essential structure of the book, without which the whole could not exist. Fielding was as superb a craftsman in his own way as Henry James. There is only one blot on the novel judged as a formal whole: the introduction of the extraneous story of the Man of the Hill, and even that can plausibly, if not convincingly, be justified.

Fielding was an innovator not only technically. Tom Jones was a new kind of hero, one might say the unheroic hero. He is handsome, brave, generous, and well meaning, it is true: "Though he did not always act rightly, yet he never did otherwise without feeling and suffering for it"; but though his heart is in the right place, his instincts are not always in his control. He is a depiction of ordinary, weak man, *l'homme moyen sensual*. When we first meet him he is a foundling, mysteriously placed in Mr. Allworthy's bed, assumed therefore to be a bastard; as Mrs. Deborah Wilkins, the servant, says: "It goes against me to touch these misbegotten wretches, whom I don't look upon as my fellow creatures. Faugh! how it stinks! It doth not smell like a Christian. If I make so bold to give my advice, I would have it put in a basket, and sent out and laid at the churchwarden's door." But Mr. Allworthy brings up the child as his ward. Tom's enemy throughout boyhood is Mr. Allworthy's heir and nephew, Master Blifil, a youth a year younger than Tom, who constantly tells tales about him, and finally, when Allworthy is ill, lies about him to such effect that Tom is turned out of the house. By now he is in love with Sophia, the neighboring Squire Western's daughter. He thinks first of going to sea, then decides to join the army marching north to meet the Scots forces of the Rebellion of Forty-five. At Upton-on-Severn he sees Sophia again; she is staying in the same inn, having run away from her father who is for compelling her to marry the detestable young Blifil. Tom follows her to London with the intention of returning a pocketbook of hers that he has found. In London, despairing of ever marrying Sophia, knowing indeed that he can do her only harm, he meets an entirely fresh set of adventures; he becomes the lover of Lady Bellaston, an elderly woman of fashion, and—something which has drawn the indignation of many critics down on Fielding—accepts money from her. It is not until after he has broken with her and been thrown into jail at the instigation of Lady Bellaston and Lord Fellamar, who wishes to marry Sophia, that everything is set right, the truth about his birth revealed, Blifil banished in disgrace, and he is able to marry Sophia.

What impresses, as always in Fielding, is the honesty of the picture of Jones. Jones, the well-intentioned sensual young man, whose "life was a constant struggle between honor and inclination, which alternately triumphed over each other," is faced squarely. It is only after he has escaped from the clutches of the gamekeeper's daughter Molly Seagrim, who has tried to father on him a bastard who, for all he can tell at first, might be his, that he realizes he loves Sophia. And then:

> It was now a pleasant evening in the latter end of June, when our hero was walking in a most delicious grove, where the gentle breezes fanning the leaves, together with the sweet trilling of a murmuring stream, and the melodious notes of nightingales, formed altogether the most enchanting harmony. In this scene, so sweetly accommodated to love, he meditated on his dear Sophia. While his wanton fancy roamed unbounded over all her beauties, and his lively imagination painted the charming maid in various ravishing forms, his warm heart melted with tenderness; and at length, throwing himself on the ground, by the side of a gently murmuring brook, he broke forth into the following ejaculation:
>
> "O Sophia, would Heaven give me thee to my arms, how blest would be my condition! . . . Was I but possessed of thee, one only suit of rags thy whole estate, is there a man on earth whom I would envy! . . . Oh! my fond heart is so wrapt in that tender bosom, that the brightest beauties would for me have no charms, nor would a hermit be colder in their embraces. Sophia, Sophia, alone shall be mine. What raptures are in that name! I will engrave it on every tree."
>
> At these words he started up, and beheld—not his Sophia, no, nor any Circassian maid richly and elegantly attired for the grand Signior's seraglio. No; without a gown, in a shift

that was somewhat of the coarsest, and none of the cleanest, bedewed likewise with some odoriferous effluvia, the produce of the day's labour, with a pitchfork in her hand, Molly Seagrim approached. Our hero had his penknife in his hand, which he had drawn for the before-mentioned purpose of carving on the bark; when the girl coming near him, cryed out with a smile, "You don't intend to kill me, squire, I hope!"—"Why should you think I would kill you?" answered Jones. "Nay," replied she, "after your cruel usage of me when I saw you last, killing me would, perhaps, be too great kindness for me to expect."

Here ensued a parley, which, as I do not think myself obliged to relate it, I shall omit. It is sufficient that it lasted a full quarter of an hour, at the conclusion of which they retired into the thickest part of the grove.

There are some extenuating circumstances in Jones's favor, but when all is said it is a case of his seeing and approving the higher and following the lower. Jones's sexual morals, allied to the fact that in the end he wins Sophia, have outraged many critics. One can only say that the eighteenth century was not the nineteenth, and at any rate it did allow Fielding to tell the truth about an average young man, as is plain when Jones is compared to Thackeray's Pendennis, who is finally unconvincing because he is incomplete exactly at those points where Jones is not. It is not that Fielding approved of Jones's sexual conduct, but he did believe, with many excellent theologians, that other sins were graver than sexual irregularity, among them malice, cruelty, meanness, hypocrisy. He was as stern a moralist as Richardson, but he was a much more generous one. He too was against the double standard in morality, as the dialogue between Tom and Sophia in the penultimate chapter of the novel makes absolutely clear, but he knew the difficulties the single standard involves. The critic who spoke of the "fortunate—the too fortunate —Mr. Jones" might have had the humility to reflect that there is no evidence that that was Sophia Western's opinion.

Jones is only one character in an enormous gallery. All are marvelously differentiated. There is Partridge, the schoolmaster-turned-barber, Jones's Sancho Panza; a crowd of innkeepers, landladies, servants, soldiers; Lady Bellaston; Harriet Fitzpatrick, a wonderfully subtle study; Mrs. Waters; Square the Deist and Thwackum the clergyman; "Black George" Seagrim, the gamekeeper who is responsible for so many of Jones's tribulations, and who, with at least a recognition of the higher, follows the lower; Nightingale; the Blifils, father and son; Squire Western and his politically minded feminist sister; Sophia herself; Mr. Allworthy. Fielding was not creating characters merely for the sake of creating characters. He populated a whole world, but it exists as a considered criticism of the real world. He is showing the age its face. Squire Western, the warmhearted, hot-tempered, fox-hunting Tory country gentleman, is as complete and rounded a personage as any in the book. His daughter is the passion of his life; he idolizes her. Yet he persecutes her, in the name of her filial duty towards him, with an odious cruelty which compels her rather than marry the hateful Blifil to emulate Clarissa Harlowe and run away from home. He is a magnificent comic character, drawn with affection but also remorselessly. Fielding has him, as we say, completely taped; no exposure could be more thorough. Consider his attitude to Sophia when she refuses to marry Blifil, and Fielding's comment:

> Mr. Western, having finished his holla, and taken a little breath, began to lament, in very pathetic terms, the unfortunate condition of men, who are, says he, "always whipt in by the humours of some d—n'd b—— or other. I think I was hard run enough by your mother for one man; but after giving her a dodge, here's another b—— follows me upon the foil; but curse my jacket if I will be run down in this manner by any o'um."
> Sophia never had a single dispute with her father, till this unlucky affair of Blifil, on any account, except in

defence of her mother, whom she had loved most tenderly, though she lost her in the seventh year of her age. The squire, to whom that poor woman had been a faithful upper-servant all the time of their marriage, had returned that behaviour by making what the world calls a good husband. He very seldom swore at her (perhaps not above once a week) and never beat her: she had not the least occasion for jealousy, and was perfect mistress of her time; for she was never interrupted by her husband, who was engaged all the morning in his field exercises, and all the evening with bottle companions. She scarce indeed ever saw him but at meals; where she had the pleasure of carving those dishes which she had before attended at the dressing. From these meals she retired about five minutes after the other servants, having only stayed to drink 'the king over the water.' Such were, it seems, Mr. Western's orders; for it was a maxim with him, that women should come in with the first dish, and go out after the first glass. Obedience to these orders was per-haps no difficult task; for the conversation (if it may be called so) was seldom such as could entertain a lady. It con-sisted chiefly of hallowing, singing, relations of sporting incidents, b—d—y, and abuse of women, and of the govern-ment.

These, however, were the only seasons when Mr. Western saw his wife; for when he repaired to her bed, he was gen-erally so drunk that he could not see; and in the sporting season he always rose from her before it was light.

Squire Western is, in fact, a drunken boor, one of those centers of arbitrary power Fielding loathed.

Fielding, it has become a cliché of criticism, was "a man's man," and his heroines are the women of a man's man. Sophia Western is scarcely likely to satisfy a feminist. But she is anything but a doll, and her behavior shows that she is neither stupid nor passive; reading of her, we are convinced equally of her beauty, her goodness, and her generosity of spirit. She is in the tradition of the Shake-spearean heroine, seen as a being at once inferior and su-perior to the male of the species, but equal never. The mainspring of her life, unless conscience is outraged, is a gracious obedience. This is to say that Fielding's conception of the relationship between the sexes was nearer to Shakespeare's than to ours. How superior it was to that of the greatest Victorian male novelists may be seen by comparing Sophia with the heroines of Dickens or, for instance, Thackeray's Laura.

Fielding's most fully drawn heroine is Amelia, in the novel of that name, his last, published in 1751. *Amelia* has always rather worried Fielding's critics. It is a much more somber book than *Tom Jones.* In that novel, as in *Jonathan Wild,* Fielding faces the human situation as steadily as any tragic writer. But in *Amelia* it is as though Fielding's resilience of spirit in the presence of the rule of wrong had been strained too far and was at the point of snapping. Perhaps his mind had been darkened by his experiences as a magistrate; certainly it had been by the death of the wife he adored, the model both for Sophia and for Amelia.

Comparison with *Tom Jones,* then, reveals *Amelia* as a falling off in what we think of as Fielding's characteristic genius. But the comparison is unjust, for he was attempting something quite different. *Amelia* is not the peregrinatory novel that *Tom Jones* is. It is much more compact, more tightly woven; the scene is set almost entirely in London, the episodes of Booth's army life being told in the long conversation between him and Miss Matthews at the beginning of the book, an interesting anticipation of the "flash-back" technique of the novelists of our own time. Then, though to nothing like the extent to which the eponymous hero is used by Smollett, Scott, and Dickens, Tom Jones himself is as it were the thread on which is hung a succession of contrasted episodes and scenes. In *Amelia,* attention is focused all the time on the situation of Booth and his wife Amelia: they occupy the foreground in a way that Jones does not; the spotlight is never played, as in the earlier novel, on a vast panorama of characters and events going on behind them. *Amelia* is, in fact, not a panoramic novel, a comic epic, at all; it is a domestic novel. That must be realized before justice can be done to it.

It contains great things. Fielding never did anything better than the first chapters, describing life in a prison of the period, a masterly episode of sardonic contempt. And there is much splendid characterization: the demoniac Miss Matthews, who is drawn with a passionate intensity satire is not allowed to qualify, and the absurd, dignified Colonel Bath, forever watching for slights on his honor and yet capable of a devotion to his sister which he angrily denies when surprised in it. These two characters show a progress in complexity beyond anything in the earlier novels. There is the host of minor characters, all as usual perfectly differentiated, but all much more somber than those of *Tom Jones* and *Joseph Andrews*: the clergyman Dr. Harrison, for instance, a Parson Adams no longer comic, expressing Parson Adams's beliefs with something like asperity and impatience. Above all, there is Amelia, a character whose quiet radiance illuminates and softens a world of viciousness and deceit. Amelia is the rarest of successful characters in literature, the absolutely good person who is credible.

Yet the novel is not quite successful, not because Fielding's ebullience of spirits has subsided or his gaiety been quenched, but because of the unsatisfactory nature of Captain Booth and of the plot as a whole. Booth, a half-pay officer turned farmer who has been forced out of his farm because of the debts he has contracted, is a Tom Jones grown older and sadder. But he is a Jones who has gained nothing in will power, who, adoring his wife, can yet betray her when he is absent from her, who promises time and again not to gamble and yet is constantly gambling their last pounds away, always to be forgiven again. He is Tom Jones become, to use Wyndham Lewis's word for Hemingway's heroes, a dumb ox, the almost passive victim of circumstances and of his own weaknesses. He is marvelously drawn; Fielding has him to the life, with his constantly growing cloud of guilt and all. But in the end it is no longer possible to feel sympathy for him; his fecklessness becomes a bore, and more and more we restively wonder how Amelia can continue to put up with him, how she can go on loving him, forgiving him, and slaving for him.

At this point the unsatisfactoriness of the plot reveals itself. By his very nature Booth is a doomed man; in reality not even an Amelia could have saved him. But in the last pages, all is put right: it is discovered that the will by which Amelia had been disinherited by her mother was a forgery. She comes into her own. The plot is not a bad plot, and it is certainly not unskillfully handled, but it is the wrong plot for the novel Fielding was writing.

The reader who comes to Fielding's fiction with some acquaintance already with the nineteenth-century novel may sometimes feel that he has read it before. In a sense he has. Fielding is the great original in English fiction, and, one way and another, more than half our novelists for more than a hundred years are packed away in him. Weakened, made fainter, sometimes made more subtle, often sentimentalized, characters like Adams, Mrs. Slipslop, Squire Western, Colonel Bath crop up time and again in later fiction. The controversies of Thwackum and Square become the novels of Peacock. The bustle, the high spirits, the rowdiness, and the horseplay which were a direct reflection of the eighteenth-century scene, survive into *Mr. Polly*. Of the kind of novel Smollett defined, and Scott, Dickens, Thackeray, and even Meredith were often to write, *Tom Jones* remains imcomparably the finest. Other novelists, Dickens in particular, added qualities that Fielding lacked, but none were so successful as he in what he invented.

What his descendants inherited they often used badly

and unsuitably. Jane Austen alone put out her legacy to really profitable interest. Very largely, the English novelists' conception of character, as it existed until seventy or eighty years ago, and as it still survives in a few isolated pockets of reaction, was derived from Fielding. But what also derived from him was the characteristic plot of much nineteenth-century fiction, the whole outfit of missing heirs, mistaken identities, stolen children, forged wills, and the rest. Fielding took these over from the theater and in *Tom Jones* turned them to brilliantly successful account. They failed him in *Amelia,* and they failed all those who may be considered in this respect his followers, whether Scott, Dickens, or Meredith in *The Adventures of Harry Richmond.* But this is no criticism of Fielding, merely evidence that for more than a century he dominated the English novel, gave it its main pattern, and pointed the direction it was to go.

3

Fielding, seeing himself as the literary equivalent of what he called the "comic-history painter"—he meant Hogarth—contrasted the comic-history painter with the caricaturist. The aim of caricature, he says, "is to exhibit monsters, not men, and all distortions and exaggerations whatever are within its proper province." Monsters are what men become in the novels of Tobias Smollett (1721-71). Lismahago, in *Humphry Clinker,* the most humane of his works, is described thus:

> He would have measured about six feet in height, had he stood upright; but he stooped very much; was very narrow in the shoulders, and very thick in the calves of his legs, which were cased in black spatterdashes. As for his thighs, they were long and slender, like those of a grasshopper; his face was, at least, half a yard in length, brown and shrivelled, with projecting cheekbones, little grey eyes of the greenish hue, a large hook nose, a pointed chin, a mouth from ear

to ear, very ill furnished with teeth, and a high narrow forehead, well furrowed with wrinkles.

Lismahago, in fact, is dehumanized; he is presented in
terms of his resemblance to an insect; nothing about his
appearance is natural or normal, and Smollett stresses the
unnaturalness not only by his description but by the words
in which he makes the description: half a yard suggests
something longer than eighteen inches, fantastically long
though that is for a human face. Characters in Smollett
have become grotesque objects and, deprived of their human appearances, turned into animals or insects, they are
deprived of their humanity. They are things to be kicked
about, the sport of any crude horseplay, the legitimate
victims of any kind of cruelty.

Smollett describes his characters, then, in terms of their
externals, grossly exaggerated and distorted, and seizes
upon those features of them that separate them from
rather than unite them to the rest of humanity; and he
does so in order to make them ridiculous. It does not matter that in the end Lismahago is rather an honorable character than otherwise; he is primarily a figure of fun; and
turning over the pages of Smollett today, the modern
reader may well decide, especially if he comes to him after
Fielding, that he is heartless. It is not quite so simple as this.
Smollett's intention, as he states it in the preface to *Roderick Random,* is to promote that "generous indignation
which ought to animate the reader against the sordid and
vicious disposition of the world." He exposes, crudely and
brutally, a brutal and crude society. He writes like a man
born with a skin too few, and affronted in all his senses by
life as he has experienced it; and he flings back at society,
with all the contempt and indignation that he can muster,
rather more than he has got. Like Swift, he was obviously
obsessed with dirt. But his brutality is homoeopathic,
that of the morbidly sensitive man who seeks to cure his

contemporaries of the filth they live in by rubbing their noses in it. His disgust is tempered neither by pity nor by charity. One feels that the spectacle of life is bearable to him only because he can find it comic, and the savagery of the disgust produces savage comedy. Smollett attacked his age precisely where it was most vulnerable, where it was dirty and diseased. If we today think of the eighteenth century in terms of its architecture, then Smollett shows us what lies beyond the sobriety and elegance of the façade. The staircase is a public privy. Through the upper windows the chamber pots are emptied into the street below. The fine ladies and gentlemen at the ball stink because they are not clean; they are the victims of gout and pox; because they eat and drink too much, they grow to look like pigs. If they are poor, if they are sailors or children, they are at the mercy of brutal, capricious authority and will be flogged and starved into insensibility or scurvy. If they lack the money with which to bribe they will remain at the mercy of anyone rich or more powerful than themselves. In any case, they will be robbed and cheated by their superiors.

Smollett was a doctor, and his works suggested the nightmare of an outraged hygienist. His first novel, *The Adventures of Roderick Random,* was published a year before *Tom Jones,* in 1748. Fielding was indebted largely to Cervantes for his conception of the novel. Smollett went to Le Sage, whose *Gil Blas* had appeared in France in 1735. Following the Spanish tradition of the picaresque, Le Sage had strung together a series of comic or farcical adventures, which together exposed the manners of society, given a unity by their happening to the same man, a rogue. In all but his last fiction, *The Expedition of Humphry Clinker,* Smollett added nothing to this primitive form of the novel. Except in *The Adventures of Ferdinand, Count Fathom,* which is not one of his better novels, the heroes are not in fact rogues as in Le Sage and the picaresque novel proper. But they do appear to the modern reader heartless toughs, given to cruel practical jokes, enemies of society in that they are always exposing hypocrisies and pretensions in a way that perhaps Smollett himself was.

Neither Roderick Random nor Peregrine Pickle in the novels of those names can be said to have much life, though Random has more than Pickle, probably because he is closer to Smollett's own experience. Like his creator, Random is a Scot of gentle birth. Neglected and ill treated by his grandfather, his father having unaccountably disappeared, he leaves home and goes to London with his old school friend Strap, now his valet, to make his fortune. In London he is cozened and cheated by a succession of rogues, tries to enter the navy as a surgeon's mate but, despite his professional qualifications, finds that entry into the service depends upon the bribing of Admiralty clerks. He becomes, instead, the assistant of a French apothecary, is seized by the press gang, manages to prove that he is a doctor and so, after all, becomes a surgeon's mate. Like Smollett, he takes part in the Cartagena expedition. For an alleged act of disobedience he is tied to the deck during a battle. He is shipwrecked, robbed, left naked on the shore, and takes service as footman to a middle-aged poetess, with whose niece, Narcissa, he falls in love. He is compelled to run away by the presence of a more prosperous suitor, is kidnaped by smugglers, and taken to France, where he falls in with Strap, now transformed into Monsieur d'Estrapes. They return to London together, where Random intends to repair his fortunes by marrying an heiress. At Bath he meets Narcissa again, but he returns to London penniless and is thrown into a debtors' prison. His uncle Tom Bowling, who has been searching for him, obtains his freedom for him, and they go abroad together on a trading voyage, in the course of which they meet a Spanish don, immensely rich, who turns out to be Random's father.

So much for the dry bones of the novel. Its value obviously lies in individual episodes rather than in any cumulative effect, and some of the episodes are very fine indeed, those describing life in the navy and at sea, and fashionable life in London and at Bath especially. They are relentless, savage cartoons inhabited by caricatures. At the same time, one cannot deny life to the caricatures; the caricature is a perfectly legitimate form of character creation, for the quality we call life in a character comes as much from the passion the author brings to its making as from truth to life, accuracy of observation, or psychological consistency. With the last Smollett was not concerned, but he united accuracy of observation with intense passion; the strength of the impression made upon him by the men and women he had observed in life is unerringly bodied forth to the reader in the characters he creates. Some are softened by humor: Tom Bowling is one of these; others, the brutal naval officer Captain Oakum, for instance, or the foppish Captain Whiffle, are not; they are, as it were, flung at the reader in terms of the most ferocious comedy.

However perfunctory his attention to plot, no one ever wrote better narrative than Smollett. The action fairly whips along, invention follows invention in the most dazzling manner, and all is told in a direct prose, stripped, muscular. As a panoramic novelist, Smollett has never been surpassed.

Roderick Random is one of his two best novels, and in a sense it represents his talent at its purest. *Peregrine Pickle*, judged as a whole, cannot be compared with it; yet it contains his best comic character and his finest piece of comedy. In form and manner it follows the earlier book closely, but there is nothing in *Roderick Random* quite to come up to the retired naval officer Hawser Trunnion, who was plainly conceived in the first instance as a figure of fun and then captured his author's affections. Commodore Trunnion thinks, feels, talks, behaves wholly in terms of his profession; he is the quintessential retired naval officer who, as far as it is possible, lives on shore as though he were still on his ship. His house is a garrison, the company sleep in hammocks, watches are kept, guns fired to welcome guests aboard. Women are not allowed on the premises after dark: the Commodore is a misogynist. It is therefore inevitable that he shall be chivvied into marriage by Peregrine's aunt Mrs. Grizzle and be henpecked ever after. The greatest comic scene in the novel is the account of Trunnion's setting out for his wedding on horseback. Since he is late a servant is sent to find him:

The valet having rode something more than a mile, espied the whole troop disposed in a long field, crossing the road obliquely and headed by the bridegroom and his friend Hatchway, who finding himself hindered by a hedge from proceeding farther in the same direction, fired a pistol, and stood over to the other side, making an obtuse angle with the line of his former course; and the rest of the squadron following his example, keeping always in the rear of each other, like a flight of wild geese.

Surprised at this strange method of journeying, the messenger came up, and told the commodore that his lady and her company expected him in the church, where they had tarried a considerable time, and were beginning to be very uneasy at his delay; and therefore desired he would proceed with more expedition. To this message Mr. Trunnion replied, "Hark ye, brother, don't you see we make all possible speed? Go back and tell those who sent you, that the wind has shifted since we weighed anchor, and that we are obliged to make very short trips in tacking, by reason of the narrowness of the channel; and that as we lie within six points of the wind, they must make some allowance for variation and leeway." "Lord, Sir," said the valet, "what occasion have you to go zig zag in that manner? Do but clap your spurs to your horses, and ride straight forward, and I'll engage you shall be at the church porch in less than a quarter of an hour." "What! right in the wind's eye?" answered the commander; "ahey! brother, where did you learn your navigation? Hawser Trunnion is not to be taught at this time of day how to lie his course, or keep his own reckoning. And as for you, brother, you know best the trim of your own frigate."

On this Smollett caps further absurdities of wild invention. The description of Tunnion's death is a rare instance of Smollett's power of pathos; it has always, and rightly, been compared with the death of Falstaff.

Smollett belonged to the glorious company of English hack writers who have turned their hands to anything. Verse, drama, travel, political writing, a treatise on midwifery, translation—he translated Cervantes, Le Sage, and Voltaire—and a history of England in many volumes poured from his pen. His novels had to take their chance with the rest, and both his notion of the novel and his craftsmanship are rudimentary compared with Fielding's. He padded mercilessly and shamelessly, inserting, for instance, into *Peregrine Pickle* a quite irrelevant story, "The Memoirs of a Lady of Quality," which he certainly did not write himself, was probably paid to put in, and which takes up more than a hundred and fifty pages. He also turned his travels into fiction, a visit to the Continent going into *Peregrine Pickle,* a tour of England forming the basis of *Humphry Clinker.* For him the novel was a branch of journalism, and nowhere in his fiction is the element of journalism, the simple aim of giving factual information, stronger than in *The Expedition of Humphry Clinker,* his last novel.

Clinker reveals a somewhat changed Smollett. That he was an exceedingly prickly fellow, who felt himself constantly persecuted and victimized, his *Travels through France and Italy,* the best known of his nonfiction works, show: wherever he went innkeepers changed into rogues as soon as they saw him; beds which he lay in immediately became hard. At the time of writing his *Travels* he was only forty-five, but when we read them it is difficult not to think of him as a testy, choleric, eccentric old gentleman. In *Clinker* it is as though he saw himself as he really was and found himself no less comic than other people. Humor therefore enters the novel as it does in no other, and softens the ferocity of the comedy. It is this, surely, that has given the book its enduring appeal, for it is quite as scatological as anything he wrote.

It recounts a tour of England and Scotland in the form of letters, but the letters are used in a way quite different from that of Richardson. They aim at a direct revelation of character—or in most instances of caricature—but they also serve to show a single incident, a place, a person from different and conflicting points of view. Five people make the tour and write the letters: Matthew Bramble (Smollett himself transformed into a Welsh squire), warmhearted, irascible, generous, a valetudinarian and a crank, the representative of common sense; his husband-hunting sister Tabitha, mean, avaricious, domineering, who gets religion in the form of Methodism en route, being converted by the footman Clinker who is picked up on the way; her maid Winifred Jenkins, who in the end marries Clinker; Bramble's nephew Jerry Melford, an Oxford undergraduate; and his sister Lydia, a girl in her teens. The least interesting is the last; Smollett was no good with well-bred virtuous young ladies. But the great characters are Matthew, Tabitha and Winifred Jenkins, and the fiercely proud, touchy, poor Scots soldier Lismahago, whom we know only through the eyes of the others and who finally wins Tabitha.

The book, then, is made up of comic episodes and of comment. The liveliest comment comes from old Matthew, who is, as his nephew says, "as tender as a man without a skin; who cannot bear the slightest touch without flinching." The following is a typical extract from his correspondence. He is describing how he fainted at a ball at Bath:

I no sooner got home, than I sent for doctor Ch——, who assured me, I need not be alarmed, for my swooning was entirely occasioned by an accidental impression of fetid effluvia upon nerves of uncommon sensibility. I know not how

other people's nerves are constructed; but one would imagine
they must be made of very coarse materials, to stand the
shock of such a horrid assault. It was, indeed, *a compound
of villainous smells,* in which the most violent stinks, and the
most powerful perfumes, contended for the mastery. Imagine
to yourself a high exalted essence of mingled odours, arising
from putrid gums, imposthumated lungs, sour flatulencies,
rank arm-pits, sweating feet, running sores and issues, plais-
ters, ointments, and embrocations, Hungary-water, spirit of
lavender, assafoetida drops, musk, hartshorn, and sal volatile;
besides a thousand frowzy streams, which I could not analyse.
Such, O Dick! is the fragrant aether we breathe in the polite
assemblies of Bath. Such is the atmosphere I have exchanged
for the pure, elastic, animating air of the Welsh mountains.
O Rus, quando te aspiciam! I wonder what the devil possessed me . . .

The views, of course, are Smollett's own, but Smollett is
seeing himself from the outside, and the humor with which
Matthew is presented gives him the extra dimension of
life that we miss in the characters of his earlier novels. So,
with his cortege, he travels through England, from
Gloucester through Bath and Clifton to London, and then
north to Edinburgh, exacerbated by noise and smells and
dirt, the stupidities of his sister, the iniquities of inns and
boarding houses, suffering in fires and in ballrooms, experiencing highwaymen, grumbling at the procedure of
magistrates' courts and Methodism, meeting old friends,
noting the crops and the state of agriculture, doing good
without fuss, and recognizing with some complacency a
bastard son in Clinker. The whole novel is a most striking panorama of English life in the 1760's.

Matthew is the subtlest of the characters. The humor of
Tabitha and her servant depends mainly on the illiteracy
and inconsequence of their letters; they are self-exposures
of pretension, vanity, and meanness. Winifred, for example, after her marriage to Clinker, now recognized as a
gentleman's son, writes to a former fellow servant:

Mrs. Jones,

Providinch hath bin pleased to make great halteration in the pasture of our affairs. We were yesterday three kiple chined, by the grease of God, in the holy bonds of matter-money, and I now subscrive myself Loyd at your service. All the parish allowed that young 'squire Dallison and his bride was a comely pear to see. As for madam Lasmiheygo, you nose her picklearities. Her head, to be sure, was fintastical; and her spouse had rapt her with a long marokin furze cloak from the land of the selvidges, thof they say it is of immense bally. The captain himself had a huge hassock of air, with three tails, and a tumtawdry coat, boddered with sulfur. Wan said he was a monkey-bank. . . . Now, Mrs. Mary, our satiety is to suppurate. Mr. Millfart goes to Bath along with the Dallisons, and the rest of us push home to Wales, to pass our Chrishmarsh at Brampleton-Hall. As our apartment is to be the yellow pepper, in the thurd story, pray carry my things thither. Present my cumpliments to Mrs. Gwyllim, and I hope she and I may live on dissent terms of civility. Being, by God's blessing, removed to a higher spear, you'll excuse my being familiar with the lower sarvants of the family; but, as I trust you'll behave respectful, and keep a proper distance, you may always depend upon the good will and purtection of

Yours,

W. Loyd.

The use of language in such a letter—and it is true of all Winifred's letters and her mistress's—goes far beyond the comic device of the malapropisms which Fielding had turned to such good account in his delineation of Mrs. Slipslop. There is a genuinely creative gusto in it, a recognition of ambiguities, a deliberate fusion and telescoping of words and hence of meanings; incongruities are linked together and found to be congruous. Whether Smollett intended it deliberately or not, he reveals hidden layers of character in Winifred when he makes her speak of, for instance, "the grease of God," "mattermoney," a "satiety" that is "to suppurate" and "dissent terms of civility." The misspellings themselves foreshadow Dickens's use of them

in such a character as Mrs. Gamp, and what we may reasonably assume was their intention leads us straight to
Lewis Carroll and James Joyce, who made a technique
out of a linguistic device that Smollett probably stumbled
upon by accident or, since he was writing of Welsh characters, may have got from Shakespeare's Fluellen.

Whether Smollett influenced Joyce or not, his influence
on later novelists has been great. He was Dickens's favorite
novelist as a boy, and Dickens took over and carried further his practice of rendering character in terms of its externals, of reducing it to caricature, though I doubt if
Dickens did so consciously or for Smollett's reasons. With
his seamen and avaricious spinsters, hungry for marriage
under a cloak of religiosity, Smollett populated a considerable area of the fiction that was to come. A line of writers
about the sea, from Marryat and Michael Scott to W. W.
Jacobs, is in his debt. Characters like Lismahago, suitably
modified, appear in Walter Scott. And there is no reason
to believe that as an influence, as someone to be learned
from, he is finished yet. Indeed, when one considers a
contemporary novel like Joyce Cary's *A Fearful Joy,* with
its breathless pace of narration, its succession of rapid,
restless scenes—a panoramic novel through time rather
than space—it is plain that he is not.

4

"Nothing odd will do long: Tristram Shandy did not
last." ". . . irresponsible (and nasty) trifling." The first
writer is Dr. Johnson, in 1776, nine years after the last
volumes of *Tristram Shandy* were published; the second,
Dr. Leavis in 1948. Time has proved Johnson wrong, but
the quotations together suggest that *The Life and Opinions of Tristram Shandy* presents its problems.

Laurence Sterne (1713-68) published the first two volumes in 1760, the last in 1767, and the first thing to remark is that within eleven years of the appearance of

Clarissa and ten years of that of *Tom Jones* the newly found form of the novel had been turned upside down and inside out. Yet *Tristram Shandy* is a novel and nothing else but a novel for all that it has never been found easy to pigeon-hole, a fact which should put us on our guard against interpreting the novel as a literary form too narrowly. To summarize the plot is to say even less about the book than such a procedure usually does. We may borrow E. M. Forster's word and call it a fantasy, which at least indicates that Sterne was not out to produce the simulacrum of reality both Fielding and Richardson in their different ways were after. Yet Sterne creates a world, and it is a solid world, a world that extends the reader's knowledge of the world as he himself habitually knows it. Whether we like Sterne's world or not, in his characters of Mr. Shandy and Uncle Toby Sterne brought into existence universal types that we recognize as such, so that we say, confronted with certain kinds of behavior, "This is Shandean," "He might be a modern Uncle Toby." Sterne's characters, like those of only the greatest writers, have the enduring quality of figures in myth: more is suggested by them than they actually state; they express ways of behavior, inclinations of temperament, that are permanent from generation to generation.

This is neither a trifling nor an irresponsible achievement. But as applied to Sterne, the word irresponsible is meaningless. One might as well say that the writings of that other priest of the Church of England, Robert Herrick, were irresponsible. As to nastiness, the word needs severe qualification if it is not to prevent us from seeing what Sterne was after. Sterne was a humorist in two very different senses; he was certainly "skilled in the literary or artistic expression of humor," which is one dictionary definition of the humorist, but he was also a "fantastical or whimsical person; a faddist," which is an earlier definition. E. M. Forster has brilliantly compared his literary

technique with Virginia Woolf's, and perhaps the quotation of a passage from her essay on the modern novel will
indicate, better than anything else, the nature of Sterne's
mind and its perceptions.

> Examine for a moment an ordinary mind on an ordinary
> day. The mind receives a myriad impressions—trivial, fan-
> tastic, evanescent, or engraved with the sharpness of steel.
> From all sides they come, an incessant shower of innumerable
> atoms; and as they fall, as they shape themselves into the
> life of Monday or Tuesday, the accent falls differently from
> of old; the moment of importance came not here but there;
> so that, if a writer were a free man and not a slave, if he
> could write what he chose, not what he must, if he could
> base his work upon his own feeling and not upon conven-
> tion, there would be no plot, no comedy, no tragedy, no love
> interest or catastrophe in the accepted sense, and perhaps
> not a single button sewn on as the Bond Street tailors would
> have it . . .

The passage could stand as a description of how Sterne
saw life and wished to transmit it to the printed page. Like
Mrs. Woolf, he too had come after a solid realist, and his
practice is a protest against what he plainly thought was an
arbitrary convention: life at the moment it is being lived,
he might have said, does not at all resemble life as it is
generalized after the moment has passed. The action of a
Fielding novel has finished before the book opens. It is
therefore a generalization after the event. But Sterne is
writing in the first person, he is thinking aloud—"Writing,
when properly managed," he said, "is but a different name
for conversation"—reminiscing. As Tristram Shandy, he
is setting out to tell us his life and opinions, but in the
monologue he speaks one thing reminds him of another
with which it has no apparent, logical connection; he is
forced to digress because a memory comes into his mind
that will not be suppressed; he remembers a story, a fact,
an instance of odd learning that will illustrate a point,
and having brought it out finds that it is quite beside or

beyond the point. We are reminded today, inevitably, of the stream-of-consciousness novels of the present century, of the soliloquies of Joyce's Leopold Bloom and Mrs. Bloom. But there is a fundamental difference. Shandy is Sterne, just as in *A Sentimental Journey* Yorick is Sterne; the names are merely convenient masks for the author himself; and—the real point of difference—Sterne is constantly amused at the wayward behavior of his own mind in the act of remembering, and constantly exploiting the waywardness for two ends, comedy and the deliberate intention of shocking the reader. The latter is of fundamental importance in Sterne. He is saying in effect to the reader: You believe you think logically, that one thought follows another in orderly sequence, that you are in control of your thoughts, that your mind is as it were a machine you can switch on at will to perform its appointed function. It is nothing of the kind. When you think, when you remember, this is what happens. And so, setting out to write his life and opinions, Shandy is not born until the fourth book, which is almost halfway through, and he can note with delight:

> I am this month one whole year older than I was this time twelve-month; and having got, as you may perceive, almost into the middle of my fourth volume—and no farther than to my first day's life—'tis demonstrative that I have three hundred and sixty-four days more life to write just now, than when I set out; so that instead of advancing, as a common writer, in my work with what I have been doing at it—on the contrary, I am just thrown so many volumes back—was every day of my life to be as busy a day as this—And why not?—and the transactions and opinions of it to take up as much description—And for what reason should they be cut short? as at this rate I should just live 364 times faster than I should write—It must follow, an' please your worships, that the more I write, the more I shall have to write—and consequently, the more your worships read, the more your worships will have to read.
>
> Will this be good for your worships' eyes?

It will do well for mine; and, was it not that my OPINIONS will be the death of me, I perceive I shall lead a fine life of it out of this self-same life of mine; or, in other words, shall lead a couple of fine lives together.

Sterne had good philosophical and psychological bases for his view of the mind's workings; he was writing in accord with Locke's theory that the association of ideas in the mind was an irrational process, but he was also writing as it were a gloss upon the theory, finding his examples, pointing them out, generalizing on them, making comedy out of them. To use a word once fashionable to describe some manifestations of twentieth-century literature, his was essentially a clowning spirit. He clowns all the time on the subjects of childbirth and reproduction. If he did so out of the context of his ideas and the form and style their expression takes, he might be offensive. Within his context I do not believe he is; it is in full agreement with his view of life that he should stress what lies beyond and below accepted opinion, that he should stress prenatal influences on his narrator and find them funny and absurd. To be shocked by Sterne after reading the discoveries of Freud and the psychoanalysts is tantamount to a deliberate refusal to be liberated from false shame.

The fact that he could comment on them even while recording them proves that Sterne was not at the mercy of the associations of ideas in his mind. Indeed, he uses the theory with a very definite end. Some of the feelings aroused by the flux of ideas are better, more worth having, than others; for him, the moments to be seized and dwelt upon were those that were charged with the comic, the pathetic, and the sentimental. The valuable moments are those that isolate oddity—the foibles, hobbyhorses, idiosyncrasies of behavior of his characters—and pathos. He is a pure humorist and a pure sentimentalist, and humor and feeling are alike ends in themselves. There is no satire in his humor; the laughter his characters provoke is of the gentlest. There are, for instance, Mr. Shandy, the theorist with theories on every subject under the sun, and his wife: the relation between them is implicit in the following passage:

> It was a consuming vexation to my father that my mother never asked the meaning of a thing she did not understand. That she is not a woman of science, my father would say, is her misfortune; but she might ask a question.
> My mother never did. In short, she went out of the world at last without knowing whether it turned round or stood still—my father had officiously told her above a thousand times which way it was, but she always forgot.

They live together in mutual incomprehension; and so do My Father and My Uncle Toby, that innocent, artless, childlike creation, the old soldier whose civilian life is dedicated to playing soldiers. They are creatures of fixed ideas, obsessively riding hobbyhorses they alone appreciate. They are drawn with an absolute economy of strokes, and they are utterly solid, three-dimensional characters. More real characters, in the sense that they are immediately convincing no matter how absurd and that they haunt the mind once having been encountered, do not exist in any fiction.

And perhaps they owe their success largely to Sterne's power of sentimentality, for one can speak of it as no less than that; he was a connoisseur of feeling. The sentimentalist specializes in distinguishing nuances of feeling, and when the sentimentalist is a novelist of Sterne's genius the result is bound to be an enrichment of subtlety in the expression of character. His sentimentality has been found by many critics as offensive as his indecency; along with his humor, it is part and parcel of his way of interpreting life, and the three cannot really be divorced from one another. For Sterne's mind is like a spectrum; humor, sentimentality, indecency fade into one another; it is never easy at any one moment to say which is dominant. Sterne is not out to make us laugh aloud or to weep, but when we smile he hopes there will be the suspicion of a tear as well; and if we are moved by his sentimentality, his pity for a dead donkey, Uncle Toby's benevolence towards a fly, we are to smile at the same time, because such sentimentality, for all Sterne prizes it so highly, is also a hobbyhorse, a foible, to arouse compassion and mirth.

Sterne is a novelist who must be taken as he is or not at all. What he set out to do he did consummately. Literary historians have tracked down sources for his style—Rabelais and Robert Burton. He shared with them both a delight in curious lore, an uncouthly sonorous vocabulary, and with the former a delight in the parody of pedantry. All this does not make him any the less an original writer. His style, grotesquely unsuitable as it would be for any other kind of novel, with its digressions, parentheses, dashes, eccentricities of punctuation, is the perfect expression of his mind and therefore, for him, a perfect style. After two centuries of the novel he remains an original. No one else has done what he did, though his influence on later writers has been tremendous. His discovery of the delights of sensibility, the pleasures of the feeling heart, was the discovery of a whole continent of experience which other eighteenth-century writers invaded with alacrity. The influence of his sentimentality has by now died away; Thackeray was the last great novelist to feel it, and him it did only harm. But the influence of his humor is still potent and nowhere more so than in the United States; when we read, for example, a book like Clarence Day's *Life with Father,* or for that matter much of Thurber, we glimpse behind the author the dubious shadow of the curate of Coxwold who took London—and Europe—by storm.

5

Richardson died in 1761, Fielding in 1754, Smollett in 1771, Sterne in 1768. Their work had been crowded into a span of forty years, which was followed by a relatively barren period of twenty years in which little of intrinsic literary merit was written in the form of the novel, though novels poured from the press in an ever-swelling flood.

Many reasons have been put forward for this sudden collapse in the standards of a form which had been raised to such heights in a single generation. The reviewers have been blamed for not recognizing that the novel was a serious branch of literature with its own laws, worthy of as much attention as the drama or poetry; but reviewers are always blamed when fiction finds itself in a dull period. The reading public, rapidly increasing and for the most part taking its fiction through the medium of the circulating library, has also been blamed. And perhaps with more reason; at any time the public is conventional and uncritical, and novels were becoming more and more the staple literary diet of young ladies. The key to the problem undoubtedly lies in the word "uncritical." Novelists themselves were uncritical because, for all the example of Richardson and Fielding before them, they had no real notion of what novels were capable of, what their true jobs were. They were purveyors of stock articles with a ready-made market. This is evident from titles current; close imitations of Richardson, Fielding and Smollett were stock lines. As a matter of fact, the appearance in one generation of as many as four writers of great genius and originality is commonly followed by a fallow period; it is as though great writers temporarily exhaust the language, which must be given time to recover. But so long as novelists saw themselves as no more than provision merchants, purveyors of commodities, so long as they had no proper valuation of themselves, nothing of much merit could be expected in the novel; and it is significant that the best work in fiction from the time of Fielding and Smollett until that of Jane Austen was done by men and women who were generally not professional writers or, if they were, were far from thinking of themselves as primarily novelists.

An instance is Oliver Goldsmith, whose novel *The Vicar of Wakefield,* published in 1766, has proved by far the most popular eighteenth-century novel apart from those of the Big Four. Its popularity, indeed, has been quite disproportionate to its achievement as a novel, and much of it has undoubtedly been due to its "niceness," which allowed adults to put it in the hands of young people when *Tom Jones* was considered improper. As a novel, its faults are gross. The plot is absurd, and the *deus ex machina,* Mr. Burchell (or Sir William Thornhill) is quite incredible. *The Vicar of Wakefield* survives almost in spite of Goldsmith's own intentions. We read it as a domestic idyll, and especially for the character of Dr. Primrose, that unworldly clergyman who in so many ways is a softened, sweetened, more respectable Parson Adams. But this was not quite how Goldsmith meant us to see his novel. In essential content it is obsessed with the same problem as are those of the greater novelists: the problem of arbitrary, irresponsible power. The abduction of Olivia by Harry Thornhill, the young squire, might have occurred in Richardson, Fielding, or Smollett, and Dr. Primrose's experiences in jail are likewise from the common fund of experience which went to the making of the eighteenth-century novel at its greatest. And Dr. Primrose was meant to be a figure of satire, almost a butt, a specimen of foolish optimism, of benevolence that did not know the world. Wisdom is represented by Burchell, whose job it is to save Primrose and his family from the consequences of the vicar's folly. But Goldsmith of all writers was the least cut out to be a realistic novelist, and what he achieved was something very different from what he intended; instead of the near tragedy of a man who brought himself and his family to ruin he produced something very much like a

fairy tale, an idealized picture of rural life, with a delightful Quixotic comic character at the center and with Burchell as an awkward eighteenth-century good fairy to con-
trive a happy ending. When we remember the book it is
the comic idyll of family life that comes first to mind; the
intrigue, the abduction, and the resolution of the plot require an effort of memory—inevitably, since they are carried out with hardly more conviction than similar incidents would be in a modern musical comedy.

In my view, underrated by literary historians is
Charles Johnstone's *Chrysal, or the Adventures of a
Guinea,* published in 1760. Structurally, it represented a
dead end in fiction, for the narrator, Chrysal, is a spirit,
the spirit of gold imprisoned in a guinea minted in Peru
and passed in the normal way of commerce and exchange
from hand to hand across the world to Europe. The device was not original. The use of an inanimate object as a
means of linking together a string of diverse episodes has
been traced to Le Sage. Its attraction is obvious: it enables
the author to encompass a wider range of varied and contrasted scenes than is possible even to the picaresque
novelist. Its weakness is equally obvious and so great as to
make no compensation in other directions adequate to it:
there is no possibility of any development of character
even to the modest extent found in a *Roderick Random*
or *Peregrine Pickle*.

But the device has a value as a vehicle for satire, and
Johnstone was nothing if not a satirist; the fact that he
chose as his inanimate object a piece of gold shows how
deliberate his satirical intention was, and, reading *Chrysal*,
one keeps catching glimpses of the great work that a satirist of the caliber of Swift or Fielding or Voltaire could
have written on Johnstone's plan. His aim is to expose
his age in terms of its cupidity, but this involves much
more than the mere word may suggest. What we get, in a
series of mainly vivid short episodes, is an all-embracing

view of power corrupted at all levels and the consequences in human misery. Johnstone's constant exposure of corruption becomes monotonous, and the bees in his bonnet —his hatred of Jews, Jesuits, and Dutchmen—are boring. He has the prejudices of his age as we do not find them in Fielding or even Smollett. Yet he had real powers of invention and could write a swift, effective satirical scene and follow it instantly with another; if the chapters describing how a clergyman's wife bribes a bishop's wife in order to get a vacant living for her husband and how the bishop in turn bribes a duchess in an attempt to get a vacant archbishopric had been written by Smollett, they would have been among the most admired instances of his work.

A much more genially satirical novel is the Rev. Richard Graves's *The Spiritual Quixote* (1772). The title defines its scope. Mr. Geoffrey Wildgoose, a young West Country squire, is infected with Methodism and sets off with the village cobbler as his Sancho Panza to preach the gospel and meet his hero Whitfield. It is essentially a novel of the open road; we can follow Mr. Wildgoose's itinerary as closely as Tom Jones's, and in his peregrinations he visits Gloucester, Bath, Bristol, the Midlands. *The Spiritual Quixote* is a satire not so much on Methodism as on Whitfield: he is the villain so far as the book has one, and the deadly little vignette of him at breakfast, with "a good bason of chocolate, and a plate of muffins well-buttered, before him," which is not at all as Wildgoose expects to find him, recalls irresistibly Dickens's Mr. Stiggins. Similarly, the most surprising, and effective, scene in the novel is when Wildgoose meets a traveler who attacks his beliefs, saying that "he would sooner renounce his Bible, than believe those doctrines, as Calvin of old, or Mr. Whitfield had of late, taught them." "I suppose then you are a follower of John Wesley's?" Wildgoose says. "No," replies the stranger; "I am John Wesley himself."

The Spiritual Quixote remains a very agreeable work, written in a very agreeable eighteenth-century prose. Graves was a much smaller writer than Fielding, but like him wrote as a scholar and a gentleman, with a similar urbanity and a belief in the disinfecting properties of reason.

Johnstone, like Fielding and Smollett, might have said with Wyndham Lewis: "The *external* approach to things (relying on the evidence of the *eye* rather than of the more emotional organs of sense) can make of 'the grotesque' a healthy and attractive companion. . . . Dogmatically, then, I am for the Great Without, for the method of *external* approach." But the tough-minded external approach is usually only possible so long as there is more or less general agreement, on the part of writers and the reading public alike, on what constitutes reality. It requires settled convictions on the nature of man's place in the universe and of his relations with his fellows and the rest of creation. The external approach is, in other words, an index of self-confidence, and when it dominates a literature, as in the first half of the eighteenth century, of a generally shared self-confidence. But when a common view of life breaks down, individual self-confidence wanes. The writer is thrown back on his own resources; he can no longer take it for granted that his attitude towards the external world will be generally accepted, and he is therefore forced to rely on himself, to rely on subjectivity. In a sense, it is not the world outside him that forms his subject matter so much as his own reactions to it.

Something like this happened to writers in the sixth decade of the eighteenth century, and it goes far towards explaining the decline in the novel. The Augustan order which had prevailed from the age of Anne until the end of George II's reign had passed; the reading public was no longer united in a body of commonly held assumptions about man, God, and society. In religion, Methodism was emphasizing the loneliness of man, stressing the paramount importance not of reason but of emotion. Novelists likewise began to stress the importance of emotion and to depend more and more on sensibility. Sensibility: its primary meaning is the power of sensation or perception, the specific function of the organs of sense. This meaning became overlaid with another, that of quickness and acuteness of apprehension or feeling, which in turn was extended, during the eighteenth century, to mean the capacity for refined emotion, sensitiveness generally in the face of external nature, and then the readiness to feel compassion for suffering, and to be moved by the pathetic. Plainly, this last kind of sensibility is always in danger of becoming morbid; it may become an end in itself, valued for itself, so that reality is sought only as a stimulus to the exercise of sensibility. When Jane Austen wrote *Sense and Sensibility* it was this that she had in mind:

> Marianne's abilities were, in many respects, quite equal to Elinor's. She was sensible and clever, but eager in everything: her sorrows, her joys, could have no moderation. She was generous, amiable, interesting; she was anything but prudent. The resemblance between her and her mother was strikingly great.
> Elinor saw, with concern, the excess of her sister's sensibility; but by Mrs. Dashwood it was valued and cherished. They encouraged each other now in the violence of their affliction. The agony of grief which overpowered them at first was voluntarily renewed, was sought for, was created again and again. They gave themselves up wholly to their sorrow, seeking increase of wretchedness in every reflection that could afford it, and resolved against ever admitting consolation in future. Elinor, too, was deeply afflicted; but still she could struggle, she could exert herself . . .

Jane Austen was writing very much as a belated eighteenth-century moralist; but in its beginnings in the eighteenth century sensibility was something more respectable than the self-indulgence of schoolgirls. It was another way of coping with the problem of arbitrary power. Behind the satire of Fielding and Smollett lay the idea of a rational pattern of society; abuses of power were deviations from an accepted norm and could be corrected by an appeal to reason through the voice of ridicule. But society was not static as Fielding and Smollett believed, and the middle of the century witnessed a crisis of confidence in reason. The obvious evils of society remained and did not grow less, and reason seemed powerless to correct them. The appeal was therefore to the heart, to the feelings, which Sterne had so well shown how to touch, though Sterne's great achievement, the use of sensibility for the purposes of humor, was exactly what the novelists of sensibility made no attempt to imitate. They used sensibility for moral, even political, ends. Henry Brooke's *The Fool of Quality*, the five volumes of which were published from 1766 to 1770, is a case in point. It is one of the worst novels ever written, but a remarkable book. An early instance of the influence of Rousseau's *Émile* in English, it is a treatise on education cast into fictional form. It describes the upbringing of little Harry Morland, who becomes the ideal nobleman through the fostering, by his eccentric and enormously wealthy uncle, of his sensibilities. Very long, utterly humorless (and therefore to the modern reader often funny), quite devoid of characters in any real sense, its action held up by long disquisitions on such themes as the beauties of the British Constitution and the all-important function of the merchant in society, and the narration further interrupted by "discussions" beween the author and his readers, *The Fool of Quality* is the work of a man who was less of a novelist, probably, than any who ever practiced the craft but who had a powerful and original mind. Harry Morland, who, incidentally, is probably the first instance of the child hero in fiction, is brought up to follow the dictates of his heart; he is the fool of the title. The fool, educated to act according to the generosity of his feelings and so regarded at first as little better than a half-wit, confounds and eventually converts all his critics by his irresistible goodness, the plausibility of his arguments, the attractiveness of his personality, and, possibly, his inexhaustible wealth.

> When breakfast was over, Harry called in John.—Mr. John, says he, can you tell me how many families there are in this village of yours?—Twenty-five families exactly, My lord. Then Harry turned to his father and said—If your lordship will be pleased to lend me five hundred guineas for the present, I will pay you very honestly the hour that my uncle comes to the country.—Why, sirrah! cried the earl pleasantly, what right has your uncle to pay your debts, especially to such a great amount as you speak of?—O, my lord, answered Harry, I have already squandered away above fifty thousand pounds of his money; and this is but a trifle, which I am sure I may very safely add to the rest.
>
> Here the earl looked truly astonished.—Fifty thousand pounds! he exclaimed. Impossible, Harry! Why, you had neither such ponds nor lakes as mine in London, wherein you might make ducks and drakes of them. How in the world could you contrive it? Where did you dispose of them?
>
> In hospitals and in prisons, my father, answered Harry. In streets and highways, among the wretched and indigent, supplying eyes to the blind, and limbs to the lame, and cheerfulness to the sorrowful and broken of heart; for such were my uncle's orders.
>
> Let me go, let me go from this place, my lord! cried Meekly; this boy will absolutely kill me if I stay any longer. He overpowers, he suffocates me with the weight of his sentiments.

The weight of his sentiments suffocates us too; but whatever its merits as a novel, *The Fool of Quality* has a permanent interest as an example of the literary expression of the impulses governing the humanitarian movement of the century.

A more famous book, and more successful as a novel, is Henry Mackenzie's *The Man of Feeling*, published in 1771, which exploits sensibility for much more purely aesthetic ends than Brooke's book. Both have earned the ridicule of later generations because of the excessive tendencies of their characters to burst into tears; in fairness it must be remembered that, as a matter of fact, eighteenth-century man did weep much more readily than we do. Mackenzie wrote very well indeed. His novel is presented as a series of fragments, a device he had perhaps picked up from Sterne, as the remains of a manuscript found by a sporting curate who, when the book opens, has used a considerable part of it as wadding for his gun. When rescued and pieced together, the manuscript contains the story of Harley, the Man of Feeling, to whom "a blush, a phrase of affability to an inferior, a tear at a moving tale, were . . . like the Cestus of Cythera, unequalled in conferring beauty." The story, such as it is, is a conventional eighteenth-century one: Harley's adventures in London and on the road to and from London. It is a record of disillusionment. As a man of feeling, Harley accepts expressions of feeling on the part of others as genuine and is therefore continually deceived. But he goes on feeling and doing good where he can. He rescues a prostitute and restores her to her father. He visits Bedlam, to the spectacle of which, especially where lunacy is combined with beauty, Harley pays "the tribute of some tears." Returned home, in love with a neighbor's daughter, he dares not confess his love until Miss Walton visits him on his sickbed. Then he does so, but her response is too much for so delicately organized a sensibility. She says:

> "Let not life be so indifferent to you; if my wishes can put any value on it—I will not pretend to misunderstand you—I know your worth—I have known it long—I have esteemed it—what would you have me say?—I have loved it as it deserved." He seized her hand—a languid colour reddened his cheek—a smile brightened faintly in his eye. As he gazed on her, it grew dim, it fixed, it closed. He sighed and fell back on his seat—Miss Walton screamed at the sight. His aunt and the servants rushed into the room. They found them lying motionless together. His physician happened to call at that instant. Every art was tried to recover them; with Miss Walton they succeeded—but Harley was gone for ever!

As Scott said, *The Man of Feeling* exhibits "a hero constantly obedient to every emotion of his moral sense. It is most skillfully done, and the London scenes, lightly touched in as they are, are admirable. In its way, it is almost a minor masterpiece, and what renders it perennially fascinating is its singular purity as a specimen of the cult of sensibility. Literary historians, in an attempt to impose some sort of order on the chaos in fiction during the last thirty years or so of the century, have often distinguished categories of the novel—the novel of sentiment, the Gothic novel, or novel of horror, the oriental tale, the novel of doctrine, and so on. The terms are useful so long as it is remembered that the categories are not hard and fast compartments. Underlying them all is the single quality of sensibility, which could take many forms. So *The Man of Feeling* may primarily have as its end a description of the impact of the world upon a young man "obedient to every emotion of his moral sense," but it is also, by implication, a statement of the case against the world, against society. As for Rousseau, so for Mackenzie—society is always evil, and against society is set the innocence and uncorrupted virtue of the idyllic countryside: "As to the world—I pity the men of it."

Along with this rejection of the world there goes a conscious, connoisseur's delight in landscape and the "picturesque":

An old man, who from his dress seemed to have been a soldier, lay fast asleep on the ground; a knapsack rested on a stone at his right hand, while his staff and brass-hilted sword were crossed at his left.

Harley looked on him with the most earnest attention. He was one of those figures which Salvator would have drawn; nor was the surrounding scenery unlike the wildness of that painter's backgrounds. The banks on each side were covered with fantastic shrub-wood, and at a little distance, on the top of one of them, stood a finger-post to mark the directions to two roads which diverged from the point where it was placed. A rock, with some dangling wild flowers, jutted out above where the soldier lay; on which grew the stump of a large tree, white with age, and a single twisted branch shaded his face as he slept. . . .

In the fiction of this time the inspiration derived from Salvator Rosa is almost as great as that derived from Hogarth in the novels of Fielding. Sir Kenneth Clark has written in his *Landscape Into Art*:

> Today, after a century of more intense romanticism, it is hard to see how the world of taste was so long deceived by the second-rate talents of Salvator. But we must realize that he was, in a minor degree, a kind of Byron. He opened a new vein of sentiment, and discovered the rhetorical form in which it could be conveyed. That his sentiments were exaggerated and his means of expressing them often commonplace was a factor in his popularity. The artist who invents stage properties which can be borrowed with effect, is sure of success, and the minor painters of the eighteenth century came to rely on Salvator's banditti and shaggy fir-trees as their successors of the 1930s relied on Picasso's harlequins and guitars. Neither would have obtained currency had they not also fulfilled some half-realized dream of the period. As Dr. Johnson said of Sterne, "His nonsense suited their nonsense." The nonsense which the eighteenth century required was some escape from its own oppressive rationalism.

Sensibility, which could find pleasure in the nicety and correctness of its feelings in the presence of human suffering or moral problems, found that it could find pleasure also in the wildness of nature, in the lawlessness of the exotic, and in indulgence in sensations of fear and awe before the mysterious or the inexplicable. The rationalism of the early eighteenth century no longer satisfied. Sensibility, in its various manifestations, was the contemporary expression of what Johnson called "that hunger of the imagination which preys incessantly on life."

Johnson knew all about sensibility, and for him, as for the great writers of the first part of the century, Swift and Pope, it was something emphatically not to be indulged

in, for that way madness lay. His one excursion into fiction of some length, *The History of Rasselas, Prince of
Abyssinia* (1759), for all its apparent exoticism of scene, is
a statement of values uncorrupted by the cult of sensibility. It is scarcely a novel, just as its setting bears no resemblance to Abyssinia then or now. Rather it is a philosophical fable on the vanity of human happiness. The
prince who leaves his birthplace in order to see the world
and finds virtue nowhere, man nowhere happy, returns
to his kingdom to devote himself to the duties that lie immediately at hand. *Rasselas* is Johnson's *Candide,* but a
much more somber one than Voltaire's, the expression of
a stoicism that would be the deepest pessimism were it not
for its author's almost despairing Christianity, for Johnson,
who did not know the word, knew at first hand the terrors
of the concept *Angst.* The *angst*-ridden do not cultivate
their sensibilities.

But *Rasselas* has its place in the history of modern fiction because it is the first major manifestation in English
of the oriental tale. In English fiction, indeed, the oriental
tale means simply *Rasselas* and Beckford's *Vathek.* The
Arabian Nights had been translated for the first time into
European languages at the beginning of the century. The
society, values, modes of thinking, and feeling they revealed fascinated because they were so utterly different
from those of Western Europe. A first reading of the
Arabian Nights must have been for the Augustans like the
discovery of a planet inhabited by creatures intelligent
certainly but utterly and disconcertingly unlike human
beings, and just as in the twentieth century writers have
for the purpose of satire brought Martians to the earth,
so the first literary exploitation of the discovery of the
East was for satirical ends. In France, Montesquieu wrote
his *Lettres Persanes,* and forty years later Goldsmith in
England wrote *The Citizen of the World;* both had the
same intention, to show the West how it might appear to

an intelligent man from the world outside the West. But at the same time, the fabulous world of Scheherazade began to have a value in its own right, and its value was precisely its fabulousness, its almost antipodal difference from the West with its rationalism and its roots in Greece and Rome.

Beckford's *Vathek*, written in French between 1781 and 1782, and translated into English without his permission two years later, is the perfect expression of the submission to the fabulous, submission, that is to say, without ulterior motive. Is it a novel? The question scarcely matters, except to remind us that though the novel has its roots in the reality round us it regularly aspires to the condition of fantasy, which is what *Vathek* is. But it is fantasy still rooted in the perception of the real, for Beckford's story of the caliph Vathek's pursuit of knowledge and power, in the course of which, Faustlike, he sells himself to the powers of evil, is a statement in fable of the author's own dominant impulses; in his own actual life Beckford got as near to being a Vathek as the West allowed. Of its kind of writing *Vathek* is a masterpiece; its imaginative quality and the sublimity of its end have always been praised. It is a *tour de force* of the most sustained order. But what has not received adequate attention is the quality of its writing. It is an unusually witty book, and the wit is of an unusual sort. It is, as it were, a fabulous wit depending on the juxtaposition of the unexpected, the shocking adjective to the obvious noun, to produce the bizarre or grotesque image:

> Wherever the caliph directed his course, objects of pity were sure to swarm round him; the blind, the purblind, smarts without noses, damsels without ears, each to extol the munificence of Fakreddin, who, as well as his attendant greybeards, dealt about, gratis, plasters and cataplasms to all that applied. At noon, a superb corps of cripples made its appearance; and soon after advanced, by platoons, on the plain, the completest association of invalids that had ever

been embodied till then. The blind went groping with the blind, the lame limped on together, and the maimed made gestures to each other with the only arm that remained. The sides of a considerable waterfall were crowded by the deaf; amongst whom were some from Pegu, with ears uncommonly large and handsome, but who were still less able to hear than the rest. Nor were there wanting others in abundance with hump-backs, wenny necks, and even horns of an exquisite polish.

Vathek had no direct influence on the fiction that was to follow; but the tone of voice, a similar style, and a similarly disconcerting view of life—as though the actual world had been taken to pieces and put together again in a slightly different form, which shocked and amused at the same time—was to appear more than a hundred years later in Aubrey Beardsley's unfinished *Under the Hill,* and in the novels of Ronald Firbank in the twentieth century.

Much more important than the discovery of a fictitious East, the falsity of which could always be exposed by actual acquaintance with the reality of the East, was the rediscovery of the past, of the sense of history. Until the middle of the seventeenth century men had scarcely distinguished between the present and the past. Then, with the beginning of the eighteenth century, the past, the great ages of Greece and Rome always excepted as peaks of human achievement moderns might possibly equal but could never expect to surpass, was seen as essentially different from the present and dismissed as barbaric, rude, and uncivilized. This self-complacency, which was the manifestation of a rare confidence in civilization and reason, did not last long; and when it came, the discovery of the past, of the Middle Ages in particular, was an event in the development of the Western mind second in importance only to the discovery of classical antiquity in the fourteenth and fifteenth centuries.

But as with the first cultivation of sensibility, preoccupation with the past seems to have had little more significance for many of its early discoverers than that of an amusing game. While serious and learned men like the poet Gray and Bishop Percy were diligently exploring the literature of the Dark and Middle ages, the Icelandic sagas and the ballads, wealthy dilettantes adorned the grounds of their country seats with cunningly contrived "medieval" ruins and hermits' grottoes. At Twickenham, Horace Walpole turned Strawberry Hill into a miniature Gothic castle, in the imitation baronial halls of which he wrote *The Castle of Otranto* in 1764.

The Castle of Otranto is only sketchily a novel, and if it were not for the progeny which derived from it one could dismiss it as a dilettante's freak. Read today it may easily be taken as an exercise in the absurd. It is the fate of the dilettante to seem to later generations absurd; for all that, his function, however much it may manifest itself as apparently irresponsible caprice, is highly valuable, and, given the background and atmosphere of its own time, the importance of *The Castle of Otranto* is obvious. That it is as gimcrack and synthetic as Strawberry Hill itself is beside the point. Nor is Walpole to be laughed at when he writes: "That great master of nature, Shakespeare, was the model I copied." However vast the gulf between *Hamlet* and Walpole's story, the fact that he could believe he was following Shakespeare indicates how potent a liberator Shakespeare has always been when writers have felt themselves oppressed and constricted by conventional ways of looking at life and of recording the vision seen. What Walpole thought he got from Shakespeare was the contrast, making for pathos, between the sublime "of princes and heroes" and the naiveté of "their domestics." Walpole was after that mixture of tragedy and comedy within the same work which is a feature equally of Elizabethan drama and the English novel. And in a sense, what Walpole thought he had done in *The Castle of Otranto* is as important as what he actually did.

The inspiration of the story came in a dream: he saw the hall and staircase of Strawberry Hill, which was combined with vague memories of a Cambridge college, with "a gigantic hand in armor" laid upon the banister. The gigantic hand became the gigantic helmet in the story which crushes the son of the usurper Manfred. When we know its origin it is easy to see how *The Castle of Otranto* was constructed. It is, as it were, a fabrication in daylight, and it creaks as artificial dreams commonly do. Walpole was after the marriage of the supernatural with the natural. He succeeded with neither. His use of supernatural machinery is ludicrous and far too frequent. The story is much closer to Grand Guignol than to the supernatural, and when, for instance, we read that "three drops of blood fell from the nose of Alfonso's statue," it is impossible not to smile. Indeed, it seems now that Walpole had missed the whole point of Shakespeare's use of the supernatural, which is always cautious in the extreme. As for his attempts at the natural, Walpole reveals a complete lack of aptitude for the creation of character and for the writing of convincing dialogue.

The Castle of Otranto strikes one today as an almost purely intellectual construction, a monstrous mechanism built to the specifications of a carefully thought-out blueprint. It had few direct imitators. In *The Champion of Virtue, a Gothic Tale,* published in 1777, and retitled a year later *The Old English Baron,* Mrs. Clara Reeve proposed to keep her story within "the utmost *verge* of probability." She did little more than tell a sentimental story in a sham medieval setting, with the supernatural reduced to a few hollow groans. The flowering of the Gothic novel was still to come. But the term Gothic novel must be used cautiously; it can easily be a red herring, for if we take a Gothic novelist like Mrs. Radcliffe and place her beside her contemporaries Charlotte Smith, Robert Bage, and William Godwin, who were not in any strict sense exponents of the Gothic, we shall be aware not so much of the differences between them as of the mental and emotional climate they share. Different though they are, they are much more like each other than they are like the novelists who went before them; they have much more in common with one another than they have with Fanny Burney, for instance, whose first and best novel, *Evelina,* was published in 1778, when she was twenty-six.

Fanny Burney's historical importance is undeniable, though her actual achievement has been overvalued. What Miss Burney did was to fuse part of the heritage of Richardson with that of Fielding. Her theme is always a young girl's impressions of the social world, her mistakes in society, her gradual discovery of its values, and her discovery of love, which, after some misunderstandings due to her innocence, ends in marriage. *Evelina* is told in letter form. It records naturally the gradual development of the heroine's mind as she moves in society, her hesitations, her doubts, her agonies at the social solecisms she commits, her analysis of her heart when in love. This came from Richardson. But the exploration of emotion and moral impulse was not Miss Burney's major interest; her heroine, for all her sharpness of wits and merciless eye for observation, is a conventional enough young woman, a young woman moving uncritically in the context of masculine values. This is one distinction between her and Jane Austen, who, though she does not deny those values, sees them in a wholly feminine context; and it distinguishes her also from Mrs. Inchbald, in whose admirable novel, *A Simple Story,* published in 1791, we have for the first time adequate expression of the attitude towards men of a strong-willed, imperious, beautiful young woman; beside Mrs. Inchbald's Miss Milner, a delightfully flashing and in the end tragic character, Fanny Burney's Evelina is a priggish mouse.

Fanny Burney's real strength was in social comedy,

and here she derives from Fielding. Her work represents the feminization of Fielding's art. It involved, of course, a tremendous diminution of Fielding's range. The whole world of his time was open to Tom Jones; the only one open to Fanny Burney was that accessible to a conventionally brought up upper-middle-class young lady constantly chaperoned, a world of routs, assemblies, balls, and tea parties, dominated by the quest for marriage, or rather, dominated by the maneuvering, innocent or otherwise, necessary to place a girl in the way of an eligible young man. In this world, men are awful and incalculable, when seen in the light of possible husbands or potential seducers, or ludicrous, if, as often, they think themselves possible husbands but are seen quite otherwise by the young women. To read Miss Burney is rather like having a mouse's view of the world of cats; the cats are very terrifying, but the mouse's sense of the ridiculous could not be keener. As an almost necessary corollary, the cats are only convincing as characters when they are ridiculous; Lord Orville, the hero of *Evelina,* a young girl's dream of a nobleman based on Richardson's Grandison, could scarcely be more wooden.

David Cecil has said that Fanny Burney's novels represent the entry of the lady into English fiction. They also represent the entry of the modern notion of class. In the work of the great eighteenth-century novelists class is still more or less feudal; everyone knows his place. Doubtless, this was not so in reality, but the sweep of a novelist like Fielding was too great to take in small discriminations of rank and position. Small discriminations, however, are precisely the subjects that most exercise ladies at tea parties, and Fanny Burney's fiction, like the world she lived in, is full of people who, absurd as it may seem to her, do not know their place. They are Miss Burney's natural victims; she observes them with a camera eye and picks up their speech with a microphone ear. Her vulgarians, the families of new-rich city merchants, expose themselves in their speech. Vulgarity, social pretensions on the part of the low, pain Miss Burney, but their absurdity also delights her, and her best comedy lies in the malicious rendering of the vulgar, as in this passage from *Evelina*:

"Mr. Smith, you are come in very good time," said Mr. Branghton, "to end a dispute between my son and daughter, about where they shall all go tonight."

"O fie, Tom,—dispute with a lady!" cried Mr. Smith. "Now, as for me, I'm for where you will, provided this young lady is of the party,—one place is the same as another to me, so that it be but agreeable to the ladies, I would go anywhere with you, Ma'am" (to me), "unless, indeed, it were to *church;* —ha, ha, ha,—you'll excuse me, Ma'am, but, really, I never could conquer my fear of a parson;—ha, ha, ha,—really, ladies, I beg your pardon, for being so rude, but I can't help laughing for my life!"

And later:

About ten o'clock, Mr. Smith having chosen a *box* in a very conspicuous place, we all went to supper. Much fault was found with everything that was ordered, though not a morsel of anything was left; and the dearness of provisions, with conjectures upon what profit was made by them, supplied discourse during the whole meal.

Evelina was a prodigious success when it first appeared, and very properly so. She caught in the lens of her malice all the London of her day that was fashionable or aspired to fashion. While she remained within her range—that part of a novelist's total experience of life that fructifies his imagination—she could do nothing wrong. But her range was limited, and when she goes outside it we are aware of a crudity the more glaring because of her brilliance in other directions. It was, for instance, a fatal mistake to attempt to fuse Smollett with Fielding and Richardson; in such scenes as the hold-up of Evelina's mother, tiresome as she is, by the pretended highwaymen, with the loss of her wig in the ditch, or the race between the two old crones, one is conscious now only of embarrassment.

If Fanny Burney has been overrated, Mrs. Charlotte Smith has been persistently underrated. In particular, *The Old Manor House* remains a most respectable work whose interest is more than historical. Published in 1793, it lacks few of the preoccupations that distinguish the fiction of the last years of the century, but they are all fused into an organic whole; a complete revolution of taste and feeling has occurred in which Mrs. Smith is perfectly at home. She is, for instance, probably the first novelist to use descriptions of natural scenery as a matter of course, but she does not use them merely for decoration or as backcloths; they have an emotional relationship to the characters who move through them. Similarly, she incorporated into her work a sense of history. From the comments of some literary historians one might think that *The Old Manor House* was a Gothic novel. Her manor house is of some antiquity, rapidly falling into decay and believed to be haunted, but the only ghosts, as is made clear early on in the story, are smugglers who exploit the ill repute of the house for their own purposes. Of course Mrs. Smith delights in romantic properties, deserted chapels, old cellars, family portraits, tapestries, armor, and so on; but they are all used to further the development of the story and are subordinated to it. And the story is a good one, relevant to the situation of the times. Orlando, the hero, is a young man of impoverished family compelled in the hope of becoming her heir to dance attendance on his great-aunt Miss Rayland, an old lady who lives in a fantasy world of family pride and great position. He falls in love with the ward of Miss Rayland's housekeeper, Mrs. Lennard, a love he has to keep secret for fear of offending his aunt. Mrs. Smith makes it quite clear that Miss Rayland's *is* a fantasy world; power now resides with the new rich—rich from industrial sources—who own the neighboring estate.

Neither Orlando nor Monimia, the girl he loves, has much life; but Miss Rayland is excellently drawn, and so too is Orlando's father's false friend General Tracy, the aging roué. Orlando's sister Isabella, whom the General hopes first to seduce and then decides to marry, has a vivacity and high-spiritedness akin to Mrs. Inchbald's Miss Milner. Mrs. Smith was scarcely a satirist, but her work and the characters in it spring from a considered point of view. There is implicit in *The Old Manor House* a body of ideas which gives the novel a real strength. Much less openly doctrinaire than Bage and Godwin, Mrs. Smith was all the same a radical; without in the least distorting her fiction to propaganda ends, she was using it to embody her criticism of society. This is overt in the chapters in which Orlando, a young officer, serves in America against the colonists; but it is implicit in her portraits of Miss Rayland and General Tracy, and it is this that gives them their power. They are in their different ways specimens of a decaying society. At the same time, she was a true novelist; she never allows her political sympathies to pervert these characters into figures of melodrama: Miss Rayland has in the end considerable pathetic dignity, and Tracy, though presented in terms of sober comedy, is never merely an object of ridicule. They are both solid creations.

Then Mrs. Smith has great technical skill. She was an adept at the handling of large scenes of intrigue, at the placing of her characters in situations which must inevitably put them at cross purposes one with another. So she builds up from one peak of interest to the next. And she wrote an admirable sober prose, with flashes of biting descriptive power, as in a phrase like "Her whole face was the color of bad veal." It is odd that so good a novel should not have been reprinted since 1820.

Mrs. Ann Radcliffe's best-known work, *The Mysteries*

of Udolpho, which has become almost the stock example of the Gothic novel, or the novel of horror, was published a year later than *The Old Manor House.* In it we can see, without the slightest shadow of doubt, the great change that had taken place in the novel, in its conception and scope alike, and of that change Mrs. Radcliffe's Gothic horrors are not the most important part. In her valuable document, "Notes on Writing a Novel," in *Collected Impressions,* Elizabeth Bowen has stated that the object of the novel is "the non-poetic statement of a poetic truth." Fully to disengage the implications of the epigram would require many pages. Here it can only be noted that while the description is recognizably true of an increasing number of novels it is not true of, among others, those of the great eighteenth-century writers: poetic truth was far from their end. It was, however, Mrs. Radcliffe's, and her fiction is the first of a type now very distinguished indeed. I do not mean the thriller, though *The Mysteries of Udolpho* was the first successful thriller. The novels I have in mind can best be indicated in a selection of examples, some more obvious than others: *Great Expectations* (if one thinks primarily of the early background of the Essex marshes and the house of Miss Havisham), the greater part of Hardy, almost any of William Faulkner's novels, and Miss Bowen's *The House in Paris* and *The Heat of the Day.* These novels are characterized by a peculiarly intense relationship between the characters and their immediate environments. Character and environment are impregnated each with the other. To some extent environment is, as it were, humanized, and the character himself is as he is because of the environment and cannot be detached from it; it is a necessary element for his existence, a special kind of air. The immediate environment exists, even, in a symbolic relation to the character; this is plain if one thinks of the decaying mansions in Faulkner's novels. In other words, in such novels the ambience in which the characters move is as important as the characters themselves.

Mrs. Radcliffe, though not to the same extent or in so sophisticated a manner, uses her landscape and castles in this way. There are times in *The Mysteries of Udolpho* when landscape seems merely to serve the purpose of a backcloth, when we feel that we are being taken, with Emily, on a conducted tour of the Mediterranean littoral. But even then the background of scenery exists to feed Emily's sensibility; it is material for her feeling. Judged conventionally, Mrs. Radcliffe's Emily is a dim enough character, but she is adequate to her creator's purposes; she is incarnate sensibility, and her function in the novel is simply to feel, to feel the appropriate emotions of wonder, awe, and terror. From this point of view, *The Mysteries of Udolpho* may be considered as a machine for making the reader feel similar emotions. The *Alpes maritimes* and castles in the Apennines, then, are just as important, as much essential to the novel as a novel, as the characters who haunt them. It is this that is new—new because it is successful for the first time—in the fiction of Mrs. Radcliffe. In her work the characters are wholly subordinate to environment; it plays upon them, invades them, almost takes them over altogether. By comparison with her, Richardson, Fielding, Smollett, Miss Burney play out their actions on bare boards.

We must be careful how we judge Mrs. Radcliffe. If we look for character in the eighteenth-century sense, which is still the conventional sense, character observed and rendered from the outside, we shall be disappointed. We shall, in fact, find only one such character, Mme. Montani, a scheming vulgar snob, who might almost have stepped out of the pages of Fanny Burney. We shall be disappointed, too, if we go to *The Mysteries of Udolpho* as an historical novel, noting from the first sentence of the book that the action of the book begins in Gascony in

1584. Mrs. Radcliffe has merely set her action in a past conveniently remote; her characters are of her own time, and she has made no attempt to "get up" her period or seek accuracy of detail. But these are minor matters. She placed her story, a thriller, in a situation in time where it could appear to be not improbable. And her handling of the story is brilliant. She communicates a real sense of mystery, and her management of suspense is admirable. She cheats once or twice, by modern standards, and she has been criticized for producing at the end rational explanations of what had appeared to be supernatural happenings. Here she had merely anticipated the basis of logic without which the thriller cannot exist. Her influence was enormous. M. G. Lewis, in *The Monk* (1795), and Charles Maturin, in *Melmoth the Wanderer* (1820), deriving also from German sources, defied the basis in logic of her novels and plunged headlong into the ghostly, the ghastly, and the supernatural, their aim the evocation of horror only. Scott learned from her; and, it has been said, "the man that Lord Byron tried to be was the invention of Mrs. Radcliffe." With her, indeed, we are already plumb in the middle of the romantic movement; her half-ruined castles on perilous crags, with dungeons beneath, her mountains, seas, and forests, her monks and nuns, the embodiments of hooded superstition, her bandits and her villains, were to become in a matter of years part of the territory and inhabitants of poetry proper. And beyond the first romantics she points to Poe and all the nineteenth-century novelists and storytellers who use, however subtly, the supernatural, the psychic, and even morbid psychological states in man, as well as to the great host of crude thriller writers of the present day.

The last decade of the century was, in fact, distinguished by the excellence of the fiction it produced. William Godwin's *Caleb Williams* appeared the year after *The Mysteries of Udolpho*. It remains a work which reveals fresh facets to each new generation of readers in the light of the preoccupations of the fiction of their own time. Godwin was a political philosopher, and the boldness of conception that went to the writing of *Political Justice* did Godwin no harm when he turned to fiction. Indeed, the one impulse produced both the work of philosophy and the novel, and Godwin seems to have conceived *Caleb Williams* as a sort of fictional gloss on the earlier book. In a highly interesting preface to the edition of 1832, reminiscent in many ways of Poe's essay on the writing of "The Raven," he tells how he wrote the novel:

> I formed a conception of a book of fictitious adventure that should in some way be distinguished by a very powerful interest. Pursuing this idea, I invented first the third volume of my tale, then the second, and last of all the first. I bent myself to the conception of a series of adventures of flight and pursuit; the fugitive on perpetual apprehension of being overwhelmed with the worst calamities, and the pursuer, by his ingenuity and resources, keeping his victim in a state of the most fearful alarm. . . . I was next called upon to conceive a dramatic and impressive situation adequate to account for the impulse that the pursuer should feel, incessantly to alarm and harass his victim, with an inextinguishable resolution never to allow him the least interval of peace and security. This I apprehended could best be affected by a secret murder, to the investigation of which the innocent victim should be impelled by an unconquerable spirit of curiosity . . .

So, by working backwards from the end, we come to the immediately arresting opening sentences: "My life has for several years been a theater of calamity. I have been a mark for the vigilance of tyranny, and I could not escape. My fairest prospects have been blasted. My enemy has shown himself inaccessible to entreaties, and untired in persecution. My fame, as well as my happiness, has been his victim." One may set alongside this opening that of a novel written almost one hundred and fifty years later, *Brighton Rock*: "Hale knew, before he had been in

Brighton three hours, that they meant to murder him. In *Caleb Williams* Godwin was writing the prototype of what may be called the novel of pursuit, which is seen in its crudest form in the "cops versus robbers" story and which achieves literary dignity in such works as *The Master of Ballantrae* and Graham Greene's *Brighton Rock* and *The Power and the Glory.* And like Graham Greene, Godwin was using the conception of the pursuit symbolically. His victim-hero, Caleb Williams, the victim equally of his insatiable curiosity and of his unrelenting pursuer, has happened to stumble upon the knowledge—or the half knowledge—that his employer, the noble-minded Falkland, is a murderer. But an unusual murderer. As he confesses to Williams: "I am the fool of fame . . . I am as much the fool of fame as ever. Though I be the blackest of villains, I will leave behind me a spotless and illustrious name. There is no crime so malignant, no scene of blood so horrible, in which that object cannot engage me." And he continues, having admitted his guilt: "Do you know what you have done? To gratify a foolishly inquisitive humour, you have sold yourself. You shall continue in my service, but never share my affection. I will benefit you in respect of fortune, but I shall always hate you. If ever an unguarded word escape your lips, if ever you excite my jealousy or suspicion, expect to pay for it by your death or worse."

When Williams attempts to escape from his bondage he is pursued and hounded by Falkland's agents until he becomes a pariah in society, "completely," as he says, "cut off from the whole human species" by Falkland's omnipresent machinations. And when at the end he does turn the tables on Falkland, when Falkland is arraigned before his fellow justices and confesses his guilt, to throw himself in Williams's arms and then die three days later, it comes home to Williams that: "I have been his murderer. It was fit that he should praise my patience, who has fallen a victim, life and fame, to my precipitation! It would have been merciful in comparison if I had planted a dagger in his heart."

In no novel of pursuit has the chase been more relentless or the atmosphere of persecution—for we are always inside Williams's mind—more claustrophobic. Godwin carried through his project with an intensity of imagination that anticipates Poe. But this is not all. Godwin believed he was presenting in symbolic terms the relation between government and those who incur the enmity of government. But symbols, if they are successful, transcend what we may call their prose translations. If true symbols, they can never be reduced to what their creator believes they stand for. It is an index of Godwin's successful use of symbol that the reader today, even though he knows the connection between the novel and *Political Justice,* may if he wishes see in this study of the hunter and the hunted who in the end find that their enmity is really love a profound symbolic rendering of the relation between God and man. Godwin had been brought up a Calvinist, and that fact has its importance in the genesis of *Caleb Williams.*

Godwin is by far the greatest of what have been called the "doctrinaire" novelists, though where he is concerned the term is a misnomer since, in *Caleb Williams* at any rate and also to a less degree in *St. Leon,* he was writing from profounder impulses than the purely political. A doctrinaire novelist proper was Robert Bage, a Staffordshire papermaker of thoroughgoing radical and French revolutionary sympathies, as his best novel, *Hermsprong, or Man As He Is Not* (1796), shows. In a sense, with Bage the class war enters fiction, for *Hermsprong* is a completely intransigent attack on feudalism and the notion of aristocracy. Against the tyrannical, avaricious Lord Grondale Bage pits "Man as he is not," man, that is to say, as he scarcely existed at the time of writing (and one might add, never will exist), in the person of the completely virtuous, wholly rational Hermsprong, who has been brought to recognize truth and tell it on all occasions by the noble redskins of North America. Hermsprong, a character inspired by Rousseau, is the criterion by which the civilization in which he finds himself is tested and found wanting. One cannot call him a prig, for he is an ideal creation, carried through with genuine intellectual power and moral passion. What gives the novel its life today is Bage's very real sardonic wit; Bage knew his Voltaire, and his novel is historically valuable because he takes us so well into the mind of the "Leftist" of the time. As a novelist, however, Bage added nothing new to fiction. His plot is a perfectly conventional eighteenth-century plot, and it is with disappointment that the reader finally learns that Hermsprong himself is the true legitimate Lord Grondale.

3

THE NINETEENTH CENTURY:
THE FIRST GENERATION

1

SIGNIFICANT CHANGES, new directions, in literature are rarely so obliging as to coincide in their appearance with such convenient points in time as the turn of a century. The year 1800, however, is a date of the first importance in the history of English fiction, indeed of world fiction, for in that year Maria Edgeworth published her short novel *Castle Rackrent*. Not her first book, it was her first work of fiction proper, and had she written nothing else, P. H. Newby's suggestive remark, in his admirable little book on her, would still hold good: "Whereas Jane Austen was so much the better novelist Maria Edgeworth may be the more important." The judgment needs expanding before it makes sense, but Maria Edgeworth herself was nearly a great novelist, and her purely historical importance must not blind us to the positive merit of her own achievement.

Miss Edgeworth occupied new territory for the novel. Before her, except when London was the scene, the locale of our fiction had been generalized, conventionalized. Outside London and Bath, the eighteenth-century novelist rarely had a sense of place; the background of his fiction is as bare of scenery almost as an Elizabethan play; and when landscape came in for its own sake, with Mrs. Radcliffe, it was there not because it was a specific landscape but because it was a romantic one. Maria Edgeworth gave fiction a local habitation and a name. And she did more than this: she perceived the relation between the local habitation and the people who dwell in it. She invented, in other words, the regional novel, in which the very nature of the novelist's characters is conditioned, receives its bias and expression, from the fact that they live in a countryside differentiated by a traditional way of life from other countrysides.

The region she discovered was Ireland, and, with Ireland, the Irish peasant. She was what would now be called Anglo-Irish, one of the ruling class, and she is the first of a long line of Anglo-Irish novelists who have exploited the humors of the Irish peasantry and its relation to the big house; Lover, Lever, Somerville and Ross were her literary descendants. But her influence goes far beyond this, as we may realize when we consider how many of the world's great novelists, from Scott through Flaubert to Mauriac, are regional novelists. Scott made no secret of his debt to her; his aim in fiction, as he said in the postscript to *Waverley,* was "in some distant degree to emulate the admirable Irish portraits drawn by Miss Edgeworth," and when we read these words we have to remember how enormous was Scott's influence on the novel throughout the western world. But her direct influence goes even beyond Scott. Turgenev is said to have stated that he was "an unconscious disciple of Miss Edgeworth in setting out on his literary career."

The originality of Maria Edgeworth's contribution to the novel is apparent as soon as one begins to read *Castle Rackrent,* short as it is. It is not so important, perhaps, that in it she wrote the first of all "saga" novels, tracing the history of a family through several generations. What matters much more is the way in which the history of the Rackrent family, who are Irish landowners, is told. The story is narrated in the first person by old Thady, a peasant who is the ancient retainer of the family. So we have at once a family history and a vivid self-portrait of an old man, simple, shrewd, possessed of native dignity, told in his own language, which, though naturally a literary version, is close enough to Irish peasant speech to retain the illusion of authenticity. And Thady is a delightful character, rich in what we now think of as typically Irish humor, the more beguiling because it is unconscious. An example is his comment on the death of Sir Patrick Rackrent:

> The whole country rang with his praises. Happy the man who could but get a sight of the hearse! But who'd have thought it? Just as all was going on right, through his own town they were passing, when the body was seized for debt.

At the same time, through Thady's voice, there is summed up the whole social history of a country over four generations. *Castle Rackrent* is a very considerable work of art in fiction, and how remarkable Maria Edgeworth was as an innovator in this novel we may probably best estimate at this point in time by setting beside it a novel that did a comparable job for its own national literature eighty years later: Mark Twain's *Huckleberry Finn,* the novel that freed American fiction from the domination of specifically English literature.

Miss Edgeworth wrote other excellent novels, and in its different way *The Absentee* seems to me no less remarkable than *Castle Rackrent,* though its weaknesses are more evident because the canvas is so much the vaster. To read *The Absentee* is to appreciate how very real the effect of Miss Edgeworth may have been on Turgenev, for, in one respect at any rate, we feel, as we read it, that we are in a world suprisingly similar to that of much nineteenth-century Russian fiction. The novel opens in London—and it might almost as easily be Moscow or St. Petersburg. There is Lady Clonbrony, the wife of an absentee Irish peer, busily at work striving to stake a claim to a position for herself in fashionable society, perverting her native Irish good humor and simplicity into a comic parody of English aristocratic manners and behavior; a figure of fun to the ladies who flock to her balls and routs; a source of endless expense to her weak-willed husband, whose Irish estates must be mortgaged to enable her to keep her foothold in the great world, and whose tenants must be fleeced and screwed for ready money to keep the usurers at bay. Lord and Lady Clonbrony might be landowners from a remote province in a Russian novel who have at last got to Moscow. For in *The Absentee* Maria Edgeworth had seized upon the essential situation of her country at the time of writing: the absence of its landowners in England and the stranglehold their agents had on a helpless peasantry. And when we visit Ireland in the company of Lord Colambre, the Clonbronys' son, whose aim it is to induce his parents to return to their native land and take up their proper duties there, we might be in nineteenth-century Russia, in that world of sequestered petty landowners, culturally almost indistinguishable from their peasants, among whom every kind of eccentricity flourished.

The Absentee, then, has a theme that was of the highest importance in its day, and it is bodied forth in a set of admirable characters. Maria Edgeworth had a most enviable gift of creating characters in the round, characters that seem, for much of the time at least, to exist independently of their author. Had she allowed them to exist independently of her all the time she would truly have been a great novelist. There is Lady Clonbrony, for instance, an object of contempt to her guests, an object of pity to her son; she has dedicated her life, one might say, to making herself ridiculous. And she is ridiculous. But she is something else, too. We see why she is a figure of fun, but we are never deluded into believing that she is only a figure of fun. She is also a suffering woman, and her sufferings are no less real because they endured for an unworthy end. Her maid, Mrs. Petito, is no less striking in her way, though she is presented from one angle only, seen always in terms of ironical comedy. But listen to her as she thinks aloud:

"It will do very well, never mind," repeated Petito, muttering to herself as she looked after the ladies whilst they ran downstairs. "I can't abide to dress any young lady who says never mind, and it will do very well. That, and her never talking to one confidentially, or trusting one with the least bit of her secrets, is the thing I can't put up with from Miss Nugent; and Miss Broadhurst holding the pins to me, as much to say, do your business, Petito, and don't talk. Now, that's so impertinent, as if one wasn't the same flesh and blood, and had not as good a right to talk of everything, and hear of everything, as themselves. And Mrs. Broadhurst, too, cabinet councilling with my lady, and pursing up her city mouth, when I come in, and turning off the discourse to snuff, forsooth, as if I was an ignoramus, to think they closeted themselves to talk of snuff. Now, I think a lady of quality's woman has as good a right to be trusted with her lady's secrets as with her jewels; and if my Lady Clonbrony was a real lady of quality, she'd know that, and consider the one as much my paraphernalia as the other. So I shall tell my lady tonight, as I always do when she vexes me, that I never lived in an Irish family before, and don't know the ways of it. Then she'll tell me she was born in Hoxfordshire; then I shall say, with my saucy look, 'Oh, was you, my lady? I always forget that you was an Englishwoman.' Then maybe she'll say, 'Forget! you forget yourself strangely, Petito.' Then I shall say, with a great deal of dignity, 'If your ladyship thinks so, my lady, I'd better go.' And I'd desire no better than that she would take me at my word, for my Lady Dashfort's is a much better place, I'm told, and she's dying to have me, I know."

In such a soliloquy as this we are not far away from the great self-isolated, continually self-communing characters of Dickens; and beyond them lies the triumphant figure of Marion Bloom. Petito is relatively a minor character in the novel, but whenever she appears we know that her interminable monologue has flowed unceasingly in her absence from the stage.

Maria Edgeworth dramatizes her characters, and she is especially good with the smaller ones, the peasants, the Irish gentlemen, and so on. Her failures are instructive, for they show why with all her gifts she was less than a great novelist. Lord Colambre and Grace Nugent, the hero and heroine, are to the point here. Colambre is a very passable attempt at a hero, for after Fielding and until we come to Meredith the great English novelists generally fail with their heroes. That he gets by is shown by our horror at his behavior towards Grace Nugent, whom he loves, his renunciation of her when he believes he has discovered that she is illegitimate and therefore, as he theorizes, that she must have inherited her mother's frailty. We are even more horror-struck, since she is such a vivid characterization, when Grace herself admits the justice of his behavior. For Grace is a young woman of high pride, vigorous common sense, and a downright flashing wit, who is not at all taken in by the fashionable world. Yet, when Miss Edgeworth requires it, she is made to behave entirely out of character.

Miss Edgeworth's characters are free, up to a point; but they are still tethered to their creator. The rope may be a long one, but they are tugged to conformity all the same. Miss Edgeworth was essentially a didactic writer for whom the virtue of the novel was that it was a particularly graphic form of tract. Fiction was an aid to education, and Miss Edgeworth's theories of human nature and right behavior trip her up as a novelist. This is most apparent in her English novels. In the Irish ones she is writing much more of what she knows at first hand, writing with her eye on the object. How her educational preoccupations spoil her as a novelist may best be seen in *Belinda*. Here she creates a woman, Lady Delacour, who, so long as she is allowed to remain alive, is one of the great achievements in English fiction. It is scarcely possible to praise her too highly, this brilliant society woman in whom tragedy, in the shape of what she thinks to be cancer of the breast, gnaws continually. "Abroad she appeared all life, spirit, and good humor—at home, listless, fretful, and melancholy; she seemed like a spoiled actress off the stage, overstimulated by applause, and exhausted by the exertions of supporting a fictitious character." She is a most striking conception, and rendered with great brilliance, a tragic heroine any novelist might have been proud to invent. But Miss Edgeworth's Belinda gets to work on her, and though her brilliance is never wholly dimmed she ends as the incarnation of the domestic virtues.

2

Jane Austen and Sir Walter Scott were born within four years of each other, in 1775 and 1771 respectively, but though Jane Austen was admired in her lifetime, by no one more generously than by Scott himself, her fame, and her prestige as a writer—which is not quite the same thing as fame—were, compared with the northern novelist's, the flicker of a candle set against the illumination of a searchlight. While Miss Austen was delineating the restricted life of a provincial lady, Scott, taking eight hundred years of Scots, English, and French history as his province, was changing the whole course of the novel throughout Europe. Indeed, he was *the* European novelist, as Byron was *the* poet, and a later generation of novelists, Balzac, Dumas, and the Russians among them, were to look back to him as to a father. Yet Jane Austen, too, was a revolutionary, however unconsciously, and few of the changes in critical opinion of this century would surprise the critic of a hundred years ago more than the comparatively sudden rise in her reputation and the equally sudden fall in Scott's. The rise and the fall are intimately connected; both are manifestations of a radical change, which first came to consciousness in England in the seventies and eighties of the last century, in their attitude towards the novel first of novelists themselves, then of critics, and in turn of an increasing number of readers. It is in the light of this change that we see Jane Austen as a modern novelist as we do not Scott. The nature of the change may be indicated in a remark Robert Liddell makes on Miss Compton-Burnett in his *A Treatise on the Novel*. Miss Compton-Burnett, he says, "is writing the pure novel, as Jane Austen did, concentrating upon human beings and their mutual reactions." The pure novel: it is not a concept that would have meant anything to Scott, and Miss Austen herself had heard of no such thing.

The writer of the pure novel sets out to delight us not by prodigality of invention, the creation of a large gallery of characters, the alternation of a large number of contrasted scenes, but by attention to the formal qualities of composition, to design, to the subordination of the parts to the whole, the whole being the exploration of the relations between his characters or of their relations to a central situation or theme. What we may call the pure novelist's criticism of life is an aspect of his design, his composition; indeed, in a very real sense it is the formal ordering of his material that constitutes his criticism of life.

Pure art of any kind has its dangers; it may degenerate into an overpreoccupation with techniques at the expense of the human quality of the content. It tends always to the abstract, and to the distortion of the reality of the artist's material for the sake of the pattern imposed upon it. Some critics find this, for instance, in the work of Henry James in his last phase. Readers who rejoice especially in the fiction of the great extraverts, Fielding, Balzac, Tolstoi, commonly find an impoverishment when they turn to the work of the pure novelists. Perfection, however, which is what the pure novelist is after, demands the recognition of severe limits. Dickens recognizes no limits at all; the art of Jane Austen is made possible precisely by the recognition of limits.

It may be asked: Did Miss Austen know what she was doing? She lived, after all, before it was common for the novelist to regard himself as an artist; she had no knowledge of the theories of fiction Flaubert and Henry James were later to state. She knew exactly what she was doing. Perfection is not obtained by blundering, and even if it were, to blunder into perfection in six consecutive works would be inconceivable. Miss Austen was a highly sophisticated artist. That her life was retired is quite beside the point. Because her subject matter is in a sense trivial—stated very superficially, it is always a young woman's finding a husband—it must not blind us to the fact that she is, with Dr. Johnson, the most forthright moralist in English; and the authority which informs every sentence Johnson wrote, that authority which comes, we feel, from vast experience of life, a massive common sense and an integrity determined to face all the facts of life without seeking refuge in illusion, is hers too.

Jane Austen was a moralist—an eighteenth-century moralist. In some respects, she was the last and finest flower of that century at its quintessential. She had escaped entirely the infection of sensibility and sentimentality; for her those qualities are material only for her satire. She is never for one moment soft in any way; indeed, there is no more intransigent, ruthless novelist in the world. She knew her limits, and the violence and crude high-spirited horseplay of the first novelists of the century are outside them. Yet the external approach that characterized Fielding and Smollett and makes them seem unfeeling to many modern readers, is hers all the same; she may not harass her stupid characters with practical jokes, as the older novelists did, but her verbal play with them is at first no less shocking to those of us who were brought up on the pieties of humanitarianism. In *Persuasion,* the tenderest of her novels, she can write:

> The real circumstances of this pathetic piece of family history were that the Musgroves had had the ill fortune of a very troublesome hopeless son, and the good fortune to lose him before he reached his twentieth year; that he had been sent to sea because he was stupid and unmanageable on shore; that he had been very little cared for at any time by his family, though quite as much as he deserved; seldom heard of, and scarcely at all regretted, when the intelligence of his death abroad had worked its way to Uppercross, two years before.

Miss Austen is never angry with her characters, but contempt for the silly and affected and stupid is constant in her work, and she found them the less funny the older she grew, for the tone of contempt becomes drier in each succeeding book. In *Pride and Prejudice,* Mr. Collins and Lady de Bourgh are figures of fun, monstrous puppets of silliness and snobbery, to be elaborated and laughed at with something like affection; Mrs. Norris, in *Mansfield Park,* and the Eltons, in *Emma,* are exposed in a withering scorn; they are comic, but in a way quite different from that of the earlier characters, and the dry scorn with which they are exposed is a moral comment.

It was from the eighteenth-century novelists, who apart from Sterne were all moralists, that Miss Austen derived her conception of the novel. She owed much to Richardson; the men she admired most, Edward Bertram, Mr. Knightley, even Darcy in *Pride and Prejudice,* are Grandisonian figures. But she owed, I think, more to Fielding. Her novels represent a feminization of Fielding's. The world they show has undergone an enormous contraction, naturally enough; the range of vision is very much smaller, but the vision is also much more intense, revealing a world composed not of large movement and broad sweeps but of minute particulars, the world of the parlor, the world of ladies to which Tom Jones is not admitted or, if admitted, so much on his best behavior as to be unrecognizable; though in certain of Miss Austen's heroines I think we can recognize figures comparable and akin to Sophia Western and Amelia, for all they are drawn from a woman's point of view.

In her own way, Miss Austen adapted and carried further Fielding's dramatic method of presenting action through a succession of short scenes in dialogue. Though keeping the right to comment, she relied more on dialogue; but, as with Fielding, the comment is not only direct but implicit in the turn of the sentence. Her fiction is as much steeped in irony, both in language and situation, as his. Both are examples of the moralist as satirist. They differ, of course, in their notions of morals. It is not quite true that for Miss Austen morals and manners are interchangeable, but the main emphasis in her work is on manners, which she sees as morals in microcosm. There are, of course, standards of reference implicit in her novels by which manners are to be judged; and sometimes they are explicit, as in *Emma,* with Mr. Knightley's "My Emma, does not everything serve to prove more and more the beauty of truth and sincerity in all our dealings with each other?" or in the statement of values implicit in the following, from *Mansfield Park*:

> The politeness which she had been brought up to practise as a duty made it impossible for her to escape; while the want of that higher species of self-command, that just consideration of others, that knowledge of her own heart, that principle of right which had not formed any essential part of her education, made her miserable under it.

These are indeed the criteria by which Miss Austen judges her characters: self-command, just consideration of others, knowledge of the heart, and a principle of right derived from education. In Miss Austen's world the errors and follies of the young are always, in part at any rate, the result of faulty upbringing; behind the wickedness of Lydia Bennet in her elopement with Wickham lie the fool-ishness of her mother and the irresponsibility of her father. Miss Austen traces the consequences of the lack of these qualities in characters set in as completely detailed a world as has been created in fiction. There is a whole larger world outside it of which she says nothing, but that does not invalidate the world she has made. The scope of her art is not in fact lessened by her ignoring of the major events in the history of her time; the reality of her world would not have been in any way intensified had she dragged in references to the Napoleonic Wars or to the industrial revolution. Her world is self-contained, but the larger context is supplied by her continual awareness and scrutiny of the values that govern the one she creates. It is by modern standards a highly formalized world with an elaborate and subtle class structure and a fairly rigid code of behavior, a code of behavior plainly incomprehensible to many modern readers. Why, for instance, was it so wrong for the young Bertrams to perform a play in their father's absence? To answer the question would be almost to write a book on the period; but unless the reader ac-cepts Miss Austen's point of view and sees that, within the setting of the time, it was wrong, he can get nothing out of *Mansfield Park*. If he does accept it, he will realize that the incident, trivial as it may seem to him now if ab-stracted from its setting, is symbolic of all deviations from an agreed code of manners, and he will realize that one of the factors that make Miss Austen the great novelist she is is just this undeviating scrutiny of behavior. And he will realize something more: she is so constantly right in her judgments of the characters and events in the small world she created that we are convinced that she would be equally right on characters and events in the larger world outside.

In many ways, because her scope is restricted in its material, more can be learned from Miss Austen about the nature of the novel than from almost any other writer. Miss Austen is praised for her delineation of character, and it is superb in its excellence; but one has only to read her to see the limitations of those critics who judge a novelist solely in terms of the ability to create character, for what gives her characters their value, what in the deepest sense "makes" them, is that it is through them that their author expresses a discriminated view of life, a highly serious criticism of life expressed in terms of comedy.

Comedy deals with the conflict between illusion and reality; "Know thyself!" is the imperative of every comic writer. Miss Austen began to write as a child and wrote all her life. In her first novels, *Sense and Sensibility* and *Northanger Abbey* (for *Pride and Prejudice,* though written in a first version more or less at the same time as those, had probably been worked over again and again before its publication in 1813), the source of her comedy is essentially the confusion in an immature mind between literature and life. Thence she proceeds, in her later novels, to the dissection and exposure of the more normal follies and illusions of mankind. It would be idle to arrange these novels in any order of merit. *Sense and Sensibility* is generally considered inferior to the others, but the second chapter, in which Mr. and Mrs. John Dashwood discuss how they may best fulfill the former's promise to his dead father to provide for his widowed mother and his sisters and, beginning by thinking of giving them three thousand pounds, end by deciding that their kinsmen's wants will be so small that they will need nothing at all except presents of fish and game when in season, is one of the high points of Miss Austen's comedy. It is a dazzling example of her dialogue, her economy of writing, and her power of making her characters expose themselves in their own words, so that we know them through and through and can imagine them in situations she has never described.

The most popular of her novels has always been *Pride and Prejudice,* because of the brilliant creation of Elizabeth Bennet, a heroine as witty as she is charming. Yet those most attached to Miss Austen's novels have usually preferred the later ones, *Mansfield Park, Emma,* and *Persuasion,* which were written after an interval of more than ten years. During that long silence, the reason for which we do not know, Miss Austen's mind grew graver; it is as though she could find folly, self-deception, irresponsibility, silliness, the individual's lack of knowledge of himself, no longer merely funny; more and more as she realized their consequences they became contemptible, even hateful, to her. The expression of this contempt, of this hatred, is always controlled, and presented in comic terms; but it is there, and the comedy is more than ever the vehicle of moral judgment. Mr. Bennet is rightly among the most admired characters in *Pride and Prejudice,* but he would be impossible in any of the later novels; there his failings as a father would have been much more severely dealt with.

In a sense, Miss Austen became concerned with justice, and her eye for the facts of reality became even more acute. This is what makes *Mansfield Park* so fascinating and so satisfying. Miss Austen's titles are always strictly relevant to the novels, and *Mansfield Park* is a study of the inhabitants of the house of that name, the country place of Sir Thomas Bertram, Bart., the values they live by, and the consequences of those values. The central character is Fanny Price, who also represents right behavior, Miss Austen's own values. Her position in the Bertram household is ambiguous. Lady Bertram's niece and ward, she is the poor relation in permanent residence, at everybody's beck and call and heeded by none except her cousin Edmund,

Sir Thomas's second son, who, destined for the church, becomes a clergyman before the novel is ended. It is Fanny alone who stands out against the plans to stage a play at Mansfield Park while Sir Thomas is away in the West Indies. She has no power to prevent their being put into effect, but her right principles on this subject are themselves enough to expose the pretensions of her odious Aunt Norris, who masks meanness and selfishness with a constant display of concern for the welfare of Sir Bertram's children and persecutes Fanny with the constant reminder that she is where she is by Sir Bertram's charity. It is from the decision to stage the play, *Lovers' Vows*, and the preparation for its production, into which Mrs. Norris throws herself wholeheartedly, that the consequences that compose the action of the novel flow: the seduction of the elder married Bertram daughter Maria by the brilliant Henry Crawford; the elopement of the younger daughter Julia with Yates; and the entanglement of Edmund, whom Fanny has always secretly loved, with Mary Crawford. Dante defines comedy as "a series of harsh complications having a prosperous conclusion," and that will stand for Miss Austen's comedy; the end of *Mansfield Park* is prosperous enough, with Fanny married to Edmund, Mrs. Norris discredited, Sir Thomas convinced of his inadequacies as a father, and his elder son a reformed character. Justice has been done. But though we know the end will be prosperous for Fanny, as we read the novel it seems touch and go.

Miss Austen has been criticized for suggesting that if Henry Crawford, who, intending merely to play with Fanny, falls seriously in love with her, had persevered in his suit, he would have won her. The criticism in my view is beside the point. One of the great merits of *Mansfield Park* is just this creation of Henry Crawford and his sister Mary. They are a brilliant couple, and they dazzle the Bertrams as they dazzle us. Mary is as seriously attracted to Edmund, for all her scorn of clergymen, whom she sees as a kind of upper servant in the old eighteenth-century way, as Henry is to Fanny. And Miss Austen concedes them much: wit, elegance, the power to please, goodness of heart, even the ability to see what is right. Their failure is a failure of character; owing to their education they lack the principles that would enable them to follow the right. Henry loses Fanny because he cannot resist the momentary temptation to test his sexual power over Maria, and Mary loses Edmund because of the flippancy with which she reacts to her brother's elopement with Maria.

Miss Austen's sense of reality is nowhere more evident than in her account of Fanny's visit to her parents' home at Portsmouth after an absence of more than ten years. Fanny goes home with all the longing in the world to see her mother. She finds herself in an atmosphere of feckless and squalid poverty. The whole passage is a masterpiece of realistic writing, and shows what Miss Austen could have done if she had not dedicated herself to comedy of manners. "Home" is a continual exacerbation of Fanny's sensibility; indeed, it is not home at all; the home she had dreamed of is exposed as a sentimental notion.

> The living in incessant noise was, to a frame and temper delicate and nervous like Fanny's, an evil which no super-added elegance or harmony could have entirely atoned for. It was the greatest misery of all. At Mansfield no sounds of contention, no raised voice, no abrupt bursts, no tread of violence, was ever heard; all proceeded in a regular course of cheerful orderliness; everybody had their due importance; everybody's feelings were consulted. If tenderness could ever be supposed wanting, good sense and good breeding supplied its place; and as to the little irritations sometimes introduced by Aunt Norris, they were short, they were trifling, they were as a drop of water to the ocean, compared with the ceaseless tumult of her present abode. Here everybody was noisy, every voice was loud (excepting, perhaps, her mother's which resembled the soft monotony of Lady Bertram's, only worn into fretfulness). Whatever was wanted was hallooed

for, and the servants hallooed out their excuses from the kitchen. The doors were in constant banging, the stairs were never at rest, nothing was done without a clatter, nobody sat still, and nobody could command attention when they spoke.

We are not made to feel that Fanny's sojourn at Mansfield has made her a snob or ashamed of her family, but simply that she is seeing the situation as it is, facing the facts, as she faces the facts about her mother: "She might have made just as good a woman of consequence as Lady Bertram, but Mrs. Norris would have been a more respectable mother of nine children on a small income." The comment, incidentally, is a striking instance of Miss Austen's fairness to her characters; she created no figure more unpleasant than Mrs. Norris, with her continual busybody nagging of Fanny and obsequiousness towards the Bertrams, yet Miss Austen will not let less than justice be done to her.

Fanny's discovery of the truth about her parents' household is, then, a step forward in her knowledge of herself. The attainment of self-knowledge on the part of the heroine is always part of Miss Austen's theme; indeed, goodness in her world may almost be equated with the capacity for self-knowledge. In *Emma,* the whole subject is the heroine's painful discovery of the truth about herself, the gradual stripping of herself of illusion. Miss Austen places Emma for us in her very first paragraphs:

Emma Woodhouse, handsome, clever, and rich, with a comfortable home and happy disposition seemed to unite some of the best blessings of existence; and had lived nearly twenty-one years in the world with very little to distress or vex her . . .

The real evils, indeed, of Emma's situation were the power of having rather too much her own way, and a disposition to think a little too well of herself: these were the disadvantages which threatened alloy to her many enjoyments.

Emma, alway surpassingly confident of being right, is in fact always embarrassingly wrong. Strong-willed, spoiled, she conceives it her duty to set the world to rights. She takes as her friend not her equal in birth and intellect, Jane Fairfax, but Harriet Smith, an amiable, stupid girl of ambiguous parentage. She persuades Harriet that her farmer sweetheart, her equal in birth and superior in intelligence, is too far below her to be acceptable, and encourages her to aspire to the vicar, Mr. Elton, only to discover to her indignation that her encouragement of the clergyman on her friend's behalf has led him to aspire to herself. She then fancies that she and Frank Churchill, who is secretly engaged to Jane Fairfax, are about to fall in love with each other, and on no real evidence at all decides Jane is in love with a married man, a suspicion she immediately communicates to Churchill. As soon as she realizes she is not in love with him she encourages Harriet to imagine that she is, but since she does not divulge his name, she merely succeeds, without knowing it, in making the girl fall in love with Mr. Knightley, the friend and adviser of the Woodhouse family who has long been in love with Emma. In her pleasure in finding she is not in love with Churchill she flirts outrageously with him and, observing none of the signs of his relation with Jane which are obvious to Knightley, brings Jane into misery and almost ruins the happiness of the secretly engaged couple. Finally, the discovery that she has led Harriet to fall in love with Knightley brings it home to her that she herself is in love with him and he with her.

The whole novel is conceived in irony. It is the high point of Miss Austen's comedy, and Emma is at the center, the most important character, as Elizabeth Bennet in *Pride and Prejudice* and Fanny Price in *Mansfield Park* are not. Yet, although the whole action of the novel is subordinated to Emma, it contains some of her best comic characters: Mr. Woodhouse, the Eltons, Miss Bates. Incidentally,

Miss Bates, the garrulous, woolly-minded spinster, is an excellent example of Miss Austen's use of the minor character. Miss Bates rambles on, innocent and silly, almost in stream-of-consciousness fashion; but she rambles on to good purpose, rambles on dramatically, in that what she says is not merely amusing in itself but furthers the course of the story by giving us information about other characters and the whole background of the book. Indeed, Miss Bates is one of the devices by which her author creates the ambience of her fictitious town of Highbury, which is as convincing a town, with as convincing a population, as any in fiction.

Miss Austen has often been attacked, usually on the lines of Charlotte Brontë's criticism:

> Anything like warmth or enthusiasm, anything energetic, poignant, heartfelt, is utterly out of place in commending these works: all such demonstrations the authoress would have met with a well-bred sneer, would have calmly scorned as *outré* or extravagant. She does her business of delineating the surface of the lives of genteel English people curiously well. There is a Chinese fidelity, a miniature delicacy, in the painting. She ruffles her reader by nothing vehement, disturbs him by nothing profound. The passions are perfectly unknown to her: she rejects even a speaking acquaintance with that stormy sisterhood . . . What sees keenly, speaks aptly, moves flexibly, it suits her to study: but what throbs fast and full, though hidden, what the blood rushes through, what is the unseen seat of life and the sentient target of death—this Miss Austen ignores.

Charlotte Brontë is really complaining that Miss Austen is not, as she herself was, a romantic novelist. The close contemporary of the great romantic poets—Wordsworth was five years, Coleridge three years older than she— Miss Austen was untouched by the romantic movement. This does not mean that she was ignorant of the power of feeling or that she despised it; it does mean that she believed it should be controlled and that in writing its expression should be intellectual. Her affinities were with Pope and the Johnson of *The Lives of the Poets*.

Today, lady novelists of some wit and concision, who concern themselves with those aspects of upper-class life which can be viewed from the tea table, are almost invariably compared by reviewers to Jane Austen. It is very rare indeed that they have anything in common with her tough eighteenth-century mind, her severity of values, her miraculous sense of form. Her influence is, rather, diffused and indirect; she has become one of the permanent points of reference by which the achievements of other novelists are measured.

3

"Scott is a novelist over whom we shall violently divide." Thus E. M. Forster, in *Aspects of the Novel:* and if we want the case against Scott we cannot do better than continue the quotation:

> He is seen to have a trivial mind and a heavy style. He cannot construct. He has neither artistic detachment nor passion, and how can a writer who is devoid of both, create characters who will move us deeply? Artistic detachment—perhaps it is priggish to ask for that. But passion—surely passion is low-brow enough, and think how all Scott's laborious mountains and scooped-out glens and carefully ruined abbeys call out for passion, passion and how it is never there! If he had passion he would be a great writer—no amount of clumsiness or artificiality would matter then. But he has only a temperate heart and gentlemanly feelings, and an intelligent affection for the countryside: and this is not basis enough for great novels. . . .

Forster concedes that Scott could tell a story—and then synopsizes *The Antiquary* in order to show how badly Scott did so.

Forster is putting the current view of Scott; and much of his case must be admitted: Scott will never again be the figure he was a century ago. Yet much more remains to him than appears from *Aspects of the Novel,* and what remains is not merely his historical influence. That was enormous; one may say, quite simply, that he made the European novel and say something much more true than such sweeping generalizations normally are. And his influence was not confined to fiction. Without being in the strict sense an historian, he revolutionized the writing of history. In religion, though not a religious man, he lay behind the Oxford Movement, as Newman himself said.

But all that is irrelevant to his present stature as a novelist: his continued greatness rests on quite other grounds. What his greatness consisted in we shall not see if we think of him as primarily an historical novelist. This may appear a paradox: it will seem less so when we remember that it was from the Waverley Novels that Balzac learned the art which gave us the *Comédie humaine,* an *œuvre* historical only if a vast, detailed picture of the author's own times may be considered historical. If we see Scott first and foremost as the writer of historical romance we may be in danger of confusing him with his later disciples Ainsworth and Lytton, with whose novels his have largely been banished to the schoolroom. As V. S. Pritchett has said in his brilliant essay on Scott, in *The Living Novel,* the historical passion was the engine of his impulse. What is important is where the engine took him.

It took him to the portrayal of man in his public and social aspects, man, that is to say, as he is conditioned by factors outside himself, by his place and function in society, his relation to an historic past. Scott's characters are embedded in a context of tradition. Historic and social processes crystallize out in his dramatis personae. It is in that sense that he made history live, but the history lives because of the characters. This may be seen in any one of his novels. *Rob Roy* is not his best, but the characters as they appear in the narrative are instructive. The time is the first years of the eighteenth century. First—to ignore, for reasons that will be plain later, Frank Osbaldistone himself—there is his father, the London merchant, the Whig. Then there is Mr. Osbaldistone's clerk, Owen, who lives and thinks wholly in terms of clerkliness. We move north, to the border, to Osbaldistone Hall, the family seat, where the family of Frank's uncle, Sir Hildebrand, consume an existence that can have changed scarcely at all since medieval times, an existence almost animal, devoted to hunting, eating, drinking, sleeping. They are Catholics and Jacobites, and of those members of the family who rise above the general boorishness, Rashleigh and Diana Vernon, an uncompromising and zealous loyalty to Pope and Pretender is the key to all their actions. And at Osbaldistone we meet the gardener Andrew Fairservice; when he plays Partridge or Sancho Panza to Frank he becomes a bore, but as we first meet him he is an astonishing revelation of the quintessential peasant: he lives triumphantly because of his very peasantness. We call on the local justice of the peace, Squire Inglewood, and he is what he is because he has opted, in a prevailingly Jacobite region, for the Hanoverian succession. We encounter—without knowing it, we have already done so —Rob Roy himself, and he too is, in all his behavior, the product of specific historic events.

There is no need further to pick out the characters of the novel. The point is that they are all rooted in the most palpable kinds of material reality, the reality of life shaped by the forces of history, or the reality of work, of traditional skills and professions. These realities give them reality. And what is remarkable is that only in very rare instances are they flat characters, extended Theophrastean types; generally they are completely alive, capable of surprising us. How is this? Partly because of Scott's intuitive insight into historic forces and traditional vocations; partly because of the intensity with which he realizes his characters through their speech. It is a commonplace of Scott criticism to say that he approached his characters from the outside, presented, so to say, the public view of them; which, after all, is very much what an historian like Macaulay did with his characters; but Scott does so with such skillfully observed detail, he makes his personages so idiosyncratic, that we are always—or nearly always, for there were private emotions outside his range altogether—able to infer their inner lives.

Scott grasped, as no other English novelist has done, the organic relationships between man and man, man and place, man and society, and man and his past, the impersonal past of history. He was enabled to do this partly because he was writing of the past; he is dealing, in a sense, with life as a finished thing, a completed process, and this is unquestionably, for all that it was the source of much of his strength, a weakness when judged by the highest standards, those established, for instance, by Tolstoi in *War and Peace*. The comparison is not irrelevant, for Scott, too, is one of the great extraverts of literature, like Tolstoi a master of the normal. On his lower level, however, Scott was triumphantly successful. At his greatest, he was writing epic, and when one considers certain specific passages, those great scenes of action such as the account of the ambush in *Rob Roy*, the pitched battles of *Old Mortality*, or the storming of the tolbooth in *The Heart of Midlothian*, one sees immediately what novelists like Tolstoi and Stendhal owed to him.

He achieved tragedy only twice, I think: in the two great short stories in *The Chronicles of the Canongate*, *The Highland Widow* and *The Two Drovers*. Both are instructive, for both are tragedies resulting from national character as shaped by historic circumstances, which are shown as forces no less impersonal than anything in Hardy. And again, when we read such a story as *The Two Drov-*

ers we can see what Scott meant to a later generation of European writers, to Mérimée, for example, with his wonderful *Mateo Falcone*.

Looking back on Scott's novels in memory, at any rate on the Scottish ones, which are his best, we tend to see them as one vast work; they coalesce in the mind into one great epic picture; so that it is not always easy to remember the precise events of single novels, and characters like old Deans, Oldbuck, and the rest seem to exist side by side bound in the one frame. It is the sign that a world has been created and populated. It is also a sign that the author has been much more interested in creating characters than in composing a formal work, which is as much as to say that, to the modern view, only half the novelist's job has been done. Scott, in fact, was a great writer of fiction who was never a good novelist. He was doing something profoundly new in fiction, but he was hamstrung all the time as a novelist by using old methods. He took over the old complex plot of the eighteenth-century novelists, with its young hero on whom the thread of action is hung and its romantic love interest. The great authority of Scott gave this kind of plot another half century of life in the English novel, to its detriment, for of all our novelists Fielding alone has been able to use it to positive advantage. Scott's plot work is poor, so that, reading him, disappointment after the first half of the book is almost inevitable; the first halves of *The Antiquary, Rob Roy, Old Mortality, Guy Mannering,* the first three quarters even of *The Heart of Midlothian,* are superb—and then how mechanically their author solves the riddles he has perfunctorily set himself.

Scott knew this himself. In his introduction to *The Fortunes of Nigel* he quotes Dryden's remark: "In short, sir, you are of opinion with Bayes—'What the devil does the plot signify, except to bring in fine things?'" But it brought in things that were not so fine, things Scott knew nothing about and cared less. It made him set at the center of his fictions the romantic hero and the romantic heroine. It is the fate of the romantic hero to be colorless, and perhaps Scott's are no more so than Nicholas Nickleby; the one hero who does emerge as a living character is Ravenswood, in *The Bride of Lammermoor*, and, as has been often pointed out, he lives as the dispossessed nobleman, not the romantic lover. Scott fails whenever he attempts to deal with romantic or sexual love. We see him, rightly enough, as a great romantic writer, indeed, with Byron, the central figure in the European romantic movement. But he was not romantic in Byron's way; passion was alien to him; he writes as a hard-headed, common-sense professional man, whose values are those of a settled society traditionally ordained. Like Fielding and Jane Austen, he accepts the world. He faces life squarely and without illusions; he is bounded, willingly, by the restrictions and limitations society imposes upon the individual. One might almost say that, if the romantic is construed only in terms of sexual emotion, he was the great antiromantic novelist. But he was anything but unaware or contemptuous of the nonrational elements of life. He took over and refined the supernatural properties of Mrs. Radcliffe's Gothic novels, and at his most successful he rooted them in actuality. Two things made this possible: his conservatism and the fact that he was a Scot. Whatever had existed in the past he approached with a sense of what can only be called piety. The past was hallowed because it was the past, and in the presence of what the past had sanctioned his own beliefs were irrelevant. Take, for instance, his description of Louis XI's adoration of the images in his hat, in *Quentin Durward*: Scot describes it soberly and factually; he calls it superstition, but he does not sneer, does not laugh; he is content with detailed statement. This is his habitual attitude towards the ritual and ceremony of the Catholic Church, and the very sobriety of his acceptance of a form of religion which he himself did not share came in the end to have a revolutionary force. What had formerly seemed to the mass of his British readers profoundly alien, even monstrous, modes of worship were made to appear natural by his acceptance of them and his unheated accounts of them. The religious fanaticism of Calvinism and its resultant distortion and intensification of character he accepted in the same way.

Similarly with the supernatural at the folklore level. It is here that the fact that he was a Scot is so important. He was able to tap a well of nationally cherished superstition, superstition still actual and operative, and he expressed what he found in its own terms. In many respects *The Bride of Lammermoor* is a farrago of traditionally Gothic and romantic properties. But consider the three "witches" in the churchyard:

> "He is a frank man and a free-handed man, the Master," said Annie Winnie, "and a comely personage—broad in the shouthers and narrow around the lungies. He wad make a bonnie corpse; I wad like to have the streaking and winding of him."
> "It is written on his brow, Annie Winnie," replied the octogenarian, her companion, "that hand of woman, or man either, will never straught him—dead deal will never be laid to his back, make your market of that, for I hae it fae a sure hand."
> "Will it be his lot to die on the battle ground then, Aislie Gourlay?"
> "Ask nae mair questions about it—he'll not be graced sae far," replied the sage.

In a sense, the three sinister old women are conventional figures; they derive pretty clearly from *Macbeth*. But the derivation is quite transcended by Scott's use of the vernacular; we are in the presence of what we may call the racial, which means that the supernatural has been given a reality it never possesses in the Gothic novel. Scott has taken into his fiction a genuine part of living national experience.

Somewhat akin to the witches of *The Bride of Lammermoor* are the bizarre nonrational, sometimes lunatic figures that haunt his novels and are so important to the working out of his plots, characters like Meg Merrilies, Madge Wildfire and her mother, even Edie Ochiltree. They are, or are often on the verge of being, elementals. Scott accepts them, and it is worth observing that their existence causes no surprise even to his most hard-headed characters, Jonathan Oldbuck, for instance. He never quite explains them, and they are the more powerful for that. They are surprisingly at home in his world of mundane common sense and condition the events that take place in it; they are, as it were, dramatizations of those aspects of life that are outside reason and inexplicable in terms of reason.

They always talk in the vernacular; their speech is racy in the strict sense of the word, for they are, as it were, organic growths of the Scottish earth. And here we come across another clue to Scott's failure with romantic young gentlemen and ladies: they habitually speak English, and very stilted, nerveless English at that. Generally his characters are alive in their dialogue only in the vernacular. Then it is not easy to imagine richer dialogue. It is, therefore, untrue to say that Scott could not create women characters. He creates most vivid ones, so long as they are Scots-speaking Scots. There are of course exceptions: Diana Vernon is a romantic heroine who is fully alive. But she is alive, imperiously alive, not because she loves Frank Osbaldistone but because she is a woman of action, possessed of masculine intelligence, and dedicated to a cause outside herself. Scott's peasant women are always admirable. Jeanie Deans, in *The Heart of Midlothian*, is superb; in her simplicity, her native dignity, and moral courage she

is one of the great heroines of fiction. But Scott is as successful with his women characters on a lower level. There
is his vast gallery of peasant women, fishwives, old maids,
tradesmen's wives, servant girls—Miss Bellenden's maid,
in *Old Mortality*, Jenny Dennison, for example; it seems
to me that no English novelist for many years to come was
capable of so excellent a piece of humorous realism. When
Scott is writing in his own language he is quite free of the
taboos that were already inhibiting novelists south of the
border. He was a man of naturally conventional mind, but
it was not a genteel mind, nor are the minds of his characters, except when they speak genteel English.

   Scott's attitude towards his characters, like his acceptance of the world in which he lived, is very much akin to
Chaucer's. He has an ease, he conveys a feeling of being at
home in his world, the whole of his world, that is rare in
English fiction. He accepted and rendered quite naturally
the contrasts of class; as Bagehot, discussing Scott's treatment of the poor, says: "He sympathizes with their rough
industry and plain joys or sorrows. He does not fatigue
himself or excite their wondering smile by theoretical
plans of impossible relief. He makes the best of the life
which is given, and by a sanguine sympathy makes it still
better. A hard life many characters in Scott seem to lead;
but he appreciates, and makes his readers appreciate, the
full value of natural feelings, plain thoughts, and applied
sagacity."

   Again Scott appears as an antiromantic. He is in fact a
sturdy humorist, as writers must be who accept the world
as he did. He delights in foible and idiosyncrasy, in the
contrast between the character as he sees himself and as he
actually is. *The Antiquary* is a good instance of this, in the
character of the antiquary himself and in those of his sister
and of the snobbish, gullible Sir Arthur, with his constantly strained and yet almost parasitical relationship to
the antiquary. All this is easy, natural, springing directly

out of appreciation of character; the deliberate attempts at comedy, the gulling of Sir Arthur by Dousterswivel, are much less good and are indeed generally absurd.

The cream of Scott's work lies in the fiction inspired by the life and history of his own country: *Guy Mannering, Rob Roy, The Antiquary, Old Mortality, The Heart of Midlothian, St. Roman's Well,* and, for some things, *The Bride of Lammermoor.* Writing of events, scenes, and characters outside Scotland, he was cut off from nine tenths of his power, though *Quentin Durward* is still remarkable for its study of Louis XI and as a picture of the breakup of the feudal order in France.

What one values in Scott is the great gallery of characters, characters shaped by an historic living past, molded by the forces of religion and religious strife: heroic figures like Claverhouse, humorous delineations of eccentricity accreting round a hard core of common sense like Jonathan Oldbuck, portraits of fanaticism like Balfour of Burley and old Deans, and all the long line of surely realized minor figures such as the Laird of Dumbiedikes and Sergeant Bothwell. Through them the past of a country comes to life and is presented epically and humorously by turns.

Scott is one of the great imperfect novelists, and his imperfections are exactly those most offensive to present-day taste. His influence on later novelists in English was mainly bad. It was he, by gathering a popular audience such as no novelist had had before, who made the novel respectable. Perhaps his weaknesses had something to do with that. At any rate, his weaknesses were more easily copied by his successors than his virtues. He hardened writers like Dickens in the English preference for the arbitrary, complicated plot that Fielding took over from the theater, and helped to establish unreal romantic heroes and heroines as a convention. His defects of form and his artistic laziness became, as it were, authoritative in the novel for two generations after him. It may have been part of the price the novel had to pay for becoming *the* popular literary art in Victorian England, but it is significant that the great European novelists did not follow him in this, and one suspects, looking at the achievement of Balzac, Mérimée, and Tolstoi, that they understood his real contribution to the growth of the novel better than did the English.

4

A consequence of Scott's enormous popular success was that he made the Scottish novel itself possible. Though the greatest Scottish novelist of his time, Scott was not the only one; but *Waverley* had first to conquer the world— and Scotland—before publishers even in Edinburgh could believe that novels of Scottish life might be worth-while commercial speculations. *Waverley* was published in 1814, but Susan Ferrier had practically finished her novel *Marriage* three years earlier, and, having written *The Annals of the Parish* in 1813, John Galt had been assured by Constable that there was no market for Scottish fiction. The success of Miss Ferrier and Galt was therefore an index of the commercial success of Scott himself.

Susan Ferrier (1782-1854) is an admirable talent that scarcely took itself seriously enough. *Marriage*, published in 1818, is typical of the three novels she wrote. It is disconcerting in its mixture of the completely conventional and the genuinely racy. On one side Miss Ferrier was a feminine, better tempered Smollett, on the other a minor Maria Edgeworth at her most pedagogically moral. The writer she bears absolutely no resemblance to, whatever some critics have written, is Jane Austen. The genesis of *Marriage* may be seen in a letter Miss Ferrier wrote to a friend with whom she proposed to collaborate: "I do not recollect ever to have seen the sudden transition of a high-bred English beauty, who thinks she can sacrifice all to

love, to an uncomfortable solitary Highland dwelling
among tall red-haired sisters and grim-faced aunts. Don't
you think that would make a good opening of the piece?"
It does indeed make a good opening. The first chapter, a
discussion on marriage between the silly and affected young
Lady Juliana and her worldly and tyrannical father Lord
Courtland, is admirable, and so are the scenes immediately
following, of the acute discomfort of Lady Juliana, married to the disinherited second son of a Highland laird, at
Glenfern Castle. It is excellent fun; Miss Ferrier produces
a series of good-humored grotesques of Highland characters: the three aunts Miss Jackie, Miss Grizzie, and Miss
Nicky, the old laird, Lady McLaughlin and Sir Sampson.
There is no subtlety in this comedy of cross purposes, in
which Lady Juliana's sensibilities are constantly being
outraged by the homely crudities of life in the Highlands;
it is the high-spirited exploitation at the level of farce of a
good comic idea, and it is carried out with gusto. But when
in the course of time Lady Juliana's twin daughter Mary,
who has been left behind in the Highlands when her
mother returns to fashionable society in London, joins
her, the nature of the novel changes. Mary is now a girl in
her teens, a creature of impossible virtue who knows always what is right, a shadow indeed of Miss Edgeworth's
Belinda. It is not that Miss Ferrier's sharp eye for silliness
and affectation fail her, but they are inoperative where
Mary is concerned, and then *Marriage* becomes a perfectly
conventional, colorless novel.

There remain compensations. There is a wonderful
scene of a gathering of literary ladies in Bath, in which the
nature of Byron's genius is ecstatically analyzed. And there
is, too, one character of real achievement, the gourmand
Dr. Redgill. It is the measure of Miss Ferrier's success with
him that he can be imagined among Peacock's gatherings
of epicures, as when he discourses on the breakfasts of
Scotland:

"But the breakfasts! That's what redeems the land—and every country has its own peculiar excellence. In Argyllshire you have the Lochfine herring—fat, luscious, and delicious, just out of the water, falling to pieces with its own richness—melting away like butter in your mouth. In Aberdeenshire you have the Finnan haddo', with a flavour all its own, vastly relishing—just salt enough to be *piquant,* without parching you up with thirst. In Perthshire there is the Tay salmon, kippered, crisp, and juicy—a very magnificent morsel—a leetle heavy, but that's easily counteracted by a teaspoonful of the Athole whisky. In other places you have the exquisite mutton of the country, made into hams of a most delicate flavour; flour scones, soft and white; oat-cake, thin and crisp; marmalade and jams of every description; and—But I beg your pardon!—your ladyship was upon the subject of this young lady's health . . ."

One of the excellent things about Miss Ferrier is the eighteenth-century vigor which informs her delineation of manners. This is true also of Galt (1779-1839). Neither indulged in anything like the savage comedy of Smollett, but their approach to life was still that of the comic writer who has his eye firmly fixed on externals. Sentimentality, which had already infected the English novel, and which was to bear quite nauseating offspring in the works of later nineteenth-century Scottish writers, is absent from them. There is, instead, a robust grasp of the facts of everyday reality and a raciness in the rendering of it that reminds us that we are much closer to the Scotland of Burns than to the Scotland of Sir Harry Lauder and Sir James Barrie. Galt's first novel, *Annals of the Parish,* is a good example of this. Its author set out apparently to write something that would be a Scottish equivalent to *The Vicar of Wakefield*: he produced a very different book. His Rev. Mr. Balwhidder has nothing of the charm of Dr. Primrose, but he makes a most effective narrator of the novel, which is no less than the history of the events of his parish during his ministry from his "placing" in 1760 to his retirement in 1810. *Annals of the Parish* is an early example of the chronicle novel, and while there are a number of characters more or less running through the book, the real character is the parish of Dalmailing itself. And here Galt's is still an outstanding performance, for we see, in considerable detail and year by year, the change from a small, static country community existing in isolation to a busy industrial town in the main stream of the social and economic history of its time, with cotton mills, Irish laborers, Jacobin workmen, a dissenting chapel, and even an Irish Catholic priest saying mass. It is the first novel I know in English of the impact of the industrial revolution on a village community written more or less at the time it was happening. Dalmailing is a living village, with vigorous inhabitants; *Annals of the Parish* cannot fail to impress as an authentic rendering of the life of its time. And the humor is uninhibited. An example is the account of the death of Mr. Cayenne, the fiery American loyalist who has settled in the parish and established the first mill there:

When I had been seated some time, the power was given him to raise his head as it were a-jee; and he looked at me with the tail of his eye, which I saw was glittering and glassy. "Doctor," for he always called me doctor, though I am not of that degree, "I am glad to see you," were his words, uttered with some difficulty.

"How do you find yourself, sir?" I replied, in a sympathizing manner.

"Damned bad," said he, as if I had been the cause of his suffering. I was daunted to the very heart to hear him in such an unregenerate state; but after a short pause I addressed myself to him again, saying, that "I hoped he would soon be more at ease; and he should bear in mind that the Lord chasteneth whom he loveth."

"The devil take such love!" was his awful answer, which was to me as a blow on the forehead with a mell. However, I was resolved to do my duty to the miserable sinner, let him say what he would. Accordingly, I stooped towards him with my hands on my knees, and said, in a compassionate voice, "It's very true, sir, that you are in great agony; but the goodness of God is without bound."

"Curse me if I think so, doctor," replied the dying un-circumcised Philistine. . . .

Within its limits, *Annals of the Parish* is scarcely to be praised too highly. Much longer and more complex, *The Entail* suffers from the arbitrary nature of the plot. But it is still a remarkable work. It is an early example of the "saga" novel, covering three generations of the life of one family. What is especially interesting is Galt's attitude towards his story and characters. His theme is avarice and land hunger, the efforts first of Claud Walkinshaw, and then of his third son George, to win back and increase the family lands that have been lost to the family by their ancestor's speculation in the Darien scheme. To this end, father and son are prepared to sacrifice every consideration of family feeling. The comedy indeed is comedy of circumstance; nature, which includes human nature, cannot be regulated, even by the most single-minded vice, and justice is done in the end.

In this novel Galt mingles tragedy with comedy. The virtuous or attractive characters are not much more than sticks, but the vicious, the hypocritical, the miserly are kicking with life. The idiot Wattie, who is never quite such an idiot as it is to George's advantage to make him out to be—witness the legal inquiry into his incapacity, a splendid piece of comic writing—is admirably done and is genuinely moving. But the masterpiece of the novel is the old woman Grippy who can believe whatever she wants to believe, who is an adept at looking after her own interests, sanctimonious and coarse by turn and always garrulous with a fine flow of language derived from scripture and sermon. "Life is but a vapor, a puff out o' the stroop o' the tea-kettle o' Time."

The Entail bustles with raw life. Reading it, one is constantly getting glimpses of how later novelists would have tackled the theme and the scene. Both are sordid enough; but Galt accepts them with the warm appreciation of a

Breughel or a Burns; his realism is not a product of outraged sensibility. He has suffered, as indeed have all the
Scottish novelists, including Scott himself, the limitation
of readers that writing in dialect imposes, but he was anything but a provincial writer. A novel like *The Entail* has
in many ways much closer affinity with the work of Gogol
or even Dostoevski in some of his phases than with that
of the great majority of his English contemporaries.

Michael Scott (1789-1835), whose *Tom Cringle's Log*
was published in 1833, was perhaps no great shakes as a
novelist. *Tom Cringle's Log* was begun in its serial form
in *Blackwood's* as a series of travel sketches. It is indeed
the old aboriginal novel of a sequence of disparate adventures linked together only by the fact that they happen to
the same hero, transferred to the sea. Smollett was Scott's
master, and his characters are caricatures in the mode of
Smollett. But he wrote with the experience of a lifetime at
sea and in the West Indies behind him, and his novels
render that experience, with all its robustness, crudity, and
horseplay, in plain terms.

Much more interesting now is James Hogg's *The Private
Memoirs and Confessions of a Justified Sinner* (1824).
This is a remarkable work by any standard, a novel probably only a Scot could have written, a most powerful
criticism of a type of religious fanaticism we may think
characteristically Scottish, at least in recent centuries.

Hogg's justified sinner, Robert Wringhim, is the spiritual descendant of the Calvinist fanatics of Scott, of such a
character as Habbakuk Mucklewrath or MacBriar, in *Old
Mortality*. He is "justified" because, having been assured
that he is one of God's elect, promised salvation uncondi-
tionally, as it were, he conceives himself free from the
normal moral restraints. In this belief he is abetted by
a mysterious young man with whom at a first meeting he
feels extraordinary sympathy and who encourages him,
with arguments so persuasive as to be irresistible, to mur-

der those whom the Lord has undoubtedly already damned and may be thought to work against His power. The chief object of Wringhim's persecution is his half-brother, the heir to their father the Laird of Dalcastle, who is in the end murdered. Wringhim succeeds to his estates, and as he finds himself growing skeptical of his friend's good intentions towards him finds himself also more and more at his mercy, until, in a final effort to free himself from the mysterious young man's domination, he kills himself.

The mysterious young man is of course the devil, and it is doubtful whether a more convincing representation of the power of evil exists in our literature. As André Gide has said: "The power that sets him in action is always of a psychological nature; in other words, always admissible, even by unbelievers. It is the exteriorized development of our own desires, of our pride, of our most secret thoughts."

The novel is interesting technically. It is in two parts. The first consists of what might be called the public view of the slaying of the young Laird of Dalcastle, of Wringhim's accession, and his curious behavior afterwards; it presents a relation of fact something in the manner of a detective story, with no solution at the end, for Wringhim disappears as he is about to be arrested for the murder of his mother and is never seen again. The second part consists of his own confession, an astonishing self-exposure of religious aberration and delusion.

It seems to me quite certain that Hogg conceived his novel as satire; his own point of view is made plain in the story Wringhim's servant tells him, by way of warning, of the strange events that occurred in the village of Auchtermuchty, whose inhabitants were deceived by the devil in the guise of an extraordinarily powerful preacher. It is a brilliant story, brilliantly told, and it furthers the disillusionment of Wringhim. But what is surprising is that, conceived as satire—Dorothy Bussy rightly pointed out to Gide the book's affinity with "Holy Willie's Prayer"—*The*

Confessions of a Justified Sinner should have turned into a psychological document compared with which Stevenson's *Dr. Jekyll and Mr. Hyde* is a crude morality.

The Irish novelists of the time, who had found their exemplars in Maria Edgeworth and Scott, are much less interesting. Their natural talents were smaller and their interpretation of life crude. They were folklorists rather than novelists, and what is most valuable in their fiction exists at the level of personal reminiscence of peasant life and of the travel sketch. The work of the brothers Banim, the first series of whose O'Hara Tales appeared in 1825, is a good instance. Their fiction, judged as fiction, is conventional; the interest lies in the first-hand observation and rendering of life as they had seen it which fills up the interstices of the plot. Gerald Griffin's *The Collegians* (1828) had fame in its own day, indeed an extended fame, since one of the most popular of Victorian melodramas, *The Colleen Bawn,* was based on it. It is almost unreadable now: garrulous, the working out of the plot buried beneath a mass of unselected detail, and with altogether too much scope given to the *longueurs* of the humor of comic Irish peasants. William Carleton was less preoccupied with comic Irishmen; even so, his most famous novel, *Fardorougha the Miser,* does not bear much examination. Dimly, in this story of a miser's obsession and the brutal revenge wreaked upon him and his family by one of his victims, one discerns a real tragic impulse; but Carleton tells his story in tones of loquacious piety and horror, underscoring every incident in the action with moral comment; and none of the characters achieves much reality.

Two Irish novelists achieved great popularity in England, Samuel Lover and Charles Lever, both for the same reason: they indulged their readers in the Englishman's traditional self-complacent conception of the Irish and things Irish. Seen in relation to the novel as it had existed since Richardson and as it was being written in Scotland

and England in their time, their work represented degeneracy. Not that they set out to be more than popular entertainers. Lover's *Handy Andy* needs no critical comment; it is merely a recounting of the farcical adventures of the comic Irish servant who had been a figure on the London stage for a century and a half. Lever (1806-72) had rather more talent. In his way he was a professional. His attitude to his work and his public he summed up in his preface to *Charles O'Malley*:

> The success of *Harry Lorrequer* was the reason for writing *Charles O'Malley*. . . . The ease with which I strung my stories together—and in reality *The Confessions of Harry Lorrequer* are little more than a notebook of absurd and laughable situations—led me to believe that I could draw on this vein of composition without any limit whatever. I felt, or thought I felt, an inexhaustible store of fun and buoyancy within me, and I began to have a misty, half-confused impression that Englishmen generally laboured under a sad-coloured temperament, took depressing views of life, and were proportionately grateful to anyone who would rally them, even passingly, out of their despondency, and give them a laugh without much trouble for going in search of it.

Stories strung together; "a notebook of absurd and laughable situations": Lever's own words describe his work. *Harry Lorrequer* and *Charles O'Malley* are essentially returns to the old rogue stories suitably gelded for nineteenth-century consumption. In each case the hero is a young Irish officer, feckless, poor, irresponsible, gallant; his adventures among what he would call the fair sex, his duels, his practical jokes, and the practical jokes played on him, form the stuff of these novels. *Charles O'Malley* (1841) is much the better of the two, and the character Major Monsoon, an attempt at a contemporary Falstaff, is not at all bad. The scenes at Waterloo retain their interest. And from time to time, in the pictures of life in the army, of happy-go-lucky, drinking Irish gentlemen, one glimpses Lever's relation to a very much greater novelist;

it is as though one has been presented with the raw material of some part of Thackeray's art.

5

Thomas Love Peacock (1785-1866) stands alone and apart not only from the novelists who were his contemporaries—and his career overlapped Jane Austen's at the one end and his son-in-law Meredith's at the other—but also from the whole sequence of English novelists. He has been imitated but he has never been seriously rivaled. His work exists in a purity his disciples have not been able to match; his limits were narrow and strict, and to attempt to broaden them is merely to destroy the delicately poised world they contain. In his way Peacock achieved perfection, and more than once.

Nothing is easier than to construe affinities as influences. Peacock's affinities are plain: Aristophanes, Lucian, Rabelais. He could conceivably have been influenced by the characters of Thwackum and Square in *Tom Jones*; had he known, as is not likely, Blake's squib *An Island in the Moon*, he might have found in it anticipations of his own work. When one has listed affinities and possible influences one has only said that he was a satirist, a satirist of a specific kind. In his preface to a new edition that appeared in 1837 of four of his novels, Peacock notes that in some details they may appear to be dated, but adds:

Perfectibilians, deteriorationists, statu-quo-ites, phrenologists, transcendentalists, political economists, theorists in all sciences, projectors in all arts, morbid visionaries, romantic enthusiasts, lovers of music, lovers of the picturesque, and lovers of good dinners, march, and will march for ever, *pari passu* with the march of mechanics, which some facetiously call the march of intellect. The fastidious in old wine are a race that does not decay. Literary violators of the confidences of private life still gain a disreputable livelihood and an unenviable notoriety. Match-makers from interest, and the disappointed in love and in friendship, are varieties of which specimens are extant. The great principle of the Right of Might is as flourishing now as in the days of Maid Marian: the array of false pretensions, moral, political, and literary, is as imposing as ever: the rulers of the world still feel things in their effects, and never foresee them in their causes: and political mountebanks continue, and will continue, to puff nostrums and practise legerdemain under the eyes of the multitude . . .

It is an exhaustive list of Peacock's victims, but his satire at their expense is not that of the censor or the moralist. Its end is laughter, good-humored, tolerant laughter at that. As Friar John, in *Maid Marian,* says:

"The worst thing is good enough to be laughed at, though it be good for nothing else; and the best thing, though it be good for something else, is good for nothing better."

Peacock's satire arises out of pure joy in the spectacle of the excesses to be satirized.

His first novel, *Headlong Hall* (1816), though not his best, is typical of all his satirical fiction. A miscellaneous gathering of intellectuals—philosophers, men of letters, scientists, a musician, a painter, a landscape artist, and so on—gather for Christmas at Squire Headlong's in North Wales. They argue, eat and drink, dance, and in the end pair off with the available young ladies and marry. The plot is as slight as possible, but it is an extremely efficient machine for providing the necessary minimum of action. The characters are intellectual types, or types of intellectuals: Mr. Foster, the perfectibilian, who believes that the world and man are constantly improving; Mr. Escot, the deteriorationist, who believes the opposite; Mr. Jenkinson, the statu-quo-ite, who believes there is much to be said on both sides; Dr. Gaster, an orthodox clergyman who has won the Squire's fancy by "a learned discourse on the art of stuffing a turkey," among others. They talk, and they do very little else, and they expose themselves in their talk.

For Peacock, in the conversations he puts into their mouths, indulges in exaggeration exactly as a writer like Smollett or Dickens does, but what he exaggerates is the element of absurdity in the ideas they are propounding, or rather, he carries their ideas to the logical end and so reduces them to absurdity. The comedy lies, as always, in taking the exaggeration beyond the point where we would expect to stop; as in the following speech of the deteriorationist Mr. Escot's:

> "The natural and original man lived in the woods: the roots and fruits of the earth supplied his simple nutriment: he had few desires, and no diseases. But, when he began to sacrifice victims on the altar of superstition, to pursue the goat and the deer, and, by the pernicious invention of fire, to pervert their flesh into food, luxury, disease, and premature death, were let loose upon the world. Such is clearly the correct interpretation of the fable of Prometheus, which is the symbolical portraiture of that disastrous epoch, when man first applied fire to culinary purposes, and thereby surrendered his liver to the vulture of disease. From that period the stature of mankind has been in a state of gradual diminution, and I have not the least doubt that it will continue to grow *small by degrees, and lamentably less,* till the whole race shall vanish imperceptibly from the face of the earth."

Peacock is full of such sublimely comic passages in which a congeries of events is explained and the future forecast in terms of a single overriding theory. His novels form a comic dramatization of the intellectual notions of his age. For anything comparable in our time we would need to imagine a novelist intellectually powerful enough to satirize in one book the exponents of, say, Marxism, psychoanalysis, the psychology of Jung, logical positivism, neo-Catholicism, Existentialism, Christian Science, abstract painting. Peacock's intellectual ability, together with the neutral position he himself seems to hold, makes him a devastating critic of the theories of his day, and since the counterparts of those theories always exist he remains a formidable critic whose work, because of his insight into the implications of the ideas he satirizes, is permanently topical.

Headlong Hall, however, is still in a sense not much more than the bare bones of Peacock: everything is there, down to the often exquisite lyrics and drinking songs which customarily intersperse his symposia, but the especial charm, the bloom, the bouquet, of his later work is lacking. This quality is not easy to define, but it is evident in his second novel *Nightmare Abbey* (1818), and perhaps in part it is a product of the awareness manifest in that book of the organic connection between ideas and the men who hold them. For *Nightmare Abbey* is a satire on the English romantic movement, which Peacock knew at first hand. Some of the characters at least are suggested by life: Scythrop is based on Shelley, and not only in his inability to choose between two equally loved young ladies; Mr. Flosky is Coleridge; Mr. Cypress, Byron. The satire dazzles; the various aspects of romanticism are unerringly hit off; the invention is constant; and one part at least of Coleridge is completely caught, that part of him which replies to Marionetta's question, "Will you oblige me, Mr. Flosky, by giving me a plain answer to a plain question?" with "It is impossible, my dear Miss O'Carroll. I never gave a plain answer to a question in my life." But there is something else present in the novel, something that does not in the least detract from the force of the satire but sets it in an extra dimension, the dimension of what I can only call poetic ambiguity. In Chapter XI, Cypress announces after dinner his intention of leaving England, and the assembled company discuss among other things love, ideal beauty, and cheerfulness. The chapter ends, first, with a song from Mr. Cypress:

> There is a fever of the spirit,
>   The brand of Cain's unresting doom,
> Which in the lone dark souls that bear it

Glows like the lamp in Tullia's tomb:
Unlike that lamp, its subtle fire
   Burns, blasts, consumes its cell, the heart,
Till, one by one, hope, joy, desire,
   Like dreams of shadowy smoke depart.

When hope, love, life itself, are only
   Dust—spectral memories—dead and cold—
The unfed fire burns bright and lonely,
   Like that undying lamp of old:
And by that drear illumination,
   Till time its clay-built home has rent,
Thought broods on feeling's desolation—
   The soul is its own monument.

It is followed after an interval of half a dozen short lines of dialogue by the admirable drinking song, sung by the two cheerful men of the party, Mr. Hilary and the Reverend Mr. Larynx, the first stanza of which is:

Seaman three! What men be ye?
Gotham's three wise men we be.
Whither in your bowl so free?
To rake the moon from out the sea.
The bowl goes trim. The moon doth shine.
And our ballast is old wine;
And your ballast is old wine.

It is not simply that the songs, so contrasted in their moods, are placed in juxtaposition or that, as in all Peacock's novels, they aerate the dialogue and keep it bubbling with a liveliness additional to that of the text, so that, when we look back on a Peacock novel, we first of all remember a dancing gaiety rather than the satire of ideas. This in itself would be much, but there is more. Mr. Cypress's song is a most beautiful pastiche of Byron; the essence of Byronism is caught in it; it could have been written only by a man who, however he might intellectually find it comic, had an intuitive understanding of and sympathy with Byronism. Peacock clowns his sympathy as soon as it has been expressed by capping it with a drinking song, but it is there all the same, and in a way the drinking song adds a poignancy to its expression.

And this is true not merely in this single instance. It is the law of Peacock's being. In all the speeches of his characters, however absurd they may be, there is a kind of passion, the passion of the self-absorbed, the crank. For the moment, Peacock has *become* the crank in question, Mr. Escot, Mr. Flosky. He has apprehended the essence of a theory, a dogmatic point of view, and it is as though the theory, the dogmatic point of view, is parodying itself. This makes Peacock's satire the best-natured in the world. It glows with sympathy, and, when appropriate, bursts into beauty in its own right.

For Peacock was always a poet, and he is never more a poet than in his satirical novels. It is sometimes debated whether he was a romantic. The question gets us nowhere. What he had was an exquisite sense of beauty. He has an aesthetic appreciation, for instance, of certain kinds of landscape which have become almost conventional romantic properties; the settings of his novels are always beautiful; he is an admirable landscape painter, though the scale he works on is small. This gives his work an idyllic quality which is the last thing we associate with satire. He exploited it to the furthest in his charming pastoral *Maid Marian,* but it is there in his satires of contemporary theory; they are satire within an idyll.

A still beauty combined with the high spirits of debate that satirizes itself is the essence of Peacock's art. We are moved to laughter, but we are also moved by the atmosphere of poetry in which the debate is enclosed. It is this that none of his imitators has ever succeeded in achieving.

Peacock's art was perfect from *Nightmare Abbey* onwards. Variation was possible, but not progression. After *Headlong Hall* his main characters are always more than the opinions they express; they have, however slightly sketched, that kind of life which makes them imaginable as living beings outside the contexts in which they exist. Peacock keeps them severely within bounds, but we are always conscious of the potentialities of life within them. One at least, Dr. Folliott in *Crotchet Castle,* we can imagine in any conceivable situation: he is full length and exists in the round. As a character, he is a glorious achievement, and the source of some of Peacock's best comedy, with his constant girding at "the March of Mind" and the Steam Intellect Society, Peacock's name for the newly founded Society for the diffusion of Useful Knowledge. Sometimes, indeed, in his comments on the consequences of technology, he is profound in a way that we may appreciate more thoroughly than Peacock's own contemporaries, for his utterances are prophetic. As a character of pure comedy he is seen at his most amusing probably in his encounter with the robbers:

> The reverend gentleman recoiled two or three paces, and saw before him a couple of ruffians, who were preparing to renew the attack, but whom, with two swings of his bamboo, he laid with cracked sconces on the earth, where he proceeded to deal with them like corn beneath the flail of the thresher. One of them drew a pistol, which went off in the very act of being struck aside by the bamboo, and lodged a bullet in the brain of the other. There was then only one enemy, who vainly struggled to rise, every effort being attended with a new and more signal prostration. The fellow roared for mercy. "Mercy, rascal!" cried the divine; "what mercy were you going to show me, villain? What! I warrant me, you thought it would be an easy matter, and no sin, to rob and murder a parson on his way home from dinner. You said to yourself, doubtless, 'We'll waylay the fat parson (you irreverent knave) as he waddles home (you disparaging ruffian) half-seas-over' (you calumnious vagabond)." And with every dyslogistic term, which he supposed had been applied to himself, he inflicted a new bruise on his rolling and roaring antagonist.

Confronted with the triumphant figure of Dr. Folliott, one sees that one part at least of Peacock's art as a novelist sprang out of Fielding.

But there is another aspect of Peacock and his characterization that needs noting: he is one of the very few men novelists between Fielding and Meredith who can draw a satisfying woman. Like Fielding's and Meredith's, and quite unlike Dickens's, Peacock's young women exist in their own right. If not as learned as the men of his novels, they are as witty; they have minds and wills of their own; they are independent spirits. Witness the sparkling Lady Clarinda, in *Crotchet Castle,* or—portrayed rather more fully—Miss Gryll and Miss Nimet in *Gryll Grange,* Peacock's last and mellowest novel, written when he was seventy-five, after a silence of thirty years. And he is just as good with old maiden ladies—Miss Ilex, for instance, in the same book. Of his contemporaries, only Disraeli has anything like the same courtesy towards and appreciation of women. It is one of the indices of Peacock's truly civilized nature. He is a novelist—one of a very small number —whose work attracts us more, and is increasingly more important, the longer the period of time since its first appearance; and as the existence of civilization becomes the more precarious the more precious it will be.

THE EARLY VICTORIANS

1

THACKERAY was born in 1811, Dickens in 1812, Trollope in 1815, Charlotte Brontë in 1816, Emily Brontë in 1818, George Eliot in 1819. Mrs. Gaskell had been born in 1810, and lesser novelists born in the Regency period include Charles Reade (1814) and Charles Kingsley (1819). Together, they are the names that first come to mind when we think of the Victorian novelists. They do not form a coherent body, and Emily Brontë will prove an exception to all generalizations we care to make about the rest of them. Yet if we set them beside the chief novelists born in the generation after the Regency, Samuel Butler (1835), George Meredith (1828), Thomas Hardy (1840), we shall see that they have much more in common with one another than they have with the younger men. What they have in common is a special climate of ideas and feelings, a set of fundamental assumptions. It was this special climate, these assumptions, that the later novelists of the century were to question, even though the great mass of the reading public still took them for granted.

And this points to another main difference between the novelists of the first half of the Victorian age and those of the second half. The former were at one with their public to a quite remarkable degree; they were conditioned by it, as of course any novelists must be, but for the most part were willingly conditioned by it. They identified themselves with their age and were its spokesmen. The later novelists, however, were writing in some sense against their age; they were critical, even hostile, to its dominant assumptions. Their relation to the reading public was nearer to that of the twentieth-century novelist than to the early Victorians. The difference may be indicated easily enough. "It was part of the felicity of the fifties to possess a literature which was at once topical, contemporary, and classic," G. M. Young has written; "to meet the Immortals in the street, and to read them with added zest for the encounter." The Immortals in question were men and women in early middle age. Within thirty years they had departed, and with them perhaps the public sense of the possibility of further Immortals; at any rate, Meredith, for all his great reputation and his enormous influence at the end of his life, was always a small seller, Hardy so outraged the conventional opinion of his day as to impel a bishop to demand the burning of *Jude the Obscure,* while Butler, ignored as a crank, never saw the publication of *The Way of All Flesh* in his lifetime, though it had been finished twenty years before his death.

This sense of identity with their times is of cardinal importance in any consideration of the early Victorian novelists. It was the source alike of their strengths and of their weaknesses, and it distinguishes them both from their successors and from their great European contemporaries. It is not that the Victorians were uncritical of their country and age, but their criticisms are much less radical than those of, say, Balzac, Stendhal, Turgenev, Flaubert, and Dostoevski, and of a different kind. For a good reason: the condition of England as compared with that of France and of Russia. Flaubert believed that human history fell into three phases: paganism, Christianity, and *muflisme,* which we may perhaps translate as "swinishness." He had no doubt that his age was that of *muflisme.* This fundamental dissatisfaction with his time was partly a matter of temperament; what is important is that it was also shared largely by his great predecessors Balzac and Stendhal. France had suffered a steep descent from the heroic ages of the Revolution and of Napoleon. Glory had departed, and the descent was the descent into vulgarity, into everything that could be epitomized in the word *bourgeois*. Balzac, Stendhal, and Flaubert were great Romantics who, instead of turning away from the world in disgust, turned *towards* it in disgust and fought it with its own weapons. In them realism as an aesthetic creed was born.

In Russia things were yet more different. There, the novel was seen as a weapon in the fight against a ramshackle feudal despotism whose main defense was a rigorous though not efficient censorship. The distinction between art and propaganda, art conceived, that is, as an instrument of persuasion, has never existed in Russia. For the most part, the nineteenth-century Russian novel was propaganda for progressive ideas, but it was not inevitably so, as the fiction of Dostoevski shows. Yet, since fiction was often the only place in which dangerous thoughts could be discussed, not always with perfect safety to the novelist, the novel became the main vehicle of criticism— of society, of morals, of the Russian attitude to the West, of man's relation to God and to his fellows, indeed, of Russian man in relation to the whole world, visible and invisible, in which he lived.

Nineteenth-century Russian fiction, then, has a sweep and range of subject, an audacity of inquiry, that we do not find in early Victorian fiction. Like the French, though at a later date, it was to have a profound effect on the English novel; but the great Victorians themselves were untouched by foreign influence.

They accepted the society in which they lived without question, or rather, when they criticized it, they criticized it as many of their readers were doing. They voiced their doubts and fears; the assumptions of their age they fully shared. When the reaction against the age set in, among intellectuals in the nineties, among the general public in the first twenty years of the present century, the Victorians were commonly charged with smugness, complacency, hypocrisy, and foolish optimism. It is now possible for us to see the Victorians more justly. They were as conscious as we are, looking back, of the tensions and contradictions of their times, the havoc caused by the industrial revolution, the presence of mass poverty, the existence side by side of what Disraeli called the two nations; and in the forties they feared revolution. The forces set in motion by the industrial revolution they did not know how to control, and the working of what seemed the iron laws of economics outraged the consciences of the best and most intelligent of the time. They were, then, thoroughly aware of the evils of their age; yet they could hardly not believe that these evils, awkward though they were to surmount, would prove to be merely temporary; for on all sides was the plainest possible evidence of enormous increase in material wealth and the physical amenities of civilization. There seemed no good reason why this progress should not continue indefinitely. There were, of course, dissident voices: Carlyle, Ruskin, Newman, and, later, Matthew Arnold. But broadly, the early Victorians accepted the idea of progress without much question. The age represented the triumph of protestantism, and perhaps its great achievement was the universal acceptance of the idea of respectability. It *was* a great achievement, no matter how dingy may be our present associations with the word— lace curtains, aspidistras, and a prudential self-regarding morality summed up in such sayings as "Honesty is the best policy" and "Nothing for nothing, and remarkably little for sixpence."

The idea of respectability needs discussing because it so thoroughly permeates the Victorian novel. In the middle of the eighteenth century the word "respectable" was applied to persons worthy of respect for moral excellence. Then the meaning changed somewhat; the word was applied to people of "good or fair social standing," with the moral qualities appropriate to this. A further shift of meaning occurred, and the word was applied to anyone who was honest and decent in behavior and clean in habits, irrespective of social position. This last meaning reveals how the idea behind the word had captured all classes of society. The respectable artisan, in work and not in debt, who took his wife and family to the Great Exhibition, was respectable in the same way as the Queen with her Consort and young family. A middle-class idea, born in the eighteenth century, had prevailed. The first great spokesman of the idea of respectability was the self-made man, the printer, Richardson. In the shape of the Evangelical Movement, the idea swept over England on a flood tide; by the 1780's it had received brilliant literary expression in Cowper's poem *The Task.* Jane Austen's novels had reinforced it; and it is amusing to reflect that the Prince Regent, who admired her work so much, should have strengthened its appeal by the disreputableness of his own behavior and that of his friends.

What we often think of as typically Victorian, especially in its attitude towards sex, had become dominant years before the Queen came to the throne. The taboo on the frank recognition and expression of sex had come into existence slowly and, as it were, almost unawares. It was in 1818 that Thomas Bowdler published his *Family Shakespeare,* in which, as he stated, "nothing is added to the original text, but those words and expressions are omitted which cannot with propriety be read aloud in a family."

One symbol of this aspect of Victorian respectability was the banishment of Fielding. He was read, and much admired, but he was no longer public reading. *Tom Jones* was kept on the top shelf of the study, or relegated to the billiard room or the smoking room, out of the way of women and children. Thackeray wistfully said that Fielding was the last writer to be "permitted to depict to his utmost power a man," and the taboo on sex represented the triumph of woman. In the eighteenth century, though Fielding had protested against it in *Tom Jones,* a double standard of morality had been generally taken for granted; there was one law for the man, another for the woman, and in each case the law seemed to be the translation into morals of biological fact. In the Victorian age, publicly at any rate, the law for man and for woman became the same law. If Victorian morality did not in truth square with the facts of life and the actual state of Victorian morals, it was certainly not for want of zeal and will on the part of the Victorians themselves. And the novelists were not behind in propagating the Victorian ideal, though it is plain that Thackeray for one did not find it particularly convincing. But here the spokesman is Trollope, in his *Autobiography*:

> The writer of stories must please, or he will be nothing. And he must teach whether he wish to teach or no. How shall he teach lessons of virtue and at the same time make himself a delight to his readers? . . . But the novelist, if he have a conscience, must preach his sermons with the same purpose as the clergyman, and must have his own system of ethics. If he can do this efficiently, if he can make virtue alluring and vice ugly, while he charms his readers instead of wearying them, then I think Mr. Carlyle need not call him distressed. . . .
>
> I think that many have done so; so many that we English novelists may boast as a class that such has been the general result of our own work . . . I find such to have been the teaching of Thackeray, of Dickens, and of George Eliot . . . Can anyone by search through the works of the . . . great English novelists I have named, find a scene, a passage, or a word that would teach a girl to be immodest, or a man to be dishonest? When men in their pages have been described as dishonest and women as immodest, have they not ever been punished?

From one point of view, the notion of respectability may be regarded as the apotheosis of wishful thinking; from another and more rewarding, as a violent and heroic attempt to correct the vices and weaknesses of the age. One may ask why the triumph of the Evangelical Movement, with its emphasis on the responsibility of the individual human being, should have been delayed until Victoria came to the throne and should then have been so sudden and apparently irresistible. One reason was the rapid progress of the industrial revolution, with its wholesale shifting of population and its enormous speeding up of communications. In a sense, the industrial revolution changed nothing; but it did bring to public attention, in the most startling way, evils that had always existed. There had always been overcrowding, there had always been drunkenness, there had always been sweatshops in cellars, and exploitation of children in industry. But now they existed on so colossal a scale that awareness of them had become unavoidable, and the viciousness and misery they bred were such as no man of good will could contemplate without horror. It is significant that industrial reform and legislation to curb the worst excesses of the factory system were often first prompted by millowners themselves, who had not made the industrial system so much as inherited it. It had grown up piecemeal and at haphazard, and out of the public view. Its consequences, as soon as seen, were plain to all, though how they might be amended was another matter.

In the eighteenth century the abuse of power had been comparatively simple; it was man's tyranny over man that had moved Fielding and Smollett. In the nineteenth century that tyranny had been displaced by the much more complex tyranny of economic forces. The effects of the new tyranny could be mitigated in part by legislation, and within limits, or so it was believed, a man could further escape them by the cultivation of the virtues of industry, thrift, and self-control, on which the notion of respectability was based. Behind the notion was the full force of public opinion, the opinion of the middle classes and the skilled working class. Outside those classes lay, at the one extreme, the aristocracy, at the other the poor, the lumpish proletariat, the mob; from the excess of both the middle and working classes revolted in horror. How real and ever present the danger from these excesses was is proved by the very fervor with which the notion of respectability was clung to. It is said that in 1816 the number of prostitutes in London amounted to a thirtieth of the population. Thirty years later Carlyle, at John Forster's house, declared that chastity among men was as good as dead, and Dickens, a fellow guest, said that "incontinence was so much the rule in England that if his own son were particularly chaste, he should be alarmed on his account as if he could not be in good health." And it was in the eighties that W. T. Stead, the editor of *The Pall Mall Gazette*, went to prison for his unorthodox way of exposing the traffic in young girls for the purposes of prostitution.

It is against the background indicated in such facts that the heroic nature of the Victorian protest against sexual license and promiscuity must be judged. At its lowest, the respectability of the age was a code governed by considerations of "good form," of what was publicly sanctioned; at its highest, it represented the conscious desire for betterment, moral and economic, the controlled impulse to self-improvement. Numerically, the respectable may not have been large; it is unlikely that the majority of working men ever subscribed to Mechanics' Institutes or attended Sunday school. But it was the respectable who were articulate, who made public opinion; and at their head were the Queen and the Prince Consort. To be respectable was to be at once orthodox and fashionable.

It was the respectable who composed the reading public,

and it was for the respectable that the great Victorian novelists wrote. Perhaps they flattered the illusions of their public, encouraged them in their black-and-white view of morals; all of them, to a greater or less degree, were inhibited by the assumptions of their public, and there is a case for maintaining that Thackeray was crippled by them. All the same, this identification on the part of the novelists with their public undoubtedly gave them great strength and confidence; they addressed the whole of the literate public, and if they interpreted that public in almost wholly middle-class terms, their intuition was right, for their working-class readers also aspired to middle-class status. The distinction between novelists as artists and novelists as public entertainers had not yet been made, and their power and authority were the greater because of that. Sharing the preoccupations and obsessions of their time, rooted in the popular life of their age, they produced an art that was truly national, that satisfied, if not at all levels, certainly at more than have been possible to the English novelists who have followed them.

"Whenever I am thinking of a character, in public life it may be, or in literature," G. M. Young has said, "I always ask 'What was happening in the world when he was twenty?'" What was happening in the world in 1832, when Dickens was twenty and Thackeray twenty-one? The first long phase of the struggle for parliamentary reform and the extension of the franchise had ended with the passing of the Reform Act. It was not a very revolutionary measure, but it put an end to the threat of revolution that had been swelling for the past decade, and it put power, if and when they cared to use it, into the hands of the middle class. Within a year, the first Factory Act was to be passed and slavery abolished in British possessions. Two years earlier the Manchester and Liverpool Railway had been opened, and a year earlier Faraday had made his discovery of the electromagnetic current.

And what was happening in the novel? What was **the** current fiction the young Thackeray and Dickens were reading? Jane Austen had been dead fifteen years, Scott was to die in 1832 itself. *Crotchet Castle* had appeared in 1831, Peacock's last novel for thirty years. It was a poor time for fiction, indeed, for writing generally. Peacock apart, of the novelists who emerged in the years between Scott's first novels and those of Dickens only two seem to me to have merit enough to keep their works still worth reading in their own right; the others whose names survive in literary history have only the wannest kind of historical interest. You may say that Pierce Egan, whose *Life in London* appeared in serial form between 1821 and 1828, and Theodore Hook, whose collections of stories, *Sayings and Doings,* began to come out in 1824 and whose novel *Gilbert Gurney* was published in 1836, influenced Dickens, and it will be true in an insignificant way: Egan and Hook were popular journalists supplying a staple commodity, and Dickens began in the same kind of journalism. There were bound to be points of superficial similarity between the man of genius and the hacks, since the man of genius began as a hack himself. But it does not really matter that Hook in certain of his characters may have anticipated Mr. Jingle. Egan and Hook gave Dickens nothing that he could not have equally well gotten out of himself or from earlier writers. As novelists, though Egan was only dubiously one, they wrote debased Smollett for a newly literate public, whose interest in high life and low they sought to gratify. But Dickens had read Smollett for himself, probably before he read Egan, and he knew at first hand, because he was born in it, the lower middle-class life that Hook snobbishly satirized. Both Hook and Egan are today readable only by people who for one reason or another have to read them. So too are the historical novelists G. P. R. James and Harrison Ainsworth, who cashed in on the sudden and enormous appetite for historical fiction that Scott had brought into being. It is true that some Ainsworth has been read by the young until quite recently, probably because of the respectability historical fiction has always had in the eyes of teachers and parents, who, by stressing the adjective, have been able to soft-pedal the noun.

Perhaps Hook should be given some credit for extending the scene of fiction to take in the suburban lower middle class of London, though that would have happened anyway. By the side of his middle-class fiction the novel of high life continued to flourish in the work of Mrs. Gore, but here again nothing was done that had not been or was to be done better by other writers. And there was, of course, the occasional novel of distinction by a writer outside the main tendencies of the age, the perennially delightful novel of Persian life, J. J. Morier's *The Adventures of Hajji Baba,* for instance, which appeared in 1824, and Mary Russell Mitford's charming stories of village life, written in what is really an eighteenth-century tradition, *Our Village,* which was published between 1812 and 1832, and her novel *Belford Regis* (1835).

There remain three names of greater weight: Frederick Marryat (1782-1848), Bulwer-Lytton (1803-73) and Benjamin Disraeli (1804-81), novelists who, however different in talent and achievement, have one thing in common: they seem in some strange way to stand apart from the Victorian age and ethos, and this though Lytton played a distinguished part in its public life and Disraeli was one of its two loftiest political figures. Marryat, of course, was of a different generation, and came to fiction in middle age after a distinguished career as a naval officer, but Lytton and Disraeli were born in the decade before that which saw the births of the great Victorians. Yet those few years were to make all the difference, and for all that they both went on writing fiction as long as they lived, they remained curiously impervious to the Victorian spirit.

Marryat is a most attractive minor novelist. He is usually seen as in the tradition of Smollett, mainly, I suspect, because both are novelists of the sea, though Marryat had infinitely greater knowledge of what he was writing about. But all the association of the two names means is that for the most part, in novels like *Peter Simple,* Marryat is content to set down a string of adventures loosely tied up by a perfunctory plot which the reader scarcely remembers when the novel is read, though its tone and feel remain vivid. The tone and feel are nothing like Smollett's. Marryat is the most good-humored of novelists, possessed of an exuberance that is rarely overplayed; there is a largeness of mind about him; a natural gallantry informs his work. It was this, I believe, that so impressed Conrad. Often his attitude and his humor anticipate surprisingly some aspects of Dickens. *Peter Simple* is a charming story, and a most vivid account of life in the Royal Navy in the early years of the century. But what gives it its distinction is not so much the episodes of adventure as the way in which they are related. We see everything through the eyes of Peter himself, the young midshipman who is accepted as, and believes himself to be, the fool of the family. Peter's innocence, which is the outcome not at all of stupidity but of a truly touching trust, is beautifully rendered. He is probably the first convincing boy in our fiction, and much of the humor of the book lies in the contrast between the world as it is and as it imposes itself on the boy's naivety. This humor, of course, is often of a very simple kind, as when the other midshipmen scare Peter, on his joining his first ship, with tales of the cruelty of the captain, who the reader has already guessed is the best-hearted and most scrupulous man in the service. Yet even here Peter is a universal character, a figure of fable; he is the boy who, in English factories, is sent off by his fellow apprentices to the shop round the corner for a pint of pigeon's milk or an ounce of elbow grease. But when Peter goes on board the humor becomes less primitive. When he is exploited by Mr. and Mrs. Trotter, and the latter, inspecting his clothes, says:

> "Now these worsted stockings will be very comfortable in cold weather, and in the summer time these brown cotton socks will be delightfully cool, and you have enough of each to last until you outgrow them; but as for these fine cotton stockings, they are of no use—only catch the dirt when the decks are swept, and always look untidy. I wonder how they could be so foolish as to send them; nobody wears them on board ship nowadays. They are fit only for women —I wonder if they would fit me,"

we know where we are. Peter shares with David Copperfield the same innocent wonderment at and acceptance of the world of grown-ups who can always fleece them with a kind word, a show of reason, and a monstrous tall story which must be true to a boy who cannot believe that falsity exists. And though he is a smaller character than David, Peter convinces and moves us in the same way.

There is, too, as in *Copperfield,* a singular purity in the drawing of the adult characters as they are seen through the boy's eyes. They are, in fact, a boy's characters: fabulous beings, drawn not critically but in wonder. And one of them is quite excellent, the gentlemanly boatswain Mr. Chucks, a comic creation Dickens would not have been ashamed of.

Marryat's talent was not confined to the kind of book *Peter Simple* is. There is nothing quite like his *Snarleyyow, or The Dog Fiend* in the language, though in characterization it anticipates the grotesques of Dickens. Smallbones, for instance, who is perhaps the hero, has obvious affinities with Dickens's oppressed and friendless waifs, Pip and Smike and poor Jo and the rest, though it is going altogether too far to say that he is the prototype of these characters, since in fact *Snarleyyow* and *Oliver Twist*, where the Dickens waif appears for the first time, came out in the same year, 1837. But here he is:

> . . . a thin, shambling personage, apparently about twenty years old—a pale, cadaverous face, high cheek-bones, goggle eyes, with lank hair very thinly sown upon a head, which, like bad soil, would return but a scanty harvest. He looked like Famine's eldest son just arriving to years of discretion. His long lanky legs were pulled so far through his trowsers, that his bare feet, and half way up to his knees, were exposed to the chilling blast. The sleeves of his jacket were so short, that four inches of bone above the wrist were bared to view —hat he had none—his ears were very large, and the rims of them red with cold, and his neck was immeasurably long and thin, that his head appeared to topple for want of support.

But Smallbones, half starved though he is, the victim of Captain Vanslyperken's brutality and meanness, the victim too of the captain's dog Snarleyyow, which is regarded by the crew as an incarnate imp of the devil, is not passive as the Dickens waifs are; he gives as much as he receives. Indeed, the main thread of the novel, which is sketchily historical, set in England and Holland and the seas between in the year 1699, is the series of attempts on the one hand of Vanslyperken to kill Smallbones and on the other of Smallbones to kill Vanslyperken's dog. Neither will be killed; apparently drowned, hanged, bashed on the head, hacked about, they bear charmed lives; each, in the eyes of his enemies, must be in league with the supernatural. Marryat was writing farce, and, like a true farce writer, he piles on situation after ludicrous situation, so that his comic invention seems inexhaustible. But the farce he was writing is of a very rare kind indeed. It is macabre farce, farce that arises out of the superstitious natures of the characters, and what is surprising is that the reader, though he is never meant to be deceived into thinking the farcical events described spring from supernatural causes, is none the less impressed by the genuine macabre quality of the novel.

A most eerie work, which one day may be generally discovered, it contains besides its grotesques some good characterization in the round and, in the reformed prostitute Nancy, one of the earliest appearances in fiction of a stock character in the nineteenth-century novel from Dickens to Gissing. Marryat's rendering of it shows his freedom both from Victorian prudery and sentimentality. Nancy is neither wept over nor apologized for; she is accepted frankly, by his characters no less than by Marryat himself. In the last years of his life he devoted himself mainly to the writing of his books for children, such as *Masterman Ready* and *The Children of the New Forest*. They are admirable; yet that he gave up the novel proper for children's fiction may be regretted. Perhaps it was forced upon him by the feeling of the age. One remembers the scene in *Peter Simple* in which the hero goes to a polite ball in the Barbados:

> Supper was now announced, and having danced the last country dance with Miss Minerva, I of course had the pleasure of handing her into the supper-room. It was my fate to sit opposite to a fine turkey, and I asked my partner if I should have the pleasure of helping her to a piece of the breast. She looked at me very indignantly, and said, "Curse your impudence, sar, I wonder where you larn manners. Sar, I take a lilly turkey *bosom,* if you please. Talk of *breast* to a lady, sar; really quite *horrid.*"

Such a passage, so unaffected in its amusement at the pruderies of pseudorefinement, could not have been written much later than 1834. After that, the joke was on the Victorians quite as much as on the genteel mulattoes of West Indian islands.

Lytton is an instance of the novelist who is good in and for his own time but, as later generations realize, does nothing that has not been better done before. Unlike the great novelists, who have usually been concerned with the examination and exploration of the moral implications of, in Conrad's phrase, "a few simple ideas," and have accordingly been content to plough a single furrow, narrow but also deep, Lytton pursued at least four very different lines of fiction. His was an ambitious, restless talent, but that of the popularizer rather than that of the creator; he may be compared in this, as in other respects, with Aldous Huxley today. Like Huxley, he had little sense of literary tact; he borrowed largely of the techniques and attitudes of other writers and applied them to quite inappropriate material. In his own time he seemed an original novelist; he was in fact a profoundly derivative one, though this does not, of course, reduce his merit for his own time.

He came first under the influence of Godwin; his first novel, published in 1827, was significantly called *Falkland. Pelham* (1828) is much more interesting and remains very readable. It is an attempt to combine the novel of fashion with that of Godwin. An index of its modish success is the fact that it is a result of its hero's taste in clothes that black is still the conventional color of men's evening dress. It is a young man's novel, bright, smart, insolent. It owed something perhaps to Disraeli's *Vivian Grey,* which had been published the year before. Pelham, who tells his story in the first person, is a young aristocrat ambitious for political power, and masking his ambition under flippancy, cynicism and dandyism. "What a damnation puppy!" one of the characters exclaims of him, and Pelham rejoices in the outburst as at a compliment. His adventures in society in Paris and London, his excursions into the underworld of the day, are told in a lively style overstudded with epigrams. Reading *Pelham,* one cannot forget that the epoch described is still pre-Victorian; Lytton is out to shock, and at times, when the underworld is being exposed, the point of view and the tone, when allowance is made for Lytton's much greater sophistication, are uncommonly like Egan's in *Life in London*.

But to this story of a young man's successful imposition of himself upon the world of fashion and politics is added that of Sir Richard Glanville, a young man of enormous talents obsessed with Byronic guilt and dedicated to revenge, revenge on the man who has raped his mistress and driven her into insanity. It is Pelham's detective work that saves him from the gallows. This part of the novel is plainly from Godwin, but it is the superficies of Godwin, Godwin without the compelling myth that lifted his finest novel out of the class of horror literature into the ranks of symbolic fiction.

Eugene Aram (1832) is also a product of Godwin's influence. Lytton took over the philosopher's latinate, abstract, chilly style which, when applied to the theme of high-minded murder, became highfalutin. As far as characterization and psychology are concerned, no novel could be less convincing than *Aram*, which was written, Thackeray said, to show "how Eugene Aram, though a thief, a liar, and a murderer, yet being intellectual was amongst the noblest of mankind."

These novels, and those for which they may stand as types, were really exercises in rhetoric, attempts at heightened narrative, at a bastard poetry, in fact. They seem grotesquely inflated now. Round about 1849, perhaps in an effort to emulate Dickens, Mrs. Gaskell, and Thackeray, Lytton published *The Caxtons,* the first of a series of novels much of a kind. *The Caxtons* offers resemblances enough to the characteristic works of the great Victorians. But Lytton was not content with this, for the basis of the novel is a close and elaborate imitation of *Tristram Shandy*, amazingly like it in small details and fantastically unlike in its spirit as a whole. All the main characters of Sterne's masterpiece may be matched in Lytton's book, the sentimental passages are carefully copied, and Lytton even goes one better than Sterne by giving his hero the absurd name of Pisastratus. Once or twice he does produce a few lines that one could believe Sterne had written, but the total effect is ludicrous. To speak of a sentimentalization of Sterne's work may suggest the impossible; but that is essentially what *The Caxtons* is. Lytton made a careful imitation of the husk of Sterne, but there is little sign that he understood its spirit. Sterne's novel is the apotheosis of the irrational; Lytton's is altogether too rational. One might say that *Tristram Shandy* is epitomized in the single remark: "A cow broke in tomorrow morning to my Uncle Toby's fortifications." Such a sentence, and its implications, are beyond Lytton, as is shown by his attempt to use Sterne's methods in order to relate a perfectly conventional story of the estrangement of a misunderstood father from his son. *The Caxtons* stands out as a most illuminating example of the misuse of literary sources, of a crashing, totally disastrous failure in literary tact. It is one of the monumental curiosities of literature.

As an historical novelist Lytton was at any rate painstaking in research, and the genre gave him full scope for his sense of the grandiose, his melodramatic attitude to life.

"A feeling of stage properties, a smell of hair-oil, an aspect of buhl, a remembrance of tailors, and that pricking of the conscience which must be the general accompaniment of paste diamonds": so Trollope summed up the impression Disraeli's novels made on him. There was something else, of course, that Trollope did not reckon with; without it, Disraeli's fiction would not have survived, nor would he have been three times prime minister.

From birth Disraeli was an outsider in England. His grandfather, the descendant of a family of Spanish Jews, had come to London from Venice in the mid-eighteenth century, and established a financial house that for a time rivaled the Rothschilds'. Disraeli's father, Isaac, had other ambitions; he is remembered as the author of *Curiosities of Literature*. A freethinker, he allowed the future prime minister and novelist to be baptized as a child into the Church of England. The young Disraeli, by virtue not only of racial origin—and physically he was very much the Jew—but also of education and social status, was outside the classes in which power resided. His position was inevitably ambiguous. And he had to impose himself on a class much more ready to jeer at him than to admire. He was ambitious, and the only means he had by which to achieve his ambitions were his native cleverness and his effrontery. He imposed himself, not by conforming to English notions of good form, but by differing from them as violently as possible.

His first novel, *Vivian Grey,* published in 1826, when its author was only twenty-two, was a prophetic work.

The theme is the incursion into politics of a young and brilliant adventurer just out of his teens whose first principle is that everything is possible. "In England, personal distinction is the only passport to the society of the great. Whether this distinction arise from fortune, family or talent, is immaterial; but certain it is, to enter into high society, a man must have blood, a million, or genius." Vivian Grey has the last. The son of a man of letters, he meets at his father's dinner table a famous and stupid politician, the Marquis of Carabas, whom he inveigles into a political intrigue against the government of the day, to which the marquis belongs. The intrigue and counterintrigue, the hero's resource, daring, and political brilliance, form the best part of the book. The new party is defeated by the treachery of a woman, the members retire, the group breaks up, and Vivian, having killed a man in a duel, is forced to flee the country. The rest of the novel recounts his marvelous adventures on the Continent.

The main interest of *Vivian Grey* now is in its foreshadowing of Disraeli's later work. As a novel it is fantastic; Disraeli when he wrote it had no practical experience of politics. Lath-and-paper personae, masks for the author himself, engage in scintillating conversation against a two-dimensional background, a world whose law is wit. Disraeli was never to be a realistic writer in the sense that, say, Trollope was. His imagination needed the artificial, the grandiose, before it could function. His heroes are always larger than life, possessed of an impossible array of talents; the estates of his country houses seem to stretch over whole counties; his principal characters tend to be either of the finest Norman blood or millionaires. In *Vivian Grey* these characteristics are carried to their logical conclusions, so that the story bears no more relation to reality than the dream it was. The description of the country house Chateau Désir is fantastic in its artificiality, but scarcely more so than descriptions of other country houses in the mature novels, which to a modern reader irresistibly suggest possible *décors* for unwritten novels by Ronald Firbank.

But *Vivian Grey* is a monstrously witty book, conceived in wit. In the scene of the dinner party at which Vivian meets Carabas is to be heard unmistakably the authentic satirical note of the later novels. And the style, though thinner than what it was to be, is at bottom the same, an eighteenth-century prose in sentences of balanced antitheses that of themselves produce epigrams: "At length, an exception to axiom the second started up in the establishment of Mr. Dallas. The gentleman was a clergyman, a profound Grecian, and a poor man. He had edited the Alcestis, and married his laundress; lost money by his edition, and his fellowship by his match."

After *Vivian Grey* Disraeli wrote some amusing Lucianic satires, a novel of fashionable life in *Henrietta Temple* and a *roman à clef*, *Venetia*, on the lives of Byron and Shelley. But the novels one thinks of as the real Disraeli novels are the Young England trilogy *Coningsby, Sybil,* and *Tancred.* They are political novels, almost the only true political novels in the language. Other novelists have attempted political novels, among them Trollope. But what Trollope concentrates on, in books like *Phineas Finn* and *The Prime Minister,* is the social background of Parliament; he is indifferent to political theory. Wells, too, essayed the political novel in *The New Machiavelli,* but the day-to-day works of politics, politics as an end in itself, was exactly what disgusted him. Disraeli's novels, however, spring out of politics and nothing else; characters and action come alive only through politics.

Coningsby was published in 1844. Its author was already a power in Parliament, the leader of the Tory schismatics. He could no longer afford the open cynicism of *Vivian Grey,* and when it appeared, *Coningsby* was at once a tract for the times, a political manifesto, and an expression of the grossest flattery towards its author's young supporters, four men of great families who were nicknamed, disparagingly, "Young England." Since their movement came to nothing, it now seems pretty silly; a modern historian has described it as "an ephemeral hotch-potch of bogus maypoles and real vested interests." In fact, Young England was in some measure the Cambridge counterpart of the Oxford Movement. Like that, and like the Pre-Raphaelite Brotherhood, it was an expression of that general reaction against the industrial revolution, utilitarianism, and the ideas of the French Revolution which was a feature of the early years of Victoria's reign, and fundamental to it was an ideal conception of feudalism.

Disraeli combined a curiously romantic, indeed histrionic, imagination with a genius for the necessary compromises and calculating realism of ordinary politics. This romantic imagination is seen at its most grandiose not in *Coningsby* but in *Tancred,* in the scene in which the young Emir Fakredeen Shehaab expounds his plan for the Queen of England to transfer the seat of her empire from London to Delhi. As presented, it is fantastic, yet twenty years after writing *Tancred,* Disraeli did in his own way bring the Emir's plan to fulfillment; he did make Victoria Empress of India. Grandiose and improbable as his imagination was, it was always applied to the world outside it, and it was always moved by certain abstract ideas, the ideas of greatness and nobility, kingship, ancient families, and youth. The young men who composed the Young England group, glorying in the spirit of *noblesse oblige,* were behaving, to Disraeli's romantic imagination, as young noblemen should behave. Idealistic and generous, and what was just as important, very rich and of high birth, they fitted naturally into Disraeli's ideal world.

In *Coningsby* the ideal and the real exist side by side. The part that is ideal is so far removed from reality as generally to seem comic now. Coningsby himself, so ardent, so high-minded, and so handsome, is almost a servant girl's hero, and the descriptions of his appropriate backgrounds —Eton, the almsgivings at Eustace Lyle's, Christmas at Beaumanoir—read today almost as burlesque, as deliberate fantasy. For Disraeli's imagination magnified, exaggerated, simplified everything it focused on, and his prose style, sweeping, rhetorical, seeking the immediate effect, abetted the process.

This is apparent especially in the character of Sidonia. Disraeli was an outsider, a parvenu; he was also a man of fierce pride, of pride in race. Coningsby and his friends may be sprigs of aristocracy, but as Sidonia tells Coningsby, the English aristocracy is itself parvenu compared with the lineage of the Jew. And Sidonia, the mysterious horseman who is richer than Rothschild, who is the adviser of kings and the maker of governments, who is immune from ordinary human passion, is—Disraeli himself. It was cunning of him. He was expounding the beliefs of his young followers who were to save England from the Whigs and the professional place seekers, but the theory behind the actions was to come from the enigmatic Jew Sidonia: "Nurture your mind with great thoughts. To believe in the heroic makes heroes."

A highly romantic figure, Sidonia cannot be said to live, but to ignore him in any consideration of his creator would be a fatal error. The racial dream represented what was probably the stabilizing factor in Disraeli's character. It makes the difference between the Disraeli of history and Disraeli as Vivian Grey.

But Disraeli, the constructor of an ideal, chivalric world inhabited by noble and noble-minded youths, was also a satirist, and as a satirist his province was the actual, the sordid day-to-day intrigues of politics. In *Coningsby* the actual exists as a foil to the ideal—and it has survived a century with much less wear. The actual is the world of Coningsby's uncle Lord Monmouth and his hangers-on. Monmouth is not satirized; he is too large in Disraeli's eyes for that. Monmouth is the eighteenth-century oligarch, a figure from the old regime. His motives are purely selfish, but he is on the grand scale. He is no aristocratic villain of melodrama, nothing like the caricature Thackeray drew from the same model and called the Marquis of Steyne. Disraeli treats him with the respect due to him. His contempt is reserved for his creature, Rigby, and for the party hacks, Tadpole and Taper.

Rigby is the embodiment of an eternal type, the cold-blooded underling; a yes man, but a particularly formidable yes man. Disraeli scorns him, but scarcely underrates him:

> The world took him at his word, for he was bold, acute, and voluble; with no thought, but a good deal of desultory information; and though destitute of all imagination and noble sentiment, was blessed with a vigorous, mendacious fancy, fruitful in small expedients, and never happier than when devising shifts for great man's scrapes. . . . He was

just the animal that Lord Monmouth wanted, for Lord Monmouth always looked upon human nature with the callous eye of a jockey. He surveyed Rigby, and he determined to buy him. He bought him; with his clear head, his indefatigable industry, his audacious tongue, and his ready and unscrupulous pen; with all his dates, all his lampoons; all his private memoirs, and all his political intrigues. It was a good purchase.

In a novel that is full of the larger than life Rigby is depicted so justly, with such accuracy of observation, as to appear something of a miniature. With Rigby, Disraeli's art diminishes. Reading of him one is reminded of the exact and wounding observation of Pope's portraits in the "Prologue to the Satires."

Tadpole and Taper are twin dummies, no more to be differentiated, as their names indicate, than Tweedledum and Tweedledee. But what admirable dummies they are:

> "I tell you what, Mr. Taper, the time is gone by when a Marquis of Monmouth was letter A, No. 1."
>
> "Very true, Mr. Tadpole. A wise man would do well now to look to the great middle class, as I said the other day to the electors of Shabbytown . . ."
>
> "And now for our cry," said Mr. Taper . . . "Ancient institutions and modern improvements, I suppose, Mr. Tadpole?"
>
> "Ameliorations is the better word; ameliorations. Nobody knows exactly what it means . . . That we should ever live to see a Tory government again! We have reason to be very thankful!"
>
> "Hush!" said Mr. Tadpole. "The time has gone by for Tory governments; what the country requires is a sound Conservative government."
>
> "A sound Conservative government," said Taper, musingly. "I understand: Tory men and Whig measures."

Disraeli is at his most impressive in the great set scenes: the scene in the first book of *Coningsby*, where, after being led through apartment after apartment of the great house, the boy Coningsby bursts into tears when he finally is presented to his noble kinsman Monmouth; the account of

Monmouth's house party at Coningsby Castle; the passage in which Rigby breaks it to Lucretia that Monmouth has left her. In these, all his talents come into play, his power of vivid description, his sense of theater, his irony, his ability to build up to a sustained climax. And what gives these passages so much of their effect, as it does the back-stage political scenes, is his style. That formal epigram-matic eighteenth-century prose, which is hollow with rheto-ric and which falsifies whenever he attempts natural description or the rendering of high ideals or psychological states, has, when he is dealing with the actual world of politics and intrigue, what one may call an historian's quality. It affects us as Gibbon's does, or Macaulay's; it admits of no hesitations, no half lights; it is completely sure, completely dogmatic. Above all, it is witty. The very structure of his sentences is witty, and his epigrams invite the reader into his confidence: "Although the best of wives and mothers, she had some charity for her neighbors." Again: "England is unrivalled for two things, sporting and politics. They were combined at Beaumanoir; for the guests came not merely to slaughter the Duke's pheasants, but to hold council on the prospects of the party, which, it was supposed by the initiated, began at this time to in-dicate some symptoms of brightening." It is when we con-sider his wit and the part it plays in his novels that we realize that Disraeli was truly the alien outsider, that he was only half taken in by what he saw and that, even when most impressed, he still found the spectacle rich enough in its oddity to give us other outsiders a huge wink. He was the outsider who got inside.

One other quality of Disraeli as a novelist must be noted: his attitude to women. Here he is remote from all the other early Victorian novelists. "All his ladies are rav-ishing," but they are also all highly intelligent; there is nothing of Amelia Sedley or Dora Copperfield about Madame Colonna, the Princess Lucretia, and Lady Everingham. They have minds and wills of their own, and here surely Disraeli, who began his career by flattering the Countess of Blessington and ended by flattering Queen Victoria—laying it on like a trowel, as he said himself—was nearer the truth about women than Thackeray and Dickens.

Coningsby is remarkable as a picture of the actual working of politics at the time of the first reform bill, *Sybil* as a picture of the state of industrial England at the time. The true theme of the novel is the class struggle and its solution in terms of the policy of Young England. The subtitle, *The Two Nations,* explains the book. It was the first novel, for Mrs. Gaskell's *Mary Barton* did not appear until 1848, to expose the conditions of the industrial working classes at their worst. It was a horrifying exposure, and it was accurate. It still has great power to move, in the descriptions of miners and mines, above all in that of the riots.

As a novelist Disraeli's limitations were many and obvious. His strength lay in his specialized knowledge; it would be almost true to say that he had to become a politician before he could become a novelist. But within his limitations he grasped and expressed the essential situation of his times with a boldness beyond that of much greater novelists.

2

"That Dickens was a great genius and is permanently among the classics is certain. But the genius was that of a great entertainer, and he had for the most part no profounder responsibility as a creative artist than this description suggests." Thus F. R. Leavis, who no one can say fails to appreciate Dickens. Yet Dickens poses a most awkward problem for him. He is "a great poet"; "in range and ease [of command of word, phrase, rhythm, and image] there is surely no greater master of English except Shakespeare." What could be more handsome? But this is not enough to place him in Dr. Leavis's "great tradition" of the English novel, for he lacks, as compared with Jane Austen, George Eliot, James, Conrad, and D. H. Lawrence, "a total significance of a profoundly serious kind." The word "tradition," of course, can mean whatever a critic wants it to mean. But a tradition of the English novel which has to leave out the only novelist of a Shakespearean order is a pretty shaky one, and to call Dickens a great popular entertainer rather than a great novelist is blatantly to beg the question.

The distinction between the entertainer and the novelist is a sophistication. There have been great entertainers in fiction who have not been great novelists, but there has never been a great novelist who was not first of all a great entertainer, for the end of the novel, like that of poetry, is delight, and "total significance," however "profoundly serious," will go for nothing, will not indeed exist, unless the novel has primary and overriding value as entertainment. That it should delight, whether at the most naive and unreflecting level or as a "superior amusement," is the first thing we ask of any novel.

Dickens was the great novelist who was also the great entertainer, the greatest entertainer, probably, in the history of fiction. Much of the misapprehension of him comes from this fact, and from the related fact that, formally, he was a man of little education writing for a public often more poorly educated than himself. The public he wrote for was largely a new public brought to consciousness by the industrial revolution, a public to which magazine proprietors had not catered before 1832, when *Chambers's Journal* and *Knight's Penny Magazine* first appeared. His success, right from the beginning, was unprecedented, and it cut across all social classes. His power was more akin to the great actor's, orator's, or demagogue's than to the writer's as we normally conceive it. The nature of his genius was such that he had to identify himself with his public;

without the sense of an audience in intimate relation with him he was less than himself. His public readings have been deplored, but they indicate the intensity of his craving for what was almost a symbiotic relation with his public. It was one of the conditions necessary to his art. And the very nature of his art made for closeness with his public. His novels were all issued serially, generally in monthly parts. This alone explains many of the structural deficiencies of his work. Every installment had to come to a climax of suspense, action and excitement must be maintained at all costs, so that the fluctuations of public demand tended to dictate the course future action would take. The one test of success was—success, which could only be interpreted by sales. When circulation dropped, something was plainly wrong with the author-public relationship and had to be mended. Thus, when the sales of *Martin Chuzzlewit* fell from 60,000 to 20,000 there was only one thing to do: Martin had to be packed off to America, however irrelevant to the main action of the novel the proceeding was.

In nothing is Dickens's almost mediumistic relationship with his public more clearly seen than in his role of reformer. The word is not quite right for him; it suggests a Shaftesbury or a Plimsoll, which Dickens never was. He attacked the injustices of the poor law, delays in administration of justice, the cruelties of schoolmasters, imprisonment for debt, and so on. But he was not a pioneer in these attacks. Dickens's relation to his age in these respects, his beliefs, his moral and political philosophies, have been brilliantly charted by Humphry House in *The Dickens World,* one of the most valuable books we possess on him. Of Dickens the reformer House says:

> He seemed topical to thousands: he was not too topical for them to see the point, nor too advanced to have the public conscience on his side. Detached now from his time he may seem more original and adventurous than he was; for then

he was only giving wider publicity in "inimitable" form to a number of social facts and social abuses which had already been recognized if not explored before him. He shared a great deal of common experience with his public, so that it could gratefully and proudly say, "How true!"; he so exploited his knowledge that the public recognized its master in knowing; but he also shared with it an attitude to what they both knew, and caught exactly the tone which clarified and reinforced the public's sense of right and wrong, and flattered its moral feelings.

In a very special sense, then, owing to the peculiar nature of his connection with his public, Dickens more than any of his contemporaries was the expression of the conscience —untutored, baffled, muddled as it doubtless often was— of his age. It was as such that he was accepted and loved. "The master of our sunniest smiles and our most unselfish tears," whom it was "impossible to read without the most ready and pliant sympathy," he showed his readers what they themselves thought and felt of the great social problems which confronted them; or rather, reading him, they discovered what they thought and felt.

"Make 'em laugh, make 'em cry, make 'em wait," was his friend Wilkie Collins's formula for the novel. Dickens first caught his readers by making them laugh. He began his writing career as a journalist, and the book with which he first captured the world began as a piece of journalism; incidentally, it still defines the conventional conception of Dickens. He was called in, in 1836, after the success of *Sketches by Boz,* to provide the letterpress for "Cockney sporting plates of a superior sort." These "plates" were a stock commercial line of the publishers of the day: Egan's *Life in London* had been running serially from 1821 to 1828; Surtees's *Jorrocks's Jaunts and Jollities,* the episodic adventures of a Cockney sportsman, had been appearing in the *New Sporting Magazine* between 1831 and 1834. Dickens's commission was to provide text for drawings of similar comic sportsmen by the artist Robert Seymour. He persuaded the publishers, however, to change the original idea somewhat and invented the character of Mr. Pickwick. As he wrote himself, the *Posthumous Papers of the Pickwick Club* "were designed for the introduction of diverting characters and incidents." "No ingenuity of plot was attempted . . . or even considered very feasible by the author in connection with the desultory mode of publication adopted; . . . the machinery of the Club, proving cumbrous in the management, was gradually abandoned as the work progressed." The book began as improvisation. Dickens soon became the senior partner in the collaboration of artist and writer, and his position was strengthened when Seymour committed suicide and "Phiz" took his place. But nothing like enormous success attended the publication until the appearance of Sam Weller in Chapter X. Immediately Dickens's problem was solved; he was no longer at the mercy of constant improvisation; the diverging incidents could be governed by the characters whom they befell. As soon as Pickwick and Sam Weller were set in juxtaposition, the kind of book he was writing must have become apparent to him: the benevolent, idealistic, unworldly master, the hard-bitten, humorous, realistic servant; it was an archetypal situation in fiction, the latest variant on the Quixote-Sancho Panza, Tom Jones-Partridge theme. It provided its own impetus and what began as not much more than a version of Surtees took its place, as soon as the Wellers were introduced, straightway in the mythology of the English.

With *The Pickwick Papers* one side of Dickens's genius was made manifest. Here is Dickens the pure humorist, rejoicing in his ability to dash off character after character, a whole world of them, his and none other's, rejoicing too in the language he puts in their mouths, a language so fertile and exuberant in comic invention as to have a lyrical quality almost of poetry. Mr. Pickwick undergoes the rigors of trial for breach of promise; he is confined in the Fleet; he is fleeced by rogues; humbugs, charlatans, snobs run riot through the book. Yet the world of *Pickwick* is a world as "innocent as Beatrix Potter's." Buzfuz, Jingle, Dodson, and Fogg are no more terrifying than Peter Rabbit's Mr. McGregor, for the world of *Pickwick* is the world of fairy tale, with the bad fairies not monstrous but absurd. It is the product of an enormously rich and zestful experience of the human scene, the work, one would say, of a young man without a care in the world, creating a world of his own in which the crudities and miseries of the real world are sterilized by humor, so that a hypocrite like Stiggins, the first of the great Dickens gallery of hypocrites, is seen as a good thing in himself without reference to moral judgment, just as Tony Weller, the most superb figure in the book, is a good thing in himself. Stiggins, the Wellers, the rest of them, are, so to say, their own reward, virtues in their own right.

But they represent only one side of Dickens. While *Pickwick* was appearing in its monthly parts, *Oliver Twist* was coming out in *Bentley's Miscellany,* and *Oliver Twist* is a very different work. Fairyland has become nightmare; the bad fairies are merely absurd no longer; they have become ogres.

"Make 'em laugh, make 'em cry . . ." In *Oliver Twist* the emphasis is wholly on the second precept of the formula. There is laughter, but very different in aim and kind from that of *Pickwick*. On the surface, *Oliver Twist* is an exposure novel, an attack on the working of the poor law. But the poor law itself is merely symbolic of the fate of innocence and weakness. *Oliver Twist,* like so much in Dickens, in his later work especially, is a fantasy of good and evil. Graham Greene, in his essay on the novel, has suggested that Dickens was a Manichee and was much more convinced of the reality of evil than of good. Certainly the rendering of evil in the book is immeasurably more vivid than that of good. No one has ever believed in Rose Maylie and Mr. Brownlow; the reality of Sikes and Fagin and Claypole is inescapable. Perhaps it ought not to be so. "Wolves tear your throats!" mutters Sikes; he is, one would say, a figure of the sheerest melodrama. And so in the context of a realistic novel, in the context of Flaubert or Arnold Bennett, he would be. But Dickens's way of character creation was not that of the realist novelist; he was after another kind of reality. It is often said that his characters are caricatures, either caricatures of comedy or monstrous puppets of melodrama. He is then seen as essentially a disciple of Smollett, greater than his master. Certainly Smollett was his favorite novelist, as Ben Jonson seems to have been his favorite dramatist. I suspect that he liked them because of their undoubted incidental resemblance to himself as artist, but that they reinforced his own predilections rather than directly influenced him. We limit Dickens unduly when we interpret his characters as humors in the Jonsonian sense. Santayana, in his fine essay on Dickens in *Soliloquies in England,* has partly answered the charge that Dickens deals in caricatures:

> When people say Dickens exaggerates, it seems to me they can have no eyes and no ears. They probably have only *notions* of what things and people are; they accept them conventionally at their diplomatic value. Their minds run on in the region of discourse, where there are masks only, and no faces; ideas and no facts; they have little sense for those living grimaces that play from moment to moment on the countenance of the world.

Santayana sees Dickens as the supreme *mimic* of people as they really are. What seems to me certain is that he caught and rendered them in the way children see grown-ups. As adults, we no longer, or only very rarely, meet people who might have stepped out of the pages of Dickens, but childhood, when we look back on it, appears to have been full of genuine Dickens figures. The child sees adults through a mind and eye unobscured by the associations we bring to the contemplation of people in later life. Simply because he is inexperienced in life he cannot accept them conventionally, at "their diplomatic value"; they are, because they must be, odd, arbitrary, incomprehensible, sometimes absurdly comic, sometimes terrifying, sometimes both at once. Scarcely ever are they ordinary; the very notion of the ordinary is foreign to the child, to whom everyone encountered is unique. When people have very powerfully impressed us in childhood they remain forever so fixed in the memory, with the sharp idiosyncrasy of the Dickens character. How many men, for instance, remember certain of their early schoolmasters as ogres or as figures of wild rib-cracking comedy. They go back to the school years later and find these same masters not much older than when they were taught by them—but strangely dwindled, seedy, ordinary, perhaps a little pathetic.

The child's view of human beings is not less real than the adult's, and it is the child's that Dickens captures so unerringly. He catches with merciless delight the externals, the apparently meaningless gestures and nervous tricks we all have without knowing we have them, and he catches too the habits of speech, repetitions of favorite words and phrases, obsessional harpings on single themes whose victims we all tend unconsciously to be and which, taken together, make us in some degree walking caricatures of ourselves. And he does this not only with his great characters, the Micawbers, Gamps, Pecksniffs, Weggs, and the rest, but almost all the time, with characters who appear only for a page or so and are then dropped altogether. They are all, within the limits set, perfectly rendered. Old Mr. Turveydrop, for instance, the aged Regency buck in *Bleak House,* is a merely marginal figure, but he is pinned down completely, with his Deportment and his marvelous phrase "Woomen, lovely woomen, what a sex You are!"

When he attempts to draw character not as the child sees it but as the adult does, as neither comic nor melodramatic, when he tries to present the "normal" view of human beings, he fails, and generally fails badly. Rose Maylie and Mr. Brownlow fall into this category of his characters, as do Agnes Wickfield and her father in *David Copperfield*, Little Em'ly, and all the host of good women and of women more sinned against than sinning. They are so hopelessly conventionalized as scarcely to come to life at all; he has accepted them at their diplomatic value with a vengeance. It is only when writing more or less in his own person, as David Copperfield or as Pip, that he succeeds in presenting character as commonly seen. Then he can do so in the most masterly fashion; but then he is writing as an adult remembering his childhood.

This childlike vision of human beings conditioned his view of the world and made it a universe at times crude in conflicting black and white, at times sinister, a heightened version of the squalid, brutal, smelly, rowdy London of his boyhood.

There is nothing surprising in his retention of this childlike vision, for he was exposed to the full horrors of life in Regency London in the cruelest possible way at the most impressionable age. His being sent out at twelve to work at Warren's blacking factory at Hungerford Stairs, near Charing Cross, is too well known to need relating. The important fact is that it left a wound in him that never healed. We could guess as much if the passionate indignation of the second chapter of *David Copperfield* were our only evidence; and David was in a sense more fortunate than Dickens had been. At least his parents were dead. It was precisely Dickens's parents who had banished him, as it must have seemed, to the blacking factory.

When he found himself, a boy of "good ability, quick, eager, delicate," suddenly thrust into the rat-ridden warehouse by the Thames, he was conscious, he tells us in an autobiographical fragment written just before *Copperfield,* of "a deep sense of abandonment."

He was so affected by the experience that he never even spoke of it to his children; they discovered it for the first time from Forster's life of him. And the feeling of abandonment was not due simply to the fact that he, a middle-class child who was always highly conscious of class, had been consigned to work among the laboring poor. What haunted him was the sense of emotional abandonment. He worked at the blacking factory only for six months, and then was taken away because his father had quarreled with the manager. But his mother tried to patch up the quarrel so that he could return to his job. That was the wound that did not heal. Years later he wrote: "I never afterwards forgot, I never shall forget, I never can forget, that my mother was warm for my being sent back." He never forgot, and he never forgave, and he put his mother in *Nicholas Nickleby* as the exquisitely ridiculous Mrs. Nickleby. It seems certain that the experience, with the circumstances attending it, the abandonment by his family, the feeling that he was no longer loved or wanted, set up in him a neurotic condition from which he was never able to free himself.

The blacking factory episode does not account for Dickens's genius, but it does, I believe, explain some of the forms his genius took, and it throws light on much that is otherwise baffling both in his art and his life. It explains why we so often find at the center of his novels the figure of the lost, persecuted, or helpless child: Oliver Twist, Little Nell, David, Paul Dombey, Pip, and their near relations Smike and Jo, in *Bleak House.* It explains, too, why their rescue, when there is rescue, so often has the appearance of a fairy-story ending, the result of what is sometimes called wishful thinking, just as the deaths of Little Nell, Paul Dombey, and Jo are dramatizations of his own self-pity. And it explains the dominant mood in which his world is created. It was not at all one of good-humored acceptance of things, but a mood of nightmare compounded of lurid melodrama and savage comedy, relieved from time to time by unreflecting joy in the absurd and the comic for their own sakes.

In *The Way of All Flesh* Samuel Butler apostrophized schoolmasters as follows: "Never see a wretched little heavy-eyed mite sitting on the edge of a chair against your study wall without saying to yourselves, 'Perhaps this boy is he who, if I am not careful, will one day tell the world what manner of man I am.'" Dickens was the wretched little heavy-eyed mite the nineteenth century neglected and who told it just what manner of age it was. It made him without realizing it a violent revolutionary. In novels like *Dombey and Son, Bleak House, Hard Times, Little Dorrit,* and *Great Expectations* the onslaught on the age is fundamental. Not much is left of the established order when Dickens has done with it. He is attacking a whole social system in all its complexity wherever it seems to him to impede or prevent the flow of generous impulse between man and man, the exercise of natural kindliness and trust.

This is why to see Dickens simply as a reformer is to put the emphasis on the wrong place. In *Oliver Twist,* for instance, it does not really matter whether Dickens was justified in his attack on the poor law or whether he was writing of workhouses already obsolete at the time of writing. He is concerned not with actual institutions but symbolic ones. Bumble, the first instance of savage comedy in Dickens, a grotesque puppet larger than life and rendered ridiculous because it is only by seeing him as ridiculous that Dickens can bear to contemplate him at all, is not merely a workhouse master; he is any unimaginative and corrupt bureaucratic underling in any system of society to whom power is given, seen from the point of view of the victim. Bumble, in other words, is a symbolic character. Similarly with Uriah Heep. David Copperfield hates his guts, and so does Dickens. He is the epitome of slimy hypocrisy, of malevolent rancorous envy masking itself under professions of duty and humility. But he is something more as well. "I'm not fond," says David, "of professions of humility"; and Heep's answer floods one whole aspect of Victorian England with light:

> "There now," said Uriah, looking flabby and lead-coloured in the moonlight. "Didn't I know it? But how little you know of the rightful umbleness of a person in my station, Master Copperfield! Father and me was both brought up at a foundation school for boys; and mother, she was likewise brought up at a public, sort of charitable establishment. They taught us a deal of umbleness; we was to be umble to this person, and umble to that; and to pull off our caps here, and to make bows there; and always to know our place and abase ourselves before our betters. Father got the monitor medal for being umble. So did I. Father got made a sexton by being umble. 'Be umble, Uriah,' says father to me, 'and you'll get on. It was what was always being dinned into you and me at school; it's what goes down best. Be umble,' says father, 'and you'll do.' And really it ain't done bad. . . . I'm very umble to the present moment, Master Copperfield, but I've got a little power."

Heep's speech is a profound comment on the charity system of the age and on the concept of the deserving poor, and Heep is much more than a comic figure: he is the symbolic representation of the victim of early nineteenth-century good works having his own back on the nineteenth century. He is, properly, terrifying.

Heep is a good example of Dickens's savage comedy. His comic characters fall into two groups. When he accepts them without intervention of moral scruples, rejoices in them for their own sake, the result is pure humor: Pickwick, the Wellers, Micawber, Boffin, or, greatest of them all, Mrs. Gamp. When sympathy is withheld or he feels a strong moral disgust or contempt, the result is a character not so much of humor as of savage comedy with no good nature in it at all. These characters are most evident when he is attacking social injustice or flaws in the social code. Bumble, Heep, and Gradgrind are typical figures of savage comedy; ridicule and contempt are poured upon them, but they remain monstrous and they terrify. I suspect, too, that in original intention such characters as Pecksniff, Squeers, Chadband, Silas Wegg, were to be characters of savage comedy, but something happened to them in the process of creation. Humor softens them; it is as though Dickens has forgotten the full extent of the viciousness he has set out to satirize in his sheer exuberant joy in the character he has invented; joy in turn has begotten a kind of sympathy, even a kind of love, so that in the end these characters also exist for their own sake, without reference to moral considerations. Silas Wegg is an instance of this process. When he comes out with such a magnificently comic phrase as "Since I called upon you that evening when you were, as I may say, floating your powerful mind in tea," we feel that the current of satire, of moral indignation, has been inhibited, for the character, through the poetry of the comic placed in his mouth, has been translated to a realm in which moral considerations are strictly irrelevant. Mrs. Gamp, of course, is the shining example in Dickens of what I have called the poetry of the comic; only a great poet could have invented her; she belongs to the same order of creation as Falstaff.

It has often been noted that there is no communication between the characters in a Dickens novel: they are isolated, self-soliloquizing beings borne along each upon his balloon of individual fantasy. Here, it seems to me, Dickens is much truer to the facts of human behavior than we are generally prepared to admit, truer at a deeper level than, say, Thackeray or Trollope, with all their greater success in rendering the everyday appearances of people. For what Dickens always concentrates on is the obsessional element in his characters. This is so regardless of whether he is describing characters that are formally comic. In Dombey, for instance, or Carker in the same novel, or Headstone in *Our Mutual Friend*, Dickens is concentrating so exclusively on the obsessional element in behavior that he is inventing characters that we should today call psychopaths, and psychopaths are more common than we like to think. In fact, no hard and fast line can be drawn between them and the comic characters; the psychopathic nature of Heep, for instance, may be obscured by the savage comedy, but it is fundamental to it. It is when the obsessional strikes us as mechanically contrived, as with Captain Cuttle, that Dickens's comic characters fail, and it is then, incidentally, that the resulting character is closest to Smollett's.

The great psychopathic characters are profoundly disturbing, especially since they are a manifestation of Dickens's increasing dissatisfaction with the society of his day. So that very early in Dickens criticism, at any rate from the time of Bagehot's essay, the later, darker manifestations of Dickens's genius began to be deplored. Chesterton regretted them, and Hesketh Pearson, in his popular biography, goes so far as to state that when Dickens "decided to abandon the picaresque type of work in which he excelled . . . the unique portrayer of comical eccentrics had become a commonplace novelist." I find this view absurd. Dickens began, of course, as a picaresque novelist with his titular hero the merest cypher. Nicholas Nickleby and Martin Chuzzlewit are young men seeking their fortunes; they take to the road precisely as Tom Jones or Roderick Random did; but we are not interested in them, we are interested in the people they meet in their travels. These early novels are brilliant improvisations, in which the only characters and scenes that matter to us now are, very largely, the incidental, whose relation to the plot, which is in any case perfunctory, is purely casual. So we read *Nickleby* for the pleasure of meeting the Crummles, the Mantalinis, the Squeerses, and Mrs. Nickleby, *Chuzzlewit* for the sake of Pecksniff, Mrs. Gamp, and the American scenes. We are, rightly, concerned mainly with the wonderful gallery of comic characters. But the monstrous error of even so fine a critic as Chesterton is that he sees Dickens almost wholly in terms of this wonderful gallery. Here a comment by Humphry House in *The Dickens World* is apt:

It is sometimes said in discussions of Dickens's technique as a novelist that any of his great characters could step out of one book into another without materially disturbing the arrangement of either. But if we try to imagine Sam Weller in *Our Mutual Friend* the limitations of this formal criticism are at once plain. The physique, features, and complexion of the characters have changed between the two books almost as much as their clothes: the grimaces of villains have conformed to a new fashion; manners are so altered that one would as little expect that Boffin should get drunk as that John Harmon should fight a duel . . . Everybody is more restrained. The eccentrics and monsters in the earlier books walk through a crowd without exciting particular attention: in the latter they are likely to be pointed at in the streets, and are forced into bitter seclusion; social conformity has taken on a new meaning. Silas Wegg and Mr. Venus are at odds and ends with their world as Daniel Quilp was not. The middle classes are more self-important, the lower less self-assured. London, though vastly bigger in extent, is smaller in mystery: it has been opened up by the police. The whole scene seems narrower, more crowded, and, in a pecular way, more stuffy. The very air seems to have changed in quality, and to tax the powers of Sanitary Reform to the uttermost. In *Pickwick* a bad smell was a bad smell; in *Our Mutual Friend* it is a problem.

That is a first-rate analysis of the change in the Dickens world. The first novel in which the change is apparent, in which the old, loose, episodic, picaresque form is replaced by formal plot, and the subordination of everything in the book to the working out of the plot, is *Dombey and Son.*

Perhaps he was influenced by Mrs. Gaskell, as in later novels he was certainly influenced by Wilkie Collins, who was the greatest master of plot of his time; the indebtednesses are unimportant because the change had to come. The great symbol of the change, in Dickens's fiction as in the history of the period, is, as House points out, the development of the railways; they made, more quickly and more thoroughly than it is easy for us to imagine, a new England, as the institution of an efficient Metropolitan Police Force made a new London. And the railways killed the picaresque novel. It had been an admirably flexible form for the portrayal of contrasting social classes: the road cut a cross section through national life. But the coach, and pedestrianism for those who could not afford the coach, gave way before the train with its first-, second-, and third-class compartments, its much greater speed and its much greater cheapness. And the arrival of the train quite literally changed the face of England, which is why it is so powerful a symbol of change in *Dombey and Son*.

Dickens was essentially a comprehensive novelist; he had to take in all classes of society; the world he was creating was indeed a world with all the variety of the actual world. So it was necessary that he should find a substitute for picaresque. He found it in the novel of highly organized plot. Again House sums up: "One of the reasons why, in the fifties, his novels begin to show a greater complication of plot than before, is that he was intending to use them as a vehicle for more concentrated sociological argument." He was, in fact, using the novel quite deliberately as a vehicle for the criticism of society, and plot—mechanical if you like, artificial, melodramatic, contrived out of all resemblance to probability—enabled him to represent in the mirror of his own world a fuller picture of the total society of his day than any English novelist has achieved before or since.

It is possible to make far too many difficulties about the

plots of the later novels. They were a necessary structure for him. Dickens was not a realistic novelist: his one attempt at something that may be called realistic, *David Copperfield,* is marvelous but a failure: "He begins," as Chesterton says, "his story in a new style and then slips back into an old one"; and he did nothing finer than those opening chapters that are in a new style. However inadequate we find the plots of the novels from *Dombey and Son* onwards, we should not be blind to the fact that as novels they are superbly well planned. They move, these novels, on two distinct and sometimes opposed planes. There is the movement of the plot, which is mechanical and often distorts, as in *Great Expectations* and *Our Mutual Friend,* the true shape of the book. But there is also the movement of the symbolism, and this is something entirely different and something new in our fiction. It means that in the last analysis we respond to the later novels as to great poems, for their effect is that of poetry, the poetry, as David Cecil has suggested, of the late Elizabethan drama, the plays of Webster and Ford and Tourneur.

As Dickens grew older his mood became darker; success could not heal the wound of his childhood. So, in the later novels, those foreshadowed by *Dombey and Son,* the criticism of his age becomes increasingly more radical, the savage comedy more savage, ferocious, and contemptuous. The comedy becomes more integrated with the melodrama, and the whole more and more saturated with his symbolism. And his symbolism can only be described by examples.

The overriding single subject of these later novels is money, which is itself a symbol, and the things that go with money, power, position, and so on. (In passing, one may point out, because Dickens himself seemed unconsciously aware of it, the symbolic role of money in the psychological interpretations of the psychoanalysts, who relate it to the feces.) In *Dombey and Son,* the symbol of money power is Mr. Dombey himself, to whose pride of position as the British merchant everything must be sacrificed—affections, wife, children. The money power he represents drags classes higher, as well as lower, than his own into his orbit; he can buy an aristocratic young woman as his second wife. But Dombey, though he does not know it, himself represents a form of power in its declension; he is the British merchant; the man of the future is the industrialist. And one of the two great symbols in the book is precisely that of contemporary industrialization at its most dramatic: railway development. Throughout the novel London is being torn down and rebuilt to make way for the railways, and it is wholly right and proper, and the more powerful in its effect for the immense preparation that has gone to it, that Carker, the underling who ruins Dombey, should be killed by a train.

The other great symbol, that of the sea—"What are the wild waves saying?"—the symbol of death and also of life and regeneration, is less effective, perhaps because it is less capable of particularization and so is more conventional, but also because it is associated with the weakest parts of the novel, the self-pity that dictated the death of Paul Dombey and the unconvincing nature of the Dickensian hero, the good young man Walter Gay.

There are many other instances of symbolism in the novel; sometimes, for instance, it emerges as an extraordinary intensification of atmosphere, as in the descriptions of Dombey's house. Even in *Dombey and Son,* we are in the presence of a rich texture of symbolism such as normally we only find in great poetry.

Money, the lust for money, this time through inheritance, is the theme of *Bleak House;* the attack on the Chancery Court is really secondary. The Court of Chancery, Dickens believed, existed to befog the hapless litigants who found themselves caught up in it; and as one looks back at the novel, after that wonderful first chapter describing November in the City, all the Chancery parts of the book seem to be shrouded in fog. The first chapter, in other words, establishes the mood of the whole. But among other things, *Bleak House* is also about Lady Dedlock, who hides a love-starved heart under a mask of aristocratic boredom, and as Robert Liddell has said in *A Treatise on the Novel*: "If it rains in Lincolnshire, it is because it rains in the heart of Lady Dedlock." Another instance of symbolism from *Bleak House* is the horrible and fantastic account of the death by spontaneous combustion of the gin-sodden rag-and-bottle collector Krook, who by virtue of his name symbolizes the whole Chancery system.

Great Expectations is another variant on the theme of money, money as the agent of isolation, for Pip, perhaps Dickens's finest character in a more or less naturalistic mode, is perverted in his natural affections and cut off from those nearest and most loyal to him by the expectation of money. Again, the wonderful opening chapter, the description of the marshes and the confrontation of the boy Pip with the escaped convict, sets the key to the whole book. And here one might note how in Dickens individual characters take on enormous symbolic significance, for example, the crazed figure of Miss Havisham, dressed always in her wedding finery. Characters such as these haunt the imagination as no naturalistically conceived personages could do; they haunt because they are not wholly rationally explicable; they have the magical compulsion of figures from the unconscious.

It is the final irony of Pip's fate that the money to which he owes everything is ill-gotten, a convict's horde. In *Our Mutual Friend* the criticism of money is even more radical. There the sources of Boffin's wealth are the dust piles of his miserly old employer Harmon. Humphry House makes it plain that these dust piles cannot be taken as a simple euphemism for rubbish: "One of the main jobs of a dust-collector in Early Victorian London was to collect the contents of the privies and the piles of mixed dung and ashes which were made in the poorer streets; and the term 'dust' was often used as a euphemism for decaying human excrement, which was exceedingly valuable as a fertilizer." It is from these extraordinarily sinister dumps of refuse that the whole action of *Our Mutual Friend* springs. They loom over the book like pit banks and slag heaps in an industrial area, and they symbolize what for Dickens was the basis of the society of his day. This can scarcely be questioned when one remembers the characters of the novel, those sharp, scathing sketches of the money-conscious, the Veneerings, Podsnap, Fledgeby, the Lammles.

Any account of Dickens is inadequate. He is the greatest comic novelist in English; he is also the most truly poetic novelist. So far as we can label him at all, he was a fantasist, and he forces us to accept the world he creates by the sheer compelling power of the intensity of his imagination. It was an hallucinatory imagination, and so long as he remains within the comic and satiric or the melodramatic he forces us to share the hallucination. His defects are many and yet scarcely matter. He was a great original. He owed something, in his early books particularly, to the eighteenth-century novelists—high spirits, the joy in rough-and-tumble, the picaresque sequence of events; and these he transmitted to later novelists, to Wells, for instance, in *Mr. Polly*. But he owed much more to himself. To find anything comparable in fiction to his own especial contribution to the novel, his sense of symbolism, the hallucinatory intensity of his imagination, the huge self-soliloquizing monsters he created, we have to go to Dostoevski and, to a lesser degree, Kafka and James Joyce. As for his influence, how can it be estimated? His work has become part of the literary climate within which western man lives.

3

"I do not hesitate to name Thackeray the first," said Trollope, writing of his contemporaries in the *Autobiography*. Posterity has a different opinion. In his lifetime, and for three or four decades after, Thackeray divided the empire of Victorian fiction with Dickens, with whom he was paired as inevitably as Browning with Tennyson. What has happened that Thackeray should have toppled from his eminence, whereas contemporaries of inferior talent, like Trollope, should today be read with an enthusiasm which would have been incomprehensible to Victorian critics?

The short answer is that his talents were so great and the ends he set himself such that he has to be judged by reference to the highest levels of the kind of fiction he proposed to write. A great innovator, Scott set standards for Europe. A great original, Dickens set his own standards. But Thackeray was neither an original nor an innovator; what he set out to do had been done before and would be done again, so it is impossible not to see him in some way in competition with Fielding, with Tolstoi, even with Proust. It is a tribute to his achievement that we do see him in these terms; but once the comparisons are made it is clear that he suffered from a failure of nerve the peculiar conditions of nineteenth-century England are not by themselves enough to explain, even though it was this very failure that was responsible for his immediate immense popularity.

Take *Vanity Fair,* which began serial publication in 1847. In this dazzlingly brilliant novel Thackeray was consciously attempting what no other English novelist of the time was doing, though George Eliot was to essay something similar a decade later. As a contributor to *Punch* he had shown himself as a parodist a blistering critic of the falsity, the romantic nonsense, pervading the fiction of the day. With *Vanity Fair* the ends he proposed for himself were realistic, a study of men and women as they actually had their being in society, and the result was a marvelous panorama of upper middle-class London life of the generation beginning about 1810. The subtitle of the novel is "A Novel without a Hero": Thackeray aimed at a consciously unheroic novel, a portrayal of modern manners. He succeeded superbly. The enormous canvas vibrates with most vividly realized characters, one of whom, Becky Sharp, is among the greatest in world fiction; and her husband Rawdon Crawley is not much inferior. Thackeray conveys the passage of time as few other novelists have been able, and this though the actual time span of the novel is not much more than ten years; we have the illusion of watching his characters change from youth to middle age and grow old; they are plastic to the pressure of events and the years. There are great scenes, the greatest the account of Waterloo, the Waterloo of the civilian hangers-on of the army. There is brilliant comedy. And always there is the utmost vividness, characters caught as it were in mid-gesture, and a wonderful ease of narration, a wonderful ability to make rapid transitions from scene to contrasted scene. Here is the social life of man: money is made, money is lost; marriages are contracted, husbands and wives prove no better than they should be; children disappoint, and are then the stay of their parents in old age; ambitions are thwarted; the whole business of getting, of social climbing, and of putting one over the neighbor is in full swing. And everything has the appearance of being completely natural; this is social life as it is. The only analogue to the novel is *War and Peace,* and that said, *Vanity Fair* is exposed in its inadequacy.

Where does the inadequacy lie? Not in the technique. Thackeray began his writing career as an essayist, and his approach to fiction was that of the natural-born essayist. His style, urbane, flexible, elegant, exquisitely modulated, was based on that of the eighteenth-century essayists, Steele and Addison and Goldsmith, and like theirs it captures the spirit, the tone, of civilized conversation. *Vanity Fair* is an extended conversation, a monologue. Thackeray, at ease, middle-aged, a man who has seen the world and has no illusions, is talking to his readers. "This," he is saying, "is life as I have known it"; and he comments on the action and characters as he goes along, makes a generalization, and illustrates it with a brilliant scene, a passage of dialogue, which always takes the action a little further and a little more brightly illuminates the characters. As a way of writing a novel, there is nothing at all wrong with it. Everything is open and above board. Thackeray is not to be condemned because he generalizes and moralizes or even because he buttonholes that "man and brother" his reader, though he certainly does so to excess. There is only one drawback to his method. Since we are presented with action and character through the author's conversation, which is the direct expression of the author's mind, we are conscious all the time of the quality of his mind. We cannot escape it. We cannot escape the point of view expressed or the attitude towards life that dictates the selection of incident and the comment.

No novelist of genius has given us an analysis of man in society based on so trivial a view of life. This is implicit in the very title *Vanity Fair*, which has a very different meaning for Thackeray from that which it had for Bunyan. For Bunyan Vanity Fair represents the whole of society and indeed all men's activities except one. For him, it is the World itself, and therefore of the Devil. The world's activities are vanity because they lead to damnation; every moment in Bunyan immortal souls are in the balance. With Thackeray the word vanity and the whole concept of Vanity Fair have undergone a change in meaning. In effect he is taking Bunyan's Vanity Fair at the valuation not of Christian but of its most respected inhabitants.

He is not approving, but neither is he disapproving—
much. Vanity is no longer that which is empty and worth-
less, a snare and a delusion, a trip wire on the path to salvation; it is simply self-esteem, the desire to be thought
well of by the world. This, for Thackeray, has become the
motive of human behavior. "Wherever there was a man,
he saw a snob"; and snobbery, the jockeying for social position and the pretense to a status rather higher than the
person's true one he saw as the main driving force of man
in society.

This view of man has satisfied none of his critics; the
amassing of "petty details," as Bagehot tartly observed,
"to prove that tenth-rate people were ever striving to be
ninth-rate people." No doubt early nineteenth-century
England was ridden with snobbery. There was a whole
upward movement of social classes and a rapid increase in
wealth that led its possessors to vie for position with those
who claimed prestige on the strength of birth or inheritance, and when Thackeray describes the life of Mr.
Osborne, "the honest British merchant," and his family in
Russell Square, he is being an accurate observer of social
behavior. It is true also that the cult of respectability must
have been the cover for wholesale snobbery on many
fronts, social, moral, intellectual. Yet the cult contained its
element of the heroic, and it is the heroic, the exercise of
virtues for their own sake, that finds no place in Thackeray's view of the world. Disinterestedness, where it exists,
is the prerogative of the stupid and the dull, of the Amel-
ias and the Dobbins.

Thackeray's novels are saturated with a most curious
ambiguity; even the famous irony, and he was a genuine
ironist, is often only a device by which Thackeray is
enabled as it were both to have his cake and eat it. This
ambiguity, which takes many forms, was noticed by his
earliest critics. "No one," wrote Bagehot, "can read Mr.
Thackeray's writings without feeling that he is perpetu·

ally treading as close as he dare to the borderline that separates the world which may be described in books from the
world which it is prohibited so to describe." It has often
been said that Thackeray was in spirit an eighteenth-century novelist born out of his time and in the wrong period,
that the Victorian age crippled him. This is implied in his
preface to *Pendennis,* with its appearance of protest against
the prudery of the age: "Since the author of *Tom Jones*
was buried, no writer of fiction among us has been permitted to depict to his utmost power a MAN. We must
drape him, and give him a certain conventional simper.
. . . You will not hear—it is best to know it—what moves
in the real world, what passes in society, in the clubs, col-
leges, mess-room—what is the life and talk of your sons."

This is special pleading. *The History of Pendennis: His
Fortunes and Misfortunes, His Friends and His Greatest
Enemy* was published in monthly parts from 1848 to 1850.
It was, the preface suggests, to have been Thackeray's
Tom Jones to the extent the age would allow him to write
it. The excuse would be more convincing if we did not
have *Adam Bede* to set beside it. As an embodiment of a
sensual and sexually attractive girl, Hetty Sorrel is worth
all Thackeray's young women put together, and it is her
intensely natural effect on Arthur Donnithorne that
makes him, as *l'homme moyen sensuel,* a much finer rendering of a young man than Arthur Pendennis is ever permitted to be.

As a novelist, Thackeray was completely inhibited where
the portrayal of women and of sex was concerned. For a
novelist purporting to give a realistic representation of
men and women in society, this was fatal. His was truly a
crippled talent; for this the age cannot be blamed, though
the effects of his psychological lameness chimed with the
sentiment of the age. In Thackeray's novels women are
either good or bad: either Amelia Sedley or Becky Sharp,
either Laura Bell or Blanche Amory, either Lady Castle-

wood or Beatrix. There is no doubt which of the two kinds stimulated his imagination: it is on Becky, Blanche, and Beatrix that his creative love is bestowed; they steal all the scenes in which they appear. Of the good women, Amelia and Mrs. Pendennis are quite frankly depicted as stupid almost to the point of imbecility. Yet again the ambiguity intervenes; their stupidity and its consequences, their lives as doting mothers and "tender little parasites" are condoned and even applauded at the very moment that they are being remorselessly exposed. In the presence of the "good woman," however moronic, Thackeray's satire is suspended in favor of his sentimentality.

Professor Greig, in his *Thackeray. A Reconsideration,* convincingly lays bare the sources of Thackeray's inhibition. When dealing with women, "he was dominated and controlled by his tutelary spirit, his mother"; and this condition was intensified by his marriage, which, after four years, was no marriage. There is even evidence, in his comment on Mrs. Pendennis's attitude to Blanche Amory, "I have no doubt there is sexual jealousy on the mother's part," that he was aware of something of the significance of his relation to his mother. In any case, it meant that he was not master of a large area of his material, and that area was one of the utmost importance in a novelist who wished to describe men and women as they are. Professor Greig notes further that the "purity" of his heroes is "almost as obtrusive as King Charles's head in the compositions of Mr. Dick." Which may be indicative of his feelings of guilt not only towards his mother but also towards the insane wife to whom he remained faithful. Amelia Sedley was modeled on her; and perhaps the lapses into sentimentality in the presence of good women were a necessary defense mechanism. So too, perhaps, his attitude towards his "bad women." For one of the striking things about them, about Becky and Blanche and Beatrix, is that though we are always and immediately convinced of their brilliance and their magnetism, they never appear to us as sexually magnetic. There are times when this works to Thackeray's advantage. Rationally, it is obvious that Becky is Steyne's mistress. Yet, since she is rendered quite without sexuality, Thackeray's disingenuous comment, "What *had* happened? Was she guilty or not? She said not; but who could tell what was truth which came from those lips; or if that corrupt heart was in this case pure?" is made to seem rather less preposterous than it otherwise would be. Thackeray's "bad women" are cold, even when beautiful. They are egoists, on the make socially, not sexually. This means that the temptations Thackeray's young men, weak though they may be in other respects, triumphantly withstand are not particularly convincing as temptations.

This emotional fixation on the "good woman," for all it was the "bad" that aroused his creative energy, had another result, especially apparent in *Vanity Fair,* in the character of Becky. Becky is one of the most completely and roundly conceived in all fiction. She is for the most part so unerringly drawn that she enters into our knowledge as a creature of flesh and blood might do, so much so that we know for a certainty when Thackeray's pencil slips, when—and this is how we feel then—he lies about her. Perhaps the core of Becky is her good humor; ambition is secondary. The truth about her is surely contained in her soliloquy on visiting Sir Pitt and Lady Crawley: "I think I could be a good woman if I had five thousand a year." Thackeray lies about her three times: when she boxes her son's ears for listening to her sing (the whole relationship between her and young Rawdon is suspect: it is as though Thackeray cannot allow a "bad woman" to have, however faintly, the normal feelings of a mother); when she blames her husband, in the most melodramatic terms, to Steyne, after he has discovered she had embezzled the money he gave her to pay Briggs; and when in the last pages it is alleged that she murdered Jos Sedley for his insurance money. These actions are flagrantly out of character.

But perhaps the simplest test of Thackeray's comparative failure as a novelist is merely to turn from *Vanity Fair, Esmond,* and *The Newcomes* to *Adam Bede, The Mill on the Floss,* and *Middlemarch.* George Eliot was a much more severe moralist, and she felt herself as free to comment on her characters and their behavior. She too was attempting a broad picture of life that should be recognizably true to life as generally observed. She is just as aware of the power of money and of the nuances of class distinction. Yet hers is an enormously richer picture of human behavior. Her characters are suffering, thinking beings; they are the battleground of moral struggle. So that, though she lacks the brilliance and surface graces of Thackeray, George Eliot satisfies us much more completely. For what finally distinguishes one novelist from another, what makes one greater than another, is the sense we have of the author's response to life. It is difficult not to see Thackeray as a man defeated by life: his response to it was muffled and faint, inadequate either to a great realist or to a great satirist. Had he been a lesser writer it would have mattered less; but reading him, we are conscious always of the gulf between his native talent and what the talent produced.

He is, then, in the second rank of our novelists. Once this is recognized, his merits stand out in shining clarity. Though marred in execution, partly as a result of his own laziness, to which the demands of serial publication contributed, partly because he was not creatively a free agent, *Vanity Fair* remains a most impressive achievement. For the most part it is superbly organized, built up on a complex system of contrasts, at the center of which are Becky and Amelia. It is the interrelation between these two sharply opposed types of womanhood, who are yet intimately linked, that sets the plot in motion and winds it up, and round them are grouped any number of characters who range themselves in balanced opposites: old Sedley and old Osborne, George and Rawdon, old Sir Pitt and the Marquis of Steyne, and so on; with, as Professor Greig has pointed out in his admirable analysis of the structure of the novel, cross groupings introduced so as to avoid the monotony of too formal a pattern: George and Dobbin, Rawdon and young Sir Pitt, old Sir Pitt and Bute, and many others. At the same time, there is a symmetry and balance of action, one half of each paired couple rising in fortune as the other falls.

It is not wholly sustained. After Waterloo, the book appears rather as a sandwich made out of two distinct novels; the principle of contrast, between Becky and Amelia, is kept up, but the organic relationship between them is gone, to be resumed in the last chapters when they come together again at Pumpernickel. But what stands out is the bold originality of the work. In the execution of its design it falls short of *Tom Jones,* to which in this respect it is obviously indebted. But in another, just as important, Thackeray had broken clean away from Fielding, as no other novelist in English had done. Thackeray sweeps away completely the whole mechanism of mystery in the form of dubious births, missing heirs, suppressed wills, and so on. The movement that carries the novel forward derives entirely from the characters and their relations to one another. And here, indeed, *Vanity Fair* has never been surpassed. Where, before him, could you find a principal character killed off off-stage before the novel has run half its course: "No more firing was heard at Brussels—the pursuit rolled miles away. Darkness came down on the field and city; and Amelia was praying for George, who was lying on his face, dead, with a bullet through his heart." Even today, more than a century after it was written, it strikes one as one reads by its boldness, and also its fidelity to the experience of life.

In those areas of experience where he is, creatively, a free agent, where he is dealing with the social life of man purely and simply, Thackeray is unassailable, and no novel is richer than *Vanity Fair* in beauties of sharp, satirical characterization embodied in incisive scenes and swift and flawless dialogue. They are so many, to recite them would be tedious, but the chapters leading up to Waterloo must be picked out. They make one of the most sustained—perhaps the most sustained—pieces of narrative writing in English fiction; a triumph, and a very complex triumph at that, of ironical comedy shot through with pathos and with the sense of life going on in spite of suffering.

Vanity Fair remains the quintessential Thackeray. As he grew older he became more and more at the mercy of his defects, and his creative range was much more limited than we might first suppose from the size of his canvases, so that his last fully complete novel, *Philip*, is now almost unreadable. *Pendennis* is a brilliant wreck, a wreck because from its very theme—it is a strongly autobiographical novel —it is dominated by his inhibitions. Where he is able to dodge these it is as good as anything he wrote, apart from the Waterloo passages of *Vanity Fair*. The opening chapters are wonderful—the scenes with Major Pendennis, young Pen's infatuation with the splendid La Fotheringay, and Pen at Oxford. Thereafter, we read on for the sake of more of Major Pendennis, of Costigan, and of Pen's adventures as a journalist.

Many critics have considered Thackeray's finest work to be *Esmond*. It is certainly his most considered and contains some of his finest effects. It gains in structure by not having been written for serialization, while the technical problem it presented, that of narrating events which had occurred in the reign of Queen Anne from the standpoint of one who had taken part in them but was writing in the days of George II, helped greatly to overcome some of Thack·

eray's weaknesses in dealing with his own time. At least we are free of the obsession with snobs and snobbery. This story of love set in the Augustan age is, indeed, a remarkable *tour de force,* and in Beatrix it contains one of Thackeray's best characters. It is a richly composed book and exists in the memory perhaps as a series of glowing pictures, like the famous virtuoso description of Beatrix descending the staircase at Walcote House. This is in fact just how Esmond remembers the events he shared in thirty years earlier; he is transcribing memories that are still colored for him with the romantic ardor his boyhood brought to the incidents themselves. Thackeray reconstructs the life of Queen Anne's London and Queen Anne's army with consummate skill; his mastery of its detail is complete. Yet it may be doubted whether *Esmond* succeeds in being more than a reconstruction, whether it becomes a recreation. Trollope especially admired Thackeray's style in this novel, his solution of the problem that faces all historical novelists, the devising of a language that shall be an acceptable compromise between the idiom of the times written about and that of the time of writing. With a skill and literary sensibility that dazzle, Thackeray modulated his own prose to that of the early eighteenth century, and he succeeded in producing something that is not pastiche, recognizably his own, and yet suggests Steele. It is an impressive achievement, but for all that, *Esmond* never suggests what it sets out to be, an eighteenth-century work written by a man who is an elderly contemporary of Fielding and Smollett. It is thoroughly mid-nineteenth century in feeling, and the central weakness of the novel lies in the character of Esmond himself, an early Victorian if ever there was one.

4

Mrs. Gaskell as a novelist is not quite easy to judge. One's first impulse is always to overpraise her, because there shines through her work the personality of a wholly admirable woman in harmony with the society in which she finds herself. Apart from her writing, she had a full life as the wife of a Unitarian minister in Manchester and the mother of a large family; she had, in large measure, what may be called the serenity of the fulfilled, and in her writing her twin qualities of compassion and humor appear as aspects of her serenity.

This is most apparent in her most successful works, *Cranford* (1853) and *Wives and Daughters* (1864-66). Here, she is content to do what she can do well, and the results are charming. In *Cranford* the quiet humors and the equally quiet disasters of the lives of middle-class ladies in a small country town are caught perfectly. The society delineated is almost entirely feminine, and the work is a little triumph of literary tact. The narrator is at once of and outside the society described, detached enough to know that it is comic and to rejoice in the comedy, but her affection for it such that no comedy was ever less satirical; the humor is an expression of love, the love that would not have its object changed however absurd it may seem to the world outside.

Mrs. Gaskell is only less successful in *Wives and Daughters* because she is working on a larger scale. *Wives and Daughters* is a very perceptive rendering of the class structure of a provincial society as seen from the position of a doctor's daughter. It is, in other words, exactly the kind of social comedy in which women novelists traditionally excel. It contains in the character of Cynthia Kirkpatrick one of the most striking young women in English fiction. Where Mrs. Gaskell fails is where so many women novelists have failed: in the convincing delineation of men. The failure is by no means absolute, but one is aware, even at the best, of discontinuities in presentation; she cannot see all the way round them.

Yet if Mrs. Gaskell had kept within the limits of her

talent, as in *Cranford* and *Wives and Daughters*, it is very doubtful whether her claim to importance as a novelist would seem much more than Miss Mitford's. It was, in a sense, a virtue in Mrs. Gaskell that she did not know her place as a novelist, and very imperfect as *Mary Barton* (1848) and *North and South* (1855) are, it is on these novels that her reputation mainly rests.

For her serenity existed side by side with a vigorous and courageous social conscience, of which these novels are the fine expression. They are flawed, as so many Victorian novels are, because of the author's obligation to fill up three volumes irrespective of whether her talent could sustain them. Mrs. Gaskell's could not, and she had to fall back on the "properties" of the novel of the period and on the sensationalism, the set pieces of violence, expected of the novelist almost as a matter of course. Mrs. Gaskell failed when it came to violence, but *Mary Barton* and *North and South* are carried along on the depth of her pity and her understanding. Her theme in these novels was what was called "the Condition of England" question, the clash between capital and labor. Why there should be unemployment and how working men should behave when their families were starving were questions to which she could give no convincing answer, but she knew exactly why the condition of England was worse than it need be, why, in fact, it led to class war. In *Mary Barton*, the heroine's father John Barton becomes a murderer and her aunt Esther a prostitute, a fate Mary herself narrowly escapes, and for two of these disasters the personal irresponsibility of a capitalist is to blame. When the workers' deputation met the millowners,

> . . . up sprang Mr. Henry Carson, the head and voice of the violent party among the masters, and addressing the chairman, even before the scowling operatives, he proposed some resolutions, which he, and those who agreed with him, had been concocting during this absence of the deputation.

They were, firstly, withdrawing the proposal just made, and declaring all communication between the masters and that particular Trades Union at an end; secondly, declaring that no master would employ any workman in future, unless he signed a declaration that he did not belong to any Trades Union, and pledged himself not to assist or subscribe to any society, having for its object interference with the master's powers; and, thirdly, that the masters should pledge themselves to protect and encourage all workmen willing to accept employment on those conditions, and at the rate of wages first offered . . . Harry Carson went on to characterize the conduct of the workmen in no measured terms; every word he spoke rendering their looks more livid, their glaring eyes more fierce . . .

Now there had been some by-play at this meeting, not recorded in the Manchester newspapers . . .

While the men had stood grouped near the door, on their first entrance, Mr. Harry Carson had taken out his silver pencil, and had drawn an admirable caricature of them—lank, ragged, dispirited, and famine-stricken. Underneath he wrote a hasty quotation from the fat knight's well-known speech in Henry IV.

Having shown the drawing to the others, he throws it carelessly into the fire. It falls short, and after the meeting one of the workmen returns and says to the waiter: "There's a bit on a picture up yonder, as one o' the gentlemen threw away; I've got a little lad at home as dearly loves a picture; by your leave I'll go up for it." It is the shock to the workers of the insensitiveness and brutality towards hungry men revealed in the caricature that precipitates the murder John Barton commits. The episode—and in this respect it is one of many—still has power to move.

Mary Barton was Mrs. Gaskell's first novel. *North and South* was her fourth and a much better one; it has an interest today beyond that of *Mary Barton,* which survives largely as an historical document illustrating early Victorian attitudes to a social problem and the early Victorian fear, which amounted almost to hysteria, of the poor. *North and South,* for one thing, remains much more closely in its author's range of talent. The most important theme is still the class war, but we are allowed to see it from the point of view of someone who is an outsider and a woman. Margaret Hale, one of Mrs. Gaskell's most spirited heroines and an excellent delineation of a serious and proud young woman, comes to Milton (Manchester) because her father, having been led by intellectual doubt to resign his clergyman's orders, has found a post there as tutor to a young millowner, John Thornton. It is typical of Mrs. Gaskell's limitations as a novelist that while she very well conveys the consequences in terms of material prosperity of Hale's honesty, we are given no clue to the nature of his doubt, so that in effect the doubt itself becomes unreal to us and Hale himself unmotivated. But his behavior brings Margaret to Manchester, and in the clash between her and Thornton we have a first-rate study, still relevant, of the clash between the South and the North. To Margaret the North is barbarous and uncouth, the negation of civilization. In no other Victorian novel does one get the sense so strongly of England as two nations, not Disraeli's two nations of the rich and the poor, but the two nations of the agricultural, feudal, Trollopean South and the industrial North. This approach to the North from the outside gives her novel real authority; we discover the North as Margaret Hale discovers it.

We discover it especially in the hard, self-confident manufacturer John Thornton. Thornton is much Mrs. Gaskell's most successful male character and as a man is much more convincing than any of Charlotte Brontë's. He is not a dream figure; he has been observed by a woman who knows the world and is judged in the novel by a girl of high spirits, intelligence, and assured values. They are not his, and out of the clash between their values arises a good part of Thornton's reality. And Mrs. Gaskell is particularly successful in rendering him in his public aspects, through those qualities that make him a Manchester millowner of the period. There is, for example, the remarkably accurate scene in which Thornton and the strike leader Higgins come together, through Margaret's mediation, in a sort of wary friendship based on their knowledge of each other as enemies:

"Yo've called me impudent, and a liar, and a mischief-maker, and yo' might ha' said wi' some truth, as I were now and then given to drink. An' I ha' called you a tyrant, an' an oud bull-dog, and a hard, cruel master; that's where it stands. But for th' childer. Measter, do yo' think we can e'er get on together?"

"Well!" said Mr. Thornton, half laughing, "it was not my proposal that we should come together. But there's one comfort, on your own showing. We neither of us can think much worse of the other than we do now."

"That's true," said Higgins, reflectively. "I've been thinking, ever sin' I saw you, what a mercy it were yo' did na take me on, for that I ne'er saw a man whom I could less abide. But that's maybe been a hasty judgment; and work's work to such as me. So, measter, I'll come; and what's more, I thank yo'; and that's a deal fro' me," said he, more frankly, suddenly turning round and facing Mr. Thornton fully for the first time.

"And this is a deal from me," said Mr. Thornton, giving Higgins's hand a good grip. "Now mind you, come sharp to your time," continued he, resuming the master. "I'll have no laggards at my mill. What fines we have, we keep pretty sharply. And the first time I catch you making mischief, off you go. So now you know where you are."

"Yo' spoke of my wisdom this morning. I reckon I may bring it wi' me; or would yo' rayther have me 'bout my brains?"

" 'Bout your brains if you use them for meddling with my business; with your brains if you can keep them to your own."

"I shall need a deal o' brains to settle where my business ends and yo'rs begins."

It is for the perception of passages such as this that we value Mrs. Gaskell. In them she is rivaled by no other novelist of her time or for many years after.

Mrs. Gaskell's merit lies in her recognition of the actual situation of the world she lived in. What she knew at first hand she could describe freshly and with a due sense of its importance. It was a considerable achievement, but not one by which we may adequately measure that of the Brontës, except perhaps that of Anne, with her study of the governess' life in *Agnes Grey* and her portrait of a drunkard's degeneration in *The Tenant of Wildfell Hall*. In both she was writing out of her own observation; but if it were not for the fame of her greater sisters, Anne would hardly be read today. Of her sisters, Charlotte failed when she attempted anything comparable to Mrs. Gaskell, such as *Shirley*, while Emily never had to try anything comparable at all. In a sense, Charlotte's greatness consists entirely in her deviation from the Gaskell norm. Emily, a much greater writer, was a law to herself.

With the exception only of Dickens, the Brontës have proved the most widely popular of English novelists. One reason for this is doubtless the story of their lives with its circumstances of loneliness and tragedy. It haunts the memory of all who encounter it like a powerful romantic novel, but a novel which if written would certainly appear too romantic, charged with too great an intensity, to be convincing; four geniuses and four tragic deaths in one novel are three too many of each. The Brontës, then, have become the objects of a cult. It is natural enough that it should be so, though it makes more difficult the estimation of Charlotte's worth as a novelist; Emily's not even the most idolatrous worship can affect.

We know a great deal about the self-contained, self-absorbed early family life of the Brontës in the isolation of the rectory at Haworth; we know how they grew up in the private worlds of daydream, the ideal universes of the Great Glass Town of Angria, which was originally the common property of the four of them but later shared by

Charlotte and Branwell only, and the Gondal of Emily and Anne. The booklets which contain them, of which a hundred survive, amounting in length to the total published output of the three sisters, have enormous value for the light they throw on the psychology of literary creation; yet the novels themselves are as revelatory. They are the products of immense solitude, of the imagination turned inwards upon itself, and of ignorance of the world outside Haworth and literature. With Emily this does not matter; *Wuthering Heights* is a work of art self-contained and complete as very few novels are: one can only read and wonder. It is perhaps the index of Charlotte's achievement, however, that she needs to be read in adolescence; come to her work after that and a considerable act of imagination is called for before she can be read with sympathy.

Fundamental to all her novels is the pupil-master relationship, which is her rationalization, based on her own limited experience of life outside Haworth, of one of the commonest sexual dreams of women: the desire to be mastered, but to be mastered by a man so lofty in his scorn for women as to make the very fact of being mastered a powerful adjunct to the woman's self-esteem. It is a fantasy with obvious affinities with the Cinderella story: the man stoops down, as it were, from a great height. But it goes a step beyond the Cinderella story in sophistication. The woman triumphs not merely because she compels the proud man to stoop. Phyllis Bentley has argued that *Jane Eyre* is much more than "a mere 'escape' romance" because Jane does not "enjoy a complete, unreal triumph"; she is left with a half-blind husband. It would indeed be absurd to condemn *Jane Eyre* as a novel of escape, yet that Rochester should be half blind and almost helpless at the end is the sign of the uncompromising nature of Charlotte Brontë's fantasy: the proud man is struck in his pride by

Nemesis. When he is helpless it is the woman's turn to stoop; Rochester's mutilation is the symbol of Jane's triumph in the battle of the sexes.

Synopsize it, and the story of *Jane Eyre* immediately becomes nonsense. For years Mr. Rochester has kept a lunatic wife on the third floor of his country house, in the charge of a gin-drinking servant, and none of the other servants, or Jane Eyre, the governess of Rochester's illegitimate child, in the least suspects her existence. The house resounds with demoniac laughter; she attempts to burn her husband in his bed; she bites her brother when he visits her; and on the eve of Jane's marriage to Rochester she comes into Jane's room at the dead of night and tears her bridal veil in half. Again, Rochester has no scruples about bigamy; he calmly proposes—having wooed her under the guise of a fortune-telling old gipsy woman at one of his own dinner parties—to marry Jane, who is eighteen years old, and when he has failed to trick her into a bogus marriage, proposes that she should become his mistress. She refuses, and still adoring him and unresentful of his behavior, runs away, spends her last coin on her coach fare, and scours the country on foot until, worn out, half starved, and soaked to the skin, she drops down at the front door of the house of her three cousins, whose existence she has not known before. There she finds she is the heiress of an uncle who has left her £20,000, which she promptly shares between her cousins and herself. One of them, the Rev. St. John Rivers, is going to India as a missionary and decides Jane must accompany him, and, though neither is in love with the other, marry him. Jane, with no interest in missions, agrees to go with him, but not as his wife. Rivers insists on marriage, and just as she is on the point of yielding Jane hears a phantom voice calling out of the night, "'Jane! Jane! Jane!'" She recognizes Rochester's voice and runs into the garden crying, "'Where are you?'" There is no reply. "'Down superstition!' " she tells herself. " 'This is not thy deception, nor thy witchcraft, it is the work of nature. She was roused, and did—no miracle—but her best.' " Jane hastens back to Thornfield, learns that Mrs. Rochester has again fired the house and that a burning beam has fallen on Rochester and blinded him, the wretched woman having been killed jumping off the roof. Jane finds Rochester and marries him. He partially recovers his sight, and they have a child.

Jane Eyre is as absurd in its own way as *The Castle of Otranto* or anything in Mrs. Radcliffe. Yet to describe it simply as a wish-fulfillment dream is to fail to take into account the caliber of the dreamer. Dream it may be, but the dream of a tremendously real person. Of Jane Eyre's reality there is never the slightest question; she is there from beginning to end, a young woman not of passion alone but of genuine intellectual quality too. She is not a particularly attractive heroine; she is much too conscious of her moral and mental superiority; she has wit but neither humor nor self-criticism, and her creator is as unaware of her deficiencies as she is herself. This is merely to say that *Jane Eyre* is a highly subjective novel, as subjective as Byron's *Childe Harold* or Lawrence's *Sons and Lovers,* and Jane as much a projection of her author as Harold and Paul Morel are of theirs. Indeed, Charlotte Brontë's resemblance to Byron is quite striking; one might say that she is the female answer to Byron; and it is in this sense that *Jane Eyre* is the first romantic novel in English. Everything in the novel is staked upon the validity of its author's sensibility; Charlotte Brontë is concerned with truth to her own feelings; the value of the feelings she never questions; it is taken for granted because they are her own.

It is in this intense, intransigent subjectivity that the tremendous power of *Jane Eyre,* together with its unity, resides. As a novel it derives at least as much from literature as from life, and perhaps Charlotte Brontë drew no very clear distinction between the two. In the whole conception and rendering of the incarceration of the mad Mrs. Rochester in the attic at Thornfield are recapitulated, more vividly than they had ever been before, the horrors of the Gothic novel of Mrs. Radcliffe. If it were not for the unity of tone, *Jane Eyre* would be incoherent, for as a construction it is artless. Yet because of the unity of tone, the melodramatic incredibilities scarcely matter; they are false to observed reality but not false to Charlotte Brontë's shaping dream; they represent, indeed, the triumph of the dream over reality. And the unity of tone is established on the first page of the novel, when we meet Jane Eyre as a small girl at the Reeds, the terrifyingly lonely child in the alien atmosphere, already a rebel, defying the world about her on the strength of her own feelings of right and wrong and of her innate consciousness of superiority. This first part of *Jane Eyre* is one of the finest and most moving renderings of lonely and proud childhood we have, a high peak in English fiction; and however improbable the situations in which Jane finds herself later, it is the same Jane who is among them, dominating them, and since we are inside her mind we accept the improbabilities as subjective distortions of reality. Mr. Rochester is a monster; the dialogues between him and Jane are absurd, but they are absurd only on his side, because he is a figment of Charlotte Brontë's imagination, a dream figure, whereas the author herself, or her projection of herself in Jane, is wholly real. Rochester is not so much a man as a most powerful symbol of virility. If, as has been said, he is a schoolgirl's dream of a man, then one can only retort that the schoolgirl who dreamed him may not have been very pleasant but was certainly very remarkable.

Shirley is much more susceptible to criticism because there Charlotte Brontë, in an attempt to write a novel that should give a picture of a certain society at a certain time, went outside the limits of her genius. She was essaying a work strictly comparable with Mrs. Gaskell's, a study of the conflict between workers and employers in the West Riding weaving industry during the years immediately before 1815. Its weakness is that, from its very nature, she could no longer rely on her subjectivity. There is once again the pupil-master theme, indeed two variants of it, and in the brothers Moore there are two Rochesters, diminished and tamed to fit an action and a background that had to be broadly realistic. The older men characters—the Tory parson Mr. Helstone, and the Yorkshire mill-owner Mr. Yorke—are well enough done, but the trio of curates, a race Charlotte Brontë held in especial contempt, are a bore and show how small a sense of the comic she possessed. The omniscient narrator is also a bore; we are nagged, bullied, lectured endlessly. What remains—and it is considerable—is the rendering of the two heroines of the novel, Caroline Helstone and Shirley Keeldar. Shirley Keeldar is always supposed to be a representation of Emily Brontë as she might have been had she been born to wealth and social position. She is truly one of the most vital and attractive of Victorian heroines; she has all Jane Eyre's and Lucy Snowe's spirit, pride, and wit without their envy and rancor. Wealth has made her any man's equal, and she is in awe of no man except perhaps Louis Moore.

Yet excellent as Shirley is, I find the much more subdued Caroline as interesting. She has no money and no position, is merely Helstone's niece and ward, the offspring of an unfortunate marriage. We may take her as Charlotte Brontë's *cri de coeur* in this novel. She is a rebel, although for the most part a silent one, a rebel against the ordained position of the Victorian middle-class unmarried woman. Conscious of talent in herself, she is also conscious of its waste, and she seeks the right to work, the right to economic independence even if it is only that of the governess; but until Shirley comes to live in the

village, her isolation is such that her dreams are incom-
municable, as we see when she tells her uncle she wishes
to be a governess. "You shall go to Cliff Bridge," he tells
her; "and there are two guineas to buy a new frock . . ."

> "Uncle, I wish you were less generous, and more——"
> "More what?"
> Sympathizing was the word on Caroline's lips, but it was
> not uttered; she checked herself in time. Her uncle would
> indeed have laughed if that namby-pamby word had escaped
> her. Finding her silent, he said:
> "The fact is, you don't know precisely what you want."
> "Only to be a governess."
> "Pooh! mere nonsense! I'll not hear of governessing. Don't
> mention it again. It is rather too feminine a fancy. I have
> finished breakfast, ring the bell; put all crotchets out of
> your head, and run away and amuse yourself."
> "What with? My doll?" asked Caroline to herself as she
> quitted the room.

The distinctive atmosphere that pervades the lives of
Charlotte Brontë's heroines is loneliness, a loneliness almost intolerable; they are marooned in themselves by circumstances and also by their very sensibility and intelligence, and they are forced to eat their souls out in waiting
and inaction. The virtue of Caroline Helstone is that she
is, as it were, a much more generalized example of this,
whereas Jane and Lucy Snowe are special cases. All are in
revolt against their circumstances, and they are in revolt
as women. This is the most obvious difference between
Charlotte Brontë and the women novelists who preceded
her; the latter, Jane Austen as much as any, had accepted
without question their place as women in a man-made
world; they had fitted in. Charlotte Brontë's characters do
not. Caroline's revolt, or impulse to revolt, is partly economic, but more an impulse towards a newly discovered
sense of dignity, of self-regard. In *Jane Eyre* and *Villette*
the self-regard is also and perhaps fundamentally a sexual
self-regard, though the revolt is one of the whole woman.

Caroline moves us because we feel she is typical; she is one character among many in a realistic picture of society. We are moved by her more than by Jane Eyre and Lucy Snowe; their passionate intensity sweeps pity aside.

In *Villette* she went back to the wholly subjective novel. Lucy Snowe tells her own story, and we are always in her mind. In events it is closer to reality as commonly observed than *Jane Eyre,* doubtless because Charlotte Brontë was so closely following actual occurrences in her own life. The pupil-master relationship she bore to M. Heger in Brussels is reproduced in that between Lucy and M. Paul Emanuel, and the latter, because he had a living original, is much more convincing as a man, though not as a symbol of masculinity, than Mr. Rochester. This relationship is the heart of the novel, and everything to do with Lucy's life at Mme. Beck's school is described with an almost hallucinatory intensity. The other elements in the novel, Lucy's love for Dr. John, and the mystery of Ginevra Fanshawe and her lover, are much less compelling or convincing. There are fewer implausibilities than in *Jane Eyre,* but there is an increase in the heroine's moral righteousness; more than Jane, she appears as a stiff-necked, humorless prig, whose passionate feelings are counterbalanced by an equally passionate concern for conventional morality, as in the absurd scene in which Lucy, called to take part at short notice in a schoolgirls' play, refuses to wear men's clothes and sets off her tail coat by a purple skirt. As an artist Charlotte Brontë had no taste, no restraint, and no sense of the ridiculous. But these defects were the defects of her virtues, and what her virtues were we see when, in this novel, we contemplate her wonderful embodying of the sinister Mme. Beck and, above all, the terrible account of human loneliness when Lucy is left alone at the school during the vacation with the imbecile girl, a scene culminating in the protestant Lucy's going into the confessional box in a Catholic church in order, however desperately, to break down the barriers of her isolation and communicate with at any rate one other human being.

Charlotte Brontë is to be judged as romantic writers, whether poets or novelists, always must be, by the intensity with which she expresses her response to life and experience. Her response is total and uninhibited. Her appearance represents something new in English fiction; with her, passion enters the novel. Before her, the treatment of sexual love had been of two kinds: as a scarcely tempestuous affection between man and wife on the one hand and as a healthy animal sensuality, such as we find in *Tom Jones,* on the other. But passion as the romantic poets have expressed it, something transcending sensuality because a blending of the spiritual with the physical, was unknown. Where love between man and woman is concerned, what is new in Charlotte Brontë is precisely such a passage as this, from *Jane Eyre:*

> No sooner did I see that his attention was riveted on them [some ladies], and that I might gaze without being observed, than my eyes were drawn involuntarily to his face: I could not keep their lids under control: they would rise and the irids would fix upon him. I looked, and had an acute pleasure in looking,—a precious, yet poignant pleasure; pure gold, with a steely point of agony: a pleasure like what the thirst-perishing man might feel who knows the well to which he has crept is poisoned, yet stoops and drinks divine draughts nevertheless.

In such a phrase as "poignant pleasure; pure gold, with a steely point of agony" we find the same grappling with language to express feeling normally inexpressible in prose that we meet seventy years later in D. H. Lawrence. And, as with Lawrence, the passionate response is not to sex alone but to all experience, to the whole living world. What Charlotte Brontë is really concerned with in *The Professor, Jane Eyre,* and *Villette* is one thing only: the depiction of the isolated, naked soul responding to the experience of life with a maximum of intensity. The pleasantness or otherwise of the revelation is immaterial; the nakedness is everything. This means that, different though her experience was from theirs, in the last analysis Charlotte Brontë belongs to the same tiny group of novelists as Dostoevski and Lawrence.

Wuthering Heights is the most remarkable novel in English. It is perfect, and perfect in the rarest way: it is the complete bodying forth of an intensely individual apprehension of the nature of man and life. That is to say, the content is strange enough, indeed baffling enough, while the artistic expression of it is flawless. Artistically, neither Jane Austen nor Henry James nor Joseph Conrad, the great masters of form in the English novel, did anything to surpass it. And this combination of an intensely individual apprehension and a wonderfully complete formal rendering of it gives it a uniqueness which makes even the fullest and most sensitive discussion of it less than adequate. F. R. Leavis in *The Great Tradition* has called it a sport. Therein lies the primary difficulty in dealing with it. It is utterly unlike any other novel. There is nothing one can compare it to, for the great masters of form have chosen subjects so different from it as to make *Wuthering Heights* exist in a category of creation all its own. It can be translated into no alternative terms; the usual compass bearings of criticism do not apply, nor do the usual abstractions the critic makes from the totality of a work go far towards piercing the mystery. No novel is more imbued with the spirit of place than *Wuthering Heights,* but Emily Brontë makes use of no such set descriptive passages as we find variously in Scott, Dickens, George Eliot, Hardy, or Lawrence. The reality of her characters cannot be questioned, but their reality is of an utterly different kind from Dickens's, Thackeray's, Trollope's, George Eliot's, or Henry James's. Nor does the style, which is a novelist's speaking voice, help; it is perfect for her purpose, but it is as plain as the most limpid of spring water.

More than with any other novel we are faced, in *Wuthering Heights,* with a totality, a work that is whole as a great lyric poem is whole and that cannot be separated into parts. And in a sense the author is not there at all: this most individual of novels is also the least idiosyncratic.

The central fact about Emily Brontë is that she is a mystic. *Wuthering Heights* itself is not the record of a mystical experience—for indications of that we must go to her poems—but the novel is the statement of the conclusions derived from her experience. What they are it is not easy to say; she was neither a philosopher nor a theologian, but a novelist; in *Wuthering Heights* she symbolizes the findings of her intuition into the nature of things, but not in a way from which we can generalize. Interpretation of the novel, therefore, will differ with every reader who approaches it. But we are surely shown the universe as the scene and expression of two opposed principles which, even though they seek to devour each other, yet ultimately compose a harmony. They are symbolized in the novel in the two houses and their occupants, Wuthering Heights on its bleak eminence, " 'wuthering' being a significant provincial adjective descriptive of the atmospheric tumult to which its station is exposed in stormy weather," and Thrushcross Grange in the fat valley below. They stand respectively, though any label is inadequate and is "shorthand" only, for the principle of energy and storm on the one hand and the principle of calm, of settled assurance, on the other. And they are not only principles; they are, as it were, elements: the children of one cannot breathe in the other. As Catherine Linton says of her relation with Linton Heathcliff:

> "One time, however, we were near quarreling. He said the pleasantest manner of spending a hot July day was lying from morning till evening on a bank of heath in the middle of the moors, with the bees humming dreamily about among the bloom, and the larks singing high up overhead, and the

blue sky and bright sun shining steadily and cloudlessly. That was his most perfect idea of heaven's happiness: mine was rocking in a rustling green tree, with a west wind blowing, and bright white clouds flitting rapidly overhead; and not only larks, but throstles, and blackbirds, and linnets, and cuckoos pouring out music on every side, and the moors seen at a distance, broken into cool dusky dells; but close by great swells of long grass undulating in waves to the breeze; and woods and sounding water, and the whole world awake and wild with joy. He wanted all to lie in an ecstasy of peace; I wanted all to sparkle and dance in a glorious jubilee. I said his heaven would be only half alive; and he said mine would be drunk: I said I should fall asleep in his; and he said he could not breathe in mine. . . ."

These two principles, these two worlds, might have existed side by side in peace if the outsider Heathcliff had not been introduced into Wuthering Heights by Mr. Earnshaw, "the old master." His history, as Nelly Dean says, is "a cuckoo's." Yet Nelly is scarcely fair to Heathcliff. Circumstances have made him a cuckoo. On one level *Wuthering Heights* is a novel of revenge, with Heathcliff the revenger, but he has become one solely because of his treatment at the hands of Hindley Earnshaw and the resulting frustration of his passionate affinity with Catherine Earnshaw. It is the frustration that leads to his great scheme of revenge on Earnshaws and Lintons alike and his winning of their properties. Heathcliff is not a monster; he is much more a primordial figure of energy. He and Catherine Earnshaw may be compared to two rivers that ought by every configuration of territory to flow into each other, but their courses are diverted, their proper channels damned, and for Heathcliff the consequence is the destruction of everything lying in his path; energy obstructed is energy perverted. When in the end Heathcliff is joined with Catherine, the harmony, the balance, is restored; the evil set up by obstructed energy has worked itself out.

By then, however, Catherine Earnshaw has been dead

for several years and is a ghost. Our first introduction to
her in the novel is as to a ghost, and almost our first introduction to Heathcliff is as to a haunted man. Emily
Brontë's province is reality, but spiritual reality; in *Wuthering Heights* death is not an end but a liberation of the
spirit, and in the world of *Wuthering Heights* those we
normally call the living and the dead exist side by side and
are in communication. Yet we do not think of *Wuthering
Heights* as an exercise in the supernatural, as some of
Stevenson's and James's stories are, because Emily Brontë
makes no distinction between the natural and the supernatural; her world is one and, rendered ever so concretely
as it may be, it is a spiritual world.

This explains why the characters and their actions, on
the face of it so incredible, convince as they do. Heathcliff
and Catherine Earnshaw are as "real" as any personages
in fiction, but they are real in a way different from any
others; those that have the closest relationship to them are
some of Dostoevski's and Herman Melville's. The reality
of Fielding's characters, or Jane Austen's, Thackeray's,
Trollope's, or Arnold Bennett's, might be called a sociological reality; the reality of George Eliot's characters, like
those of James and Lawrence, is primarily psychological,
though no hard and fast separation between the two kinds
can be made. But Emily Brontë's world and its inhabitants have nothing to do either with sociology or with
psychology; her world is determined by spiritual values
which are embodied in the characters. This does not make
them less real; it does make them real in a unique way.
They convince because they so completely express in themselves and their behavior the laws of their being, which
are their creator's deductions—artistic deductions—from
the findings of her intuition into the nature of things. The
intuition was grasped with complete certainty and in detail; if it came as a flash of light, then it lit up the whole
of life, and what was seen thus illuminated was remem-

bered as well as the illumination. The proof of this is the very concreteness of *Wuthering Heights* and its flawlessness as a totality. Everything in the novel works together to produce the concreteness, the characters, the action, the kinetic prose that renders a whole landscape and geography and climate without ever becoming, except for phrases, "descriptive." "*Wuthering Heights,*" E. M. Forster has said in *Aspects of the Novel*, "is filled with sound—storm and rushing wind." The storm and rushing wind are conveyed by no set pieces but are in the words themselves of the novel, in its imagery of bent thorn trees, and in the characters. *Wuthering Heights* is a novel conceived at the highest poetic level, and its great characters are dynamisms of a kind we find normally only in the greatest dramatic poetry.

Yet superb as the conception of *Wuthering Heights* is, it is easy to imagine one similarly superb being botched in its execution. *Wuthering Heights* is anything but botched; the conception is matched by a technique equally superb. To find anything to rival it we have to wait for the arrival of Conrad half a century later; in fact, Emily Brontë anticipates uncannily Conrad's characteristic methods of narration as we find them in *Lord Jim* and *Chance* and goes into even subtler degrees of complexity. As we begin to read the novel the action is already approaching its end, poised on the edge of climax. We first see Heathcliff through the eyes of the narrator Mr. Lockwood, the outsider from the south who has rented Thrushcross Grange from him. We share in Lockwood's bewilderment and curiosity at the strange situation at Wuthering Heights, and through him we feel the full impact of Heathcliff's intransigent spirit. But it is from Nelly Dean, the housekeeper at Thrushcross Grange and a former servant at Wuthering Heights, that Lockwood hears the whole apparently tragic story—one says "apparently" because finally the novel is not tragic but something for which we lack a word, though perhaps heroic is the nearest we can get—through the years down to the actual time of narration. Nelly has been the closer observer of the action, of Heathcliff's arrival, his brutalization by Hindley Earnshaw, his revenge on him and on Edgar Linton, who marries Catherine Earnshaw, and his deliberate attempts to bring down and degrade both families as he himself had been degraded. To some extent Nelly has even been Heathcliff's confidante, as she has certainly been both Catherine Earnshaw's and her daughter Catherine Linton's; she has also, as servant and tool, played her small part in the action, though she is spiritually outside it; she is at once narrator and chorus, and what she narrates she does with awe. Emily Brontë incorporates within Nelly's account other narratives in the first person, young Catherine Linton's and Isabella Linton's. Then Lockwood abruptly leaves Thrushcross Grange, disgusted with the weather. When he returns to the neighborhood some months later curiosity again drives him to Wuthering Heights. He finds the atmosphere and situation there curiously changed, and Nelly, installed there as housekeeper, again tells him what has occurred.

As in Conrad, this complex method of relating the story serves a complex purpose. The device of plunging us into the action while it is well under way is as old as epic, but it always dramatizes it and keys up the suspense; our curiosity is piqued as Lockwood's was. We are compelled to identify ourselves with Lockwood, and the effect of our seeing everything partly through his eyes and partly through Nelly Dean's is, as it were, to see the action framed, almost as though on a stage, while the enormous curiosity of the sophisticated southerner and the awe of the simple peasant woman become themselves a tribute to the intensity of the drama whose unfolding is being reported; they serve not merely to heighten the drama but to underline its significance and its scope, for Lockwood and

Nelly are essentially spectators. That is the role forced on us, the readers, and their comments, their function as chorus, become ours too. Emily Brontë puts us, so to speak, in our place at the very beginning; her technique dictates what we shall see and also how we shall respond to what we see. It is this that gives *Wuthering Heights* its singular richness, which can only be compared in its total effect to that of Shakespearean tragedy, for at the end of the novel, which as novels go is quite short, all we can say is something like the last lines of *Lear*:

> we that are young
> Shall never see so much, nor live so long.

Set beside Mrs. Gaskell and the Brontës, Charlotte M. Yonge (1823-1901) calls for little attention. She still has her small band of admirers, who make fantastic claims for her. Every age has its novelist who sets down a portrait of the age as it would like to see itself. Miss Yonge, with her High Anglican piety, did this for the Victorians, depicting idealized family life in numerous novels. Books like *The Daisy Chain, The Heir of Redclyffe*, and *Heartsease* remain interesting as revelations of the mid-century's notion of itself, and they are still very readable, for Miss Yonge had the gift of creating characters understandable at first glance and the power of placing her idealizations in circumstances and surroundings drawn from actual observation. These qualities enable her precariously to survive as once famous ladies like Mrs. Craik and Mrs. Oliphant no longer do.

5

Trollope, it has often been said, is a lesser Thackeray. But the two novelists cannot be linked in this kind of way. Trollope is big enough to exist in his own right, and however inferior he may be to Thackeray as a writer, there are grounds for considering him a more satisfying novelist.

Michael Sadleir has noted in his *Trollope: A Commentary* that his work lies "athwart the pattern of modern literary criticism." This is true, and with him, more than with any of his English contemporaries even, it is essential to remember that the novel was an unself-conscious, even a primitive, form. A great part of his strength comes from this. He was, more than any other English novelist of his time, completely at one with his age, critical of it in comparatively small details but in the main accepting it as he accepted the air he breathed. His political position is revelatory: a right-wing Liberal. He knew exactly what the novel should be; it was what the great majority of readers have always wanted it to be: "a picture of common life enlivened by humor and sweetened by pathos." His failings are obvious. His style is commonplace, so that he relies wholly on the interest of his subject matter; when the subject matter is dull Trollope is dull. He has no sense of form; he was content to produce a story that would, somehow, fill three volumes of a novel, a novel, moreover, that was to appear as a magazine serial before publication. As he realized himself, he had little skill in plot construction, which was both an asset to him and a liability. Everything conspired to make him a superb improvisator; one reads him from chapter to chapter, with little sense of the whole.

The effect of this is curious. "The chronicler of small beer," Richard Garnett called him, and this is almost certainly the impression a single novel read in isolation does make. It is not, however, the impression made by ten. Then it is very different: it is that of the creation of nothing less than a world. With no theory behind him, and with only a modest ambition, Trollope produced a *Comédie humaine,* and though it would be absurd to set him up against Balzac the fact remains the world he created is almost as capacious as Balzac's and as solid in its reality.

When allowance is made for the difference in degree of talent and creative energy, Trollope is not unlike the writers—or teams of writers—of modern radio "soap opera." Though he did not have to produce a daily installment, he worked in much the same way, and a modern writer of Trollope's temperament and combination of talents would probably find greater scope in serial writing for broadcasting than in the novel as we now know it. In the kind of action represented, a soap opera like the B.B.C.'s *Mrs. Dale's Diary* is at least superficially Trollopean.

In fact, the canvas of *Mrs. Dale's Diary*, as a social picture of the times, is nothing like so wide as Trollope's. Trollope's focal point is the upper middle class, but with that as the center of his picture, he can draw round it the whole of the society of his day down to peasants and brickmakers, though his view of society is essentially confined to the south of England; the changes made by the industrial revolution lie outside the frame. But, as in *Mrs. Dale*, he is keeping several parallel and only tenuously related stories going the whole time, and, again like the soap opera, each chapter, each installment, has to hold the attention almost irrespective of what has gone before or is to come. It holds the attention, like *Mrs. Dale*, because it is seen as a faithful image of ordinary life. Nothing is outside the reader's experience or potential experience—or his knowledge; the characters are ordinary enough in mind, feeling, ambitions, fears, for the reader to be able to identify himself with them without difficulty. They awake in him the emotion of delighted recognition.

Again like the soap opera, a single installment of which will sound banal and trivial in the extreme, Trollope's is an art of the cumulative. "His great, his inestimable merit," wrote Henry James, "was a complete appreciation of the usual . . . He *felt* all daily and immediate things as well as he saw them; felt them in a simple, direct, salubrious way, with their sadness, their gladness, their charm, their comicality, all their obvious and measurable meanings." A complete appreciation of the usual: this can only be rendered at length, for the usual is usual because it is repetitive, its effect cumulative. The aim of most novelists is to heighten, to intensify. In a way, rather like Arnold Bennett's in *The Old Wives' Tale,* Trollope's is the opposite of this, and this is why one cannot in the end even condemn his dullnesses and *longueurs,* for, wittingly or not, they help his purpose. At first the rhythms of his novels seem intolerably slow; they end by wearing us down to their own pace, as time does in life.

One thing only made possible this rendering of his complete appreciation of the usual: his extraordinary facility and brilliance as a creator of character. Here, in range, diversity, and number, he is unsurpassed by any English novelists save Scott and Dickens. This is due doubtless to the fact that he approached life without theories and preconceptions; he is both the least intellectual and the least romantic of novelists. In nineteenth-century England, too, he was the one with the widest experience of life, experience as an important civil servant, as a man who delighted in the social pleasures of the hunting field, cards, and the table, as a magazine editor and highly professional man of letters, as an indefatigable and eager traveler throughout the English-speaking world, even as a Parliamentary candidate.

This sense of the world, the world as public and social activity, is carried over into his fiction. It is one of the prime sources of its strength. His novels are often classified according to their setting and subject, so that we speak of the Barsetshire novels, the political novels, and so on. The classification has its conveniences and is probably unavoidable in an author who wrote more than fifty books of fiction. But it has done its harm because, by enforcing a distinction where none really exists, it has tended to concentrate attention on the Barchester novels at the expense of the later books. In fact, the historical novels apart, and these are of no importance, all Trollope's work makes a whole, of which Barset is a province only. Even in the Barset books, in *The Warden* itself, Trollope's interest in and approach to his story may well be considered political in the sense that he is delineating struggles for power and position. His theme is the world and the way of the world, and this is the more strongly emphasized by the role of such characters as Mr. Harding and Mr. Crawley, in whom the way of the world is inoperative.

James thought *The Warden* the best of Trollope. It is more nearly a unity than any other of his novels. But Trollope became a better novelist the more he wrote, or rather, the more he wrote the more he surmounted certain of his weaknesses. Perched as he is on the edge of the over-pathetic, Mr. Harding is a very considerable achievement; yet he is conceived in too much sweetness, and so is Eleanor Bold. Trollope was not a sentimental man, but in *The Warden* he gave full rein to the sentimentality that perhaps the age expected of him, and in this novel as in *Barchester Towers* he allowed himself to be much more familiar with his readers than was his practice later. Astringency grew in him, and the early Barset books would be the better for more than they possess.

But *The Warden* is merely the gateway to Barsetshire, and his full powers are not seen until later in the series. The note of these early books, of *Barchester Towers,* for instance, is an easy humor, and there is always the suspicion that the humor is a little too easy. Mrs. Proudie and Mr. Slope, praised though they have always been, are somewhat overdone, as is Madame Neroni; and the young women are, by comparison with those we are to meet later, pallid creatures. The real achievements are Archdeacon Grantley and Bertie Stanhope. In them, and in the Archdeacon especially, we encounter the real source of Trollope's strength. This is a quite unsentimental charity, the off-spring of an unillusioned knowledge of men as they are and of a firm moral code. The result is a magnificent fairness. There is no either/or in Trollope; there is a "this" and "this" existing side by side and simultaneously. The Archdeacon is a most ambitious man and a worldly one; as his father, the old Bishop, lies dying, he is genuinely stricken with filial grief while yet doing all he can to secure the bishopric for himself. But Trollope does not condemn; there is, in fact, nothing to condemn, for Trollope was always conscious of what may be called the discontinuities of the moral life; he knew, even if he did not know the words, all about rationalization of motive and wish. According to his lights, the Archdeacon is a good Christian; Trollope sees the incongruities of his behavior, but he respects him.

It is this charity, this recognition of the gap between ideal behavior and the actual behavior of men, that makes him the true successor to Fielding, the Fielding particularly of *Amelia*. In the accuracy of their delineation, Trollope's young men are the best, as *hommes moyen sensuels*, in Victorian fiction, for George Eliot was too rigid a moralist to allow Arthur Donnithorne, for example, to remain unscathed by the consequences of his sin. But there is something most impressive in Trollope's rendering of a certain type of young man. It is a recurring type in his novels: the young man, generally ambitious, whose susceptibility to women leads him to be at any rate half unfaithful to the girl who loves him and with whom he has an understanding. There are Phineas Finn in the novels of that name, Frank Greystock in *The Eustace Diamonds,* and Paul Montague in *The Way We Live Now,* while Johnny Eames of *The Small House at Allington* and *The Last Chronicle of Barset* is a near relation, in spite of the fact that fidelity to a hopeless love is his strong suit.

Because he is akin to Fielding, Trollope is also akin to Jane Austen. James, noting his "complete appreciation of the usual," added that "this gift is not rare in the annals of English fiction; it would naturally be found in a walk of literature in which the feminine mind has laboured so fruitfully. Women are delicate and patient observers; they hold their noses close, as it were, to the texture of life. They feel and perceive the real with a kind of personal tact." But Trollope's affinity with Jane Austen goes beyond this. His discriminations are much less fine and subtle than hers, but when allowance is made for this, he judges his characters in a similar way, and like hers, his view of life is hierarchic; every one of his characters has his place in a graduated social order. Trollope may on occasion mildly satirize it, but he accepts it as fully as Jane Austen does, and he is probably the last English novelist to do so.

His relation both to Fielding and Miss Austen can be summarized very much as follows: just as Jane Austen represents a feminization of Fielding, so Trollope is a masculinization of Miss Austen. His inferiority to them both as an artist is so obvious as not to need stating, but the kinship is real. When he deals with women he is, naturally enough, much nearer to Fielding. His women are often excellent, and Mary Thorne and Lily Dale are something more than that, as are his spirited old ladies like Miss Stansbury in *He Knew He Was Right*; but they are women as men see them and want to see them; they are, in other words, conceptions ever so slightly chivalrous. Behind them stand the heroines of Shakespeare, Sophia Western, and Amelia.

In the Barset novels Trollope populated a whole county in the most satisfying detail and diversity, but there is no hard and fast distinction between the later novels of the series and those that have been classified as political and satirical. They are linked by characters common to all, though their importance may be much greater in one kind of novel than in another. For Trollope was not a political novelist in the sense that Disraeli was or even Wells, in *The New Machiavelli*. In *Phineas Finn* and *The Prime Minister* he is a political novelist to the same degree as you could call him a religious novelist in *Barchester Towers*; in other words, he is political only inasmuch as his main characters are men and women actively engaged in politics. The categories, never watertight, overlap, but the novels of the second half of his career develop certain tendencies evident in the last Barset books. The great character of *The Last Chronicle*, for instance, is Mr. Crawley, a character of a depth quite beyond Archdeacon Grantley or Mr. Harding. With Mr. Crawley, the ascetic scholar almost fatally doomed to failure in life, we stand on the threshold of abnormal psychology. Trollope handles him beautifully; he all but achieves the stature of a tragic hero; in his suspicions of his own sanity and his humble acceptance of it, there is a touch of Lear. Similarly there is Louis Trevelyan in *He Knew He Was Right*. The initial quarrel between Trevelyan and his wife is scarcely credible, strikes one as too much *voulu*, but nothing could be more convincing than the gradual intensification of Trevelyan's obsession from a rectitudinous egoism to the isolation of madness. In the same way the dominant figure in *Phineas Finn* is the Scottish millionaire landowner Mr. Kennedy, a relentless study of jealousy and religious dementia.

For, as his career progressed, Trollope's grasp of reality became stronger and stronger. Barset, in its beginnings at any rate, was an imagined world. When in the course of his post office duties he visited Salisbury and wandered "one mid-summer evening round the purlieus of the Cathedral" to conceive the story of *The Warden*, he had no special knowledge of life in cathedral cities or of ecclesiastical politics. But Salisbury—and Barchester—was a challenge to the imagination, and this comes out in the characterization in the early books, which shows signs of self-indulgence on the part of their creator. There is, in all but the best of characters, somewhat too much play with foible and idiosyncrasy. Trollope is enjoying himself hugely, delighting in the creation of characters humorous, comic, pathetic, and sinister for the sake of creation itself. To this delight readers always respond; yet it *is* a self-indulgence in a novelist, and it produces neither the most surely conceived characters nor the greatest novels. When Trollope turned increasingly to the London scene and Barset became more and more impregnated by the great world, his work deepened. He could no longer indulge in the luxury of character creation for its own sake since he was now compelled to match himself against an actual social scene; his creative gusto and its results had to be checked against the facts of observed reality. Trollope wrote nothing better than some of the episodes in the Barchester novels; but the best of the political novels and those roughly related to them are, as a whole, superior to the Barchester books because there is, in the later novels, a much greater unity of tone; and the tone is increasingly critical.

It is here that comparison with Thackeray becomes possible. As a prose writer, Thackeray makes Trollope look a bumbling, clodhopping amateur. Yet, in his later novels, Trollope, it seems to me, reveals an insight and a depth of penetration into the realities of social life beyond Thackeray's. He was doubtless lucky in being handicapped by no general view of life; a novelist is much better off with no philosophy at all than with a superficial one. What he did have was a strong and shrewd grasp of right and wrong in social behavior and this adds immeasurably to the truth of his picture of society. Take his very fine near-tragic novel *He Knew He Was Right*. In a way, the action is precipitated because the two central characters, Louis and Emily Trevelyan, insist on standing on what they claim are their rights. Neither is capable of compromise. But the tragedy would not have been precipitated if it had not been for the behavior of Colonel Osborne. Osborne is not a wicked man, he is merely a man of the world, much respected by the world; he simply "liked that which was pleasant; and of all pleasant things the company of a pretty, clever

woman was to him the pleasantest." He is, in fact, irre-
deemably selfish, and it is his irresponsibility of behavior,
not his wickedness, that sets the action on its tragic course.

There was something else Trollope possessed, that fascinated him the more the older he grew: the recognition
of the obsessional. This cuts right across any easy shallow
moralism. We see the obsessive operating in *He Knew He
Was Right* in the character of Louis Trevelyan; we see
it at work also in *Phineas Finn* and *Phineas Redux,* in
the character of the melancholy Mr. Kennedy; indeed,
Phineas's tribulations are the direct result of Kennedy's
insane jealousy of him. Trollope has never received anything like adequate recognition for his sober appraisals of
the psychologically abnormal and the part they play in
society. Yet they add greatly to the depth of his rendering
of the social scene, for, among other things, they hint at
the instability underlying the surface of society.

They point too to another quality of Trollope's, the
disinterestedness of his imagination. It operates only intermittently, but it is there all the same, and is one of the
rarest qualities in fiction: the ability to see a character
wholly in the round, and without preconceived opinions,
without theories of behavior, so that the character is shown
as behaving at once credibly and yet mysteriously; one
thinks of Madame Max Goesler and her relationship to
the old Duke of Omnium.

Trollope's later novels have not received the attention
they deserve. They show him as the steady and, for all his
tolerance, the relentless observer of his time and, in the
end, one of its sharpest critics. Remarkable is not a word
one normally applies to Trollope; his own special province
in fiction was essentially the unremarkable, yet *The Way
We Live Now* is one of the remarkable novels of the language. A very long book, even for Trollope, it is a detailed
study of corruption in society in all its aspects, literary,
journalistic, financial, though at bottom what we are faced

with is always corruption of manners, of the code of behavior in decent society. At the center of the novel is the tremendous figure of the great, shady financier Melmotte, the magnet of all society, the man for whose support both parties bid. Trollope's point of view is put by his spokesman, Roger Carbury:

> "What are we coming to when such as Melmotte is an honoured guest at our tables? You can keep your house from him and so can I. But we set no example to the nation at large. Those who do set the example go to his feasts, and of course he is seen at theirs in return. And yet these leaders of fashion know—or at any rate they believe—that he is what he is because he has been a swindler greater than other swindlers. Men reconcile themselves to swindling. Though they themselves mean to be honest, dishonesty is of itself no longer odious to them."

Carbury, for such is the fate of the good man in fiction, is the weakest character in the novel; he is there only to express Trollope's views. But the novel, as a sardonic, disillusioned panorama of Victorian society in the seventies, is brilliant and prophetic; thirty or more years later Belloc and Chesterton were to attack English life from a similar point of view. Melmotte himself is a superb character, and the noblemen and their heirs who hang on to him are admirably sketched in contemptuous comedy. The greatness of *The Way We Live Now* is shown by the fact that, though written in an entirely different mode of fiction from Dickens, it is the only other novel in English of the century that, as a study of the role of money in society, can stand with *Our Mutual Friend*.

6

Of the novelists born in the fertile second decade of the century one very great writer remains for consideration: George Eliot. But George Eliot was already middle-aged when she turned to fiction, and her work belongs to a later phase of the Victorian novel, and first a handful of minor

writers must be discussed, writers who remain interesting
at any rate in part of their work, or for individual books,
not because of their art but because of flashes of talent that
still leap across and above their lack of art.

The first of these, Robert Smith Surtees, was born as
early as 1803 and died in 1864. Perhaps he is only dubiously a novelist, but he has survived better than most. His
first book, *Jorrocks's Jaunts and Jollities* (1838), was a re-
printing of sketches contributed to the *New Sporting
Magazine,* of which he was editor. As episodic as *Pickwick*
in its beginnings, it recounted with great gusto and a racy
humor the adventures of the Cockney sportsman Mr. Jorrocks in the hunting field. In the end, Surtees was writing
works as much novels as Lever's, and as formless. But a
passionate sportsman himself, he knew what he was writing
about, and if the enthusiasm with which hunting people
have always read him is any guide, he caught and rendered
the pleasures and perils of fox hunting better than anyone
has done before or since. Of the richness of his humor there
can be no doubt, and Jorrocks and Pigg, the huntsmen,
though minor immortals, are immortals none the less.

George Borrow (1803-81) is perhaps even less a novelist
than Surtees. *Lavengro* (1851) and *Romany Rye* (1857)
in fact compose a single work, which even so is incomplete.
Conceived as an autobiography, it is essentially fiction-
alized autobiography, cast, reasonably enough since Borrow
wrote it, in the form of the picaresque novel of Smollett.
The interest is wholly in the episodes. As a novel it fails
because of its mixed origins: Borrow does not bother to
establish the character of his hero-narrator, George, so
that the work is never detached from the personality of
Borrow himself and is only thoroughly comprehensible
in terms of our knowledge of its author. Nor does he create
his other characters in any real sense: Petulengro, Isopel
Berners, and the rest are potential rather than actual character; as shown, they are caught each in his permanent

gesture and do not bear close examination. Isopel, for
example, is made to talk in a highly literary language
which quite belies her workhouse upbringing, and it is a
flaw that goes to the heart of Borrow that she must be the
daughter of an aristocratic father. Structurally, the book
is naive beyond the picaresque model, which indeed need
not be naive at all. But Borrow attempts to impose a pattern of significance on the picaresque by the introduction
at intervals of a certain set of characters, Petulengro and
the Man in Black in particular. Actually, no true pattern
is established; instead, the reader is aware only of a monstrous misuse of coincidence.

Lavengro-Romany Rye is a crotchety, "impossible" book,
the work of an "impossible" man, full of the author's King
Charles's Heads and private persecutions. It is often exe-
crably written. Its initial appeal is easily understood; it
was the appeal to the same romantic impulse as caused
Cambridge dons to climb the Alps and Birmingham busi-
nessmen to walk up Snowdon. It is a minor manifestation
of the cult of the sublime in landscape that so many Victorians took over from Wordsworth and Ruskin almost
as a religion, but cranky and uncouth as it is, it is a genuine
manifestation, for Borrow was an original. The critic of
the *Athenaeum* said on the first publication of *Lavengro*:
"It can hardly be called a book at all." In a way he was
right. He also said it was merely a "collection of bold
picaresque sketches." It is for these—or for the best of them,
the descriptions of the street fights in Edinburgh, the fight
with the Flaming Tinman—and for Borrow's fresh eye
for nature that the book is read today.

There are still Borrovians; but what remains in general
circulation of Charles Kingsley's fiction has long been relegated to the nursery. Yet *Alton Locke* (1850) is by no
means a despicable novel. It is always called a tract, and
so it plainly is; Kingsley was not a natural novelist like
Mrs. Gaskell, who could at her best embody the social,

industrial, and economic conflicts of the day in excellently realized characters, nor had he the brilliance and power of imagination of Disraeli. Yet in *Alton Locke,* his fictitious autobiography of a Chartist working man, he produced something unique in his time. Kingsley was a very good descriptive writer, though not of the highest class, and his scenes in the East End sweat shops are still horrifying to read, while his account of a Chartist riot is a very considerable bravura piece. But what gives *Alton Locke* its vitality is the passion with which Kingsley conceived his hero, the tailor-poet and working-class leader. Locke may be largely an intellectual construction, but he lives, and he does so because Kingsley has entered into a state of mind, indeed into a state of being, that his much greater contemporaries were unable imaginatively to realize, for all their depth of sympathy with the poor. This state of mind, state of being, is class consciousness. In the end, through the ministrations of one of those noble-minded aristocratic ladies that so haunted the Victorian imagination—and, after a surfeit of Carlyle, Disraeli, Kingsley, and Tennyson, did the Victorians recognize her when she turned up in the flesh in the formidable and far from Pre-Raphaelite figure of Florence Nightingale?—Locke renounces his belief in direct action and is converted to Christianity, becomes, in fact, such another Christian Socialist as Kingsley himself. Kingsley is writing a *roman à thèse,* and characters and plot alike have to be forced to fit the thesis, but this does not prevent his rendering in the fiercest terms the agony of class consciousness, and Locke's reactions to his first sight of Cambridge and the brute insensitivity with which he is ducked in the Cam by a group of undergraduates are described so vividly that, even when read today, they get under the skin. They remain true, and pathetically right; and here Locke stands out as the prototype of the class-conscious characters, their minds rankling with pride, envy, and above all the sense of injustice, of Gissing and, in a somewhat different way, because they were aware they belonged to a class in process of taking over power, of Wells and Lawrence.

It is sometimes said that Kingsley's younger brother Henry (1830-76) was the better novelist. I cannot find him so. At least Charles Kingsley was conscious of the real situation of his time in one of its most important and least heeded aspects. It is this that gives *Alton Locke* the authority it still has. Henry's work lacks this authority. His values may be described as sub-Kingsleyan, that is to say, he is recognizably of the "Muscular Christian" group of writers to which Tom Hughes, of *Tom Brown's Schooldays,* also belonged: curates are namby-pamby unless they make a habit of leaping five-barred gates, and then they are universally adored; fictional heroes are one and all nature's boy scouts, pure in thought, word, and deed. That he had no power of construction is perhaps a minor matter; it was the great early Victorian fault, and novelists of more talent transcended it. He wrote agreeably, and his descriptive gifts have been rightly praised, by Michael Sadleir in particular. His sensitivity, too, was keener than his brother's. Yet the real and only interest in his novels today is their documentary interest. Rather obscurely the black sheep of the family, he went out to Australia and spent part of his five years there as a policeman in what was still a pioneer country. The best and freshest parts of his novel *Geoffrey Hamlyn* are those that describe pioneer life in New South Wales. Mid-Victorian novelists were fascinated by the idea of Australia; it was the place where dispossessed gentlemen, ambitious artisans, and repentant convicts could all go and make good. It was therefore highly convenient for the purposes of fiction, and Lytton and Reade both made use of it. In their works it is improbable enough, as we might suspect from the fact that Mr. Micawber of all people became a successful magistrate there. But Henry Kingsley was describing what he knew at first hand,

and his accounts of the country bear the impress of reality. It was, after all, a country made for the Muscular Christian to take his exercise in, and one of the bemusing things about *Geoffrey Hamlyn* is the way in which all the characters in the novel, virtuous and wicked alike, ultimately turn up in Australia.

But apart from this ability to render, pastorally and charmingly, a new scene, Henry Kingsley had another real talent: he could most graphically describe violent action and maintain the suspense while doing so. Here again he was writing of what he knew; as a policeman he had fought bushrangers, and the chapters in *Hamlyn* describing the terrorizing of the countryside by bushrangers and their final defeat after a long chase by the settlers and police in the romantic fastnesses of the Snowy Mountains are a fine, sustained piece of genuinely heroic narrative. After Australia, he was to become a war correspondent in the Crimea, and again he made good use of his experiences, for his glimpses of the war there, in *Ravenshoe,* are among the most vivid we have.

Sheridan Le Fanu (1814-73) is of considerably greater stature. Indeed, his talents, when separated out and seen in isolation, were such that it is not easy to understand why he failed to be more significant than in fact he is. It is likely that his very versatility was against him; he could do many things well and too often attempted to do them simultaneously in a single book. More important, because fundamental, he lacked any conception of the novel as a form of art and of the novelist as an artist. Here he resembled almost all his contemporaries who were born in the second decade of the century. It was a disability that only the very greatest among them could compensate for. To conceive of the novel merely as a vehicle of popular entertainment or of propaganda, meant in practice that the novelist did not sufficiently respect either his source of strength or his weaknesses. Unless a towering genius, like

Dickens, or a being possessed, like Emily Brontë, he was never truly braced for action. What he did was too easy, and the result is plain now, when we read all but the greatest early Victorians not for their work as a whole but for episodes of characters and groups of characters that exist in the mind after reading almost in a void, detached from the novel as a totality. The lesser Victorians survive, when they do, in spite of, not because of, their lack of an adequate conception of the art. They practically never, except by a lucky fluke, produced work commensurate with their talents.

Le Fanu is a case in point. And with him there was a complicating factor. Perhaps because he was an Irishman who spent most of his life in Dublin, he was old-fashioned in the practice of his craft even by contemporary English standards, so that, except in his best work, his short stories, he seems to be vying with writers of an earlier generation, inevitably, since the eighteenth century lingered on in Ireland long after the century ended according to the calendar.

All his talents are displayed as it were in a farrago in *The House by the Churchyard* (1863). It is a charming, at times brilliant, hotchpotch, the action set in the middle years of the eighteenth century in the village of Chapelizod just outside Dublin, a village in which everyone knows everyone else's business and has a flourishing trade in gossip. In this novel, which purports to be the memories of an old man, Le Fanu appears as an antiquated provincial Thackeray; he writes in that strain of wisdom and elderly experience which is really a combination of sentimentality and nostalgia. But the characters of the novel belong to Lever rather than to Thackeray, and almost all the characters and properties Lever took over from the eighteenth-century novel are there: the garrison of comic officers, the comic doctors, the spinster ladies, the widows lusting after marriage, the young man of sensibility, the clergyman who is second cousin to Dr. Primrose, and the specifically Irish types—the jolly, fat Roman Catholic priest, something of a hypocrite but the best fellow in the world all the same, and the Irish officer still wet from his bog and farcically punctilious about his honor; all these, together with the routs and dances and dinners, the horse play, the crude surgery and purges, the comic duels prompted by bewildered misunderstandings. The novel bustles with activity, flickers and jumps about like an old film, and it is all handled in a most genial and sprightly way. It is impossible not to admire the ease with which Le Fanu brings his characters to life under his pen, especially in his dialogue.

But *The House by the Churchyard* is also a horror story, and the horror and the comic extravaganza do not fuse at all. Le Fanu was expert in touching the nerve that twitches to the fearful, as expert as anyone who has written. His effects of horror are the more powerful because of their simplicity. The haunting of the house by a fat white hand could hardly be bettered. "The hand was rather short, but handsomely formed, and white and plump." But good though both the suggestion of horror and the rendering of his comic scenes are, Le Fanu ruins his novel because he is attempting incompatible things simultaneously.

He fails in *Uncle Silas* (1864) for a rather different reason. Here there is no comedy. We have instead, as the central character, a young girl, who tells the story from the vantage point of years later, caught in a Mrs. Radcliffe-like situation of imprisonment in an old, derelict house in the wilds of Derbyshire. In fact, though the dangers are real enough, the effect of the supernatural is supplied by the girl herself; she is terrified as a result of misunderstanding her dead father's Swedenborgianism. Le Fanu's use of the ideas of Swedenborg is brilliant; it sets his story naturally, as it were, in terms of the supernatural.

But despite the excellence of some of the characterization, that of the Swedenborgian Dr. Bryerly, the chattering, shrewd Lady Knollys, and the wholly sinister Uncle Silas himself, the story fails in the end because it drops from its original truly haunted level to a mechanical ingenuity of explanation and solution in the Wilkie Collins manner though worked out with much less than Collins's skill.

Uncle Silas represents the horror story in transition to the modern story of detection. So far as I know it is the first novel to include the now familiar puzzle of murder in a sealed room. But in fact, the supernatural and the purely rational—and the modern detective novel is in its way a manifestation of the scientific attitude—can never exist easily side by side, for they are irreconcilable. The rational must prove the supernatural an illusion; I do not think Le Fanu was convinced the supernatural was an illusion. The problem always for a writer like Le Fanu is to show the supernatural in action in the context of a larger whole that includes reason. He solved it with real success in what is undoubtedly his best book, *In a Glass Darkly* (1872). This is not a novel but a group of stories, a collection of "cases," cases investigated by an alienist, Dr. Martin Hesselius, whose theories on the relation of body to mind are perhaps not so very different from Swedenborg's. When, in the story "Green Tea," for instance, Le Fanu relates the case of the clergyman who is haunted by a monkey and finally driven to suicide, the narrator may explain away the clergyman's own theory of diabolic possession, but for the reader today the monkey will probably seem a striking projection of the unconscious. And indeed the power of these stories in *In a Glass Darkly* has increased because of our increased knowledge of the unconscious workings of the mind. Le Fanu was right finally to explore the supernatural in terms of psychopathology. Dr. Hesselius's theories may no longer convince, but the cases he describes quite triumphantly remain.

Charles Reade is a considerably less interesting writer; he can be read with pleasure if one is young enough, but after that, in my experience, scarcely at all. He was praised by his contemporaries and by later critics for his ability to tell a story and for his "realism." If by story is meant "a narrative of events arranged in their time sequence," as E. M. Forster defines it, then the ability may be conceded him. Even so, one can only stare goggle-eyed at the effrontery of a novelist who can baldly, and early on in his narrative, write: "He drew George aside, and made him a secret communication," the secret of which, of considerable importance to the plot, is not to be revealed until several hundred pages later. As for the "realism," the critics meant something rather different from what the word normally stands for. Reade was always a novelist with a mission, bent on exposing current evils. So in *It Is Never Too Late To Mend* (1856) he exposed the brutalities of the prison system; in *Foul Play* (1869), the practice of the scuttling of ships in order to obtain the insurance money; in *Put Yourself in His Place* (1870), the iniquities of trade union-ism. He always began with an actual case in mind and worked from a dossier of evidence in the form of news-paper reports, books, and so on. But no matter how well authenticated the bases of his novels may be, their docu-mentary quality is now the least obvious thing about them, and they certainly evoke no illusion of the reality of ob-served life itself.

It was by way of the theater that Reade came to the novel, and writing for the stage was always his chief love. What he learned in the theater he applied to the novel. But the Victorian theater was not exactly the best and subtlest of schools for a writer. Reade's short scenes are immediately effective—as effective as a blunt instrument banged on the back of the head; and he could carry action swiftly forward in terse dialogue. But the total impression of his novels is always theatrical in the worst sense, an impression at the furthest remove from that realism aims at. He thought in terms of strong situations, melodramatic situations, and not in terms of human beings, and he was intent, too, on exhibiting, as it were, all the effects that the mechanism of the stage could produce. *Foul Play* is as good an illustration of his fiction as any. A young clergyman is falsely accused of murder, is sentenced and transported to Botany Bay. He falls in love with the governor's daughter and later finds himself on board ship with her in the South Seas. The ship is scuttled and he and the girl are cast away to live like Crusoes on a desert island. There is much more—the girl is tubercular, among other things —but that is enough for our purpose. It is writing of the most crudely sensational order, and is none the less sensational because Reade subscribes to a conventional black-and-white view of character. At times the story sags to a depth of absurdity that makes one wonder how it ever imposed itself on even the naivest of readers. For sheer credibility, the account of the clergyman-convict and the consumptive young lady on their desert island exists considerably below the level of *The Swiss Family Robinson.*

That Reade had genuine powers of description, shown, for example, by the description of the bursting of the dam and the flood in *Put Yourself in His Place,* cannot be denied; but again it is description of the coarsest theatrical kind. One is impressed by it in the same way as one is by parallel spectacles on the stage. One admires, but never for a moment does one think it has anything to do with reality. The test of this is simple: read Reade's flood, and then the account of the flood in *The Mill on the Floss.*

His best book no doubt is the only one generally read today: *The Cloister and the Hearth* (1861). In this novel of fifteenth-century Europe his capacity for research stood him in good stead. Children enjoy it still. Whether it is an adequate representation of the breakup of the medieval order is quite another matter.

In their own time, Charles Reade's name was generally linked with that of Wilkie Collins, and both were seen as in some respects disciples of Dickens. Nothing much is left of Reade, but at least two novels, *The Woman in White* (1860) and *The Moonstone* (1868), keep Collins's memory sweet. Both novelists were working at the opposite pole of manner and intention to Trollope, and this itself gives interest to his note on Collins in the *Autobiography*:

> When I sit down to write a novel I do not at all know, and I do not very much care, how it is to end. Wilkie Collins seems so to construct his that he not only, before writing, plans everything on paper, down to the minutest detail, from the beginning to the end; but then plots it all back again, to see that there is no piece of necessary dove-tailing which does not dove-tail with absolute accuracy. The construction is most minute and most wonderful. But I can never lose the taste of the construction. The author seems always to be warning me to remember that something happened at exactly half-past two o'clock on Tuesday morning; or that a woman disappeared from the road just fifteen yards beyond the fourth milestone. One is constrained by mysteries and hemmed in by difficulties, knowing, however, that the mysteries will be made clear, and the difficulties overcome by the end of the third volume.

The criticism goes to the heart of Collins's work and helps to explain the sources of his success and his failure. Trollope is really criticizing, and criticizing fundamentally, the whole genre of fiction we now call the detective novel. The genre was unknown to Trollope, as it was to Collins, even though *The Woman in White* and *The Moonstone* are the most brilliant detective novels ever written; and they are that partly because the genre was unknown to him. The detective novel, of which there were then very few instances extant at all, had not yet split away from the body of fiction proper. Collins had to combine with his extremely ingenious plots all the qualities of a good "straight" novel, and the combination he made was masterly. *The Woman in White* and *The Moonstone* represent an almost miraculous balance between the novel of mechanical plot and the novel of character. They satisfy completely as detective novels, but the exigencies of detection are not allowed to cripple the characters: they spring, at any rate for the most part, from genuine observation and invention. Technically, these novels remain of the greatest interest; by allowing the stories to be told in the words and from the points of view of the characters involved, Collins at once sharply dramatizes the characters and presents them from various angles. This gives an admirable illusion of solidity and reality to his work, for we are taken in succession into the minds of the personages in the action. This means, to put it at its lowest, that it was essential his characterization should be adequate. In these two novels it is much more than merely adequate. Marion Halcombe, in *The Woman in White,* is one of the best and most original characters in our fiction: she exists in her own right as a courageous, determined, generous person; and Rachel Verinder, in *The Moonstone,* is a fine rendering of a well-born young woman of decided mind.

Count Fosco, of *A Woman in White,* has always been admired, and he is one of the great grotesques of our fiction. He cannot be said precisely to live; it is impossible to imagine him outside the confines of the novel he was devised for; but he is a wonderful piece of invention and a most original and attractive villain, many times reproduced since his creation by later novelists and film script writers, though never so well as Collins managed him. Sergeant Cuff, in *The Moonstone,* is another of Collins's prototypes.

Collins is much more satisfying a novelist in his two detective novels than he ever is outside them. There, plot rules everything, and this was fatal to those novels in which Collins was intending seriously to deal with serious questions. Trollope's criticism was then just. Perhaps it scarcely affects *Armadale* (1866), which is generally considered his best book after *The Woman in White* and *The Moonstone*, for *Armadale* is an exercise in pure melodrama based on the notion of doom. Collins presents us with all the facts of the case in the first chapters; after that, we read on in order to find out how Collins is going to bring us to the end that we know is predetermined. The book has the fascination of a diabolically ingenious puzzle, and our only real concern is to see how Collins will solve the puzzle.

Armadale justifies itself on its own plane. This cannot be said of his propaganda novels such as *No Name* (1862) and *The New Magdalen* (1873). The latter is a novel on a favorite Victorian theme, the redemption of the "fallen woman"; it is a protest against the hostility of Victorian society to the woman known to have fallen. It is done with consummate skill, but with the wrong kind of skill, for the initial situation, that of a woman who has taken over another's identity so thoroughly that she can pass herself off as the other even among people who have known her, is so improbable as to remove the novel immediately from the category in which Collins would have us consider it.

Collins was always a superb storyteller, yet his main significance for us today, *The Woman in White* and *The Moonstone* apart, is, like Reade's, that he shows how necessary, inevitable, and salutary was the reaction against the kind of novels he wrote. He and Reade were damnably efficient in a very narrow way; they thought, felt, and expressed themselves in stereotyped forms which may originally have had some relation to the observed conditions of existence but had precious little when used by them. Before they died, Reade in 1884 and Collins five years later, they could have read the first works in fiction of Gissing and George Moore. What they made of them, if they did read them, it is pointless to speculate.

THE LATER VICTORIANS

1

Georgе Eliot's first novel, *Adam Bede*, was published in 1859. She has been described as the first modern English novelist. Put thus baldly, the statement begs too many questions to have much meaning. Yet it is true that her work marks a change in the nature of the English novel, a change so significant as almost to amount to a mutation in the form. She did not herself make the change; it would have occurred had she never written a word of fiction, and it was not spectacular in its operation. Moreover, it was a complex change, and not all its manifestations appear in her work. But 1859 saw the publication not only of *Adam Bede* but also of another first novel, by a younger writer: George Meredith's *The Ordeal of Richard Feverel*. Together, vastly different though they are, they stand in sharp contrast to the works of established novelists that appeared in the same year, *A Tale of Two Cities*, *The Virginians*, *The Bertrams*. It is precisely these works that make the publication of *Adam Bede* and *Richard Feverel* so significant, for, by contrast with the fiction of Dickens, Thackeray, and Trollope, George Eliot's and George Meredith's first novels appear as new points of growth in our literature.

They were the counterparts of new growing points already visible in European fiction generally. Here dates are relevant. A translation of Turgenev's *Sportsman's Sketches* had come out in English in 1855; in that year Tolstoi's *Sevastopol* had been published in Russia and Flaubert's *Madame Bovary* in France. Dostoevski's *The House of the Dead* was to follow in 1861 and Turgenev's *Fathers and Sons* two years later. None of these works had any influence on George Eliot or Meredith, but looking back we can see that the English writers belonged to the same broad movement that was shaping the novel anew in Europe, and henceforward, for English novelists younger than they, the usable past of fiction was to include, besides the traditional English novel from Defoe onwards, nineteenth-century French and Russian fiction. The result, so far as England was concerned, was the mutation of which the modern English novel was the product.

In what did the mutation consist? We can see roughly if we contrast Flaubert, Turgenev, Tolstoi, and Dostoevski with Dickens, Thackeray, and Trollope. The difference is not one of talent; rather it lies in the end the novelists have proposed for themselves. The English saw themselves sometimes as preachers and reformers, always as public entertainers. Their conception of themselves was modest, their conscious aim nothing much more elevated than Wilkie Collins's "Make 'em laugh, make 'em cry, make 'em wait." Set against this innocent notion of the novelist's function Flaubert's description of his ambition: "To desire to give verse-rhythm to prose, yet to leave it prose and very much prose, and to write about ordinary life as histories and epics are written, yet without falsifying the subject, is perhaps an absurd idea. . . . But it may also be a great experiment and very original." The French novelist has arrogated to himself the rights and privileges of the poet; he is taking his talent and his medium as seriously as poets do theirs. Flaubert's words show the nineteenth-century novelist catching up, in the claims he makes for his vocation, with the Romantic poets at the beginning of the century. Flaubert's aims, it is true, were not those of Dostoevski or Tolstoi; yet in spite of the genuineness of his affinity with Dickens, Dostoevski, with his tremendous subject matter of man in relation to God, is plainly using the novel with a depth of seriousness quite beyond anything the early Victorians proposed for it.

The seriousness of these European writers was both moral and aesthetic; it is not always a simple matter to distinguish one from the other. But it is not by accident that this seriousness of intent came into our fiction consciously with George Eliot and Meredith. In education and interests both were out of the common run of English novelists. George Eliot was thirty-eight when she wrote her first fictions. Until then, she had worked as a rationalist journalist, reviewing learned books on religion and philosophy. A woman of formidable learning herself, she was the friend of men more learned, like Herbert Spencer, and shared their interests. Dickens's and Thackeray's associates had been men like themselves, journalists, artists, actors, not intellectuals and philosophers. George Eliot lived in a much larger world of ideas, ideas which conditioned her views of fiction, the shape her novels took, and the very imagery of her prose.

So with Meredith. Educated partly in Germany, influenced by French writers, a critical attitude towards England and its literature was second nature to him.

George Eliot was the greater novelist, though the work of the two is so different as to make them scarcely comparable. But Meredith brought into our fiction consciously, as Emily Brontë had introduced it unconsciously, a quality of poetry which later novelists were to weave into the fabric they had inherited from George Eliot.

George Eliot was that common English type, the radical tory. Her radicalism, at once cautious and courageous, lay in the spheres of theology and ethics. Born in the Established Church, she had become a Calvinistic Methodist as a girl; essentially religious, she was brought by her intellectual honesty to a reluctant agnosticism, an agnosticism that laid as remorseless a stress on morals, on right behavior, as had the dissent of her youth. She writes, in *Silas Marner*: "Favorable chance is the god of all men who follow their own devices instead of obeying a law they believe in. . . . The evil principle deprecated in that religion, is the orderly sequence by which the seed brings forth a crop after its kind." George Eliot believed, almost like a fanatic of determinism, in "the orderly sequence by which the seed brings forth a crop after its kind." Human beings were made for good or ill by their actions and in the last analysis by their characters, and the consequences of their actions were remorseless. She accepted implicitly Edgar's words:

> The gods are just, and of our pleasant vices
> Make instruments to plague us

and did so perhaps the more firmly because she could see no evidence for the existence of gods.

George Eliot's moral beliefs chimed with what appeared to be the findings of contemporary science, particularly heredity, which appeared as a scientific—and scientifically proved—determinism. This gave her fiction great authority in its day; later, it was to make it seem dated; now, when she is again seen as a great novelist, we realize how much of her strength is derived from the very intransigence of her view of human beings. It was a view too mechanistic to allow her to write tragedy. But, by placing the responsibility for a man's life and fate firmly on the individual and his moral choices, she changed the nature of the English novel. If it is the individual's choice of actions that shape his life, then plot in the old sense of something external to character and often working unknown to it is irrelevant and unnecessary. Character, in fact, itself becomes plot, though in her greatest novel character itself is discovered to be conditioned by environment, or rather, its capacity for growth and scope to be limited, almost to the point of tragedy, by the world around it.

George Eliot's toryism is evident in her traditionalism, her delight in an ordered, hierarchical way of life in which everyone has his prescribed place and duties. In her youth she had been a great reader of Scott, and Scott is probably the greatest single influence on her fiction. She wrote for the most part of a society and a way of life over and done with; it was indeed the society and way of life she knew in her childhood, that of midland England before the first Reform Bill. The values that informed the mid-century, however, were already operating in the world she described. Yet, like Scott, she gained from the fact that the world she described was a finished one. Since it was finished, it was static. It could therefore be described completely, and in the solidity and comprehensiveness with which she created her fictional world she has no peer in English except Scott.

Joan Bennett has noted, in her admirable *George Eliot: Her Mind and Art,* "the organic form of her novels—an inner circle (a small group of individuals involved in a moral dilemma) surrounded by an outer circle (the social world within which the dilemma has to be resolved)." This is evident from the first in *Adam Bede,* which is, among other things, a novel about a whole village and a whole social structure; we are given the freedom of the squire's hall, the rectory, the tenant farmer's farmhouse, the carpenter's cottage, all of which exist in a distinct relation to one another; all, one might say, are part of the others' lives. Yet, in this novel especially, George Eliot's imagination is not of a piece. It is much more free when working on the figures of the outer circle; with the major characters of the smaller circle within it is sharply curbed by her intellectual, which are her moral, preoccupations. These she allows to become unnecessarily overt. She retained the old privilege, of course, of commenting on, explaining, even upbraiding her characters; in *Adam Bede* she carries it to quite excessive proportions. And here she suffers from the defects of her prose style. Fielding and Thackeray, who had similarly indulged themselves, were writers who could not help being graceful and witty. George Eliot's prose has neither grace nor wit; it is serviceable, but lacks the conversational ease that alone makes the author's interventions in the story in his own voice tolerable for long. It is not altogether pleasant to be lectured by George Eliot.

To state the matter too extremely, *Adam Bede* falls into two parts. They may be summed up in two sentences that occur in the novel. She writes, in her capacity of narrator: "It is for this rare, precious quality of truthfulness that I delight in many Dutch paintings, which lofty-minded people despise. I find a source of delicious sympathy in these faithful pictures of a monotonous homely existence, which has been the fate of so many more among my fellow mortals than a life of pomp or of absolute indigence, of tragic suffering or of world-stirring actions." "This rare, precious quality of truthfulness" perfectly describes the ambience of the novel and makes it, *Far from the Madding Crowd* apart, the finest pastoral novel in English. Then there are the Rector Mr. Irwine's words: "Consequences are unpitying. Our deeds carry their terrible consequences, quite apart from any fluctuations that went before—consequences that are hardly ever confined to ourselves." These sentences define the inner action: the fall of Hetty Sorrel, her seduction by Arthur Donnithorne, the consequent wretchedness of Adam Bede, and his subsequent marriage to Dinah Morris. This is handled with great temperateness —up to a point. Arthur Donnithorne, the young squire, is admirably done; this is no Steerforth seducing Little Em'ly, but a touching, idyllic love affair in which both young people are caught. Yet one cannot help revolting against what seems her creator's vindictiveness towards Hetty. Hetty's pretty sensuality is beautifully rendered;

everyone in the novel who meets her feels it, and so does the reader. But for George Eliot it seems to be a bad mark against her, something in itself reprehensible. George Eliot, we learn from her biographers, was perhaps overconscious of what she construed as her own ugliness, and it sometimes appears that in her fiction she had to mortify women beautiful as she herself was not. She could not, one feels, forgive sexual passion. Hetty has to suffer because she has fallen a victim to it herself and arouses it in others.

The lack of feeling for sexual passion, indeed, this deliberate turning away from it, makes Adam Bede's marriage to Dinah at the end of the book difficult to accept. And here a further complication obtrudes: neither Adam nor Dinah quite convinces. The "good" characters set in contrast to Donnithorne and Hetty, they are too good to be true. The novel is a wonderful study of the impact of Methodism on English life, but that is not to say that the characterization of Dinah is successful. Conscious goodness in a character is the most difficult quality a novelist can portray, for goodness conscious of itself is surely the most treacherous quality a human being can feel; its most likely consequences are those that appear in Mauriac's Brigitte Pian, in *La Pharisienne*. Dinah is never Pharisaic, because she is shown in the very actions of goodness. But for the modern reader she is almost fatally handicapped by the dialogue she has to speak, what the eighteenth century called "Methodistical cant": the words put into her mouth are of a kind that has been parodied and burlesqued so many times in fiction before and after George Eliot that it is now extremely hard to imagine them spoken with passion and sincerity.

George Eliot tried too hard with Dinah, and she tried too hard with Adam Bede, who seems now a humorless, hectoring, loquacious prig. In this novel, as elsewhere, she is most successful in convincing us of human goodness when she does not go all out to do so; in such a character as the Rector Mr. Irwine, not at all a model parish priest by evangelical standards.

What is memorable in *Adam Bede* is its ambience, the pastoral outer circle of life in Broxton that encloses the moral action: the scenes in Mrs. Poyser's farmhouse and at the Rectory, the harvest supper, and the rest. It is these that warm the inner moral action into life. The "Dutch interiors" of the Poysers have always been praised, and could scarcely be overpraised, for the endless rhythm of one kind of "monotonous homely existence" is caught forever. Doubtless George Eliot was using the memories of her childhood, but it seems to me as certain as such things can be that she is remembering her childhood through Scott. It has been debated endlessly which is the better in the rendering of rural speech and character, George Eliot or Hardy. No answer can be given, if only because we are confronted with dialects now dead; at any rate we may confidently say that no one speaks like Mrs. Poyser in Warwickshire today. Yet Hardy surely renders his rustic speech more freshly than George Eliot. George Eliot formalizes it, stylizes it. There is a rich humorous appreciation of it, but it is the delighted appreciation of someone recording it from the outside and from a superior station. George Eliot is at pains to render her rural speech idiosyncratic not only of individuals but of specific groups. Here are Mr. and Mrs. Poyser discussing Hetty Sorrel:

"Nay, nay," said Mr. Poyser, "thee mustn't judge Hetty too hard. Them young gells are like th'unripe grain; they'll make a good meal by-and-by, but they're squashy as yet. Thee't see Hetty'll be all right when she's got a good husband and children of her own."

"*I* don't want to be hard upo' the gell. She's got cliver fingers of her own, and can be useful enough when she likes, and I should miss her wi' the butter, for she's got a cool hand. An' let be what may I'd strive to do my part by a niece of yours, and *that* I've done; for I've taught her everything as belongs to a house, an' I've told her her duty often enough, though, God knows, I've no breath to spare, an' that catchin' pain comes on dreadful by times. Wi' them three gells in the house I'd need have twice the strength to keep 'em up to their work. It's like having roast-meat at three fires; as soon as you've basted one, another's burnin'."

What gives their speech its character are the images the Poysers call upon. But they are different images; Mr. Poyser's, with his similes from unripe grain, are those of the farmer, Mrs. Poyser's those of the housewife. Mrs. Poyser is certainly individualized beyond this; but both gain strength from the fact that their speech is, as it were, generic: the speech of a special category of being of which each is an individual member. Scott did the same with his peasant characters, and as with Scott, the result is that such characters take on a universality; in a way, they come to represent the enduring norms of life in society. Much of the solidity of George Eliot's recreation of the scene of pastoral Warwickshire comes from this: Mrs. Poyser is not only one quite sharply individualized farmer's wife, she is every farmer's wife. And perhaps part of Adam Bede's failure comes from a false application of the same convention. Adam too is made habitually to express himself in the terms of his craft, but it is not Adam's place to be a representative carpenter, and in his mouth his analogies from joinery and building emerge as platitudes and copybook maxims.

George Eliot's fiction falls naturally into two parts. *Scenes of Clerical Life, Adam Bede, The Mill on the Floss,* and *Silas Marner* were all published between 1858 and 1861. *Romola,* three years later, heralded her more ambitious period, which comprised *Felix Holt the Radical* in 1866, *Middlemarch* in 1871-72, and *Daniel Deronda* in 1876. The speed with which the novels of her first period were produced shows how accessible was the vein of imagination on which she drew. *Romola* suggests her realization that it had been exhausted, and her later work proves that she felt the necessity to dig more deeply.

In *The Mill on the Floss,* however, George Eliot had only to remember. The nucleus of *Adam Bede,* the action of which begins in 1799, was an anecdote told to the author by her Methodist aunt of a visit she had paid to an ignorant girl condemned to death for murdering her child. *The Mill on the Floss* had no such origin. It may not be an autobiographical novel as *Sons and Lovers* is, but Maggie Tulliver bears a much closer relationship to George Eliot than any character in the earlier novel does. Indeed, it is not going too far to say that Maggie is the essential Mary Ann Evans that George Eliot was born, and this close relationship between the author and her heroine gives the novel a warmth and immediacy *Adam Bede* lacks. It is from the identification that *The Mill on the Floss* gets its power and its charm. As a detailed rendering of the growth of a girl to young womanhood, a girl marked by intellectual distinction, a generously ardent nature, and a strong capacity for feeling, Maggie has never been surpassed. We do not for one moment question the intellectual ability or the spiritual quality of this girl, her craving for a larger world of the mind and the emotions or—what exists almost by reflex action—her dedication to self-sacrifice. "I was never satisfied with a little of anything," she tells Philip Wakem. "That is why it is better for me to do without earthly happiness altogether . . . I never felt that I had enough music—I wanted more instruments playing together—I wanted voices to be fuller and deeper." And she is set perfectly in her yeoman background on the edge of the country town, set perfectly in her relations to her parents, her adored brother, and circle of aunts and uncles. The world recreated in it is a much more deeply felt one than that of *Adam Bede.* In a sense, it is a more real one, and never has the conservatism, the self-complacency, the lack of imagination of a long-estab-lished provincial society been better rendered. It is ren-dered with affection, with humor, and with complete un-derstanding.

Yet it seems that George Eliot's identification with her heroine was too complete for the novel to be more than partially successful. Maggie's childhood is wonderfully described; because of this we can accept her devotion to her brother, the coarse-fibered, arrogant Tom. Our doubts begin when Maggie reaches young womanhood. For it is evident that Maggie's spiritual ardors are in fact excessive, her desire for self-abnegation too willful. Intellectually, George Eliot herself recognized this, for it is one of the functions of Philip Wakem, who loves her, to act as Mag-gie's confidant; he is in part "the reader's friend," and his job is to elucidate Maggie both to herself and to the reader, to set her and her ardors of emotion in perspective. So when Maggie says to him: "Is it not right to resign our-selves entirely, whatever may be denied us? I have found great peace in that for the last two or three years—even joy in subduing my own will," he can retort, as the reader wishes to:

> "Yes, and you are shutting yourself up in a narrow self-delusive fanaticism, which is only a way of escaping pain by starving into dullness all the highest powers of your na-ture . . . *You* are not resigned: you are only trying to stu-pefy yourself."

But the criticism of Maggie remains intellectual; as a character she is not seen critically by her creator at all. This comes out clearly when Maggie, tacitly engaged to Philip, falls in love with and is swept off her feet by Ste-phen Guest, who is tacitly engaged to her cousin Lucy. The situation is necessary so that Maggie may be made to make a moral choice. It is weakened, for us, because the nature of the choice as George Eliot sees it is rather different from what it would be for a young woman placed in similar circumstances today. But that is relatively unimportant. What is important is the character of Stephen Guest and the light Maggie's attitude towards him throws on her.

Stephen Guest has always been attacked. Leslie Stephen described him as "a mere hairdresser's block." Swinburne called him a "cur" for whom horsewhipping was too good. As a self-satisfied, superior, rather bounderish young man, Stephen Guest is convincing enough, and it is also well within the order of things that even so fine a spirit as Maggie should be sexually attracted by him. She might well be deluded by him. But that the delusion should persist is quite another matter. It does, and it does so because George Eliot herself is deluded by him. She does not, in other words, recognize that she has created a young man of vulgar pretentiousness. If this was a sign of immaturity on her part, in the novel it can only appear as immaturity on Maggie's, immaturity of which her author is quite unaware. Stephen Guest is simply not adequate to a young woman of Maggie's fineness of sensibility and discrimination, and his role in the novel forces us to question whether we haven't been wrong all along in our estimate of her.

In the third volume of *The Mill on the Floss*, then, George Eliot lets herself, and her heroine, down very badly. She spoils her novel, and to make things worse, goes on to ruin it by the quite arbitrary "tragic" ending, the flood of the Floss, Maggie's rescue of her estranged brother, and their reunion in death. If you have a river in a novel, a flood is always tempting; but by yielding to the temptation, George Eliot, instead of allowing Maggie to resolve the moral dilemma in which she found herself, and live by its consequences, took the easy way and substituted for a genuine resolution a cliché ending from the stock of Victorian fiction.

George Eliot concluded this first period of her career with a work which, though slight, is as perfect as any prose fiction in the language. *Silas Marner* is a small miracle. The story of a poor dissenting weaver who, betrayed by his friend, is accused of theft, loses his future wife, goes into exile in a remote country district and becomes a miser, is robbed of his gold, and redeemed and brought back to human fellowship by the discovery and adoption of a golden-haired baby girl: only George Eliot could have succeeded with it in her own time, and no novelist of any seriousness since her day would have dared attempt it. It has the charm of a fairy story with the solidity of a completely created fictitious society. One scarcely knows which to admire the more: the sureness of George Eliot's feelings or the fineness of her literary tact. They are not of course to be separated; the sureness of her feelings is expressed through her literary tact, and one sign of her tact is how she handles Marner. He is the central character of the novel, but his appearance in the book is never continuous; he is off stage rather more often than he is on, and the normality of the scene which is his background is such that we always see him in two distinct ways at once: as the pathetic figure he in truth is, which is how George Eliot shows him, and as the essentially alien creature, the outsider, that he is for the villagers. The norm of life in the novel is expressed in the wonderful conversations in the Rainbow Inn, which embody George Eliot's finest delineations of rustic characters and her finest humor. To this life Marner is always marginal; and in a sense he remains marginal to us until he finally finds his place in human fellowship again. *Silas Marner* is a novel of redemption, but the redemption is not Marner's alone, for the novel has a double action, Marner's and the young squire Godfrey Cass's, in which Marner is the unwitting agent.

Silas Marner is the most Wordsworthian of novels, comparable in its effect and in its feeling for natural piety with such poems as "Simon Lee," "The Idiot Boy," "Michael," and "Resolution and Independence."

Of the four novels of her second period the only one that is a success is *Middlemarch*. *Romola*, her novel of Renaissance Florence, everyone has agreed was a mistake; by turning her attention to fifteenth-century Italy she cut herself off from what was the main source of her power as a novelist, the loving, accepting contemplation of early nineteenth-century Warwickshire and its inhabitants. As much as Wordsworth or Hardy, she depended for the full exercise of her creative scope on a particular place at a particular time. In *Romola* she had to rely excessively on her intellect. It was a formidable one, but great novels are not the product of intellect alone, and with George Eliot especially there is always a clash, except when she is at her greatest, between her intellect and her imagination.

This is no less evident in *Felix Holt the Radical*, though it is much less a failure than *Romola*. A failure it was bound to be because of the plot George Eliot saddled herself with, a plot based upon the minutiae of the law which, in itself, would be enough to have made the novel an exposition of a special case rather than of general interest. In fact, no reader's interest has ever been engaged by the plot of *Felix Holt*. Holt himself is a bore, and this against the reader's will, for intrinsically he is an interesting character. He is never, however, quite allowed to establish himself. Instead, a point of view is established. It is a valuable one: that the working man's power to vote will count for nothing without the power to use it wisely. But it is no longer exactly new, and it wasn't when George Eliot was writing, and Felix Holt remains as it were a frozen attitude, almost a propagandist's dummy, as may be seen if he is compared with his silly old mother, who is alive from the first complaining word she utters.

The excitement of *Felix Holt* is intermittent, but the excitement when felt is real, and of a kind not commonly experienced in fiction. There are few truer or more touching characters in our literature, for example, than Mr.

Lyon, the dissenting minister; he is a splendid instance of George Eliot's intuitive understanding of spiritual and intellectual ardor. And reading of Esther Lyon's relation with Felix, one sees how George Eliot enters and occupies an area of experience novelists have commonly ignored: the simple and enduring human aspiration towards goodness. When she writes of Esther:

> She heard the doors close behind him, and felt free to be miserable. She cried bitterly. If she might have married Felix Holt, she could have been a good woman. She felt no trust that she could ever be good without him . . .

we realize that we have been shown an aspect of love generally neglected but which here impresses by its very truth.

But the great character of *Felix Holt* is Mrs. Transome, in whom George Eliot's abiding preoccupation with the effects on the individual of his past actions here finds intensest expression. Mrs. Transome has sinned long before the action of the book begins. She stands before us immediately and dramatically as the embodiment of the wasted life, wasted because committed to a sin the consequences of which she cannot evade and the knowledge of which shapes her whole being. Secret remorse eats her away like a cancer. All George Eliot's most passionate apprehension of the results of sin on character go into the rendering of her; she is, Gwendolen Harleth apart, her creator's most powerful symbol of the bleakness and bitterness of despair, of guilt that consumes its possessor.

The figure of Mrs. Transome shows how George Eliot's vision of human fate had darkened, deepened, and intensified in this second period of her work. But, except in *Middlemarch,* this intensified vision of a personal nemesis received, in terms of her novels judged as wholes, flawed expression. Her last book, *Daniel Deronda,* succeeds and fails in much the same way as *Felix Holt,* and for similar reasons. Its weakness is self-evident: it is the clash between the imaginatively conceived character of Gwendolen Harleth and the action in which she is centered on the one hand and the intellectually fabricated plea for Zionism on the other. This latter is purely propagandist; Zionism has turned out in result different from anything George Eliot imagined, and the very fact that we now have an actual Zionism and an actual Zionist state to set against her imaginations makes them the less convincing. But Gwendolen Harleth is as convincing today as ever she was. She is a magnificent creation, as great as any in our literature, and she is the product of sheer imaginative power. She is nothing like George Eliot herself, as Maggie Tulliver and Dorothea Brooke may fairly be claimed to be. She is cold, arrogant, calculating, self-willed, where they are warm, impulsive, self-sacrificing; she is indeed much nearer Mrs. Transome, and nemesis, in the shape of marriage to Grandcourt and her belief that she is responsible for his death, inevitably comes down on her. And she is realized in all her complexity; she is not simply an upper-middle-class Rosamond Vincy. She is a wonderful symbol of the sacrifice to false gods and its consequences, wonderful because of the greatness of her stature and the complexity of her motives. She will keep *Daniel Deronda* permanently interesting.

There remains *Middlemarch*. It has become the fashion to murmur "Tolstoi" when this great novel is mentioned and to speak of "a provincial *War and Peace*." George Eliot was not a Tolstoi; whole areas of experience Tolstoi effortlessly illuminated were quite outside her knowledge. Part of her genius, as *Middlemarch* shows more plainly than any of her novels, was a genius for analysis totally unlike his. Yet the almost inevitable reference to *War and Peace* does indicate the largeness of scale of *Middlemarch*. In it she creates a provincial society of greater scope than any she had attempted before, the society of Coventry and its rural environs in the years immediately before the first Reform Act of 1832. It is the most comprehensive of her novels and the most successful, because in it she was able, as she was not elsewhere except in the very much smaller range of *Silas Marner,* to integrate all its parts. *Middlemarch* is among other things a beautiful composition. And this despite the fact that it is built up of four major plots: the story of Dorothea Brooke; the story of Lydgate's marriage; the history of Mary Garth; and the fall of the banker Bulstrode. All these are related one to another without strain, and all have as it were their satellite minor centers of interest; together, they make a network that encloses the whole life and movement of opinion and events in a provincial city.

Yet two of the plots, those cohering about Dorothea and Lydgate are more important than the others in the sense that without them the novel would be unthinkable, and of these Dorothea's takes first place, simply because Dorothea stands at the heart of George Eliot's conception. She is the largest character and the one nearest to the heroic. The wonder is that we do not think George Eliot's claims for her are inordinate. For in *Middlemarch* George Eliot is investigating human aspirations, in particular the aspirations to serve and to be good, under two aspects; there is the part played in their realization by the individual human being himself, with all his frailties, his imperfect self-knowledge and his will power, and there are the limits set by the society in which he is born. To both Dorothea Brooke is central in a way that Lydgate is not, not only because of the passion with which she is conceived but also because of the magnitude of the conception. Writing on St. Theresa in the prelude to the novel, George Eliot says:

> That Spanish woman who lived three hundred years ago, was certainly not the last of her kind. Many Theresas have been born who found for themselves no epic life wherein there was a constant unfolding of far-resonant action; perhaps only a life of mistakes, the offspring of a certain spiritual grandeur ill-matched with the meanness of opportunity.

Dorothea is seen as a St. Theresa born in the wrong place at the wrong time. She is, as it were, a heightened Maggie Tulliver, a Maggie Tulliver with the advantages of social position, wealth, and independence. In a sense, these are her undoing, for she is, one can't help thinking, drunk with the splendor of her aspirations, and it is a valid criticism of George Eliot's presentation of her that so often to the modern reader her zeal for self-sacrifice, her lust almost to serve the highest where she sees it, should seem spiritual arrogance, the pride of self-righteousness. She is to a degree self-deceived; the intensity of her vision makes her blind to what lies outside its illumination. As George Eliot writes:

> All Dorothea's passion was transfused through a mind struggling towards an ideal life; the radiance of her transfigured girlhood fell on the first object that came within its level. The impetus with which inclination became resolution was heightened by those little events of the day which had aroused her discontent with the actual conditions of her life.

The first object which comes within her level is the scholar Mr. Casaubon. Her passion for the ideal transfigures him, and it is part of the irony of her fate that the truth about him is seen not by her but by comparatively imperceptive characters like Sir James Chettam and Mrs. Cadwallader, people of no vast ambitions or insights but content merely to do their duty according to the positions in which they find themselves. "She says," Mrs. Cadwallader remarks, "he is a great soul. A great bladder for dried peas to rattle in!" She is not quite right, but nearly so, and Dorothea's disillusionment, having married Mr. Casaubon, is inevitable and bitter. Casaubon is one of George Eliot's supreme achievements, and it is difficult to think of any other English novelist who could, having conceived him, have drawn him so unerringly. Never has desiccated pedantry been more devastatingly rendered. He has obvious affinities with Mrs. Transome; like her, he is living a lie, the knowledge of which he dare not divulge but which haunts him ceaselessly. His very jealousy of Dorothea springs out of fear that she has penetrated his secret; for his great book, which has become the reason of his existence, in his own eyes, in Dorothea's and the world's, is, as he knows, a work of no significance.

Casaubon is a terrifying figure of haunted futility. George Eliot's comprehension of him and pity for him are such that he exists on the grand scale. He too—and we are made almost against our will to feel this—has within him "a certain spiritual grandeur," but one "ill-matched with the meanness of opportunity." We cannot, any more than we can Dorothea, call him a tragic figure; yet, like Dorothea, he impresses us as a being capable of suffering tragedy, and we are moved to compassion by the sense of waste that informs his being.

In the shape of the novel as a whole, the figure of Dorothea is balanced by that of Lydgate. Interesting as he is, he is a lesser character, a smaller conception; he does not strike us as being capable of tragedy. George Eliot notes that "in the multitude of middle-aged men who go about their vocations in a daily course determined for them much in the same way as the tie of their cravats, there is always a good number who once meant to shape their own deeds and alter the world a little." Lydgate, the young doctor, is of this number. He is ambitious, indeed he has settled in Middlemarch because of his ambition:

> He went to study in Paris with the determination that when he came home again he would settle in some provincial town as a general practitioner, and resist the irrational severance between medical and surgical knowledge in the interest of his own scientific pursuits, as well as of the general advance: he would keep away from the range of London intrigues, jealousies, and social truckling, and win celebrity, however slowly, as Jenner had done, by the independent value of his work.

By gaining the support of the philanthropic banker Bulstrode, who is building a new hospital, Lydgate seems to be in a fair way to achieving his ambitions. He is defeated partly by himself, partly by the very provincial circumstances in which he has opted to settle. As far as the man himself is concerned, he has what George Eliot calls "spots of commonness." It is these "spots of commonness," this discontinuity in the fineness of his texture, which lead to his marrying Rosamond Vincy, that magnificent image of the self-satisfied acceptance of a mean notion of social behavior. Rosamond is adamant in her idea of what is owing to her. But the frustration of Lydgate's ambitions is not by any means due wholly to the spots of commonness of which his disastrous marriage is a symbol; it arises quite as much from the life of Middlemarch itself, with its professional jealousies and intrigues, its political oppositions, and, above all perhaps, from his association with Bulstrode. It arises, in other words, partly from the nature of things.

If we take Dorothea and Lydgate as the poles of *Middlemarch,* in between them, clustered about them, and clustered about the two other main plots is as large and diverse a collection of characters as exists in any English novel. There are failures, of course. Bulstrode is a striking representation of one side of the Evangelical Movement, its relation to capitalism and economic and social power, but the crime that eats at Bulstrode's heart is too melodramatic for its context and to that extent unconvincing. Then the Garth family tends to suffer from the monotony of goodness. Yet the gallery is a brilliant one, its members far too numerous to be itemized; one may only mention representative members, Dorothea's sister Celia, her husband Sir James, Mr. Brooke, and that splendid comic character the auctioneer Mr. Trumbull, who astonishes whenever he appears.

In one part of her conception, however, George Eliot fails. This is the character of Ladislaw. Her failure here is akin to her failure with Stephen Guest. Both George Eliot and her heroine see qualities in him that no reader has succeeded in perceiving. He is plainly meant to stand for the free spirit, and here his role is like that of Philip Wakem. He is the voice, where Dorothea is concerned, of common sense. When he tells Dorothea: "The best piety is to enjoy—when you can . . . It is of no use to try and take care of all the world; that is being taken care of when you feel delight—in art or in anything else. Would you turn all the youth of the world into a tragic chorus, wailing and moralizing over misery?" he is obviously speaking for George Eliot herself, and, incidentally, striking a note heard far too rarely in her work. But as a lover and husband for Dorothea he appears as totally inadequate, the product, one can only think, of his author's dream fantasies.

George Eliot is seen at her greatest in *Middlemarch*. Not all her qualities are manifest in it; it lacks the charm of the first part of *The Mill on the Floss* and *Silas Marner*, and the humor is much more severely controlled. But it expresses, as the earlier books do not, a complete experience of life, experience in the widest sense, imaginative and intellectual alike. The view of life expressed is a somber one, and one that cannot be wholly accepted; much of value is lost if, as George Eliot seems to conceive it, life is seen as primarily a gymnasium for the exercise of the moral faculties.

Perhaps this is not much more than to say that George Eliot has to pay the price of her earnestness. One says it is excessive, yet, fused with her remarkable imagination and her intellectual power, it made her the great novelist she is. It meant that she had a comprehensive view of life, a view that could take in every variety of experience that she knew. And, like an ardently held religious belief, it made every action of her characters important. Agnostic though she was, it isn't going too far to say that in this sense she is a religious novelist, as Bunyan is, or Mauriac today. In consequence, the characters themselves achieve a new importance in her novels, almost as though their eternal well-being is constantly in the balance. And one of the signs of this new importance of the characters is her relentless and scrupulous analysis of them; when we meet Dorothea, Casaubon, and Lydgate we realize that it is the very thoroughness and intensity of her analysis that creates them. This is something new in English fiction, which later novelists, such as Gissing and Henry James, Conrad and Lawrence, were to take up. It is indeed precisely here that her essential modernity lies.

2

Shelley wrote: "The distinction between poets and prose-writers is a vulgar error," and for him Plato, Bacon, and Rousseau are poets, for their appeal primarily is to the imagination. In this sense all novelists might be considered poets. Yet it is obvious that the pleasure we get from Jane Austen, for instance, is not the kind of pleasure we normally expect to get from poetry. Matthew Arnold picked out, as one of the essentials of poetry, what he called "natural magic," the recognition of which is one of the ways, perhaps ultimately the only way, by which we know a work is poetry. We do not find it in Jane Austen. We are delighted by her, we rejoice in the unerringness of her perceptions and discriminations, in the truth and accuracy of her delineation of character and society within the limits she has set herself. But we do not get from her the surprise of magic, the flash of revelation in the light of which we see something we realize is new; it is the sense of its being new that causes the surprise. This we get repeatedly in Dickens, in individual characters and in general effect. Here he stands in contrast to all his immediate contemporaries except Emily Brontë. We cannot avoid calling him poetic—poetic in a way that Thackeray, Trollope, and George Eliot are not.

Dickens is poetic not as a result of any especial use of language, but by virtue of the intensity of his visual sense and his awareness of relationships below the conscious level. He is a symbolist; his work is poetic as dreams are poetic. When Flaubert, however, wrote to Louise Colet of his ambition "to give verse-rhythm to prose" and to write about ordinary life as epics are written, he meant exactly what he said. His concern was with words; his aim was to give the prose paragraph the texture and exactitude of classical poetry; he wanted to get into prose the "peculiar property of poetry" as Coleridge defined it: "the property of exciting a more continuous and equal attention than the language of prose aims at." Sometimes, then, poetry in novels will appear in the novelist's visionary intensity, as in Dickens and in a somewhat different way Hardy; sometimes it will appear in his use of language, which, though not in the conventional form of poetry, will enable him to express moments of consciousness in his characters common to all but hitherto only expressible in poetry. We find examples of both in Meredith.

But Meredith was also a poet in the technical sense, and whether we look on him as a poet first and a novelist second, or vice versa, his fiction exists in the larger context of his work as a whole; for Meredith his novels were merely one form his poetry took. His work is not nearly so highly rated now as it was at the beginning of the century. When one looks at his fiction as a whole, however, it seems much more likely than not that Meredith's present eclipse will prove only temporary. The reasons for the eclipse are obvious enough. His philosophy has worn badly. Its essence is contained in his lines:

> Into the breast that gives the rose,
> Shall I with shuddering fall?

He identified himself with the spirit of evolution as he conceived it, and one can see how exhilarating he must have been until Shaw's Creative Evolution stole a considerable part of his thunder. Then, in style and attitude alike, he must have appeared as something like a later Carlyle, but an optimistic Carlyle, saying "Yea" to life not as a categorical imperative but out of sheer exuberance of spirit. But today, E. M. Forster's devastating comment on his attitude, "the home counties posing as the universe," seems an accurate summing-up.

His prose, besides, is as far removed as it can be from our present ideas of what constitutes good style. At its worst, it is rebarbatively Teutonic and vulgar, and at its best, except when it fuses into poetry, it is too brilliant, fatiguing because of excess of epigram and metaphor; it dazzles, and because it dazzles, tires the mind.

But there is another reason for the present neglect of him. We approach him in the wrong way. We look for the rendering of social life that we find in Thackeray, Trollope, George Eliot, Henry James, and Gissing, to mention his immediate contemporaries, and it is not there, even when we suspect that it is precisely what he is intending. The fault is not entirely ours. In his famous essay, *The Idea of Comedy,* he restates the classical conception of comedy, and reading it, we naturally expect Meredith to show in his fiction the grasp of the social scene that characterizes Jonson and Congreve. We do not find it at all. In the essay he talks much of society, but there is no very convincing society in his books, and often, if we are looking for a representation of society and of typical behavior, there is something that looks like willful freakishness.

Take the novel that in some respects is his least Meredithean, *The Adventures of Harry Richmond* (1871). There is an obvious indebtedness to Fielding, and since it is supposed to be written in the first person by Harry Richmond himself it appears much more naturalistic and therefore more conventional in style than most of his work. One third of the way through occurs the astonishing chapter,

"The Statue on the Promontory." Harry has gone to visit his father Richmond Roy at the court of a tiny German principality and, looking for him, watches the Prince of Eppenwelzen unveil the statue of his ancestor Prince Albrecht Wohlgemuth.

The statue was superb—horse and rider in new bronze polished by sunlight . . . The horse gave us a gleam of his neck as he pawed a forefoot, just reined in. We knew him: he was a gallant horse; but it was the figure of Prince Albrecht that was so fine. I had always laughed at sculptured figures on horse-back. This one overawed me. The Marshal was acknowledging the salute of his army after a famous victory over the Turks. He sat upright, almost imperceptibly but effectively bending his head in harmony with the curve of his horse's neck, and his baton swept the air in proud submission to the honours cast on him by his acclaiming soldiery. His three-cornered lace hat, curled wig, heavy-trimmed surcoat, and high boots, reminded me of Prince Eugene. No Prince Eugene—nay, nor Marlborough, had such a martial figure, such an animated high old warrior's visage. The bronze features reeked of battle.

The ceremony goes on; a poet reads an ode; and then, as Harry gazes at this masterpiece, suddenly:

The head of the statue turned from Temple to me . . . The eyes, from being an instant ago dull carved balls, were animated. They were fixed on me. I was unable to give out a breath. Its chest heaved; both bronze hands struck against the bosom.
"Richmond! my son! Richie! Harry Richmond! Richmond Roy!"
That was what the statue gave forth.

The statue is none other than Richmond Roy made up for the occasion, and his son's presence ruins the carefully planned illusion.

Literally examined, and seen in the context of a more or less realistic novel, the scene is preposterous. But it would not be preposterous in the comedies of Shakespeare or the plays of Shaw, and this is a pointer to the nature of Meredith's art. He is, in part, though only in part, a fantasist. The background of his fiction and the events in it may be implausible, devised with no regard to probability; but as in Shakespearean comedy, the figures in the foreground are real enough. Stevenson, an enthusiastic admirer, called the view of life thus expressed "the romantically comic," and the phrase is good enough; and in the same letter to W. E. Henley in which he describes his own view of life at the time of writing and quotes Meredith's work as an exemplar of it, he dashes off a sentence that sums up much of the best in Meredith: "To me these things are the good: beauty, touched with sex and laughter; beauty with God's earth for the background."

In fact, the scene in which the statue comes to life is not preposterous in *Harry Richmond*. Rather, it has genuine poetic power, for it symbolizes the truth about Richmond Roy as realism could not do. Roy is a character who by his very nature is larger than life; Meredith conveys this by his poetic device at the same time as he keeps him credible. Meredith's fantasy, though it distorts the novels when seen as a panorama of society, serves his purpose, which is to disengage and expose his characters at highly significant moments in their careers. As he wrote himself: "My method has been to prepare my readers for a crucial exhibition of the personae, and then to give the scene in the fullest of the blood and brain under stress of a fiery situation." How he arrives at the situation he seems scarcely to care.

Meredith's general theme is the eternal one of comedy, the clash between illusion and reality, and the central character's painful progress to knowledge of reality and himself. The characters walk in a kind of fairyland, an enchanted land, and in describing Menander's and Molière's characters in *The Idea of Comedy*, he defines his own: "The foundation of their types is real and in the quick, but they are painted with spiritual strength, which is the solid in Art." They are, then, always not exactly larger than life but of a fineness of perception, a potential greatness of spirit, that lifts them far above the ordinary. In a sense, they are spiritualized; men and women alike have Meredith's own uncommon cleverness and wit, and the men have a lofty conception of honor, while the beauty of the women is matched only by their ardor and their pride in themselves. And Meredith's attitude towards his characters differs according to their sex; the men, even when the objects of his satire, are transfigured by his wit, the women, by his poetry.

His first novel, *The Ordeal of Richard Feverel* (1859), is purely Meredithean in its fundamentals, even though these are to some extent overlaid by extraneous matter, borrowings from Dickens and an arbitrary ending to the book that has pleased no one. Ignore these, and what remains is quintessential. There is the object of the satire, Sir Austin Feverel, the man with an ideal system of education, who is to be chastened into an awareness of the truth about life; there is his son, Richard, the hero, for whom the action of the novel is essentially a discipline through which reality is learned; there is the girl he loves, Lucy. The machinery by which the scene is staged "in the fullest of the blood and brain under stress of a fiery situation" is clumsy in the extreme, but *Richard Feverel* remains remarkable for the poetry which informs it and, in particular, illuminates Richard and Lucy. It idealizes them and universalizes them in their moments of intensest experience, as in the chapters "An Attraction" and "Ferdinand and Miranda," which render the birth of love between them; the transfiguration they share is depicted not directly but in the beauty of the rhythm and imagery of the prose that describes the natural background to them.

The most popular of Meredith's novels have probably always been *Evan Harrington* and *The Adventures of Harry Richmond*. In both, the comedy is less ideal and there is a greater striving after surface realism, doubtless because the source of the comedy was an actual situation very close to the author. Indeed, in its most vital parts *Evan Harrington* (1861) is a fictionizing of his own family history. Meredith's was itself Meredithean comedy. To his contemporaries he was a man without a background. He suppressed it so effectively as to cause his origins to be the subject of speculations that appear to us, who know the facts, quite fantastic. He was believed, at any rate by some, to be the illegitimate son variously of George IV, William IV, and Bulwer-Lytton. In fact, Meredith had already made public the truth about his origins in *Evan Harrington*. He had not bothered even to change the Christian names of some of the characters he had taken from real life. Like Evan, Meredith was the son of a tailor of Portsmouth. The "Great Mel" who, though dead before the action begins, dominates the novel, the gentleman tailor who shook hands with his customers as an equal and never sent out a bill, who rode to hounds, was an officer in the Yeomanry, and when visiting Bath was taken for a marquis, was his grandfather; and at the time of writing his novel Meredith, like Evan, actually numbered among his aunts one who was the wife of an officer of Marines later to become a general and be knighted, and another who was married to the Portuguese ambassador to the Vatican.

So much then was straight family history. In *The Adventures of Harry Richmond* an obviously related situation is explored. There, Harry is caught between his allegiance to his mother's family, a family of honest country squires, and his loyalty to his father, the adventurer Richmond Roy, who is the bastard son of a royal duke by an actress and whose aim in life is to see himself legitimized and his claim to rank vindicated.

The problem of the hero in both novels is one of integrity. Evan Harrington is in love with the aristocratic Rose Jocelyn and, being in love with her, has to decide whether to pass himself off as a gentleman, as his sister the Countess de Saldar intrigues that he shall, or become a tailor to pay off the "Great Mel's" debts, as his mother urges him. *Harry Richmond* is the better novel. Part of the trouble with *Evan Harrington* is that the figure dominating the book, the "Great Mel," is dead before the action begins, and Evan himself is not much more than a chopping block for Meredith's strokes of wit and generalizations on life and conduct. For the most part the grand people at Beckley Court appear as unreal; the girls, Rose Jocelyn and Juliana Bonner, are a different matter, for reasons that will be clear later. What saves the novel is the character of Evan's sister, the countess, a great comic figure on whom Meredith, moved to delight by the contemplation of her, has lavished his inventive genius.

The Adventures of Harry Richmond gains by the presence in it the whole time of Richmond Roy. A fabulous figure, he is one of the greatest achievements in nineteenth-century fiction. His success in imposing himself on his son, who is his fascinated slave to the last tremendous denouement, is the more credible because of his success in imposing himself on the reader. A charlatan, he is a charlatan of greatness, almost of nobility, and in the final encounter with Squire Beltham, a scene blistering in its effect, his fall is very nearly that of a tragic character. And in Squire Beltham he has a worthy adversary, for the squire has a John Bull-like strength reminiscent of Fielding; he possesses great authority because he is drawn with great authority. In the clash between these two redoubtable characters and the loyalty each inspires, Harry Richmond's dilemma is much more powerfully dramatized than is the similar one in which Evan is caught.

Meredith's mind was naturally lofty, and his work, *Beauchamp's Career* (1876) and *Diana of the Crossways* (1885) especilly, is marked by a most engaging largeness of spirit. His finest work, however, is *The Egoist* (1879).

There, his talents for once are in perfect balance; and the style, though more ornate and convoluted than in the earlier books, is still just this side of the fantastic rococo extravagance of those that followed. And elaborate though the novel may appear at first sight, in it Meredith has at last solved the problem of plot. Indeed, one can scarcely speak of plot at all; what we have instead is design, pattern, the pattern, as the hero's name suggests, of the Willow Pattern Plate. Sir Willoughby Patterne, that adored Admirable Crichton, the hero of self-regard, having been jilted by Constantia Durham, jilts Laetitia Dale in order to marry Clara Middleton, is jilted by her, and in the end, stripped of his pretensions, cast into abject nakedness, is compelled to marry Laetitia on her own terms. It is as simple as that.

In essence, indeed, the novel is even more simple; there is a sense in which it might be said to be all contained in Mr. Collins's proposal to Elizabeth Bennet in *Pride and Prejudice,* and Sir Willoughby, though on the grand scale, is hardly more subtle a character than Mr. Collins. He is almost completely static, yet the illusion of life he presents is extraordinarily vivid. It is so from the thoroughness of Meredith's examination and dissection of him. Here he was certainly helped by the simplicity, symmetry, and tautness of the novel's design, which brought all his powers into the sharpest focus. So intensely is Sir Willoughby felt and seen by his creator, so strongly realized in his singleness of mind and habitualness of stance, that, for all he is a monster, he does become something of a universal figure. The concentration brought to bear on this single aspect of humanity, for such Sir Willoughby is, makes him the complete representation of quintessential self-approval. And here one difference between Meredith's way of characterization and George Eliot's is plain. George Eliot creates her characters through her analysis of them, but it is of a character caught in a highly individualized situation, implicated in one particular moral problem. Meredith's analysis of Sir Willoughby applies to all egoists by virtue of their being egoists. Analysis does not create him; in a sense indeed, it is as it were detachable from him, almost as though it were an essayist's running commentary on the inimitably dramatized action. But it does illuminate him as the representative of a type.

Sir Willoughby, then, is an intellectual creation. With young women Meredith's creative method is different. Clara Middleton is "real" in a way Sir Willoughby is not. The difference is evident in the effects the two characters have on us. By Sir Willoughby we are amused and scarified, or rather, we are amused and scarified not so much by him as by Meredith's exhibition of him. But by Clara Middleton we are moved, moved by the sense of a human destiny in the balance; and this is something quite different. There are several reasons for this. One is that, caught between Sir Willoughby and her egregious but most entertaining father, an egoist who somehow escapes all the penalties of egoism, Clara is in an intolerable position. Then, and more important since it causes her fate profoundly to matter to us, Meredith's attitude to young women is always poetic, and the poetic individualizes, concretizes. Meredith's analysis of Clara therefore is specific, not general, the analysis of an individual young woman in a particular situation. It serves, in other words, to intensify his arrowlike perception into her character. From beginning to end of the novel, Clara is growing, her mind is in a crisis of constant discovery about herself and the world around her. And from her very nature, she is pledged to self-discovery and to action in accordance with what she discovers. Seen from this point, it is she, not Sir Willoughby, who is at the novel's center; Sir Willoughby falls into position as one of the jailors who, like her father, bar the way to right action.

But Clara is not created through analysis alone. There

are times when Meredith is not content with analysis; and
then her perceptions are dramatized in such a way that we
are taken right inside her mind. When this happens Meredith soars into poetry, for poetry is the medium by which
the dramatization is made to occur. The obvious example
is the singularly beautiful passage in which Clara sur-
prises Vernon Whitford asleep beneath the wild cherry
tree.

> She asked the boy where Mr. Whitford was. Crossjay
> pointed very secretly in the direction of the double-blossom
> wild cherry. Coming within gaze of the stem she beheld
> Vernon stretched at length, reading, she supposed; asleep,
> she discovered: his finger in the leaves of a book; and what
> book? She had a curiosity to know the title of the book he
> would read beneath these boughs, and grasping Crossjay's
> hand fast she craned her neck, as one timorous of a fall in
> peeping over chasms, for a glimpse of the page; but imme-
> diately, and still with a bent head, she turned her face to
> where the load of virginal blossom, whiter than summer
> cloud on the sky, showered and drooped and clustered so
> thick as to claim colour and seem, like higher Alpine snows
> in noon-sunlight, a flush of white. From deep to deeper
> heavens of white, her eyes perched and soared. Wonder
> lived in her. Happiness in the beauty of the tree pressed to
> supplant it, and was more mortal and narrower. Reflection
> came, contracting her vision and weighing her to earth.
> Her reflection was: "He must be good who loves to lie and
> sleep beneath the branches of this tree!" She would rather
> have clung to her first impression: wonder so divine, so un-
> bounded, was like soaring into homes of angel-crowded
> space, sweeping through folded and on to folded white
> fountain-bow of wings, in innumerable columns: but the
> thought of it was no recovery of it; she might as well have
> striven to be a child. The sensation of happiness promised
> to be less short-lived in memory, and would have been, had
> not her present disease of the longing for happiness ravaged
> every corner of it for the secret of its existence. The reflec-
> tion took root. "He must be good . . . !" That reflection
> vowed to endure. Poor by comparison with what it dis-
> placed, it presented itself to her as conferring something on
> him, and she would not have had it absent though it robbed
> her.

Passages comparable may be found in Meredith's other novels, in *Beauchamp's Career* especially. Unless we may call them poetry we have no word adequately to describe them. The passage is complex, but the complexity is that of poetry. A perception, "He must be good . . ." with all its implications, has crystallized. We have, in fact, something like a lyric poem in reverse. Such perceptions, so embodied, Meredith reserved mainly for his young women, which is why they are unique in our fiction in their blending of seriousness, ardor, passion, and dedication; and Clara Middleton may stand for them all, since she is queen of them all. It is her presence, side by side with the brilliantly exposed Sir Willoughby and his entourage of witty ladies who function as a kind of *corps de ballet* to the action, that gives *The Egoist* its permanently fascinating subtlety.

Wit and poetry exist side by side, and each irradiates the other. It is this combination that gives Meredith his special place in the novel. In the history of the novel, however, it is the poetry that is important. A mind come suddenly to obscure consciousness of itself, trembling on the verge of half-apprehended self-discovery, can be shown directly only through poetry. Meredith is the first master of this kind of poetry in the English novel, and in this respect he stands behind Henry James, with what Stephen Spender has called his "described poetry," D. H. Lawrence, Virginia Woolf, and later novelists like Elizabeth Bowen.

3

Thomas Hardy's first novel, *Desperate Remedies*, was published in 1871. He was then thirty-one. His career as a novelist ended twenty-five years later, with *Jude the Obscure*. Thereafter his life, right up to his death in 1928, was devoted to poetry, which had been his first love. He turned to the novel primarily because it was the domi

nant literary form of the time; writing novels was a way
of earning a living. It is often said that he had little interest in the novel as an art form, but the statement needs
constant qualification. His outspokenness where sex was
concerned, in *Tess* and *Jude,* made him, in the eyes of his
contemporaries, the English counterpart of the great European novelists, Flaubert, Tolstoi, Zola. But his was an
older art of storytelling than theirs, and perhaps it is on
the word storytelling that the emphasis should fall. Of current theories of realism he was highly critical. He turned
naturally for his standard of reference to the primitive
oral tale: "We story-tellers," he said, "are all Ancient Mar-
iners," and just as so much of his lyric poetry is based on
the rhythms of country dances, country airs, and folk songs,
is a new expression of an ancient music, so behind his novels we feel the shaping presence of the ballads of love,
passion, and betrayal he knew as a boy when he was a
notable fiddler at dances.

Hardy was a provincial, a countryman; indeed, despite
his training as an architect and his wide knowledge of
literature and of the science and philosophy of his age,
almost a naif, a primitive. This differentiates him from
contemporaries like George Eliot and Henry James.
Their work represents "the tone of the center," to use
Arnold's phrase. Hardy is strictly an eccentric. It is in his
provincialism and naivety, one could almost say his uncouthness, that his strength lies. When he leaves the intensely local world he knew to ape the tone of the center
and try to render fashionable life, as in *The Hand of
Ethelberta* (1876), he fails as badly as any novelist. But on
his own ground he is practically unassailable.

In some respects he is like Scott. When he revived the
word Wessex to denote a region of England, he did so in
full consciousness of the historical weight of the name.
Apart from *The Trumpet-Major* (1880), he wrote nothing
that can be called an historical novel, yet his characters,

like Scott's, live in the additional dimension of history; peasants for the most part, they are close to an earth that has changed little over centuries. Most of them as they live in our memory, the principal characters in *Jude* being the great exception, seem to live in a timeless era in which actual historical events and persons have assumed the vagueness and largeness of myth. Like Scott, Hardy was fortunate for his art in being born just as an age was ending. Acutely, painfully conscious of the modern world as he was, he looked back to the past and summed up in his fiction a life that was dying when he was a child, a life cut off from the main stream of national life, more primitive, more pagan. Set George Eliot's renderings of rural life beside Hardy's: hers are generally slightly earlier in time, yet however sequestered the scenes described may be, they strike one as much more modern. The industrial revolution is not far away, nor is the religion that came out of it, nor is eighteenth-century rationalism. The scenes of witchcraft in *The Return of the Native* would be incredible in any Midland village, however remote, in which a Dolly Winthrop lived.

Hardy was attempting something very different from the aims of most novelists. The art of the novelist who sets out to display human beings in the context of social life must be one of constant differentiation and discrimination between characters. But social life as we find it depicted variously in Jane Austen, Thackeray, Trollope, George Eliot, and James, scarcely exists in Hardy. His characters stand in relation to other things, the weather, the seasons, a traditional craft. He sees his characters much as Scott does his, first in their generic aspects; thus, before he is anything else, Giles Winterbourne is the peasant good with trees, Gabriel Oak the good shepherd, Tess the dairymaid. Individuality, as such, is not at all what he is after; what concerns him most in human beings is their response to the deep-rooted passions, above all sexual love.

Intellectually, Hardy was very much an advanced man of his time. That he was a pessimist seems to me to need no proof. But reading his work one can scarcely fail to see him as a soul naturally Christian. This involves no contradiction; as David Cecil has written in *Hardy the Novelist:* "Christian teachers have always said that there was no alternative to Christianity but pessimism, that if Christian doctrine was not true, life was a tragedy. Hardy agreed with them."

He did so because he lived at a time when the intellectual assent to Christianity was probably more difficult than it has ever been, and however much he hoped, in the words of his famous poem, that "it might be so," he could never give Christianity his intellectual assent. Yet while intellectually he was "advanced," emotionally he was a traditionalist. He wrote in a letter in 1915: "You must not think me a hard-headed rationalist for all this. Half my time—particularly when writing verse—I 'believe' (in the modern sense of the word) . . . in spectres, mysterious voices, intuitions, omens, dreams, haunted places, etc. But I do not believe in them in the old sense any more for that." He did not believe because, as G. M. Young says in *Last Essays,* the total effect of Darwin, Mill, Huxley, and Herbert Spencer on their age was to make it "almost impossible for their younger contemporaries to retain the notion of a transcendent, governing Providence." Hardy was the quintessential younger, as George Eliot had been the quintessential strict, contemporary of these scientists and philosophers, and therein lies a considerable part of the difference in their attitudes to life and to their fictional characters. Loss of faith compelled George Eliot to stress, far beyond orthodox Christianity, the individual's responsibility for his actions. For her, the choice between right and wrong was open for every human being to make; the basis of her ethics is the belief in the freedom of the will. But Hardy was scarcely a moralist at all, because in his universe morals were beside the point; between the forces of nature, including therein the forces of his own nature, and man's aspirations there could be no reconciliation; they were eternally opposed, and from the human view the workings of nature must appear hostile and malign.

What Hardy found in the science and philosophy of his day reinforced the findings of his temperament and of his observations of a largely traditional way of life, and his greatness is due to this marriage between his philosophic pessimism and his habit of seeing human behavior in its more abiding aspects. It was not an easy or harmonious marriage, but its tensions were part of its strength. Without the philosophical interpretation of what he saw and felt his work might have approximated in scope to the traditional ballad; but if he had not seen human beings in depth, in their relation to traditional skills, the work and rhythm of the seasons and the force of the great nonrational, instinctual urgencies, he would probably not have been the superior of other novelists of much the same time, Gissing in England and Dreiser in America, who interpreted man according to the deterministic philosophy of the day. They, for all their pity for mankind, do not achieve more than the pathetic; Hardy rises to tragedy, and his tragedy is an arraignment of the nature of the universe as he saw it.

Believing that where man was concerned the very nature of things was malign, he believed also that it was the more malign the more sensitive, the more intelligent, the more finely organized the human being. The only characters in Hardy who need fear no fall are those already down, those who live close to earth without aspirations to rise, the wonderful gallery of peasants whose attitude to existence is unillusioned, accepting, and humorous. These Hardy portrays and records through their speech with a warmth and sympathy equivalent to love. His second novel, the delightful pastoral *Under the Greenwood Tree*

(1872), he devoted to them entirely; elsewhere, they act as the chorus to the tragedy.

If any single novel may be taken as the key to Hardy's mind and art it is probably *The Return of the Native,* his sixth book, published in 1878. A tragic love story, like almost all his fiction, it is extremely simple in plot. Clym Yeobright, who has been a diamond merchant in Paris, comes home to serve his fellow men as teacher and preacher. He falls in love with and marries Eustacia Vye, who has had a secret love affair with Damon Wildeve, the husband of Clym's cousin, Thomasin. Eustacia and Wildeve resume their affair and, after their death by drowning, Thomasin marries Diggory Venn, the traveling raddleman, who has throughout brooded over the action of the novel like a guardian but not always effectual angel. The significant characters are Clym and Eustacia. Clym is the first of Hardy's idealists, the first of what have been called his "prig heroes," a man conscious all the time of what Hardy himself called "the ache of modernism." In a sense, he represents Hardy's own values:

> In Clym Yeobright's face could be dimly seen the typical countenance of the future. Should there be a classic period to art hereafter, its Pheidias may produce such faces. The view of life as a thing to be put up with, replacing that zest for existence which was so intense in early civilizations, must enter so thoroughly into the constitution of the advanced races that its facial expression will become accepted as a new artistic departure. People already feel that a man who lives without disturbing a curve of feature, or setting a mark of mental concern anywhere upon himself, is too far removed from modern perceptiveness to be a modern type. Physically beautiful men—the glory of the race when it was young—are almost an anachronism now; and we may wonder whether, at some time or other, physically beautiful women may not be an anachronism likewise.

Clym, then, is Hardy's modern man. Eustacia, however, is not his modern woman; she is woman as he most characteristically sees her. She has her affinities with Flaubert's Emma Bovary. She is a born romantic, at odds with her environment:

> To be loved to madness—such was her great desire. Love was to her the one cordial which could drive away the eating loneliness of her days. And she seemed to long for the abstraction called passionate love more than for any particular lover.

But Hardy's depiction of her is very different from Flaubert's of Emma. Emma is revealed with cruel exactitude, exposed with the clinical remorselessness of a case history. Eustacia is magnified into a splendid romantic figure. E. M. Forster says in *Aspects of the Novel* that Hardy "conceives his novels from an enormous height." He conceives his great characters from the same height, in the case of Clym by making him a representative of what he considered modern man—and the man of the future—in his most essential qualities, in the case of Eustacia by a richly romantic view of her. There is no implied criticism of her attitudes, such as is felt throughout in Flaubert's rendering of Emma. She is too big for that, and all Hardy's powers of evocation are showered upon her:

> Eustacia Vye was the raw material of a divinity. On Olympus she would have done well with a little preparation. She had the passions and instincts which make a model goddess, that is, those which make not quite a model woman. Had it been possible for the earth and mankind to be entirely in her grasp for a while, had she handled the distaff, the spindle, and the shears at her own free will, few in the world would have noticed the change of government. There would have been the same inequality of lot, the same heaping up of favours here, of contumely there, the same generosity before justice, the same perpetual dilemmas, the same captious alternation of caresses and blows that we endure now. . . .
>
> She had Pagan eyes, full of nocturnal mysteries, and their light, as it came and went, and came again, was partially hampered by their oppressive lids and lashes; and of these

the under lid was much fuller than it usually is with English women. This enabled her to indulge in reverie without seeming to do so: she might have been believed capable of sleeping without closing them up. Assuming that the souls of men and women were visible essences, you could fancy the colour of Eustacia's soul to be flame-like. The sparks from it that rose into her dark pupils gave the same impression. . . .

Her presence brought memories of such things as Bourbon roses, rubies, and tropical midnights; her moods recalled lotus-eaters and the march in *Athalie*; her motions, the ebb and flow of the sea; her voice, the viola . . .

The passage reminds us that Pater had published *The Renaissance* five years before. The wonder is that so highly romantic and mannered a piece of writing could have been successfully woven into the texture of the novel. Yet it is, and one can think of no other English novelist who could have got away with it. One thing, however, is clear: the woman so described could not possibly be a fit wife for the single-minded idealist who "had a conviction that the want of most men was knowledge of a sort which brings wisdom rather than affluence," and who, wishing "to raise the class at the expense of the individuals rather than the individuals at the expense of the class," "was ready at once to be the first unit sacrificed." And indeed Eustacia marries Clym because she cannot *not* believe that he will return to Paris, taking her with him; when his eyesight fails as a result of his studies and he takes up furze cutting rather than endure idleness, she again becomes Wildeve's mistress, as she was before her marriage.

But, as *The Return of the Native* further shows, there is another way in which Hardy conceives his novels and their tragic characters from an enormous height. The anthologists of English prose have done him no service by snipping off from the book the description of Egdon Heath with which it opens and isolating it as a purple passage. The heath is not just so much scenic backcloth to the action, it

is all-pervasive; without it, the novel would be unimagin-
able, for the heath provides it with the especial dimension
in which it has its being. The heath holds the action of the
novel and its characters as though in the hollow of the
hand. It does not matter in the least that, living on Egdon,
Eustacia dreams of Paris; that is part of her tragic destiny.
The function of the heath in the novel is to describe, as
carefully and thoroughly as Hardy can, the real circumstances in which man lives. What the individual man may
feel about those circumstances is irrelevant, for he does
not thereby escape them. The heath, one might say, is an
extended image of the nature of which man is part, in
which he is caught, which conditions his very being, and
which cares nothing for him. His life in relation to it is as
ephemeral as the bonfires the peasants make of the heath
furze.

This ephemerality of man, the insignificance of his
being, is brought out time and again in *The Return of the
Native,* generally by reference to the brooding permanence
of the vast heath. "This obscure, obsolete, superseded
country" is the world of nature under the aspect of time,
time geological and historical alike. Man has scarcely
scratched its surface. It has its own life, which is man's
only when he is content to be lowly and unassuming like
the furze cutters who live off it. Hardy shows us the heath
through all the seasons of the year and over immeasurably
greater stretches of time. At times it "seemed to belong
to the ancient world of the carboniferous period, when the
forms of plants were few, and of the fern kind; when there
was neither bud nor blossom, nothing but a monotonous
extent of leafage, amid which no bird sang."

Such is the heath in what may be called its geological
aspect. But it has another:

The month of March arrived, and the heath showed its
first faint signs of awakening from winter trance. The awakening was almost feline in its stealthiness. The pool outside

the bank by Eustacia's dwelling, which seemed as dead and
desolate as ever to an observer who moved and made noises
in his observation, would gradually disclose a state of great
animation when silently watched awhile. A timid, animal
world had come to life for the season. Little tadpoles and
efts began to bubble up through the water, and to race
along beneath it; toads made noises like very young ducks,
and advanced to the margin in twos and threes; overhead,
bumble-bees flew hither and thither in the thickening light,
their drone coming and going like the sound of a gong.

The secret life of the heath Hardy describes again and
again, with all the powers of eye and ear for nature in
which he is unrivaled among our novelists. The human
inhabitants of the heath he sees almost from an anthro-
pologist's point of view, or the specialist's in comparative
religion. When the peasants dance in August, time, as it
were, is telescoped; the centuries slip by; they behave as
their ancient ancestors did. "For the time Paganism was
revived in their hearts, the pride of life was all in all, and
they adored none other than themselves." Christian Cantle,
Granfer Cantle, Timothy Fairway, Sam the turf cutter,
and the rest are as much a part of nature, of the life
of the heath, as the toads in March that make noises like
very young ducks. Not so Clym, Eustacia, Thomasin, and
Wildeve; these are cut off from nature, and that they are
cut off means that they are undone, though in the case of
Thomasin, Hardy altered his original conclusion of the
novel to provide her with a happy ending.

Hardy's view of life, then, was cosmic. This means that
his tragic novels exist always on two planes, the plane of
design and the plane of plot. As a plotter he was often
defective. Sometimes—and then it seems the result of in-
competence—he stumbles because the course of the action
suddenly becomes implausible, as when Tess kills Alec
d'Urberville with the bread knife, an implausibility under-
lined by the failure in tact which allows him to describe
the blood seeping through the floor to the ceiling below

in the likeness of "a gigantic ace of hearts." His incursions into melodrama are similar signs of a failure in tact; the final arrest of Tess at Stonehenge is an instance. It just fails to come off; the grandiose conception is somehow blurred.

But Hardy's chief weakness in plot arises from his view of causality. He is intent to show that the stars in their courses fight against the aspiring, the man or woman who would rise above the common lot through greatness of spirit, of ambition, or passion. Here his problem was difficult indeed, and it is not surprising he never solved it. For the universe itself to become suddenly hostile to man could only be shown through the working of what may be called the freak coincidence. It is silly to blame Hardy for the emphasis he places on coincidence; simply, he believed in coincidence. To take an example from *The Return of the Native,* it is part of the conspiracy of things against the exceptional man that Clym's mother should visit Eustacia, in order to make the peace between them, at the very time that Eustacia is entertaining Wildeve; it is part of nature's enmity that she should be bitten by the snake on her way home. But Hardy, as though not wholly convinced himself, does not know where to stop. He spoils his case by overstatement; when we learn later that Eustacia's letter to Clym has not been delivered because the messenger forgot to post it, we begin to protest. We begin to feel that the author has aligned himself with the nature of things against his characters, that he is manipulating fate against them.

Hardy's worst failure here is certainly "Father Time's" killing of Sue's children in *Jude,* and his suicide: "Done because we are too menny." When we first meet "Father Time" in the train he is a memorable and poetic conception, but increasingly he becomes the author's mouthpiece; and then we realize he is the good little child of sentimental Victorian fiction, who speaks wisdom in his innocence, turned upside down. He too is a sentimental creation, and made the less convincing because, according to the doctor, he is a boy "of a sort unknown in the last generation . . . the beginning of the coming universal wish not to live." The philosophical explanation high-lights the sentimentality; and when four pages on Jude quotes Aeschylus: "Things are as they are, and will be brought to their destined issue," we feel that, in this instance, the issue is being brought about not because it is in the nature of things but because Hardy wishes it to be so. It is the one turn of the screw too many.

But these failures in the management of his plots matter less in Hardy than they would in any other novelist; they are botches, but they do not ruin the work, because though large enough when measured in terms of plot they are small when seen against the vastness and the strength of the design behind the plot. Plot in Hardy is his attempt to express the significance of the great design in purely human terms. Failure was almost inescapable, for Hardy, as a man of his time and place, had no completely adequate myth through which his view of the nature of things could be bodied forth.

But the greatness of conception, the sense of cosmic scope behind the action, put Hardy's novels apart from any other fiction written in England in the nineteenth century and send us naturally for our comparisons to works of great poetry. *The Return of the Native* was the first novel in which he achieved the tragic level, and it could be argued that it is his finest. In no other does the setting of the natural world so dominate the characters. Perhaps the dichotomy between the human being and the nature in which he lives is too acute in this novel; in the tragic works that follow, *The Mayor of Casterbridge* (1886), *Tess of the d'Urbervilles* (1891), and *Jude the Obscure* (1895), one has the feeling that the tragic heroes and heroines more and more take nature into themselves, and to this extent the importance of the natural setting as something apart from man diminishes.

As a creator of character Hardy worked in a way diametrically opposite to George Eliot's. If she is a psychological novelist, then Hardy is the reverse. When he attempts analysis he generally succeeds only in diminishing the stature of his tragic figures, as with Clym and "Father Time," for as a rule his analysis is inadequate. Sometimes, as with Sue in *Jude the Obscure,* he cannot himself adequately "explain" his character's motives. In other words, subtle and complex though she is, she has been instantly apprehended; she has, like all Hardy's great tragic characters, the authority, only dimly and half apprehended, of a force of nature.

Hardy's characters, then, tend to be differentiated only in the great emotional situation, and then their triumphant life comes from the poetry that invests them. The most obvious instance of this is Bathsheba Everdene's realization in the fir plantation at night of the presence of Sergeant Troy, in *Far from the Madding Crowd* (1874), and the miraculous description of Troy's swordplay which follows a little later:

> He flourished the sword by way of introduction number two, and the next thing of which she was conscious was that the point and blade of the sword were darting with a gleam towards her left side, just above her hip; then of their reappearance on her right side, emerging as it were from between her ribs, having apparently passed through her body. The third item of consciousness was that of seeing the same sword, perfectly clean and free from blood held vertically in Troy's hand (in the position technically called "recover swords"). All was as quick as electricity . . .
> In an instant the atmosphere was transformed to Bathsheba's eyes. Beams of light caught from the low sun's rays, above, around, in front of her, well-nigh shut out earth and heaven—all emitted in the marvellous evolutions of Troy's reflecting blade, which seemed everywhere at once, and yet nowhere specially. These circling gleams were accompanied

by a keen rush that was almost a whistling—also springing from all sides of her at once. In short, she was enclosed in a firmament of light, and of sharp hisses, resembling a sky-full of meteors close at hand.

Never since the broadsword became the national weapon had there been more dexterity shown in its management than by the hands of Sergeant Troy, and never had he been in such splendid temper for the performance as now in the evening sunshine among the ferns with Bathsheba. It may safely be asserted with regard to the closeness of his cuts, that had it been possible for the edge of the sword to leave in the air a permanent substance wherever it flew past, the space left untouched would have been almost a mould of Bathsheba's figure.

After that, there is no necessity for analysis; Bathsheba's sudden subjugation to Troy, her complete possession by him, is shown in the most striking way possible; she is as much his victim, as helpless before him, as if she had really met him in the field of battle.

Poetry is the constant attendant of Hardy's tragic characters. It is not an intellectual poetry, like Meredith's; it is much more primitive and magical, and always it heightens the significance of the characters and the reader's consciousness of their tragic stature. And, as Hardy moves away, as it were, from the norm of prose intention as traditionally conceived, so he moves his novels more and more out of the realm in which they may be criticized from the prose point of view. In some respects, his simplest and most successful tragic novel is *The Mayor of Casterbridge*. Henchard is his grandest hero, as Tess is his most moving heroine, and much of Henchard's tragic greatness comes from his impercipience. He contains all nature within himself, as a truly great bull might be described as doing. This almost animal impercipience removes him far away from the tragic heroes of Shakespeare, and yet, in one respect at any rate, it is Macbeth with whom we have to compare him. External nature fights against Henchard, but it is nature interpreted by superstition, and it is the poetic quality of the whole that makes the superstition credible. The poetry heightens and deepens our sense of Henchard's tragic fate. Two instances of this poetry may be quoted: the moment when his wedding present to Elizabeth Jane is discovered, "a new bird-cage, shrouded in newspaper, and at the bottom of the cage a little ball of feathers—the dead body of a goldfinch"; and the scene in which Henchard sees the dead body, "lying stiff and stark upon the surface of the stream":

> In the circular current imparted by the central flow the form was brought forward, till it passed under his eyes; and then he perceived with a sense of horror that it was *himself*. Not a man somewhat resembling him, but one in all respects his counterpart, his actual double, was floating as if dead in Ten Hatches Hole.

To match the first for pathos and the second for the twitch of horror felt along the nerve one has to go back to Webster.

Sometimes the poetry is the poetry of attendant and pervasive circumstances. An example of this is the description—but it is more than description, it is setting—of the Valley of the Great Dairies in *Tess of the d'Urbervilles*, the setting to Tess's meeting and falling in love with Angel Clare. Yet whatever the kind may be, the poetry and the imagery through which it is rendered are always precise, not merely with the scrupulous accuracy of a poet like Clare but with the insight, the regard for minute particulars and for the pattern which contains them, of Gerard Manley Hopkins. So, reading Hardy, one is often struck with the strangeness that characterizes something seen and rendered as it were for the first time, with the innocent eye; a small instance is the road that is seen as bisecting Egdon Heath "like the parting-line on a head of black hair." But the accuracy is no less when the object rendered is of much greater moment. Thus Hardy describes Tess as having been "caught during her days of immaturity like a bird in a springe." In another novelist this could be a sentimental cliché. It is not in Hardy. As John Holloway says in his book *The Victorian Sage*, it is "an exact and insistent image to remind us that when Tess was seduced at night in the wood, her experience really was like that of an animal caught in a trap—as might have happened in the very same place." The image goes to the heart of Tess's situation. She is caught in tragedy because she is animal, but if she had been merely animal, or if she had been Retty Priddle or Izz Huett, there would have been no tragedy.

Jude the Obscure stands somewhat apart from the rest of Hardy's fiction. It is his one attempt to write a novel strictly of his own time; we remember, reading it, that he was twelve years younger than Ibsen and nine years older than Strindberg. Jude, we are to understand, is a sensualist and a man who, at crucial times in his life, seeks escape in drink. But as we see him under these aspects in the novel he is certainly not more than *l'homme moyen sensuel*; neither his sexual nor his drinking exploits are anything out of the ordinary, and they could have had little effect on the course of his life if he had been in fact *l'homme moyen sensuel*. His tragedy lies in that he is not. What brings him down are the intellectual ambitions beyond his station, his dream of the student's life at Christminster. The common-sense advice to a man in his station, with his aspirations, is the Master of Biblioll's: ". . . judging from your description of yourself as a working man, I venture to think that you will have a much better chance of success in life by remaining in your own sphere and sticking to your trade than by adopting any other course." Had he taken the Master's advice, he might have indulged in drink and fornication far beyond anything suggested in the novel with relative impunity. The central tragedy of Jude is one of unfulfilled aims, aims, moreover, almost impossible of fulfillment at the time in which he lived, even though he had had the purity and self-control of a saint. His tragedy may be paralleled by that of the cockney workman Gilbert Grail in Gissing's *Thyrza,* which had appeared eight years before. Indeed, *Jude* should probably be considered in relation to Gissing's novels; as in them, we are conscious—admittedly for the first time in Hardy—of a strong undercurrent of what can only be called class consciousness.

It does not appear in the earlier novels because there there was no need for it; Hardy was describing events in a world still traditional. But in *Jude,* by making his tragic hero a working-class intellectual, he removed his action out of the values of Wessex altogether. He could do no other, for he had taken his theme and his hero from a strictly contemporary world, and Jude is a man who must be defeated by the contemporary world; his morbid sensibility is "planted" for us in the second chapter of the novel. Everyone has noticed the way in which the rich rustic chorus has disappeared in *Jude* (with the exceptions of Jude's aunt and the widow Edlin) and how thin, by comparison with *The Return of the Native* and *Tess,* the whole texture of the writing, of the world described, and the links that bind men to nature and the nature of things, has become. There is no place in *Jude* for the great heroic or poetic scenes such as Troy's swordplay and Gabriel Oak's fight to cover the ricks during the great storm in *Far from the Madding Crowd,* the remarkable episode of Wildeve and the raddleman gambling on the heath at night by the light of glowworms in *The Return of the Native,* or the wonderful opening of *The Mayor of Casterbridge.* All this represents an enormous loss, precisely where Hardy was strongest; but they had to go, for they stand for that way of life from which Jude and Sue Bridehead, by virtue of being working-class intellectuals, are totally uprooted.

These great poetic and heroic scenes are exactly what compose the design that lies behind Hardy's other novels and gives them their sense of timelessness. One can't say that design, as opposed to plot, is absent from *Jude,* but it is much shrunken; it has become an ironical symbolism: Arabella captures Jude first by throwing the boar's pizzle at him; when she marries him a second time, at the end of the novel, they are living above her father's pork shop. Again, as Jude passes from belief to unbelief, Sue progresses in the opposite direction. The effect of this shrinkage in design is to throw the emphasis precisely where Hardy is always weakest, his manipulation of the plot. Simply because Hardy is working much more nearly at the level of realism in *Jude,* one might say at Gissing's level, improbabilities become increasingly serious. The most explicit statement of Hardy's view of the tragic situation of man, *Jude* suffers artistically from its explicitness.

Nevertheless, *Jude* is a most powerful and impressive novel, and part of its power and impressiveness certainly derives from Hardy's very refusal to employ his great poetic qualities in it. These may, at times, mitigate or at least make more acceptable the tragic horror, but in *Jude* everything is subordinated to the depiction of the increasingly tragic situation of Jude and Sue. They are described from a much closer range than is usual with Hardy. Jude is the characteristic Hardy hero—hypersensitive, high-principled, essentially "soft-minded," to use William James's term—made actual in a Victorian working man; we know him in much more detail than we do Clym Yeobright or Angel Clare. But Sue Bridehead is a departure for Hardy. She is the opposite of Eustacia Vye, Bathsheba Everdene, and Tess not merely in the fact that she is an intellectual. But she is much more than Hardy's version of the "New

Woman," and she utterly transcends Gissing's versions of that creature. His Rhoda Nunn in *The Odd Woman* is now an oddity of history. But Sue survives because of her ambiguity, her sexual ambivalence, which she is aware of all the time and cannot quite understand:

> "At first I did not love you, Jude; that I own. When I first knew you I merely wanted you to love me. I did not exactly flirt with you; but that inborn craving which undermines some women's morals almost more than unbridled passion—the craving to attract and captivate, regardless of the injury it may do the man—was in me; and when I found I had caught you, I was frightened."

Perhaps the key to her is in Hardy's word "intellectualized." The passage, during the account of her leaving her husband Phillotson, where, ever reasonable, she quotes J. S. Mill and he replies, "What do I care about J. S. Mill! I only want to lead a quiet life!" has amused many critics, but it is absolutely right in character and tone. The reference to Mill at that particular juncture—and allowance having been made for the date of the action, it could just as well have been Freud or Lawrence—exposes her completely. Sue is a most subtle delineation of a not uncommon type of woman in the modern world, and it is significant that the only writer on Hardy who has fully understood his achievement in creating her is D. H. Lawrence.

There will probably always be those for whom Hardy is, in Henry James's phrase, "the good little Thomas Hardy." His faults are glaring enough. His plots creak. His villains have stepped off the boards of a barnstorming company peddling melodrama. His prose is often clumsy to the point of uncouthness. Yet the true index of Hardy's stature is that he is almost the only tragic novelist in our literature and that when we consider him we have ultimately to do so in relation to Shakespeare and Webster and to the Greek dramatists. His influence has been at once enormous and slight. After his discovery of Wessex a host of minor novelists opened up regions throughout the length and breadth of England and showed us man against an ancient soil; of them all the only one who has any interest for us today is perhaps Eden Phillpotts. In many ways the later novelist most akin to Hardy is D. H. Lawrence.

6

THE NOVEL FROM 1881
TO 1914

1

By the 1880's the mutation that had occurred in the novel with George Eliot and Meredith had become dominant. Novelists were conscious of a split in fiction between the old and the new, and while significant novels of the older type continued to be written—and indeed still are—they had more and more the appearance of throwbacks to the past. An indication of this consciousness of the split is Henry James's essay "The Art of Fiction," published in 1884, and if one wanted to pin-point the change in its clearest terms one could scarcely do better than quote his words on Trollope:

> Certain accomplished novelists have a habit of giving themselves away which must often bring tears to the eyes of people who take their fiction seriously. I was lately struck, in reading over many pages of Anthony Trollope, with his want of discretion in this particular. In a digression, a parenthesis or an aside, he concedes to the reader that he and this trusting friend are only "making believe." He admits that the events he narrates have not really happened, and that he can give his narrative any turn the reader may like best. Such a betrayal of a sacred office seems to me, I confess, a terrible crime; it is what I mean by the attitude of apology, and it shocks me every whit as much in Trollope as it would have shocked me in Gibbon or Macaulay.

James's criticism is not simply that of the conscious craftsman on work that seems to him botched. When he speaks of the novelist's calling as "a sacred office" he means what he says. He has just been describing the novel as history: "That is the only general description (which does it justice) that we may give the novel." And he follows the passage quoted above with the clinching statement that Trollope's habit of confessing to make believe, his attitude of apology where his art is concerned, "implies that the novelist is less occupied in looking for the truth than the historian, and in doing so it deprives him at a stroke of all his standing-room."

James is making a claim for the novelist not exactly new —in her own way George Eliot would have subscribed to it—but making it with a calmness of assertion and a confidence that show that for him it was a truth scarcely needing proof. He is saying, in effect, much what Wyndham Lewis has said in *The Writer and the Absolute*:

> . . . there is in all those arts which parallel nature something like a law obliging the artist to a fanatical scrupulosity, as it were a physical incapacity to depart from nature's truths in exchange for any other. This is as inescapable as the requirements of geometry. The writer Flaubert as much as the painter Chardin provides an impressive illustration of this law. . . . The truth of the great novelists is different from and more personal, certainly, than that of the contemporary "scientific" historian. But in any case a meticulous fidelity to life is of its essence. To ask it to falsify nature would be to destroy it.

This law of "fanatical scrupulosity," however, is operative only when the novelist sees himself as an artist, a creator of an imitation world made in some sense with regard to objective truth. The question is not one of "realism" in any narrow interpretation of the word. It is rather that the novelist must in effect be able to say, whatever the situation he has chosen to describe, "Given the nature of man. then my situation, through the characters enacting

it, can resolve itself only in this way." A novelist like
Stevenson, for example, whose material is mainly such as
we usually consider romantic, in this respect conforms to
the law of fanatical scrupulosity no less than James or
George Moore.

Stevenson is a relevant figure here, for it was with him
that James debated in 1885 the nature of the novel and
the function of the novelist. When he wrote his "Humble
Remonstrance" Stevenson was opposed to realism as it
found expression in the practice of Zola. "The root of the
whole matter," he said, "is that a novel is not a transcript
of life, to be judged by its exactitude; but a simplification
of some side or point of life, to stand or fall by its significant simplicity." With this James had no difficulty in agree-
ing. Of course, art, in which the novel is included, is a
simplification. So is the history of the historian. But just
as the work of history must be judged by its adequacy to
the raw material of its subject matter, so, simplification
though it is, the novel must be judged by how far it is
successful in standing for life itself, or of that area of life
the novelist has concerned himself with. A good novel is
untrue only in the sense that the events described in it
have not actually happened. If the novel is successful
one must feel that if they were to happen they would do
so precisely as the novelist says. The appeal, in other words,
is to our knowledge of the nature of man and of the nature
of his relations with his fellows, and this must be so however great or however limited the ambition the novelist
has set himself, whether he is consciously aiming at pro-
fundity or intent merely on entertaining his readers in a
civilized manner.

It was probably not accidental that this heightened,
more serious conception of the novel as art should have
triumphed in the eighties, for the split between the old
novel and the new coincided with a cultural revolution.
Forster's Education Acts of 1870 provided compulsory

primary education for all, and the result, over the years, was an enormous increase in the reading public. But the gap between the best education and the worst was so great that the highbrow-lowbrow dichotomy with which we are now wearisomely familiar was inevitable. Before 1870, the poor man who strove to learn to read and, having done so, went on to read beyond the newspapers, did so because he was to some degree a superior man. To be able to read was a key to enfranchisement; it opened the door to a better position as a tradesman or to success in business; it was essential to the politically minded working man who dreamed of power for his class; and for a few rare disinterested spirits it offered the freedom of a culture traditionally an upper-class preserve. But whatever the motive for learning to read, the Victorian working man, by and large, accepted the cultural standards of classes higher in the social scale. After 1870 this was no longer necessarily so. The provision of reading matter for a semiliterate public became the concern of a vast industry which set its own standards, standards which had nothing to do with literary and artistic standards as normally understood. Indeed, the notion of a single standard ceased practically to exist, and perhaps this was inevitable, for when you give a semiliterate person the vote and persuade him that thereby he is an arbiter of his country's destinies, it is not easy at the same time to convince him that he is not also the arbiter of what is excellent in art; there is a natural tendency for every man to believe that what he prefers must be the best.

From the 1880's onwards, when the results of the Act of 1870 were making themselves manifest, we are faced with a situation in the novel that scarcely existed at any time before. Certainly until 1939 more and more novels were published each year, but the great majority of these have had no pretensions to being literature. Fiction has become stratified in a way it was not in the mid-Victorian period. It was the great strength of the nineteenth-century novel that all who read could read it. Admittedly, the reading public of 1853 was much smaller than today, but what there was Dickens or Thackeray could command. Now, we have not one but many publics, some of them existing in almost complete isolation from the others. Since Trollope, it is unlikely that any single novelist has captured them all, though many excellent novelists, from Wells to Graham Greene, have captured several of them. What is important, however, is the effect of this stratification of fiction on novelists themselves. There has been, certainly, a feeling of alienation from, in some authors a complete disregard of, the public as a sort of irresponsible monster. Stevenson, an author with a large popular following, felt it. And what is significant is the part the conception of the novelist as artist plays in it. The notion of the artist as a dedicated man is very recent; it comes from the Romantic poets and its holy scripture in English is Shelley's *A Defence of Poetry*. The artist, so runs the claim, is responsible to himself and to no one else. You must take him or leave him. But when the public begins to leave him, or perhaps never finds him, then for the artist this modern conception of art has an added value: it justifies him in his own eyes; it gives him dignity and grandeur—in a word, the sense of glory—while he pursues his lonely labors which, it seems at the time, no one wants. Without such a sustaining belief, it is difficult to see how the great "minority" writers, James, Conrad, and Joyce, could have gone on writing.

Since the 1880's, probably a majority of significant novelists have tended to see themselves as apart from the public, opposed to what they have assumed to be its prejudices, and in their own minds at least always in advance of it, and this despite the fortunes it may have bestowed on them. The 1890's witnessed the triumph of the novelist as conscious artist because the period provided the circumstances which made it possible for him to behave as one. These circumstances grew out of the political and economic trends of the time. One of the latter, limited though its significance may seem when set against Forster's Education Acts, had consequences of great importance to the novel. During the eighties the traditional three-volume novel was finally displaced by the one-volume novel, that is, the normal length of a work of fiction was cut by almost two thirds. The change was not sudden, but it was the outcome, in a sense, of a struggle between two different reading publics and the middlemen who catered for them, between the raiiway bookstalls and the old established circulating libraries. In the end, the railway bookstalls won.

For some novelists who were in mid-career when it became effective, the change was disastrous; Gissing, for one, never succeeded in adapting himself to the much shorter length. Of itself it would have been enough to kill the huge sprawling novel of the Victorians; the loss is obvious if we think of *David Copperfield, Vanity Fair,* and *Middlemarch.* When we come to the secondary writers, however, it is a different matter. All but the very greatest of Victorian novels, and some of them, suffer from excessive length, from the presence of what Henry James, in another connection, called *remplissage,* rubble shoved in to fill up. The English novel in the nineteenth century had been like a hold-all into which anything could be stuffed. The one-volume novel imposed upon the novelist the necessity for a much more rigorous selection of incident and material. It was this, together with the demands of new reading publics, that led to the breakdown of the Victorian novel into the categories of fiction that we know today however we may describe them—the "straight" novel, the psychological novel, the novel of adventure, the detective novel, the thriller, the woman's romance. Where the very great were concerned, this was probably an impoverishment, but the new length of the novel was itself certainly a powerful aid to those writers, like Stevenson, James,

George Moore, Conrad, and Bennett, whose view of the novel was of an autonomous work consciously shaped.

2

The greatest figure among the generation of novelists who came to maturity during the eighties—Stevenson, Gissing, and Moore were among them—remains Henry James. Born in New York in 1843, he was the oldest of them all and, except for Moore, outlived them. He was a very prolific writer, but his pre-eminence is not due simply to that, nor even to his deeper insight into the human situation than theirs. Dying in 1916, he appears still in many ways our contemporary, the greatest of our contemporaries. We read him today as a modern novelist in a sense that Stevenson, Gissing, and Moore were not, and we do so because, for better or for worse, more than anyone else he made what seems to be the specifically modern novel. Describing Flaubert as a man who "was born a novelist, grew up, lived, died a novelist, breathing, feeling, thinking, speaking, performing every action of his life, only as that votary," he described himself. One might say that for him life itself existed for the novel; and we see the fruits of this obsession with his art not in his fiction alone but also in the Notebooks he kept all his life, in his letters, and in the great prefaces—those fascinating, gnomic, tantalizing discussions of the bases of his fiction and the technical problems it presented to him—to the individual volumes of his collected works that he composed towards the end of his career. We know James as a novelist better than any other apart from Flaubert, and in the history of the English novel James holds a position analogous to Flaubert's in the French; both strove to give the novel the aesthetic intensity of a great poem or a great painting.

James, however, if not an Englishman—he was not naturalized until 1915, the year before his death—was at any rate an Anglo-Saxon, and his fiction is as ethical in its intentions as it is aesthetic. These two aspects of his art cannot be separated.

He was from the beginning an outsider in a very special sense. His father, the son of an Ulster immigrant who was a self-made millionaire, was a philosopher who believed that conventional education made for standardization and that children should be submitted to as many influences as possible. The young James found himself at school in turn at Albany, New York, London, Paris, Geneva, Boulogne, and Bonn before going to the Harvard Law School. Rootlessness was thrust upon him; he was conditioned to the role of spectator. At the same time, he had a longing for a settled society ordered with rank and ceremony such as the United States could not offer him; he found it in England but still remained in his own eyes an outsider. In England, where he settled in 1876, he moved much in society and was a great diner-out; but as we see from the Notebooks, his dining out represented for him so many forays into enemy territory, plundering expeditions from which he would return with the germ of a story, the vague suggestion for a novel, captured from the conversation of others.

Something more must be said about his father. In England in 1844, he was visited by what was known in the James family as "the vastation." Sitting alone after dinner, he was seized by "a perfectly insane and abject terror, without ostensible cause, and only to be accounted for, to my perplexed imagination, by some damned shape squatting invisible to me within the precincts of the room, and raying out from his fetid personality influences fatal to life." The terror lasted an hour and reduced him to "almost helpless infancy." More than twenty years later, Henry's elder brother William, the philosopher, experienced a similar attack. "Drained of self-confidence and the will to live, he suffered hallucinations and was for some years familiar with thoughts of suicide and insanity." What he underwent, it has been said, was not only a "psychological seizure" but a "spiritual crisis." It was from his analysis of the seizure and the crisis that *The Varieties of Religious Experience* was born.

For the James family, then, evil was not an abstract quality but something known, painfully, at first hand, and the sense of evil is powerfully implicit in Henry James's work, felt sometimes as the corruption of innocence, as in his most popular story, *The Turn of the Screw,* and sometimes as "the black and merciless things that are behind great possessions." It is hardly too much to say that the greater part of his significant work is a dramatization of the conflict between good and evil.

James's range as a novelist was considerably greater than one might guess either from his admirers or from his detractors. But from beginning to end two themes are dominant, though they are far from being his only ones. The first is what he himself called the "international subject," which meant in effect the relationship between America and Americans on the one hand and Europe and Europeans on the other. For James, the theme was one from which the American writer could scarcely escape; it was part of the "complex fate" of being an American writer. "The burden," he said, "is necessarily greater for an American—for he *must* deal, more or less, even if only by implication, with Europe, whereas no European is obliged to deal in the least with America." The other dominant theme is related to this; it is that of the innocent, eager for life, corrupted or despoiled by the sophisticated, in whom the good things sought by the innocent appear to reside. In practice in James's fiction, the innocent tend to be American, their exploiters European. The two themes come together in his first novel *Roderick Hudson, The*

Portrait of a Lady, The Wings of the Dove, and *The Golden Bowl,* while *The Ambassadors* is a variant on them.

The Portrait of a Lady (1881), James's first great novel, is still considered by some critics his best. "The idea of the whole thing," he wrote in his Notebooks while at work on the novel, "is that the poor girl, who has dreamed of freedom and nobleness, who has done, as she believes, a generous, natural, clear-sighted thing, finds herself in reality ground in the very mill of the conventional." Most of James's novels and stories had their germ in a situation presented to him in conversation or picked up in the course of his reading; they existed in the beginning in the form of a tiny, often fragmentary anecdote. In his Notebook entry for Christmas Eve, 1893, he sets down a "little history" "related to me last night at dinner at Lady Lindsay's, by Mrs. Anstruther-Thompson. It is a small and ugly matter—but there is distinctly in it, I should judge, the subject of a little tale—a little social and psychological picture." As we read on we realize we have the genesis of *The Spoils of Poynton* (1897). *The Portrait of a Lady* began in a different way. The germ consisted, he tells us in the preface, "altogether in the sense of a single character, the character and aspect of a particular engaging young woman, to which all the usual elements of a 'subject,' certainly of a setting, were to need to be super-added . . . the conception of a certain young woman affronting her destiny." For the particular young woman he almost certainly went back to the memories of his adored cousin, Minny Temple, who died at the age of twenty-four.

The figure of Minny Temple was a most potent symbol in James's life, the symbol of youth and of all that was fine and candid, all that responded most ardently and generously to the promise of life and measured its own demands from life according to its own capacity for experience and greatly doing. Above all, perhaps, it was the symbol of something essentially American. This may not be easy to understand now; as we meet Isabel Archer, the Minny Temple figure of *The Portrait of a Lady*, she falls naturally into the same company of young women in fiction as Jane Austen's Elizabeth Bennet and Emma Wood-house, George Eliot's Gwendolen Harleth, and Meredith's Clara Middleton, and those names define her quality, her sense of the value of herself. But wherein is the American-ness? It can be most easily realized by thinking of Trol-lope's representations of American women, of Mrs. Hurtle, for example, in *The Way We Live Now*. For Trollope, Mrs. Hurtle is frightening in the freedom she claims for herself: "she had shot a man through the head somewhere in Oregon." One doesn't quite see Henry James's heroines doing that, but they are free spirits in a way that more or less contemporary English heroines are not; freedom is something they are born to, a condition of their being, as it is not, for instance, of Clara Middleton's, to say nothing of Trollope's young women. They are the product of an attitude towards woman different from the English Vic-torians'.

When Isabel Archer is brought to England by her Aunt Touchett, she has already refused the rich American busi-nessman Caspar Goodwood, and this itself is a sign that she is a free spirit; poor, she has rejected a fortune, and Goodwood loves her and is a good man. But it is not in her nature to play for safety. "She spent half her time thinking of beauty and bravery and magnanimity; she had a fixed determination to regard the world as a place of brightness, of free expansion, of irresistible action . . . She had an infinite hope that she would never do anything wrong." At the country house of the Touchetts, American bankers long resident in England but still consciously American, she meets Lord Warburton, who falls in love with her. Warburton is presented as an admirable figure, the English aristocrat at his best, a Radical in politics through sheer *noblesse oblige*. He proposes, and Isabel refuses him; why she scarcely knows; but she knows she must find her own place in the world and Warburton's is not hers. To Mrs. Touchett, her refusal of Warburton is freakish, but Mr. Touchett and his son Ralph understand. Isabel delights them, and it is Ralph who persuades his father to leave her a fortune. "I call people rich," he says, "when they're able to meet the requirements of their imagination." It seems to him a moral duty to enable Isabel to meet hers.

Actually, it is Isabel's undoing. James sees her as clearly as Jane Austen does Emma Woodhouse, though he does not see her satirically:

> Altogether, with her meagre knowledge, her inflated ideals, her confidence at once innocent and dogmatic, her temper at once exacting and indulgent, her mixture of curiosity and fastidiousness, of vivacity and indifference, her desire to look very well and to be if possible even better, her determination to see, to try, to know, her combination of the delicate desultory flame-like spirit and the eager and personal creature of conditions: she would be an easy victim of scientific criticism: if she were not intended to awaken on the reader's part an impulse more tender and more purely expectant.

Her very qualities of ardor of spirit and innocence of the world make her a born victim. She meets Mme. Merle, a woman of the world, and Gilbert Osmond, an expatriate American living in Florence in pursuit of the beautiful. She is captivated by Osmond's life of apparent disinterestedness, of seeming dedication to art. She marries him, but the hideous irony is that Osmond has married her only to get her fortune, to provide Pansy, his daughter by Mme. Merle, with a dowry. They live in Rome, in a palace, and as Isabel reflects one night:

> It was the house of darkness, the house of dumbness, the house of suffocation. Osmond's beautiful mind gave it neither light nor air; Osmond's beautiful mind indeed seemed to peep down from a small high window and mock at her.

Of course it had not been physical suffering; for physical suffering there might have been a remedy. She could come and go; she had her liberty; her husband was perfectly polite. He took himself so seriously; it was something appalling. Under all his culture, all his cleverness, his amenity, under his good-nature, his facility, his knowledge of life, his egoism lay hidden like a serpent in a bank of flowers.

She saves Pansy from an unhappy marriage which is being thrust upon her and returns to England to nurse Ralph Touchett in his last illness. There she meets Caspar Goodwood again. He is still in love with her and pleads with her to leave Osmond for him. "We can do absolutely as we please," he says; "the world's all before us—and the world's very big." "The world's very small," she answers, and returns to Osmond. Happiness and love are consciously rejected.

This ending has been criticized. Given James's conception of his heroine, it seems inevitable, and to fail to see it as such is tantamount to misunderstanding the conception, an integral part of which is the notion of honor. Isabel had "an infinite hope that she would never do anything wrong." Right and wrong are not simple matters for James's great heroes and heroines; they are related to what may be called their life style. At the moment of choice they feel a categorical imperative to behave according to their deepest idea of themselves and of what they owe to self-respect, regardless of comfort or personal happiness. Isabel returns to Osmond because no other course would be fitting to her own conception of herself, just as Fleda Vetch, in *The Spoils of Poynton,* renounces Owen and Poynton, since not to do so, however much it might further her own happiness and her material comfort, would be to compromise her moral sense. Honor, in fact, is at stake.

When James wrote *The Portrait of a Lady* a whole range of possibilities of development lay before him. In *The Great Tradition* F. R. Leavis has examined the parellels between *The Portrait of a Lady* and *Daniel Deronda* and assessed the influence of George Eliot upon him. But there was another influence as potent, Balzac's, and the two novels that follow *The Portrait, The Bostonians,* and *The Princess Casamassima,* both of which appeared in 1886, follow Balzac in that the notion of the novelist lying behind them is that of the novelist as the historian of his own time. These novels show how easily he might have become the chronicler of his age at the point at which public issues dominate, mold, and express character. Of *The Bostonians* he wrote: "I wished to write a very *American* tale, a tale very characteristic of our social conditions, and I asked myself what was the most salient and peculiar point in our social life. The answer was: the situation of women, the decline of the sentiment of sex, the agitation in their behalf." The novel relates the struggle between the Southerner Basil Ransom and the militant feminist Olive Chancellor for the possession of the mediumistic Verena Tarrant. It is in one respect James's boldest novel, for the relationship between Olive and Verena is plainly Lesbian, and here no doubt James had seized upon one of the motivating factors in the extreme feminist movement. But the whole action is rooted in and springs out of a closely observed environment at a time when it was marked by a curious mingling of idealism, charlatanry, and naive crankiness. All these are the butts of James's exposing satire, and here, as it happens, a contemporary novel gives us a measuring rod by which we may judge his achievement. His lifelong friend the American novelist William Dean Howells was not a negligible writer, particularly in his native context, and the craze for spiritualism and occultism that swept Boston in the eighties inspired his *The Undiscovered Country* as it partly did *The Bostonians.* Howells's novel may still be read with pleasure; it contains at least one excellently drawn character, the self-deceiving idealist Dr. Boynton; but *The Bostonians,* for all the weakness of Verena Tarrant, transcends the topicality of its theme and remains an important novel because the social trends dealt with are expressed strongly in terms of character, and the characters, shaped though they are by them, are more than the social trends.

The Princess Casamassima was the first fruit of James's decision to settle in England, and much of its richness comes from the thoroughness of his surrender to the spell of London, from "the assault directly made by the great city upon an imagination quick to react." The words are from his preface to the novel, where he tells us "that this fiction proceeded quite directly, during the first year of a long residence in London, from the habit and the interest of walking the streets." Hyacinth Robinson, his hero, "sprang up for me out of the London pavement." London contains the novel, and it is impregnated with London, which in its pages becomes almost a character in its own right, as Paris is in such a novel of Zola's as *L'Assommoir*. And above all, it is the London of the streets James celebrates, as he salutes its vitality in the offspring of its streets, in, for instance, the superbly vulgar and vital Millicent Henning, who becomes almost a symbol of working-class London:

> She was to her blunt, expanded finger-tips a daughter of London, of the crowded streets and the bustling traffic of the great city; she had drawn her health and strength from its dingy courts and foggy thoroughfares and peopled its parks and squares and crescents with her ambitions; it had entered into her blood and her bone, the sound of her voice and the carriage of her head; she understood it by instinct and loved it with passion; she represented its immense vulgarities and curiosities, its brutality and its knowingness, its good-nature and its impudence, and might have figured, in an allegorical procession, as a kind of glorified townswoman, a nymph of the wilderness of Middlesex, a flower of the clustered parishes, the genius of urban civilization, the muse of cockneyism.

To this London of the 1880's James was the receptive outsider, and to experience, appreciate, and absorb it in his novel he created a character of a sensibility and intelligence akin to his own. Lionel Trilling, in his brilliant revaluation of the novel in *The Liberal Imagination*, sets it in its place as one of the "great line of novels which runs through the nineteenth century as the very backbone of its fiction," those novels whose "defining hero may be known as the Young Man from the Provinces," though "his social class may constitute his province." It does so with Hyacinth Robinson, the illegitimate son of a dissolute peer and the French seamstress who murdered him and died in jail, brought up by a little dressmaker in Islington. Hyacinth is the victim of this clash of parenthood. "There was no peace for him between the two currents that flowed in his nature, the blood of his passionate, plebeian mother and that of his long-descended super-civilized sire." Trilling admirably isolates the folk-story element in Hyacinth and his situation; he is, from one point of view, the unacknowledged prince barred from his heritage and destined to strange ends by the very ambiguity of his birth.

Naturally an aesthete, he becomes a bookbinder, possibly the one skill open to a youth of his class that could satisfy his delight in making beautiful things. Through his fellow workmen he is drawn into the revolutionary movement of his day, and is taken up by the Princess Casamassima (the Christina Light of James's first novel *Roderick Hudson*), who, out of her "aversion to the banal," has left her Italian husband and the whole aristocratic way of life in order to seek reality in revolutionary activities. She is attracted to Hyacinth just because he is a fine spirit barred, not from the heritage that might be his as a nobleman's son, but from the heritage that should be every man's by virtue of being man. "Fancy the strange, bitter fate," she exclaims, "to be constituted as you're constituted, to be conscious of the capacity you must feel, and yet to look at the good things of life only through the glass of the pastry-cook's window!" His very existence justifies for her the social revolution.

Hyacinth's life may be conceived of as a series of initiations, by his adoring foster-mother Miss Pynsent into the secret of his birth, by his workmate M. Poupin, the refugee Frenchman, into the traditional glories of early nineteenth-century revolutionary idealism, by his friend Paul Muniment into the more ruthless and scientific principles of later nineteenth-century direct action, and by the Princess. But the initiation the Princess inducts him into differs from the others; her intentions, except that she takes him much more seriously, are Muniment's, to make him the dedicated soldier of the class war; her achievement is the quite involuntary one of making him see the heritage he is barred from in a wholly new light and understand the price its existence entails. He goes to spend a few days at Medley, the great country house the Princess has rented and to which she has invited him in order to bind him more closely to herself and the cause. He finds:

> There was something in the way the grey walls rose from the green lawn that brought tears to his eyes; the spectacle of long duration unassociated with some sordid infirmity or poverty was new to him; he had lived with people among whom old age meant for the most part a grudged and degraded survival. In the favoured resistance of Medley was a serenity of success, an accumulation of dignity and honour.

The full revelation comes to him, however, when he visits Europe on the tiny legacy Miss Pynsent has left him. His appreciation of the beautiful is stronger than his ardor for social justice, and Venice completes the transfer of his sympathies. He writes to the Princess of the effects the scene has on him and the results as they influence "the sacred cause":

> It's not that it hasn't been there to see, for that perhaps is the clearest result of extending one's horizon—the sense,

increasing as we go, that want and toil and suffering are
the constant lot of the immense majority of the human race.
I've found them everywhere but haven't minded them. Forgive the cynical confession. What has struck me is the great
achievements of which man has been capable in spite of
them—the splendid accumulations of the happier few, to
which doubtless the miserable many have also in their degree
contributed. . . . They seem to me inestimably precious and
beautiful and I've become conscious more than ever before
how little I understand what in the great rectification you
and Poupin propose to do with them. . . . You can't call me
a traitor, for you know the obligation I supremely, I immutably recognize. The monuments and treasures of art, the
great palaces and properties, the conquests of learning and
taste, the general fabric of civilization as we know it, based
if you will upon all the despotisms, the cruelties, the exclu-
sions, the monopolies, and the rapacities of the past, but
thanks to which, all the same, the world is less of a "bloody
sell" and life more of a lark—our friend Hoffendahl seems
to me to hold them too cheap and to wish to substitute for
them something in which I can't somehow believe as I do
in things with which the yearnings and the tears of generations have been mixed. You know how extraordinary I think
our Hoffendahl—to speak only of him; but if there's one
thing that's more clear about him than another, it's that he
wouldn't have the least feeling for this incomparable, abom-
inable old Venice. He would cut up the ceiling of the Vero-
nese into strips, so that every one might have a little piece.
. . . I don't know where it comes from, but during the last
three months there has crept over me a deep mistrust of that
same grudging attitude—the intolerance of positions and fortunes that are higher and brighter than one's own.

"You know the obligation I supremely, I immutably
recognize": Hyacinth has been chosen by the revolutionary
leader Hoffendahl to be the instrument of assassination;
Hyacinth makes no attempt to dodge the responsibility he
has voluntarily undertaken, but when the call comes, turns
the pistol on himself.

Traditionally, *The Princess Casamassima* has been
among the least regarded of James's novels. Perhaps it

never wholly recovered from the bad press it had on publication. But there is another reason. Our notion of the social revolution and of revolutionaries is Marxist. *The Princess Casamassima* is pre-Marxist; its revolutionaries are not members of the Communist Party but Anarchists, an ingratiating race of men forgotten for the most part now except in Herzen's *Memoirs,* but they were terrible in their day, which was James's in the 1880's, when assassination was a frequently employed weapon in political warfare. However removed it may be from revolutionary politics as we know them, as they are mirrored in, for example, Malraux's *Storm in Shanghai, The Princess Casamassima* is, as Trilling shows, "a brilliantly precise representation of social actuality." Within that, and not to be separated from it, is James's recognition and dramatization of the uncomfortable truth the idealistic Left has rarely faced, that the creation of certain kinds of art and styles of living, generally regarded as good in themselves, and the establishment of democratic values may be mutually exclusive, for each may exist only at the expense of the other. This clash between rival goods is dramatized in the fate of Hyacinth Robinson, and the peculiar poignancy of his fate comes from the fact that the choice he must make between rival goods necessarily involves him in a choice of betrayals.

The central weakness of the novel is that Hyacinth, for all the pathos of his end, never reaches tragic stature. He is a decidedly original creation; he is "there" all the time; he is wonderfully intelligent and wonderfully sensitive. He is seen by James and presented all the time as the victim. This is right enough; one would not expect him to be a Stendhalian hero. At the same time, there is a failure, and possibly it is a failure in James's initial conception of his novel. The whole theme of the novel seems to demand a hero who shall create a myth in the reader's mind, and this Hyacinth does not do, as the Princess herself, that fiery essence of intransigence, of pride, of craving for reality at any cost, triumphantly does.

All the same, *The Princess Casamassima* is a great novel, and one further quality of it must be noted, a characteristic of James's especially evident here because of the range of social scene he was committed to. This quality is the charity of James's mind, his truly luminous compassion. He weighs the worth of his characters as scrupulously as Jane Austen; he is never taken in by them; they are exposed with an exquisite moral clarity. But—and this is the point—the same steady constant light illuminates them whatever their social class, and this is something exceedingly rare in nineteenth-century fiction in England. James does not patronize, scorn, or sentimentalize the poor; he does not consider them *de haut enbas*: Millicent Henning and Miss Pynsent and Rosie Muniment exist as much in their own right as Lady Aurora, Madame Grandoni, and the Princess herself. This is one source of the abiding satisfaction we feel from *The Princess Casamassima,* as is apparent when we compare the novel with contemporary works like Gissing's *Thyrza* or even later novels like those of the early Wells, books written from a particular, partial, and limiting view of the lower classes as, almost, a separate order of creation.

Neither *The Bostonians* nor *The Princess Casamassima* was successful in England or America. Their failure was probably decisive for the turns James's talent was to take. "I have entered upon evil days," he wrote to W. D. Howells in 1888. "I am still staggering a good deal under the mysterious and (to me) inexplicable injury wrought—apparently—upon my situation by my two last novels." There began his long, baffling, heartbreaking, though not in the end unrewarding, affair with the theater. During this period he wrote, besides his plays, mainly short stories, those remarkable short stories, so close to his own situation, on art and the problems and fates of makers of art. He was changing, and when towards the end of the nineties he returned to the novel he did so as the great innovator. Yet his work was not so much different from what had gone before as more intensely his and no one else's. *Roderick Hudson*, *The Portrait of a Lady*, *The Bostonians*, *The Princess Casamassima* are traditional novels which only James could have written; from *What Maisie Knew* onwards his fiction is all his own; the change is akin to D. H. Lawrence's when, having written *Sons and Lovers*, in form the typical Edwardian autobiographical novel, he moved on to write *The Rainbow* and *Women in Love*.

It might be said James had fallen under "the fascination of what's difficult," since for him every new novel he ventured represented a technical problem to be solved. Yet this is only part of the truth, easily exaggerated if we rely overmuch on James's prefaces. A case in point is *What Maisie Knew* (1898), one of the most remarkable technical achievements in fiction. We are shown corruption through the eyes of innocence that will not be corrupted. Maisie is a child who must lead her life between her divorced parents, who are immoral and irresponsible. The entire action is presented through Maisie, through her developing consciousness and understanding. F. R. Leavis, who has written so well on this novel, has said that it was in Dickens that James "found the tip that taught him how he might deal, in this kind of comedy, with his moral and emotional intensities—those to which he was moved by his glimpses of late Victorian society," and suggests that the source of his treatment was *David Copperfield*. One sees how this may be so, for the theme of *Copperfield*, or at least of its first half, is innocence alive in a corrupt adult world, the contrast between the two producing the comedy; yet there is all the difference between a novel presented as the childhood memories of a grown-up man who can intervene and comment as a grown-up upon the action whenever he wishes, and a novel the action of which is registered in the consciousness of a child.

The clue to James's intention here as in his great late novels may be found in Conrad's description of him as "the historian of fine consciences," a phrase the richer for its possible ambiguity, since there seems some doubt whether Conrad was using the word "conscience" in its normal English sense or in its French meaning of perception, consciousness. To isolate and exhibit the working of the fine conscience (in both its meanings) was the motive behind James's technical innovations and all his attempts to make of the novel a self-contained whole carrying within itself a maximum significance. Ethics are one thing and aesthetics doubtless another, but it was James's principle that the ethical could be rendered successfully in fiction only when the representation was aesthetically satisfying, and to make it aesthetically satisfying he was prepared to plunder the other arts of the drama and of painting for his models. One of the constant cries of his Notebooks is "Dramatize, only dramatize!" while throughout his criticism there runs the analogy by which the novel is seen as composition or "the fictive picture." There is no contradiction; he is simply invoking, as models for what he wants to do, arts more formal, more highly organized than the novel has normally been. To dramatize meant to present intensely, so that the last drop of value could be squeezed from the scene rendered; the notion of composition, of the novel as "fictive picture," implied the right relationship of the parts to one another and to the whole, and everything the painter means by volumes, masses, and color values.

Fundamental to all this, the principle activating it, was James's belief in the necessity of what he called the Commanding Center, the unifying element in the work. In *The Spoils of Poynton,* the commanding center was the houseful of furniture, in *The Wings of the Dove* the title itself, and the whole situation of Milly Theale and her relation to the other characters it sums up. Often the commanding center lies in what James called a "fine central intelligence," Maisie's in *What Maisie Knew,* Strether's in *The Ambassadors.* As R. P. Blackmur has written in his introduction to his edition of James's prefaces called *The Art of the Novel*:

> . . . The novel was not a play however dramatic it might be, and among the distinctions between the two forms was the possibility, which belonged to the novel alone, of setting up a fine central intelligence in terms of which everything in it might be unified and upon which everything might be made to depend. No other art could do this; no other art could dramatize the individual at his finest; and James worked this possibility for all it was worth. . . . And this central intelligence served a dual purpose. . . . It made a compositional centre for art such as life never saw. If it could be created at all, then it presided over everything else, and would compel the story to be nothing but the story of what that intelligence felt about what happened. This compositional strength, in its turn, only increased the value and meaning of the intelligence *as* intelligence, and *vice versa.*

The final splendid flowering of James's genius came in his three last novels, *The Wings of the Dove* (1902), *The Ambassadors* (1903), and *The Golden Bowl* (1904), novels of a classical perfection never before achieved in English, in which practice and theory are consummately matched. Diverse as they are, *The Wings of the Dove* must stand as example of all three. In it James goes back to his abiding preoccupations of the international subject and of innocence eager for life and despoiled by the sophisticated; in theme the novel is a restatement of that of *The Portrait of a Lady,* and like that novel, though much more directly, it was inspired by James's memories of Minny Temple, who had haunted him so long. He was to say, twelve years later, that in *The Wings of the Dove* he had sought to lay her ghost "by wrapping it in the beauty and dignity of art." In his preface to the novel he tells us that the idea "is that of a young person conscious of a great capacity for life, but early stricken and doomed, condemned to death under short respite, while also enamored of the world; aware moreover of the condemnation and passionately desiring to 'put in' before extinction as many of the finer vibrations as possible, and so achieve, however briefly and brokenly, the sense of having lived." Such is Milly Theale, the dove of the title.

She is not, of course, a representation of Minny Temple; Minny's situation was enough for James. In a renaissance tragedy, Milly would undoubtedly have been a king's daughter; James does the best he can to heighten her pathos in the context of her time and place by making her a millionairess in her own right, and, her father dead and with no other relations, alone in the world except for her companion Mrs. Stringham. She is therefore completely free; she has the world at her feet. She is indeed, so far as potential of power is concerned, the equivalent of a princess, and her wealth and freedom lend her the glamor that belonged in former times to princesses. The characters in the novel, Mrs. Stringham especially, see her as one. And here the significance of James's symbolism must be noted; he builds her up as the modern counterpart of a renaissance princess in order to heighten the pathos of her lot, but by making us see her as a princess he also gives her the aura of the legendary: princesses are beings who live in fairy-land, waiting for gallant young men to submit themselves to impossible ordeals in order to claim their hand.

This particular princess, however, is doomed; she comes to Europe with her secret: she is condemned to an early death by an incurable disease. Characteristically—it is a device which infuriates some readers—James does not tell us what disease; rightly or wrongly, most readers will infer tuberculosis.

Milly comes to Europe in search of experience in the widest sense, for a taste of conscious happiness before death. In London she enters a corner of English society which Herbert Read has called "a little gamy." She meets the vibrantly brilliant Kate Croy, who introduces her to a young journalist, Merton Densher. Milly has met him in New York and falls in love with him. It is in Venice that she realizes the conspiracy in which she is caught, that Densher is secretly engaged to Kate and that they have planned that he shall marry her so that, after her death, they can share her money and marry themselves. She "turns her face to the wall" and dies. But she has the last word. "She has stretched her wings," says Kate after her death, "and it was to *that* they reached," for she has forgiven them and left Densher her fortune. But he is now stricken with self-revulsion at his behavior, and with revulsion against Kate, his bad angel. He tells her that he will marry her without the money or give it to her and stay single. She says that he has fallen in love with Milly's memory:

> ". . . Her memory's your love. You *want* no other."
> He heard her out in stillness, watching her face, but not moving. Then he only said: "I'll marry you, mind you, in an hour."
> "As we were?"
> "As we were."
> But she turned to the door, and her headshake was now the end. "We shall never be again as we were!"

So the novel ends, with the relationship between Kate and Densher shattered and the prospect before them of lives haunted by guilt and remorse. *The Wings of the Dove* is modern tragedy, one could say drawing-room tragedy, yet the characters in literature Kate Croy and Merton Densher most irresistibly call to mind are Lady Macbeth and Macbeth, as Milly Theale suggests Ophelia or Desdemona. They have, for all their background of Bayswater in the nineties, the true heroic stature of tragedy. How does James achieve this? The answer is, by his

style. James's style in his last novels has often been ridiculed, and there are times—not so much in the novels as
in the letters and the prefaces—when it does topple over
into the comic. Yet it is still the most remarkable style
achieved since the seventeenth century, and like so much
seventeenth-century prose it is an exploration and a development of the resources of the language. In consequence,
it often strains the language. Its closest nineteenth-century
analogue is probably not any prose at all but the poetic
style of G. M. Hopkins. It is meant to record the findings
of subtle sensibilities, and here, certainly, it can over-
task credence; all the characters in James's later fiction are
the possessors of subtle sensibilities because the style imposes the necessity of their being so. It was a penalty the
style exacted. But it does much more than express subtle
sensibilities or split the hairs of fine discriminations. For
one thing, it is an intensely visual style. And then, it is intensely metaphorical; extravagantly so, one would say, if
the metaphors were not there always to heighten and render more sharply the character being created or the situation being dramatized. James makes his sentences dense
with as much meaning as he can get into them, but the
meaning exists on several planes at once; it is a fusion of
meanings, so that to attempt to unravel a James sentence
is akin to analyzing a complex stanza in poetry.

Here is an example from *The Wings of the Dove* of
James's style at work:

> It was perfectly present to Kate that she might be devoured,
> and she likened herself to a trembling kid, kept apart a day
> or two till her turn should come, but sure sooner or later to
> be introduced into the cage of the lioness.
>   The cage was Aunt Maud's own rooms, her office, her
> counting-house, her especial scene, in fine, of action, situated
> on the ground-floor, opening from the main hall and figur-
> ing rather to our young woman on exit and entrance as a
> guardhouse or a toll-gate. The lioness waited—the kid had

at least that consciousness; was aware of the neighbourhood of a morsel she had reason to suppose tender. She would have been meanwhile a wonderful lioness for a show, an extraordinary figure in a cage or anywhere; majestic, magnificent, high-coloured, all brilliant gloss, perpetual satin, twinkling bugles and flashing gems, with a lustre of agate eyes, a sheen of raven hair, a polish of complexion that was like that of well-kept china and that—as if the skin were too tight—told especially at curves and corners. Her niece had a quiet name for her—she kept it quiet; thinking of her, with a free fancy, as somehow typically insular, she talked to herself of Britannia of the Market Place—Britannia unmistakable, but with a pen in her ear, and felt she should not be happy till she might on some occasion add to the rest of the panoply a helmet, a shield, a trident, and a ledger. It was not in truth, however, that the forces with which, as Kate felt, she would have to deal were those most suggested by an image simple and broad; she was learning, after all, each day, to know her companion, and what she had already most perceived was the mistake of trusting to easy analogies. There was a whole side of Britannia, the side of her florid philistinism, her plumes and her train, her fantastic furniture and heaving bosom, the false gods of her taste and the false notes of her talk, the sole contemplation of which would be dangerously misleading. She was a complex and subtle Britannia, as passionate as she was practical, with a reticule for her prejudices as deep as that other pocket, the pocket full of coins stamped in her image, that the world best knew her by. She carried on, in short, behind her aggressive and defensive front, operations determined by her wisdom. It was in fact, we have hinted, as a besieger that our young lady, in the provisioned citadel, had for the present most to think of her, and what made her formidable in this character was that she was unscrupulous and immoral. So, at all events, in silent sessions and a youthful offhand way, Kate conveniently pictured her: what this sufficiently represented being that her weight was in the scale of certain dangers—those dangers that, by our showing, made the younger women linger and lurk above, while the elder, below, both militant and diplomatic, covered as much of the ground as possible. Yet what were the dangers, after all, but just the dangers of life and of London? Mrs. Lowder *was* London, *was* life—the roar of the siege and the thick of the fray. There were some things, after all, of which Britannia was afraid; but Aunt Maud was afraid of nothing—not even, it would appear, of arduous thought.

The passage, even ripped out of its context, obviously tells us a great deal about Kate Croy, the proud, penniless girl with her high demands on life. Her mind is rich in perceptions that emerge in witty images accreting naturally round the object of her attention, here her aunt Mrs. Lowder. And we are at the center of Kate's consciousness; the figure of Mrs. Lowder affects us as she does Kate. Mrs. Lowder is comic, formidable, implacable; but she is more, for Kate's is a myth-making mind, and before it has finished with Mrs. Lowder she has become a figure of myth, one that can stand as a symbol of the implacability and the terror of life on which Kate has embarked. Here, without any strain on James's part, Mrs. Lowder has been heightened in significance far above a similar character in ordinary naturalistic fiction; she is what she is, but can stand for so much more.

James heightens all his characters in this way. Our impression of Milly Theale is the sum of the impressions made by her on Mrs. Stringham, Kate, Densher. We see Kate as an heroic figure because that is how Densher and Milly see her and how she is depicted by James, in all her splendid impatient vigor, in the marvelous first chapter of the novel, where we meet her waiting for her shifty n'er-do-well father in his seedy rooms. This seems at first straight description; it is not quite. When James wants to make us aware of Kate's beauty he does so by making us see her as she sees herself in the mirror, and all the time we are gaining our knowledge of her predicament through her own thoughts presented in *oratio obliqua*.

Much light is thrown on the function of style in James by the revisions he made in the texts of his novels when preparing them for the definitive New York edition, which began to appear in 1907. F. O. Matthiessen, in *Henry*

James: The Major Phase, has examined the changes he made in *The Portrait of a Lady.* He shows how their effect is to concretize and individualize, to make more vivid. The colloquial expression takes the place of the formal; the abstract is translated into the particular. Originally, the last sentence of his account of Ralph Touchett's ill health had been: "The truth was that he had simply accepted the situation"; in the New York edition it becomes: "His serenity was but the array of wild flowers niched in his ruin." Here in miniature we see how the change reveals the special part style plays in James. To concretize, to individualize, to make more actual and more vivid—this is to dramatize. But there is more. The change adds a pathos and a glory; it makes the character more interesting, more worthy our attention. Where his characters are concerned James's prose serves a purpose resembling that of blank verse in Shakespeare and the Elizabethan dramatists. It universalizes even as it individualizes. Without sacrifice of their observed reality, it lifts the characters right above the naturalistic convention. The style is an expression of the significance they have for James and of the intensity with which they feel and live. It is this intensity which makes us feel that they profoundly matter, that they are characters fit for tragedy, whereas the characters of novelists like Gissing, Moore, and Bennett, however much we may respect their work, undergo no such transcendence, only a sad fate.

3

From the eighties onwards, the recorder of the novel who wishes to do more than produce an annotated catalogue of names and titles must ruthlessly select. More than ever the novel became the dominant prose form attracting to itself the solicitations of almost all men of letters whether the nature of their talents were the novelist's or not; so in the eighties we have Pater writing *Marius the*

Epicurean, Wilde writing *The Picture of Dorian Gray* in the nineties, and twenty years later Chesterton his extravaganzas and Belloc his political squibs. Once, novels themselves had been the literary counterpart of Gladstone bags into which anything could be crammed; now the novel as a category of literature had become a convenient hold-all for literary talent.

In the eighties and nineties the great contemporary figures in fiction were still Meredith and Hardy, but a number of younger men came to maturity during the period. There were, besides James, R. L. Stevenson (1850-94), George Gissing (1857-1903), and George Moore (1853-1933), to each of whom a number of lesser writers now appear attached as satellites. The period also saw the emergence of another writer of fiction whose talents were certainly as great as theirs, Rudyard Kipling; but, magnificent prose writer and short-story writer as he was, Kipling's genius was not for the novel, and *Kim* (1901) remains the lonely masterpiece of his longer fictions, a novel without parallel or progeny.

Stevenson's reputation often seems the triumph of a fascinating personality rather than that of a writer. This is not in fact true, though the one work which makes us see him as a great novelist, *Weir of Hermiston* (1897), was unfinished at his death and survives as a fragment. Apart from *Weir of Hermiston,* Stevenson's significance is of a rather different nature from that of any of his contemporaries of comparable stature. It was only in the last years of his life that he found his true material; he had to go to Samoa before he really discovered Scotland, and going to Samoa, he discovered the South Seas too. Had he lived, one imagines his work would have followed the two distinct paths of *Weir* and the magnificent story of the Pacific islands, *The Beach of Falesá.*

Yet his early fiction is not negligible, and one is tempted to say that his distinctive contribution to the English novel is that he successfully married Flaubert to Dumas, the latter standing as a convenient symbol of the novel of romantic adventure. For Stevenson the novel of adventure came as much within the province of art as the novel of moral realism did for James; it was worthy of just as much seriousness in treatment. One might expect a certain disproportion between content and treatment. One does not find it; rather, treatment elevates content, brings out its true value. *Kidnapped* (1886) was written as an historical story for boys; its immediate end is to communicate excitement. In that it succeeds superbly, and it does so because of the precision and intensity with which action, character, and scene are rendered and the way in which everything in the novel is subordinated to their realization. As a result, *Kidnapped* seems to have the authenticity and authority of history itself. What began as a boy's book became one of the archetypal novels of pursuit, of the hunter and the hunted.

The Master of Ballantrae (1889) is a bigger book, more ambitious, less successful because Stevenson was in part attempting what then he could not do. The action turns on the character of Alison, and at the time of writing the novel Stevenson could not create a convincing woman. But *The Master of Ballantrae* carries the same authority of history as *Kidnapped* and it dramatizes, too, Stevenson's abiding preoccupation, one so thoroughly Scottish as to make him the born interpreter of the national character. This is his preoccupation with the doctrine of Predestination as it emphasizes the theory of divine election, with some souls damned as irretrievably as others are saved. Stevenson was haunted by the idea of damnation, of the soul condemned to evil. The Master of Ballantrae is such a soul; he is incarnate wickedness. Yet in a curious way he becomes the hero of the novel; it is the younger brother, at the beginning "neither very bad nor yet very able, but an honest, solid sort of lad," who is perverted by the Master's persecution into miserliness, repining, and the lust for revenge, so that he becomes one of the most absorbing psychological studies of degradation in our fiction.

If Stevenson had died five years earlier than he did, one would have said that his contribution to the novel was twofold. His rediscovery of the art of narrative, of conscious and cunning calculation in telling a story so that the maximum effect of clarity and suspense is achieved, meant the birth of the novel of action as we know it and the measure of the work of later writers such as John Buchan and Graham Greene; while in books like *The New Arabian Nights, Prince Otto,* and those written with Lloyd Osbourne, *The Wrong Box, The Wreckers,* and *The Ebb Tide,* he gave a wholly new literary dignity and impetus to light fiction, fiction whose end is, unaffectedly, entertainment. One wouldn't say Stevenson made Anthony Hope possible, but, as in the novel of action, he set the standard for him and those who have followed him.

In the last five years of his life, however, his creative range developed astonishingly. The remarkable thing about his long short story *The Beach at Falesá* is not that in it he brought into our fiction an exotic scene of a kind we now associate with Conrad and Maugham but that he was able to tell his story of the Pacific through a vulgar, lower-class Englishman whose wistful dream is to keep a pub, and to assume the identity completly. With *Weir of Hermiston* we are faced, of course, with an insoluble problem: could Stevenson have kept it up? What we have is a magnificent torso, as splendid a piece of writing in its own right as any in our fiction; it has immense solidity, strength, and grace; every word he uses is decisive, and chosen for euphony as well as force and precision. The Edinburgh of 1813 is wonderfully re-created; it doesn't fall by comparison with Scott's picture of Edinburgh a century earlier in *The Heart of Midlothian.* And within its context Stevenson was dramatizing one of his own most racking experiences, the conflict between father and son. That described in the novel between the Lord Justice-Clerk and Archie was not Stevenson's, but it was a perfect objective correlative for it. The Lord Justice-Clerk, the hanging judge, is a truly tremendous figure, as ruthless, as majestic in his sense of justice, as diabolical in his scorn for those who fall before it as, one is tempted to say, the God of the Covenanters; he terrifies us almost as much as he does Archie or the wretched prisoners who appear before him:

. . . My Lord Hermiston occupied the bench in the red robes of criminal jurisdiction, his face framed in the white wig. Honest all through, he did not affect the virtue of impartiality; this was no case for refinement; there was a man to be hanged, he would have said, and he was hanging him. Nor was it possible to see his lordship, and acquit him of gusto in the task. It was plain he gloried in the exercise of his trained faculties, in the clear sight which pierced at once into the joint of fact, in the rude, unvarnished gibes with which he demolished every figment of defence. He took his ease and jested, unbending in that solemn place with some of the freedom of the tavern; and the rag of man with the flannel round his neck was hunted gallowsward with jeers.

Duncan had a mistress, scarce less forlorn and greatly older than himself, who came up, whimpering and curtseying, to add the weight of her betrayal. My lord gave her the oath in his most roaring voice, and added an intolerant warning.

"Mind what ye say now, Janet," said he. "I have an e'e upon ye, I'm ill to jest with."

Presently, after she was tremblingly embarked on her story, "And what made ye do this, ye auld runt?" the Court interposed. "Do ye mean to tell me ye was the panel's mistress?"

"If you please, ma loard," whined the female.

"Godsake! ye made a bonny couple," observed his lordship; and there was something so formidable and ferocious in his scorn that not even the galleries thought to laugh.

At the same time, the women in the novel, the old Kirstie and the young, for the first time in Stevenson have reality, and their reality is vibrant.

Weir of Hermiston strikes us as a fragment of epic. We know that the Lord Justice-Clerk was based on the eighteenth-century Lord Justice-Clerk Braxfield. Stevenson's Lord Justice-Clerk, then, is the consummate expression of a national myth, of one aspect of Scotland's consciousness of itself. His novel is rooted in his country's history and feeling. Here it looks forward to a later Scottish novel, not, it is true, as finely wrought as Stevenson's, which in the quality of its writing is strictly comparable with Flaubert's, but of great power, George Douglas Brown's *The House with the Green Shutters,* published in 1902, its author's only book. Between the publication of Stevenson's last novel and Brown's, Scottish fiction had deliquesced into the sentimental effusions of the Kailyard School; its most famous works are probably Ian Maclaren's *Beside the Bonnie Brier Bush,* S. R. Crockett's *The Stickit Minister,* and Barrie's *Window in Thrums.* These novels represent Scottish small-town life in terms of a paralyzing sweetness. They had their counterpart on the music-hall stage in the songs and personality of Sir Harry Lauder. Historically, *The House with the Green Shutters* is a savagely deliberate attempt to reveal the harsh reality of Scottish provincial life behind the false façade put up by the Kailyard writers. This is now the least interesting thing about it.

Like *Weir of Hermiston, The House with the Green Shutters* is a fragment of national myth, depicted on a much smaller scale, in a narrow provincial setting, and related not with Stevenson's marmoreal dignity of style but with a sardonic scorn. Much of the novel's strength certainly comes from the freshness of the language in which it is written, for Brown relies heavily on Scots dialect words; they accentuate the provincialism described and the contempt that informs his attitude towards it; but they also introduce a quality of lyricism that lightens the somberness of the novel. The main strength, however, lies in the subject itself. At the center of the novel is Gourlay, the man of demoniac power, to use Brown's own adjective. "Brute force of character" is the secret of his strength. He is envied by his fellow townsmen; his son, in his weak, credulous way, rebels against him; and he is finally brought down by a more astute rival, of whom, in his contempt for all who live about him, he has made an enemy. His tragedy is the tragedy of the bull insulted, baited, goaded, and finally killed in the ring. Gourlay is a man with few redeeming features, except his own pride in being a man. But his stature is such that he towers over his backbiting neighbors as he does over his son, who is an extremely shrewd characterization of a youth whose genuine sensibility is matched by no corresponding intellectual ability. Gourlay, in his native intransigence of spirit, bursts the bounds of provincial conventional opinion. In his own way he is great, and because he is great he has to be hounded and brought down. This impression is so strong that we may properly call the novel tragic, though its author's own standpoint is that of a peculiarly sardonic comedy that links him with Hogg, Galt, and Burns. *The House with the Green Shutters* is not a perfect novel—it was, after all, Brown's only one, written a year before he died at the age of thirty-three, and novelists learn how to write novels by the practice of writing them—but in spite of its faults in construction and its author's tendency to generalize on the action in his own person, it has monolithic power, and the nightmare vividness with which controlled hate can illuminate its subject.

4

Mark Rutherford, whose real name was William Hale White (1831-1913), and George Gissing (1857-1903) are associated in the mind partly by some similarity in their subject matter but more by the kinship of their attitudes to life. Both were men of very considerable intellectual

attainments accompanied by a certain feebleness of vitality; they strike us as defeated by life, and defeated from
the beginning, as a consequence of temperament. At an
early age, both strayed from the paths they could have
been confidently predicted to take. If they had not done
so, they would have been spared much misery, become
much less interesting men, and probably not have written
novels at all.

Rutherford came to fiction late; he was fifty when his
first novel, *The Autobiography of Mark Rutherford,* was
published in 1881. It is his own story, and the book, which
is presented much as Gissing's *The Private Papers of
Henry Ryecroft* was to be twenty years later, as its central
character's assessment of life edited by a friend after his
death, exists very much on the borders of fiction and
autobiography. It is a record of disillusion; the point of
view from which it is written is summed up in the comment: "One-fourth of life is intelligible, the other three-
fourths is unintelligible darkness, and our earliest duty
is to cultivate the habit of not looking round the corner."
Rutherford is the son of a family of shopkeepers in a Midland town who belonged to the dissenting sect then called
Independents. He writes:

> Nothing particular happened to me till I was about four-
> teen, when I was told it was time I became converted . . .
> I knew that I had to be "a child of God," and after a
> time professed myself to be one, but I cannot call to mind that
> I was anything else than I always had been, save that I was
> perhaps a little more hypocritical. . . .

Rutherford is sent to a training college for Independent
ministers, is ordained, and appointed to a chapel in an
East Anglian town. He suffers from intellectual doubt
and finds himself unable to meet the criticisms of his beliefs made by an agnostic working man; and then, leaving
the Independents for the Unitarians, he has a short spell

as Unitarian minister before leaving the ministry to work for a Rationalist publisher in London in loneliness and poverty.

The Autobiography of Mark Rutherford is a poignant account of loneliness both spiritual and material. Its theme is the religious and intellectual bankruptcy of dissent in the forties. The great tradition of radical revolt had dwindled into a mean, self-righteous illiberality in which the letter was everything and the spirit scarcely existed.

The peculiarly affecting quality of Rutherford's fiction, however, comes from the way he sees dissent. Intellectually, he had freed himself from nonconformity, but emotionally his allegiance was still to it. For him, it was an heroic tradition, and, apart from its value as a record of spiritual crisis, *The Autobiography* is moving because it is a lament for an heroic tradition from which the glory has departed. In *The Revolution in Tanner's Lane* (1893) he takes this up explicitly. Technically, it is a broken-backed novel —Rutherford had little power of organization and construction—but it is still an historical novel of unique interest. It begins in 1814, with Zachariah Coleman, a young London printer, "a moderate Calvinist" in religion, caught up almost against his will in what were then revolutionary politics; he is, that is to say, a Radical, a Republican, against the Government, in favor of universal franchise. He is caught up so effectually that he is forced to leave London and live in Manchester, where he is arrested and sentenced to two years' imprisonment after the "Peterloo Massacre" of 1819.

Zachariah represents a dissent which is still dynamic, our of which certain political principles opposed to the established order necessarily spring. Then Rutherford—very clumsily, it must be said—leaps forward twenty years and begins what is almost a separate novel to show us dissent in stagnation, declined to a pettifogging concern with a narrow, spying morality and to a Laodicean caution in the world's affairs. Its representative is the Rev. John Broad, who writes to his son, a student for the ministry:

> A young minister, I need hardly say, my dear Thomas, ought to confine himself to what is generally accepted, and not to particularize. For this reason he should avoid not only all disputed topics, but, as far as possible, all reference to particular offences. I always myself doubted the wisdom, for example, of sermons against covetousness, or worldliness, or hypocrisy. Let us follow our Lord and Master, and warn our hearers against sin, and leave the application to the Holy Spirit.

Rutherford is not more than a minor novelist, but he did what no other English novelist was to do until Bennett did it incidentally, and from an entirely different point of view, twenty years later: he put religious dissent into fiction not as something eccentric to the main tradition of our history but as part of its main stream. He rendered it critically yet sympathetically, and, doing so, he also brought into our fiction a class of men and women who hitherto had existed only at its edge, the world of shopkeepers and small farmers—what might be called the nineteenth century's own especial yeomanry—with which dissent was, in country districts at any rate, particularly closely associated. He knew the inhabitants of this world through and through, for they were his own people, and reproduced them, as he does his intuitions about life, in a prose singularly simple and limpid.

Gissing is not a great novelist but he is considerably more than a minor one. He is one of those imperfect artists whose work inevitably leads one back to the writer in person. His fiction is not, except in perhaps three instances, sufficiently detached from its creator; it is too personal, the powerful expression, one cannot help feeling, of a grudge. The grudge expressed is a common one today, though Gissing was the first novelist directly to manifest it; and this in a way does universalize his work, in spite of its lack

of objectivity. His general view of his times was very close
to Flaubert's; he too might have used the word *muflisme*
to characterize the age, which he found vulgar, shallow,
naively self-satisfied, and which, like Flaubert, he judged
by standards drawn from his notions of classical antiquity.
But Flaubert exteriorized his disgust in novels which are
nothing if not wonderfully solid entities, whereas Gissing
remains the novelist of the special case—his own.

It is presented in an idealized form in what has always
been his most popular book, *The Private Papers of Henry
Ryecroft* (1903). Neither a straight novel nor a straight
autobiography, *Ryecroft* may best be described as an autobiographical fantasia, projected in the form of a collection
of personal essays largely composed in that curious dialect
of written English Lamb devised from the literature of the
sixteenth and seventeenth centuries and bequeathed to
the occasional essayists of the nineteenth. The character
projected is an old and battered veteran of the war of letters who has been rescued from the eternal battle against
public, publishers, and editors, by the unexpected inheritance of a small annuity which has allowed him to retire to
a cottage on the Exe. There he spends his time in blissful
solitude, mildly aestheticizing among wild flowers, reacting inordinately to the parcels the secondhand booksellers
send him, pitying himself for his former poverty and the
uncultured people it forced him to associate with, and
congratulating himself with much complacence on his
present good fortune.

"Mine be a cot," in fact; but Gissing's does not contain
even a Lucy in russet gown and apron blue. *Ryecroft* represents a dream of such irresponsibility as to amount to the
expression of a deliberate opting out of life. Read cold, as
it were, without reference to the author, it can scarcely be
anything but repellent; the old and battered veteran turns
out to be—fifty-three, and his creator forty-three. Read
in the light of one's knowledge of Gissing's life, however,

the book makes a rather different impression. He wrote it when he was well out of poverty and his reputation established, but the iron had entered his soul too early for success to change his attitude either to himself or to life. The son of a pharmaceutical chemist of Wakefield, he had been a boy academically brilliant; at fifteen, he had come first in England in the Oxford Local examinations, and he had won a scholarship to Owens College, Manchester, where he swept all before him. His future could be foretold with confidence: he would go to one of the older universities; he would get a first and a fellowship and settle down to the life of a classical scholar and a don. Nothing like this happened. He fell in love with a young prostitute, was expelled from Owens for pilfering, and packed off to the United States, where at times he practically starved. When he returned to England a year or two later it was practically to starve again, at any rate for a time. The prostitute, whom he had married, had become a dipsomaniac. They lived apart, but half his earnings went to her; and so began the life of drudgery, of coaching and writing and reading, and often of semistarvation, he later described in *New Grub Street* (1891) and *Ryecroft*. When his wife died, he picked up a servant girl in Regent's Park and married her; she proved little better than the other.

His friend H. G. Wells, who looked after him in his last months with great tenderness, wrote of him that "he had no natural customary persona for miscellaneous use"; and Gissing, in his preface, explains the title of his second novel, *The Unclassed* (1884), by saying: "Male and female, all the prominent persons of the story, swell in a limbo external to society. They refuse the statistic badge." Gissing himself dwelt in a limbo external to society, he refused the statistic badge, and it enabled him to explore a certain kind of man and woman as they have not been explored in our fiction before or since.

The weakness of *Ryecroft* is that it is a dream. Ryecroft

is the final rendering of what may be called the Gissing man; he is much less interesting when abstracted from life. In the novels at least he has to struggle with society, and he appears in all the novels as fundamentally the same character, whatever his class, calling, or education, though different aspects of him may be seized and enlarged upon from book to book. He is, primarily, a man who lives in a self-created isolation that is the result of the sense of his own difference from his fellows. If he is a working man, like Grail in *Thyrza* (1887), the difference is his all-consuming hunger and thirst for culture. Generally, it is a combination of poverty, hypersensitiveness, pride, and education. Often, the Gissing man, like Reardon in *New Grub Street,* adds to the difficulties his temperament imposes upon him, a responsibility for others he is incapable adequately of fulfilling. He has two distinguishing marks, that lack of a "natural customary persona for miscellaneous use" Wells found in Gissing himself, and a ferocity of self-regard that prevents him from compromising with the world in which he lives. Sometimes—Kingcote in *Isabel Clarendon* (1886) is a case in point—it is scarcely possible to account rationally for his behavior; then he appears as a neurotic taken at his own valuation of himself. But, with one exception among the novels in which a man is the central character, Gissing assumes all along the rightness of his heroes' attitudes. It is this that vitiates these novels as realistic representations of late nineteenth-century life. We see this in two of his most powerful novels, *Thyrza* and *New Grub Street. Thyrza* is his best novel about working-class life in London. At its center is Gilbert Grail:

> Daily his thirteen hours went to the manufacture of candles, and the evening leisure, with one free day in the week, was all he could ever hope for . . . He would eat his meal when he came from work, then take his book to a corner, and be mute, answering any needful question with a gesture or the briefest word. At such times his face had the lines of age; you would have deemed him a man weighed upon by

some vast sorrow. And was he not? His life was speeding by; already the best years were gone, the years of youth and force and hope—nay, hope he could not be said to have known, unless it were for a short space when first the purpose of his being dawned upon consciousness; and the end of that had been bitter enough. The purpose he knew was frustrated. The "Might have been," which is "also called No More, Too late, Farewell," often stared him in the eyes with those unchanging orbs of ghastliness, chilling the flow of his blood and making life the cruellest of mockeries.

With a character such as Grail Gissing's sympathies are fully engaged, as they always are with men and women exiled from their proper sphere, the sphere to which they naturally belong by their aspirations or their talents. It was this special sympathy that made him the first and perhaps the best delineator in English of a comparatively recent type of man, the proletarian intellectual, the educated man from the working classes who, for all his talents and even success, is even now often compact of feelings of inferiority, pride, and envy of those who possess by right of birth the graces and freedoms he has had laboriously to acquire. But the price of this special sympathy was a wholesale lack of sympathy with the environment—and its inhabitants—in which the exceptional being must live. From working-class life as a whole, he turns with a shuddering revulsion. There is in his novels of working-class life, *Thyrza, The Unclassed* (1884), *The Nether World* (1889), a conspicuous failure in charity, obvious when they are compared with the novels of James and George Moore. The values by which he judges the working class are literary in the narrowest sense; at times one would think that the sole end of life was that men and women should read.

Again, *New Grub Street,* that terrifying document of the miseries of authorship, exposes one facet of the literary life that seems always to be with us, but its validity as a considered representation stands or falls by the character of Reardon, who is so weak, so shrinking, and at the same time so intransigent as to be a special case. A Reardon, one feels, could survive in no form of society in which the element of risk entered. He is damned by his own temperament, and though he is a pathetic figure he is not a tragic one, merely the successful emblem of Gissing's self-pity. *New Grub Street* strikes one as special pleading for a special case. Through the Gissing man we see the world as through a distorting lens, but it is a lens of extraordinary power.

There is the one exception: *Born in Exile* (1892). In the character of the proletarian intellectual Godwin Peake, who walks out of a brilliant career as a student in a northern college because his vulgar uncle proposes to open an eating house bearing the name Peake opposite the college gates, Gissing created a counterpart of one side of himself seen and presented with such objectivity as to be thoroughly satisfying. He did so by stressing not the hypersensitivity in his make-up but the pride. Peake is a monster of egoism, but his is not the enervated egoism of Ryecroft. It is the egoism of the man who feels himself born in exile, robbed of his inheritance, and determined to win his rights. Pride grips him like a passion. As a boy he nails his colors to the mast when he exclaims: "I hate low, uneducated people! I hate them worse than the filthiest vermin. . . . They ought to be swept off the face of the earth! All the grown-up people, who can't speak proper English and don't know how to behave themselves." As an adult, he throws down his challenge to society when he tells a friend: "My one supreme desire is to marry a perfectly refined woman. Put it in the correct terms; I am a plebeian, and I aim at marrying a lady."

Peake at this time is an industrial chemist with literary ambitions. An arrogant Rationalist, he has written, with some success, an anonymous article for a review, in which he ridicules the pretensions of a popular work aiming to reconcile science and religion. Then by chance he meets

Sidwell Warricombe, the sister of a wealthy college friend. Gissing tends to write of the Warricombes, who are wealthy manufacturers of some culture, as though they were almost Renaissance princes. This scarcely matters, for if the romanticizing was part of Gissing's illusion it was also part of Peake's, who is the real center of interest. Attracted towards the Warricombes by the graciousness of life they represent, Peake plunges into a career of dissimulation simply in order to maintain relations with them. He declares his intention of being ordained as an Anglican priest and, to ingratiate himself with Sidwell and her father, settles in Exeter, where they live, to study theology; he discusses the conflict between religion and science with Mr. Warricombe and cynically shores up his battered faith. He proposes to Sidwell, but he is exposed; the attack on religion in the anonymous article is brought home to him.

In the passionately felt character of Peake, with his remarkable career of intellectual dissimulation—and of his intellectual distinction we are never in the least doubt—Gissing approaches the intensity and power of the Russian novelists he admired.

It was for women Gissing reserved his fullest sympathy; his range of women characters is considerably greater than that of his men. But he distinguishes very carefully between women. He writes in *Born in Exile*: "Godwin was one of those upon whose awaking intellect is forced a perception of the brain-defect so general in women when they are taught few of life's graces and none of its serious concerns—their paltry prepossessions, their vulgar sequaciousness, their invincible ignorance, their absorption in a petty self." No novelist has described more surely than he the miseries of matrimony as they arise from woman's jealousy, shrewishness, and sluttishness. One remembers Harriet Casti, in *The Unclassed,* in whom all those qualities are combined. But the same novel has in Ida Starr, the young prostitute, one of his most charming heroines; with great skill he reveals in her not only real intellectual ability but also the growth of moral and spiritual graciousness. Again, his normal attitude to the working classes at times breaks down in the presence of working-class girls, as it does in *Thyrza,* his tenderest novel, with its three contrasted heroines of the slums, Thyrza and Lydia Trent and Totty Nancarrow.

Artistically, his most successful novels are the two in which women dominate, *The Odd Women* (1893) and *In the Year of the Jubilee* (1894). They are his most objective works, and they are unmarred by the self-pity and special pleading of his other novels. In *The Odd Women* he achieved one of the very few novels in English that can be compared with those of the French Naturalists who were his contemporaries. The theme is implicit in the title: the fate of women who do not possess economic security. He presents the problem in terms of the three daughters of an improvident doctor who leaves them with the tiniest of legacies and no training of any kind. With these he contrasts Rhoda Nunn, an impassioned feminist who conceives it her task in life to prepare women for an active role apart from marriage. Rhoda Nunn, the "New Woman," is badly dated, but the Madden sisters are still moving, and the novel is a most impressive study of loneliness in London lodgings, of women maintaining middle-class respectability on the minimum of means. Here he exhibited the fate of the "unwanted" middle-class Victorian woman in all its pathos—he wrote nothing more poignant than his vignette of the secret gin tippler Virginia Madden—and the effect is the stronger because of his restraint and detachment.

In *In the Year of the Jubilee* Gissing's characters no longer dwell "in a limbo external to society." The novel is a frontal attack on the lower middle-class world of the London suburbs. It is his most controlled expression of his disgust with his age. He exposes its vulgarity with a wintry humor, as in the figures of the Barmbys, the elder

with his preposterous letters to the press, the younger with
his "Carlyle and Gurty! Yes, Carlyle and Gurty; those two
authors are an education in themselves." The vulgarity
is presented, too, in three of his most appalling women,
Beatrice and Fanny French and their sister Ada Peachey,
whose "features resembled Fanny's, but had a much less
amiable expression, and betokened, if the thing were possible, an inferior intellect." But *In the Year of the Jubilee*
is not simply an exposure of *muflisme,* for it contains probably his most successful heroine. Nancy Lord is not in the
least idealized; in the early chapters she is almost as unpromising human material as the Frenches, but she yet
develops through her tribulations a strength of moral character that enables her to make a success of a marriage at
first seemingly disastrous.

5

Gissing said that the novelists who had helped him most
were the French and Russian, and their influence upon
him is obvious enough: Zola in the novels of working-class
life, Maupassant in *The Odd Women,* and Turgenev in
his more tender renderings of women. Yet the influence
was intermittent; he had often to produce a novel whether
he wanted to or not, and then he slipped back, as in *A
Life's Morning* (1885), to good old-fashioned Victorian
melodramatic plots. His close contemporary George Moore,
however, who was born four years earlier than Gissing.
in 1853, and died thirty years later, in his first and to my
view most important phase as a writer took over the French
novel so wholeheartedly as almost to lead one to say that
his aim was to write the French Naturalistic novel in English. But at the word "naturalistic" one must pause.

Words applied to literary and artistic movements revolutionary in their day have seldom any precise meaning.
They are emotive words, slogans, battle cries to rouse the
faithful. Often, as with the word "Impressionist," as ap-

plied to the French painters of the second half of the nineteenth century, they come into existence quite by chance, as journalistic coinings that are seized upon and given currency as convenient labels. Naturalism, naturalistic, are such words. They have certain attributes, but the sum total of these attributes is not enough truly to describe the work of the great masters of Naturalism, Maupassant and Zola. The very difference between these writers, who as artists are poles apart, is enough to show up the inadequacy of the word as a label. Yet, when the attributes are borne in mind, it still has its value to categorize a certain kind of fiction, a kind that, often in an impure state, more or less dominated the writing of the novel throughout Europe and America from the mid-eighties to about 1914.

The word was first applied to literature by the French novelists of the second half of the century who saw themselves as the disciples and successors of Flaubert. It was an attempt to define, on a theoretical basis, what before had been called Realism. Flaubert himself refused to be called either Realist or Naturalist; he saw himself as a French classicist, and dismissed Naturalism as an "ineptitude." Certainly the theory of Naturalism leaves out a great deal that is cardinal to Flaubert, leaves out perhaps what is most important in him, his insistence on style, on the conscious making of a work of beauty. The two classic statements of Naturalism are Maupassant's preface to his novel *Pierre et Jean* and Zola's book *Le Roman experimental,* in which he defines description as "an account of environment which determines and completes man."

Naturalism, like most critical theories devised to buttress specific movements in art, was heavily pseudoscientific and bound to be discredited as soon as the scientific theories on which it was based were discovered no longer to hold. But this does not automatically invalidate the fiction written in its name. What the Naturalists were after, when the theory is stripped of its scientific verbiage, was the illusion of reality, of life as it is lived. Maupassant, less ingenuous than Zola, said that Realists ought more truly to be called Illusionists.

Naturalism was the literary equivalent of Impressionism in painting; just as the Impressionists painted objects as seen in certain conditions of light and atmosphere, so the Naturalists depicted human beings in terms of their environment. The relation between the two theories was well known to the novelists themselves, and it is part of Zola's strength, for instance, that in his novels he often sets out to describe a scene as nearly as possible as Manet might have painted it. One of the weaknesses of the Naturalistic novel in England is that the novelists had no native contemporary painters working on parallel lines they could emulate. If Zola constantly suggests Manet, George Moore in his best novel, *Esther Waters,* suggests Frith in such a painting as "Derby Day."

The Naturalists, then, placed their main emphasis on environment; it was this that led them so highly to value research and documentation. For the same reason they turned away from psychological analysis of characters; indeed, Maupassant denied its possibility. Their view of man may be summed up in the epigraph George Moore chose for his second novel, *A Mummer's Wife* (1885): "Change the surroundings in which man lives, and in two or three generations, you will have changed his physical constitution, his habits of life, and a goodly number of his ideas." As a novelist Moore owed everything to the French, so that in the tradition of the English novel he appears something of a sport. Bennett, later, was to begin his career as a novelist equipped with an impressive knowledge of nineteenth-century French fictin and almost no knowledge at all of English, but after his first novels his own sheerly English character kept on breaking into and through the novels he wrote on French models. But Moore was not English but Irish, and though he was educated in

England it was at a Roman Catholic school, and from there he went to Paris, to study painting. He became the English apostle both of the Impressionists and the Naturalists. How well his apprenticeship in Paris served him is shown by the excellence of his best fiction; it is not easy to believe that *Esther Waters* (1894) is from the pen of the man who had written the *Confessions of a Young Man* six years before and was later to write *Hail and Farewell*. Moore in his role of *enfant terrible,* dandy, great lover, the Moore who claimed to have owned as a pet in Paris "a python that made a monthly meal off guinea-pigs," is frequently a great silly, a touchingly unconscious comic figure. But this side of Moore does not enter *Esther Waters* or *A Mummer's Wife* at all. He is as much outside them as Flaubert was outside *Madame Bovary,* and he shows, too, remarkable powers of understanding of and sympathy with characters who could have found no place in his scheme of values as a man rather than as an artist.

A Mummer's Wife is a quite impressive attempt to fuse *Madame Bovary* with Zola's *L'Assommoir*; it is the study of the degradation of an actor's wife through drink. It opens with a third-rate opera company's visit to the Potteries; in other words, in part it anticipates what was to be Bennett's typical scene. Moore's descriptions of Hanley and its potteries have naturally enough nothing of the quality of felt life that distinguishes Bennett's, but comparison does bring out the thoroughness with which Moore soaked himself in his material in order to produce his "slice of life," to use the phrase the Naturalists themselves introduced to describe the effect they were after in their fiction.

The main interest of *A Mummer's Wife* is admittedly now historical. This is far from true of *Esther Waters*, a work of great poignancy and even of beauty, so lovingly —it seems the only word—does Moore subordinate himself to the task of describing his heroine's life. It is a completely unsensational life. Esther Waters, the slum girl, who, brought up as a Plymouth Brother and "at heart a thoroughly religious girl," goes into service, is seduced and deserted by the footman, has her illegitimate son, slaves as a wet nurse and servant for him, refuses a respectable and religious man for his sake, in order to marry his father, now a publican and bookmaker, and undergoes at the end a second declension in fortunes when her husband dies from tuberculosis—Esther is rendered with scrupulous fidelity. This, we feel at the end, as Moore intended us to, is the common lot of hundreds of thousands. "No, I have not changed, Fred," Esther says to the Salvationist who loves her and finds her serving in her husband's pub in Dean Street, "but things have turned out different. One doesn't do the good that one would like to in the world; one has to do the good that comes to one to do. I've my husband and my boy to look to. Them's my good. At least that's how I sees things."

Esther is the center of a large gallery of characters, all treated with the same scrupulous fidelity. There are no villains and no heroes. And Moore is the consummate master of all the changing backgrounds of the book, the great house with its racing stables and the obsession with racing that grips all who live in it, the maternity hospital, the baby farmer's, the wet nurse's life, the Derby, the betting man's pub in Soho. The novel is a triumph not only of sympathy but of empathy. Of all English novels in the Naturalistic mode this is the one that most thoroughly fulfills Maupassant's requirements. If we seek the secret of the beauty which is this novel's final effect we shall find it, I think, in two statements of Moore's. In *A Drama in Muslin* he wrote: "Seen from afar, all things are of equal worth and the meanest things when viewed with the eye of God are raised to heights of tragic awe which conventionality would limit to the deaths of kings and patriots." This is the usual Naturalist claim and it is not in fact true; tragic awe is not the emotion we feel on contemplating Esther Waters's fate. But at least the effort to see *sub specie aeternitatis,* to see as God might see, raises subject matter hitherto regarded as "low" to a wholly new dignity. Esther is accorded the rights due to the human personality. That is one thing. The other is the mode of expression, which is stated in Moore's words: "Art as I understand it is a rhythmical sequence of events described with rhythmical sequence of phrase." This sums up perfectly what Moore achieved in *Esther Waters,* and it is from the combination of it with the dignity given the subject that the beauty of the novel is born.

In his later career Moore was to pursue this idea of rhythm as the basis of prose art as far as it would go. In his fictional interpretation of the life of Jesus, *The Brook Kerith* (1916), and in his *Héloïse and Abélard* (1921), the emphasis is wholly on narrative; the usual constituents of novels, character, dialogue, milieu, are subordinated to the weaving of a seamless tapestry of prose akin in the effects obtained to Malory's *Morte d'Arthur.* Here it seems to me Moore passed out of the realm of the novel altogether; however *The Brook Kerith* and *Héloïse and Abélard* are to be judged, it is not by reference to novels as we have known them during the past two centuries.

Moore remains almost the only English Naturalist in the French sense. For the Naturalist theory stressed an attitude towards character endemic to French novelists but rare in English. It was Flaubert who said: "Art is not made to paint the exceptions," and he added that the characters most suited to fiction were the "more general" because they were the more typical. This is not the English view, which is implied in the very ambiguity of the word "character" in our language. It may mean, simply, an imaginary person invented by a novelist, but it may also mean a person distinguished by odd behavior, an eccentric. We call a man of strongly marked idiosyncrasy a "character"; and

English novelists have always tended to see their imaginary persons as eccentric persons; the two meanings constantly overlap. The French, however, rarely see their characters as "characters." The difference between the two attitudes might be put like this: the English novelists tend to work from the highly individual, the highly idiosyncratic, to the general type; the French tend to work from the general type to the individual. A French novelist, inventing a miser or a hypocrite, is interested in the quality of miserliness or hypocrisy. An English novelist is much more likely to stress the comic aspects of miserliness or hypocrisy, so much so, indeed, that both he and his readers may be in danger of forgetting the vice in their appreciation of the idiosyncrasies that are its result. For the English, there is always a tendency for character to be an end in itself, valuable in its own right; the French are interested in a character as the instance of a general law or because a general law may be deduced from it. Perhaps this is to say that whereas the French on the whole write as moralists the English write as humorists.

The theory of Naturalism, with its preoccupation with the unexceptional, the representative, reinforced the French in that inherited disposition. But it cut right across the grain of the English, so that, between the mid-eighties and 1914, while there is plenty of realism in English fiction, there is little true Naturalism.

A case in point is the work of Arthur Morrison (1863-1945). Morrison is an excellent minor novelist, and the end he proposed for himself, in novels like *A Child of the Jago* (1896) and *The Hole in the Wall* (1902), was strictly realistic: to expose the East End, and the condition of the people living there, as they really were. In this he was eminently successful; his account of life in Wapping, where the police went about in threes, in *The Hole in the Wall*, is as grim and relentless as Zola. But when we look at the characters in the novel we see they are like nothing in

Naturalism. Captain Kemp, Mr. Cripps, Mrs. Grimes, are either natural Dickens characters or characters conceived by a novelist who is so steeped in Dickens that automatically he turns his creations into Dickens characters: they look like Dickens characters, they speak like them. And though *The Hole in the Wall* is genuinely a work of realism, the whole portrayal of character in it suggests that Morrison's affinities were much less close to Moore than to W. W. Jacobs (1863-1943), who also wrote about life in the stories of London River and was a comic writer perfect within his narrow limits, stemming, certainly not out of Naturalism, but out of Dickens. Indeed, in England realism came to be associated with a positive geniality, even at times sentimentality. This is especially true of the writers of what is sometimes called "the Cockney school": Morrison himself, Zangwill, Barry Pain, W. Pett Ridge, Edwin Pugh, and later Frank Swinnerton in such a novel as *Nocturne* (1917). The early Wells, too, has his associations with the school. Those who belonged to it aimed at describing the everyday reality of the lower-middle-class and working-class London scene, and they succeeded, but their objectivity towards the backgrounds described did not extend to the characters inhabiting them. They are rendered with the humorous affection that comes from delight in idiosyncrasy.

Moore's true successor in Naturalism, apart from Bennett in one or two early novels and *Riceyman Steps* towards the end of his career, is Somerset Maugham (b. 1874), whose first novel, *Liza of Lambeth*, it is a little disconcerting to realize, was published in 1897, a year before Bennett's first and only two years after Conrad's and Wells's. But even in Maugham the influence of Naturalism, which Maugham got direct from the French, is discontinuous, for in his most ambitious novel, *Of Human Bondage,* which in part—and in its best parts—springs out of Naturalistic dogma, one is suddenly aware of the fatal intrusion of something different altogether, something that looks as though it comes from Samuel Butler's *The Way of All Flesh*.

Butler was born in 1835, but his novel was not published until 1903, a year after his death, though it had been begun in the early seventies and rewritten in the early eighties. *The Way of All Flesh* is an example of the novel as delayed action bomb. Even so, even after 1903, it might have lain inert for years if Bernard Shaw had not touched it off. Then it suddenly exploded, and out of the debris a novel of a new kind emerged, or rather, a novel with a new subject and a new hero. The subject is self-determination, the hero the young man in revolt against his family background and the values it represents. One can't say such novels would not have been written except for Butler's example; they include Bennett's *Clayhanger*, Lawrence's *Sons and Lovers*, Maugham's *Of Human Bondage*, even Joyce's *A Portrait of the Artist as a Young Man*, and certainly these authors had little affinity with Butler temperamentally or as artists. But his novel, as far as subject goes, stands as a prototype.

Now that we have passed through the period of reaction against the Victorians and can see them with eyes no longer astigmatic from emotion, *The Way of All Flesh* appears a less satisfactory novel than it did. It is in essentials autobiographical, though Butler himself never went to prison like his hero Ernest Pontifex and Ernest did not migrate to New Zealand like his creator, and its weakness as a novel is that it forces one back to Butler. It is the special case masquerading as the representative, and to understand the mechanism of the case one must go to the author's life. In *The Way of All Flesh* Butler comes forward both as prosecuting counsel and as judge; his conduct of the case is brilliant; the defendants haven't a chance; and willy-nilly the reader finds the role of defending counsel thrust upon him, which means in effect he becomes the judge of the judge as well.

The defendants are Butler's parents, represented as the Rev. Theobald Pontifex and his wife Christina. There are two Butlers, or two representatives of him, in the novel: Ernest, the little victim of his father's tyranny and his mother's emotional blackmail, and his godfather Overton, the narrator, who is the adult Butler explaining, analyzing, commenting on his own childhood. The presence of Overton was probably essential to Butler's purpose, for he was writing a novel with a thesis; one way and another, all Butler's conclusions about life and right living come into the book; it cannot therefore be judged as we judge a novel of James or Moore. But it means that we have to take into account the nature of the thesis and Butler's conclusions.

Overton is certainly used clumsily. It is not that he comes between us and the brilliantly cold comedy of Butler's exposure of Theobald and Christina, but his running commentary upon them compels us in the end to feel a sympathy for them quite opposite to Butler's intentions. We are meant to be morally horrified by the Pontifexes' unconscious hypocrisy and pious cruelty; and so we are, when instances of these are allowed to speak for themselves, when they are presented dramatically, as in such scenes as Theobald's beating of the three-year-old Ernest after Sunday evening prayers because he cannot pronounce the word "come" or Christina's famous letter to her children written to be opened after her death. In such scenes Theobald and Christina are exposed as something like moral monsters of self-righteousness, vanity, and rationalization. But the running commentary, the essays, one is tempted to call them, in which they are embedded, are altogether too much, wonderfully witty though they are. When Overton tells us of Christina, after her engagement to Theobald:

. . . Christina pictured herself and Theobald as braving the scorn of almost every human being in the achievement of some mighty task which should redound to the honour of her Redeemer. She could face anything for this. But always towards the end of her vision there came a little coronation scene high up in the golden regions of the Heavens, and a diadem was set upon her head by the Son of Man Himself, amid a host of angels and archangels who looked on with envy and admiration—and here even Theobald himself was out of it. If there could be such a thing as the Mammon of Righteousness Christina would have assuredly made friends with him—

when we are confronted with a whole sequence of passages like this, we realize that the scales have been tipped against the Pontifexes from the beginning and that Butler is going to see they remain tipped. Theobald and Christina are not to have the credit for any disinterested action and scarcely for their good intentions. They are to be allowed to do nothing right. Once this is realized, it is difficult to avoid seeing Butler's hatred and contempt for them as other than disproportionate and neurotic. The lack of charity—in a writer whose articles of belief included 1 Corinthians 13—is suffocating, and one thinks with the greater appreciation of Bennett's treatment of old Darius Clayhanger in *Clayhanger*. Darius had been a tyrant to Edwin (as indeed it seems Bennett's own father was to Bennett), but at the end Edwin's generosity of mind is such that he can see the old man as pitiable, moving as the spectacle of an empire in ruins is moving.

Then there is the thesis—one might say the purpose—of Butler in *The Way of All Flesh*. An expert in demolition, he was wholly successful in demolishing the repressive, low-church, middle-class Victorian family and its values. But what did he put in their place? As far as *The Way of All Flesh* goes, very little. Without his parents, Ernest is a thin and dim character; it is impossible to care for him or for what happens to him; and the freedom he achieves is a pretty dingy affair: parenthood without responsibility, a comfortable private income, a philosophy of life that boils down to a smug hedonism, and the conscious superiority which goes with a reputation for being an advanced thinker. There are splendid comic passages in the second half of the novel, in particular Ernest's mistake in confusing a respectable working girl with a prostitute and the trial scene that follows; but the real life of the novel lies in Christina and Theobald as the objects of Butler's hatred.

The therapeutic value of *The Way of All Flesh* for the generation that read it at its first appearance is obvious. For them it must have been as exhilarating as the early plays of Shaw; in it they saw conventional notions of traditional institutions and right behavior go down like ninepins before Butler's satire. Every age has its own brand of romanticism, its special line in cant, which the next generation must debunk, and Butler was a great debunker, and for those in revolt against the Victorian father figure a liberator. The sequence of autobiographical novels of the Edwardian period is an indication of this.

6

In many ways the true heir of Henry James was Joseph Conrad (1857-1924). By birth a Polish aristocrat, he left Cracow at seventeen to become a sailor in the French merchant service. He came to England in 1878 and thereafter sailed in British ships mainly in the Far East. In 1886, he became a naturalized British subject and obtained his Master Mariner's Certificate. He did not, however, obtain a command until two years later. He remained at sea until 1894. His first novel, *Almayer's Folly,* was published a year later.

Conrad had known French from childhood and was widely read in its literature, but he did not begin to learn English until he was twenty-three. That he should have learned it to such purpose as to become a master of our prose comparable in felicity of language and sweep of eloquence with De Quincey and Ruskin is one of the most remarkable feats recorded in literary history. Yet the feat itself, together with his romantic extraliterary career as a sailor in exotic waters, may easily blind us to the essential nature of Conrad's genius as a novelist. He is not great simply because he pulled off a remarkable feat, and though he is a novelist of the sea and of exotic places, he is much more. His life at sea provided him with a store of experiences that he drew upon for the material of his fiction, but the true value of the sea and of the exotic place was that they offered him what might almost be called the laboratory conditions in which he could make his investigations into the nature of man and the springs of action.

Like a later novelist, André Malraux, who has much in common with him in the obviously romantic quality of his career and the exoticism of his scene, Conrad is the novelist of extreme situations. In the greater part of his work his theme is man against himself, the environment, whether sea or exotic place, having a double function, to isolate the character from society and the larger world of men, so that he can be put *in extremis,* and to act as the agent of his self-confrontation. Nature itself can then become a symbol of evil, or rather, nature and the human being appear to exist almost as manifestations of each other.

In his earlier and greater work Conrad is much preoccupied with evil. The nature of the evil is never defined. At its simplest, it is seen as something inherent in the physical universe itself and malevolent towards man, as in this passage from *Lord Jim*:

> Only once in all that time he had again a glimpse of the earnestness in the anger of the sea. That truth is not so often made apparent as people might think. There are many shades in the danger of adventures and gales, and it is only now and then that there appears on the face of facts a sinis-

ter violence of intention—that indefinable something which forces it upon the mind and the heart of a man, that this complication of accidents or these elemental furies are coming at him with a purpose of malice, with a strength beyond control, with an unbridled cruelty that means to tear out of him his hope and his fear, the pain of his fatigue and his longing for rest: which means to smash, to destroy, to annihilate all he has seen, known, loved, enjoyed, or hated; all that is priceless and necessary—the sunshine, the memories, the future—which means to sweep the whole precious world utterly away from his sight by the simple and appalling act of taking his life.

But evil in Conrad can be something much more sinister, much more complex than this, which could be taken as an extreme instance of what Ruskin called "the pathetic fallacy," the reading of human attributes into nature. The nature of this complex "indefinable" evil can best be expressed by stating what is opposed to it. In a famous sentence in his preface to *A Personal Record* Conrad wrote: "Those who read me know my conviction that the world, the temporal world, rests on a few very simple ideas: so simple that they must be as old as the hills. It rests, notably, among others, on the idea of Fidelity." Douglas Hewitt has shown in his *Conrad: a Reassessment* that as a clue to Conrad these words are not to be taken precisely at their face value. Fidelity is the barrier man erects against nothingness, against corruption, against evil which is all about him, insidious, waiting to engulf him, and which is, in some sense, within him unacknowledged. But what happens to a man when the barrier breaks down, when the evil without is acknowledged by the evil within, and fidelity is submerged? This, rather than fidelity itself, is Conrad's theme at his greatest. And from the ever-present danger of having his fidelity, which in a way is his sense of his own moral value, his self-respect, submerged one kind of man only, Conrad implies, is exempt; the completely unimaginative; the truly strong man is Captain MacWhirr, of the steamer *Nan-Shan*, in *Typhoon*, who, according to

Mr. Jukes, got out of his disaster "very well for such stupid man."

Conrad's furthest exploration of evil is his short story *Heart of Darkness* (1902), which describes a voyage up the Congo into the heart of Africa closely resembling a journey Conrad had made. The heart of darkness of the title is at once the heart of Africa, the heart of evil—everything that is nihilistic, corrupt, and malign—and perhaps the heart of man. The story is told by Conrad's famous narrator Marlow and, within its positively dense atmosphere of death, decay, and the cruelties of imperialistic exploitation, it relates the effect on Marlow of the blackness of Africa, its otherness—everything that lies beyond the concept of fidelity—and of the presence, terrifying even when unseen, of Mr. Kurtz, the figure of evil who is worshiped by the natives as a god. It is nearly a story of diabolical possession, for Marlow is compelled to face the fact that in some mysterious way there is a bond between himself and Kurtz. Kurtz, who by comparison with the ordinary commercial exploiters of Africa even has an evil grandeur, is the man Marlow might become. "It is strange," Marlow says, "how I accepted this unforeseen partnership, this choice of nightmares forced upon me in the tenebrous land invaded by these mean and greedy phantoms." He is freed by Kurtz's death; but when he returns to Europe he finds it shrouded in the darkness symbolized by Africa and the mean and greedy phantoms battening on it.

In Conrad's fiction as in James's, form, content, and language cannot be separated; there is a complete interpenetration between all these parts of the novelist's art. Whatever is in the novel is there to produce a calculated effect and to cooperate towards a total impression. Ford Madox Ford, who collaborated with Conrad and was greatly indebted to him in his own fiction, has described their common attitude towards the novel in *Return to Yesterday*:

We used to say . . . that a Subject must be seized by the throat until the last drop of dramatic possibility was squeezed out of it. . . . A novel was to be the rendering of an Affair: of one embroilment, one set of embarrassments, one human coil, one psychological progression. From this the Novel got its Unity. No doubt it must have its caesura—or even several; but these must be brought about by temperamental pauses, markings of time when the treatment called for them. But the whole novel was to be an exhaustion of aspects, was to proceed to one culmination, to reveal, once for all, in the last sentences, or the penultimate; in the last phrase, or the one before it—the psychological significance of the whole.

Ford's account has a weakness: it might suggest that Conrad is a psychological novelist. He is not; he is a moralist, not a psychologist. But how point the moral without at the same time abandoning the objectivity to which he was committed as an artist? He does so in more than one way, but the commonest is by using a narrator, Marlow more often than not, to tell the story. It was not the only reason for using Marlow, for, as with Nelly Dean in *Wuthering Heights,* his presence helps to dramatize the action and compels us to see it through his eyes; it provides an intense focus. Yet the device of Marlow does enable Conrad to make overt comments of a kind he otherwise could not. But here we must be careful. Is Marlow merely a device? In origin almost certainly. To gather a number of men of the world round a dinner table and have one of them relate a strange personal experience is one of the oldest, and now one of the stalest, contrivances in English magazine fiction, and perhaps it is especially associated with *Blackwood's Magazine*. Conrad early wrote for that periodical—*Lord Jim* was serialized there— and it may be that at first he was merely conforming to a way of storytelling traditional to *Blackwood's*. Beyond that, the question does not admit of a single answer. Marlow, a sea captain and a man of vast experience of the exotic, is admittedly a *persona* for Conrad himself, but there are times, as in *Heart of Darkness* and *Lord Jim*, when he is more than a *persona*; a character in his own right involved in the action and changed by it. Later, in *Chance*, he is scarcely involved and certainly not changed. Then he is a device and nothing more. Seen as a device simply, he is most satisfactory in relatively short pieces like *Heart of Darkness*. In the novels the convention becomes a strain on credibility, and Conrad does not help by reminding us, in his preface to *Lord Jim*, that members have been known to talk for six hours at a stretch in the House of Commons. But for Conrad himself the value of such a figure as Marlow was immense; it was that of a self-dramatization that allowed him to comment and point a moral as he could not do in his own person as novelist. Conrad, like James, is the historian of fine consciences, and Marlow is the connoisseur of the fine conscience, the evaluator as well as the recorder.

His job, to use Ford's phrase, is to exhaust all the aspects of the affair. He does this in *Lord Jim* (1900). Here, the fine conscience is Jim's, the idealistic young first mate of the *Patna*, a steamer "eaten up with rust worse than a condemned water-tank" and packed with pilgrims on the way to Mecca. We see him on the bridge:

> At such times his thoughts would be full of valorous deeds: he loved these dreams and the success of his imaginary achievements. They were the best parts of life, its secret truth, its hidden reality. They had a gorgeous virility, the charm of vagueness, they passed before him with a heroic tread; they carried his soul away with them and made it drunk with the divine philtre of an unbounded confidence in itself. There was nothing he could not face. He was so pleased with the idea that he smiled, keeping perfunctorily his eyes ahead; and when he happened to glance back he saw the white streak of the wake drawn as straight by the ship's keel upon the sea as the black line drawn by the pencil upon the chart.

"There was nothing he could not face." Yet, when he thinks the steamer is sinking with its human cargo for which no boats exist, he panics and jumps into the sea. With the other officers in the one boat, he imagines he sees the ship's lights disappear. In fact, the ship and its cargo are rescued by a French warship, and Jim takes it upon himself, as a moral duty, to undergo official examination. Marlow is present in the court and describes it at length. This is the first part of the novel, and the finest.

"The bitterness of his punishment," Marlow comments, "was in its chill and mean atmosphere. The real significance of crime is in its being a breach of faith with the community of mankind, and from that point of view he was no mean traitor, but his execution was a hole-and-corner affair." His execution, in effect, consists in his drifting further and further East, seeking a personal redemption, rehabilitation of himself in his own eyes, but he is dogged always by the shadow of his guilt. He is an outcast. Then the opportunity for redemption in his own eye arrives. He becomes the ruler of a remote district in Malaya. He has achieved "the conquest of love, honour, men's confidence." And then he is suddenly undone. His territory is penetrated, as a last refuge, by a renegade Englishman, Gentleman Brown, and his gang. Brown is the figure of evil in the novel, characterized by "the arrogant temper of his misdeeds and a vehement scorn for mankind at large and for his victims in particular . . . he seemed moved by some complex intention." Against him, Tuan Jim has no chance at all. Brown is in a sense the tempter

> He asked Jim whether he had nothing fishy in his life to remember that he was so damnedly hard upon a man trying to get out of a deadly hole by the first means that came to hand—and so on and so on. And there ran through the rough talk a vein of subtle reference to their common blood, an assumption of common experience; a sickening suggestion of common guilt, of secret knowledge that was like a bond of their minds and of their hearts.

The situation is a version of the Kurtz-Marlow relation in *Heart of Darkness*. In a way Brown's words represent the opinion of the world about Jim; but they are also echoes, as it were, of a small voice within him. "We are betrayed," Conrad could have said with Meredith, "by what is false within." Bound to Brown by a shared guilt, Jim brings ruin on Patusan, and is killed himself by the villagers.

Marlow's final comment on Jim and his fate is: "He is one of us—and have I not stood up once, like an evoked ghost, to answer for his eternal constancy?" "One of us": a man of honor, a man pledged to fidelity. But if Jim is one with Marlow, Marlow is also one with him. The weakness, the breaking, could have been his. In Conrad's world, "Though he believe it, no man is strong"; the gulf of nullity is always at his feet, and the sea and exotic places are not the causes of his destruction but the agents, and to this extent counterparts of the destructive elements within him.

Useful as Marlow was to Conrad, in his novels he did his finest work when he dispensed with him and relied for the expression of his point of view on other means. For Marlow has one fatal defect: he talks too much and sometimes in the wrong way. Like his creator, he is a lord of language, but there are times when he becomes intoxicated by the exuberance of his own gorgeous verbosity. Conrad's prose is always heightened, heightened to a degree much above what is normal in English. It is essentially eloquent, a prose of peroration, to the total effect of which everything is subdued: choice of words, rhythms, balance of clauses, length of sentences, culmination of paragraph. The total effect aimed at, as in James's very different, much more intimate prose, is to heighten character. Here Conrad is certainly successful. But there are occasions, especially when Marlow is speaking for Conrad, when the prose is overdone and becomes hollow. It seems then to exist not to express meaning but to conceal it; and what is worse, sometimes to conceal absence of meaning. It becomes a splendid smoke screen, a dazzling tapestry of magnificently sonorous language. Certain words are always danger signals to the attentive reader of Conrad; when he comes across "exotic," "enigmatic," "inscrutable," he had better look out: a confidence trick is about to be played upon him.

The confidence trick occurs when, the tragic vision having failed or become momentarily blurred, the grand style falls into rhetoric. It is from about 1910 onwards that Conrad gives way to rhetoric, the tragic vision having departed. "There seems to have been within him," Douglas Hewitt has said, "a continual war between the recognition of the 'heart of darkness' and the desire to rest securely on unquestioned values." The latter won. It may be seen happening in *Under Western Eyes* (1911), though there Conrad was perhaps betrayed partly by his hatred of Russia and all things Russian. But the confidence trick may be seen at its most thoroughgoing in *Chance* (1913). Marlow is again the narrator, but it is a different Marlow, no longer the indefatigably inquisitive scrutineer of the human heart, but a character much more rigid in attitude and sympathy, who dresses up platitudes in superb clothing and is in the end curious to little purpose. In *Chance* technique has become an end in itself, and what you have is no longer a view of human beings as essentially flawed, with darkness at the heart of things, but melodrama peopled with characters morally all white or all black. And from then on, Conrad's work was melodrama, written by a man of genius but still melodrama, with the hollowness of rhetoric prevailing. It was to this declension in his art that Sir Desmond MacCarthy's friend was referring when he said of *The Rover* (1923), "I have just finished listening to a performance on the Conrad."

Even so, Conrad's best work represents a body of achievement unequaled in English fiction this century by any writer except James. And reading him today, one realizes, as one did not twenty-five years ago, when he was often regarded as a sort of bridge between boys' adventure stories and adult literature, how essentially modern he is. Wells and Bennett already date as a novelist such as Trollope does; they plainly belong to an age that is past and write out of assumptions about the nature of society and men no longer current or readily acceptable except by the deliberate exercise of the historical imagination all fiction of the past, apart from the greatest, compels us to make. The world Conrad describes, the moral dilemmas facing his characters, are those we know today, that seem to us now, as someone has said, almost to have come into existence in 1940.

His best work, it seems to me, consists of the short stories "Youth," "Heart of Darkness," "Typhoon," "Falk," and "The Secret Sharer," and the novels *The Nigger of the "Narcissus"* (1897), *Lord Jim, Nostromo* (1904), and *The Secret Agent* (1907). Of the novels, *Nostromo* is undoubtedly the finest; a good case could be made out for considering it the greatest novel in English of this century. It represents a remarkable extension of Conrad's genius. Before and after it, his concern was with man in isolation: Lord Jim, or Axel Heyst in *Victory* (1915). The environments that hemmed in their isolation and the other human beings threatening it were certainly set down in the concretest detail; there is no question of their reality; yet at the center of most of Conrad's novels and stories is the solitary man fighting against what is outside him. The characters of *Nostromo* are still in the deepest sense solitaries, but they are not detached from society; indeed, in great part the courses their lives take are dictated by the nature of the particular society in which they have their existence. *Nostromo* is a political novel in the profoundest meaning of the word and—this is the index of Conrad's achievement—it may stand as a picture of the modern world in microcosm.

In it, with the utmost plausibility, he invents a whole country, the South American republic of Costaguana, with its especial geography, history, and economy, its political struggles and its revolutions. But this is merely the beginning. Costaguana is almost as cut off from the rest of the world, by the ocean and by mountain ranges, as any ship; it provides Conrad, in other words, just as much as did the isolation of *Heart of Darkness* and *Lord Jim,* with the laboratory conditions in which he can make his investigation into the nature of man, but this time it is man in relation to society and politics. There rise up in Costaguana, or enter it from outside, all the forces that shape the modern world: nationalism, liberalism, journalism, finance capitalism, colonial exploitation; and all these, in one way or another, are there and as they are because of the existence of the silver mine at San Tomé. Silver is Costaguana's *raison d'être* in the modern world, and silver dominates the novel. As Conrad himself informed a correspondent, "silver is the pivot of the moral and material events, affecting the lives of everybody in the tale." It is, as much as the houseful of beautiful furniture in James's *The Spoils of Poynton,* the Commanding Center of *Nostromo*; it gives the novel its unity. And besides being the lever by which Conrad can set in motion in his microcosm all the forces shaping the modern world, it exists as the great betrayer, the undoer and the perverter of men and their ideals. Marlow, in *Lord Jim,* notes of sea captains forced to abandon their ships: "There was a villainy of circumstance that cut these men off more completely from the rest of mankind, whose ideal of conduct had never undergone the trial of a fiendish and appalling joke." The very existence of the silver of San Tomé provides the trial, in this novel, of a fiendish and appalling joke.

There is Charles Gould, the owner of the mine. He lives

for it from the least ignoble of motives, one of which is family piety; another he puts to his wife in these words:

> "What is wanted here is law, good faith, order, security. Any one can declaim about these things, but I pin my faith to material interests. Only let the material interests once get a firm footing, and they are bound to impose the conditions on which alone they can continue to exist. That's how your money-making is justified here in the face of lawlessness and disorder. It is justified because the security which it demands must be shared with an oppressed people. A better justice will come afterwards. That's your ray of hope."

Gould is caught in the liberal capitalist dream. But events cast their shadow before in Conrad's statement:

> Charles Gould was competent because he had no illusions. The Gould Concession had to fight for life with such weapons as could be found at once in the mire of corruption that was so universal as to almost lose its significance. He was prepared to stoop for his weapons. For a moment he felt as if the silver mine, which had killed his father, had decoyed him further than he meant to go; and with the roundabout logic of emotions, he felt that the worthiness of his life was bound up with success. There was no going back.

But as Dr. Monygham, who may be taken as one of Conrad's spokesmen, warns Mrs. Gould:

> "There is no peace and no rest in the development of material interests. They have their law, and their justice. But it is founded on expediency, and is inhuman; it is without rectitude, without the continuity and the force that can be found only in a moral principle. Mrs. Gould, the time approaches when all that the Gould Concession stands for shall weigh as heavily upon the people as the barbarism, cruelty, and misrule of a few years back."

The corruption of Gould's ideals is implicit in his very commitment to the mine; and the commitment has another consequence: in the end it separates him from his wife.

Similarly, Nostromo, the Magnificent Capataz, the Man

of the People, the heroic leader possessed by the sense of glory, is perverted by the silver and in the end comes to his death through it.

It has been suggested that the characters of *Nostromo* are "humors" rather than characters in the round. There is something in this. Each has his ruling passion, which often becomes his besetting sin. Thus Gould has his obsession with the mine, an obsession of duty. About Nostromo, Decoud, "incorrigible in his scepticism, reflected, not cynically, but with general satisfaction, that this man was made incorruptible by his enormous vanity, that finest form of egoism which can take on the aspect of every virtue." Nostromo's enormous vanity consists in his hunger and thirst for the love of the people with whom he identifies himself. Similarly, Dr. Monygham's experience of torture and imprisonment "seemed to bind him indissolubly to the land of Costaguana like an awful procedure of naturalization, involving him deep in the national life, far deeper than any amount of success and honour could have done. They did away with his Europeanism; for Dr. Monygham had made himself an ideal conception of his disgrace."

It is through their ideal conceptions of themselves that Conrad interprets his characters. We see them, therefore, from an acute angle of vision; they live intensely, but within relatively narrow limits. In the context of the novel, however, these limits do not diminish the impression they make of reality. Indeed, Conrad so sets them in the scene, so poses them, as to persuade us not only of their ordinary reality as lifelike characters but of their symbolic reality.

An obvious instance is the method of portraying Nostromo. Just before Decoud, in the passage quoted above, has noted that Nostromo has been made incorruptible by his enormous vanity, the Man of the People has assured him that "silver is an incorruptible metal that can be trusted to keep its value for ever." Conrad's irony is plain, but at the moment it is more important to realize that throughout the novel Nostromo is associated with silver and when he makes his appearance in any scene in the novel the word silver is almost certain to occur. The result —and it is true of the other characters too—may be a simplification, but it is also an intensification, and it sets up a complex system of cross references and ironies that weaves the book into a single texture.

Conrad's subject in *Nostromo* was too vast in implications, in scene, and in range and number of characters to allow him to use a narrator like Marlow. One effect of this is that the rhetoric, the retreat into grandiloquent vagueness, is almost absent, so that the novel has a strength and sinew unmatched in his other work. Another is that the absence of the narrator forced him to dramatize his point of view. So the action is reflected and interpreted in the consciousnesses of certain of the characters who, though never passive and all furthering the action, function incidentally as a chorus to the whole. These characters include Mrs. Gould, Dr. Monygham, Decoud, and also the naive, stupid Captain Mitchell, "Fussy Joe," whose heavily pompous, God-given store of cliché and platitude on the theme of progress in Costaguana represents Conrad's most ironical comment on the action of the novel.

Nostromo is the most highly organized novel in English apart from perhaps the late James and Joyce's *Ulysses*. The remarkable effects of depth and recession obtained are a result of its organization, an adequate analysis of which would be impossible in the space of anything less than an extended essay.

7

During their lifetimes H. G. Wells and Arnold Bennett achieved a public fame of a kind that has been no other English novelist's before or since. They would not have had it had they not been novelists in the first place, and yet the nature of the fame had little to do with their novels as such. It was essentially that of the journalist, the popular pundit prepared to pronounce on any subject under the sun with complete self-assurance. With Shaw, whose popular reputation was also a product of journalism, they divided between them the empire of the press, the most highly paid writers in the Anglo-Saxon world.

All that has nothing to do with their merits as novelists. Both were men of vast output in fiction; to say nothing of their short stories, Wells wrote nearly fifty novels, Bennett thirty. Of these, perhaps ten of Wells's are still valuable in their own right, if the best of the scientific romances are included, and, more certainly, five of Bennett's.

Wells was born in 1866, Bennett a year later. Both were from the lower middle class, but from very different sections of it. Wells was from the feudal south, in revolt against a traditional class system, Bennett from the industrial north, where the dominant class was the middle class, into which Bennett's father had climbed during his son's lifetime. The difference between the environments of their childhoods may be stated, admittedly in an exaggerated form, as follows: Wells came of the servant class, Bennett of the class that kept servants. The difference was to be reflected in their work. Their attitudes to the novel were also unlike. Wells was impatient of art. He had no greater admirer than James, but he reacted petulantly and brutally against James's attempts to convert him to the aesthetic view of fiction. For him, the novel was essentially a medium of ideas. "I would rather," he wrote in his *Experiment in Autobiography*, "be regarded as a journalist." Bennett's approach was nothing if not aesthetic; in the early parts of his *Journals* he is continually restating the Naturalist doctrines, as in such a passage as this:

11 *January*, 1897. The novelist of contemporary manners needs to be saturated with a sense of the picturesque in modern things. Walking down Edith Grove this afternoon,

I observed the vague, mysterious beauty of the vista of houses and bare trees melting imperceptibly into a distance of grey fog. And then, in King's Road, the figures of tradesmen at shop doors, of children romping or stealing along mournfully, of men and women each totally different from every other, and all serious, wrapt up in their own thoughts and ends—these seemed curiously strange and novel and wonderful. Every scene, even the commonest, is wonderful, if only one can detach oneself, casting off all memory of use and custom, and behold it (as it were) for the first time; in its own right, authentic colours; without making comparisons. The novelist should cherish and burnish this faculty of seeing crudely, simply, artlessly, ignorantly; of seeing like a baby or a lunatic, who lives each moment by itself and tarnishes the present by no remembrance of the past.

Wells, it seems to me, had greater genius than any other novelist of his time in England; Bennett was a man of talent and ambition. But in his best work the theories he took over from the French enabled him to make the fullest use of his talent, while Wells, for lack of any serious concern for his art, before he was halfway through his career—gave up for mankind what was meant for the novel—I cannot help thinking to mankind's ultimate loss.

Wells's work falls broadly in three phases in roughly chronological sequence. Before 1900 most of his fiction consisted of scientific romances; after 1900, though he continued on occasion to write them, until about 1910 the main stress is on comedy; and then from about 1910 his interest for the most part was in the novel of ideas. The work of the last phase can be ignored; novels like *The New Machiavelli, Joan and Peter,* and *Mr. Britling Sees It Through* had a topical value in their day, but little literary interest now; while no one is likely again to read *The World of William Clissold* (in three volumes), the fictitious autobiography of a character closely resembling Wells himself, when he can read the *Experiment in Autobiography,* which is not fiction.

The scientific romances are still unsurpassed of their

kind. They are intellectual *jeux d'esprit*; *The First Men in the Moon* (1901) may be taken as typical. Wells works out, in all its implications, what would happen, on current knowledge, if men reached the moon. It is fantasy based on logic. The first difficulty, how to get to the moon, is brilliantly jumped over. He invents—or his scientist Cavor invents—"Cavorite," a substance "opaque to all forms of radiant energy" and therefore to gravity. There is no attempt at explaining it: Wells's narrator, Bedford, is not a scientist. Cavor's calculations might have been understood by Kelvin or Professor Lodge or Professor Karl Pearson, but reduced him to a hopeless muddle:

> Suffice it for this story that he believed he might be able to manufacture this possible substance opaque to gravitation out of a complicated alloy of metals and something new—a new element, I fancy—called, I believe, *helium,* which was sent to him from London in sealed stone jars. Doubt has been thrown upon this detail, but I am almost certain it was *helium* he had sent him in sealed stone jars. It was certainly something very gaseous and thin. . . .

The characterization is as sketchy as it could be: Cavor, with his cricket cap—a headgear, if popular literature is any guide, considered tremendously funny in late Victorian and Edwardian England—is the scientist of the comic papers; Bedford is a vulgar *entrepreneur,* a very crude satire on the businessman in an age of conscious imperialism. But what matters is the sheer fertility of Wells's imagination, which in these books is moved much more by the contemplation of science and its possibilities than by human beings. The descriptions of the surface of the moon, with its extreme cold by night, its extreme heat by day, and its proliferation of plant life that rises and dies within a single day, are still wonderful to read. And even more impressive is the creation of the Selenites, the curious, anālike beings which inhabit the moon. This picture of a community based on extreme speciality of function is the

rendering of a horrible utopia, a nightmare Plato's Republic, the force of which is probably stronger for us who
have witnessed totalitarian states and tyrannies than it
could have been for its first readers.

It is easy to see what *The First Men in the Moon* ought
to be. While reading, we are constantly reminded of Swift,
not only of Laputa but, at the end, of Brobdingnag. And
the reminiscences are fatal. What one feels should be profound satire remains merely an exciting story. But all the
same, the brilliance of imagination and the sheer creative
high spirits will probably keep *The First Men in the Moon*
and the best of Wells's other scientific romances read for
many years to come.

Wells's comic novels, *Love and Mr. Lewisham* (1900),
Kipps (1905), *The History of Mr. Polly* (1910), are on a
higher plane of intention. *Mr. Polly* seems to me perfect
of its kind, Wells's undoubted masterpiece, delightful,
comic, and oddly moving. Because it is all these it is Wells's
most effective criticism of society. For its theme is education; or rather, the inadequacies of popular education,
which are summed up in the endearing figure of Mr.
Polly, who, in his delight in the resources of language and
the exuberance of his imagination, might be an uneducated Wells. He is the little man in revolt, but inasmuch
as he is a little man he is in himself an indictment of the
society which has made him, since he is plainly a representation of a human being whose potentialities have been
wasted. Norman Nicholson, in his book on Wells, has per-
ceptively suggested that the only comic character in
modern fiction to be compared to him is Joyce's Leopold
Bloom. The association of the two characters certainly
indicates the kind of thing Wells was attempting in the
creation of Mr. Polly. Polly is the perpetually soliloquiz-
ing fantasist whose environment can provide his imagination with nothing to bite on, and he is seen, as Wells does
not always see his lower-middle-class characters, with affec-

tion. The novel is conceived on a much smaller scale than anything in Dickens, but Dickens himself created no surer character than Mr. Polly. He is in many ways the hero of a fairy story, but a hero he is, and has his moment of recognition as such, when, having failed to kill himself and fire his shop for the insurance, he rescues his neighbor's aunt.

The History of Mr. Polly is very much an English novel. It recapitulates a main tradition in our fiction, that from the eighteenth century of Fielding and Smollett to Dickens. And it can stand up to the comparisons. Indeed, when one thinks of the account of Mr. Polly's father's funeral, of the wonderful character of Uncle Pentstemon, and of such remarks of Polly's as "Second—second Departed I've ever seen—not counting mummies," there is only Dickens who can be invoked; just as, in the presence of the great scenes of the fire and the Homeric fight with Uncle Jim at the Potwell Inn, we discover anew what Fielding meant by the comic epic.

The History of Mr. Polly shows Wells following his natural genius. But already, before writing that novel, he had gone astray and embarked on the novel as journalism, as topical comment, in *Ann Veronica* (1909). In the same year he had published *Tono-Bungay,* his most ambitious fiction and the bridge between his comic novels and his novels of ideas. Had he realized his ambition in this work he would have produced a novel, however different, comparable in intention and scope to *Nostromo.* But he was too impatient, too impatient of art, and *Tono-Bungay* is a novel of excellent interludes in an embarrassing muddle. It begins brilliantly, with its *David Copperfield*-like account of life in the great house, Bladesover, from the vantage point of a boy in the servants' hall. The boy is George Ponderevo, the hero and the narrator. It was probably fatal that Wells decided to tell his story in the first person, especially since Ponderevo is as much concerned with ideas as his creator; it meant almost inevi-

tably that ideas and digressions would swamp the novel,
which is partly a satire on the irresponsibility of capitalism,
partly a plea for the necessity of a planned society. The
satire on capitalism, so long as it is embodied in the figure
of George's Uncle Ponderevo, is effective, though not exactly, perhaps, as Wells intended. For Uncle Ponderevo
steals the book—Uncle Ponderevo the pinchbeck Napoleon of commerce, the little chemist who invents the pat-
ent medicine Tono-Bungay, becomes a millionaire, and
dies a fugitive from the law babbling of visionary palaces,
an end, as we know from *Experiment in Autobiography,*
Wells got from his observations at the death bed of George
Gissing. Moreover, Uncle Ponderevo steals our affections,
as Mr. Polly does. He is of Polly's breed, but a Polly given
a larger stage and allowed to translate his fantasies into
action. The results are criminal, but what one remembers
are the wistfulness and the innocence. He has the pathos
of the victim of his own fantasies.

George Ponderevo is another matter. He is the conscience of the novel, but not an adequate one. Wells was
incapable of being anything but sentimentally vulgar on
the subject of sexual love. George, like all those of his
heroes who in some sense are *personae* of Wells himself,
has the most naive and adolescent romantic notions of
love, which are presented quite uncritically and in novel-
ettish terms. The sensibility displayed is too crude for the
criticism even of the economic system to have much weight.

What *Tono-Bungay* conspicuously lacks is, of course, a
Commanding Center, the principle making for unity. It
is still readable but it reads now as improvisation. There
is, for example, the incident of George's journey to Mor-
det Island to bring back the Quap, the radioactive earth
which is to restore the Ponderevos' falling fortunes. It is
brilliantly done, but is plainly an afterthought. And the
book ends with the muddle increased, with the destroyer
George has built seen as a symbol of truth. It is one of

Wells's shoddiest and most careless pieces of writing. In the penultimate paragraph of the novel Wells refers to the "turgid degenerate Kiplingese" of the journalists. At the moment of writing it, he did not have the right to sneer.

Arnold Bennett was born at Hanley, one of the six pottery towns—Bennett in his fiction made them five, for the sake of euphony—that now make up the city of Stoke-on-Trent. This is one of the oldest industrial conurbations of England. For earlier novelists who had dealt with the industrial scene, the subject came as a moral challenge. Disraeli, Mrs. Gaskell, Dickens, were southerners for whom the industrial north was essentially alien; the revolution that had made it was new and frightening, an affront and a threat, and its towns were at once centers of a new kind of power and a new kind of man and the breeding places of a new kind of misery. For Bennett, the Potteries were neither new nor frightening; they were the perfectly familiar: home. Bennett's scene, as he realized himself, was fresh material for English fiction. It was in every way ugly, and yet however unpromising the surroundings there is a certain type of mind which craves for beauty, must find it, and where it is lacking, must create it for itself. Bennett's was such a mind. The English novelists who were his predecessors could give him singularly little help here. He was able to do what he did in the first place because of what he learned from the French, that beauty might lie not in the matter presented but in the manner in which it was presented. It was a discovery that made the Five Towns novels possible, and also it gave Bennett the strength and assuredness that comes from a writer's knowledge that he is working with the sanction of an established tradition behind him.

Bennett at his best, in *Anna of the Five Towns* (1902), *The Old Wives' Tale* (1908), and the three Clayhanger novels, *Clayhanger* (1910), *Hilda Lessways* (1911), and

These Twain (1916), is entirely a regional novelist. But he is regional in a different way from that of Hardy. Hardy was of Wessex and remained of Wessex, as Bennett was never of the Five Towns. For Hardy, Wessex was a microcosm of the universe, and we accept it as such. But for Bennett the Five Towns were provincial; he left them when he was twenty-one and never returned to them for longer than a few days at a time. Steeped as he was in them, in their atmosphere, history, and traditions, as a writer he was completely outside them. His attitude towards them is always expository; he is explaining them, exhibiting them, to an outside world that is not provincial. They exist in relation to a larger world that Bennett accepts as the norm. The result is that though the Five Towns novels transcend the Five Towns, what we get in them is a picture of the provinces. The picture is true because it is of the provinces; in Hardy the picture is true not simply because it is of Wessex. At his best Bennett does achieve universality of a kind, but it is not Hardy's kind. It is, if such a thing is possible, a limited universality, true for a certain kind of community at a certain point in time, a picture of life not only in the Five Towns but in any industrial provincial community during the last three decades of the nineteenth century. It is a very considerable achievement, but not in the class of the greatest. It is only in a few passages in *The Old Wives' Tale* and *The Clayhanger Family* that we are brought face to face not merely with the human situation at a given date and place in North Staffordshire but with the eternal human situation. This is to say that though Bennett, in three or four books, is a master, he is a minor master.

In *The Old Wives' Tale* and *The Clayhanger Family* Bennett's aim was to unroll the panorama of life in time through all the tiny, detailed incidents of its thousand acts. His was normally the opposite of the dramatic method; James compared it to "the many-fingered grasp of the orange that the author squeezes." But there is one exception among his novels to this general principle of composition: the early and much neglected *Anna of the Five Towns*, a highly organized composition dramatically presented. Anna is seen from a comparatively narrow angle of vision, rendered not full face, as are the central characters of the later novels, but from the point of view implicit in the moving last pages of the book:

> She had promised to marry Mynors, and she married him. Nothing else was possible. She who had never failed in duty did not fail then. She who had always submitted and bowed the head, submitted and bowed the head then. She had sucked in with her mother's milk the profound truth that a woman's life is always a renunciation, greater or less. Hers by chance was greater . . .

Bennett had noted in his *Journal* the "essential characteristic of the really great novelist: a Christlike, all-embracing compassion," and *Anna of the Five Towns* is an exercise in compassion. Brought up to render implicit obedience to her father, the miser Ephraim Tellwright, who had once grown "garrulous with God at prayer-meetings" but later became supreme in "the finance of salvation . . . in the negotiation of mortgages, the artful arrangement of the incidence of collections, the manufacture of special appeals, the planning of anniversaries and of mighty revivals . . . the interminable alternation of debt-raising and new liability which provides a last excitement for Nonconformists," Anna inherits her mother's money when she comes of age, and at Tellwright's behest becomes a sleeping partner in the pottery of Henry Mynors, a rising young businessman who is a pillar of Methodism. Among her other properties is the factory of Titus Price, the Sunday school superintendent. Mynors falls in love with Anna, proposes, and is accepted; and Anna realizes too late that it is Willy Price she loves, the pathetic and much contemned youth who has committed forgery in an effort to save his father, whom Tellwright and other creditors have driven to suicide.

The story is set firmly in terms of Methodism, the faith Bennett was brought up in and which he early abandoned without much sympathy for it. But he treats it with absolute fairness: Methodism was an integral part of the community in which his actions took place, the channel of its spiritual and cultural aspirations, and Bennett has dealt with it as an element in the lives of the industrial middle class more faithfully than any other novelist before or since. But he treats, too, the characters in *Anna* with scrupulous fairness. Mynors, for example, is given great natural dignity; and even the grotesque Titus Price achieves dignity in the hour of death:

> Here was a man whom no one respected, but everyone pretended to respect—who knew that he was respected by none, but pretended that he was respected by all; whose whole career was made up of dissimulations: religious, moral, and social. If any man could have been trusted to continue the decent sham to the end, and so preserve the general self-esteem, surely it was this man. But no! Suddenly abandoning all imposture, he transgresses openly, brazenly; and, snatching a bit of hemp cries: "Behold me; this is real human nature. This is the truth; the rest was lies. I lied; you lied. I confess it, and you shall confess it." Such a thunderclap shakes the very base of the microcosm.

These characters are excellently drawn, and so too are the charming Mrs. Sutton, the only truly sympathetic study of a religious person in Bennett's works, and the miser Tellwright. But the triumph of the novel is Anna, that compound of honesty, innocence, and pride who cannot bring herself to be publicly saved at the revival and who, in the greatest moment of her life, can flout her upbringing and defy her father from sheer compassion for Willy Price.

In *Anna of the Five Towns* Bennett was writing more nearly at the tragic level than ever he was to do later. His view of life was not tragic; it was a stoical acceptance of things as they are, a reluctant conformism. The great discovery of Edwin Clayhanger's life is "Injustice is a tremendous actuality! It had to be faced and accepted." And life is something for Bennett that exists wholly in time, the simplest, least philosophically construed time, time that is the ticking of the clock. The French poet Laforgue sighed: *Ah, que la vie est quotidienne!* For Bennett that life is quotidian is exactly the point about it. It is this almost loving subjection to time as the succession of minutes, hours, months, years that makes *The Old Wives' Tale* the most impressive record we have in English of life in time, of birth, change, and decay. We know that it was Bennett's most deliberately and seriously pondered work; we have its moment of conception, recorded the next day in the *Journal*; and we know that in writing it Bennett was in conscious rivalry with Maupassant in *Une Vie*. But perhaps what is much more important to realize is the simple basis of the novel, which is that of so many of the most moving lyric poems, that girls must grow old and beauty fade.

Bennett's thesis, that young girls grow into fat old women, may be a limited truth, but it is worked out with the fullest intensity; continuously throughout the novel the contrast between youth and age is illustrated in a series of instances that ends only with the end of the book. And the girls Constance and Sophia—for Bennett went one better than Maupassant by having two heroines—grow into womanhood and old age in relation not only to a succession of characters older and younger than themselves but also to the history of Bursley. The flow of time governs background as well as characters; horse trams change to steam trams and thence to electric. The novel is the history of a community as well as of two old women. Bennett describes the paralysis of John Baines as "a tragedy in ten thousand acts." The use of the word tragedy is journalistic, but as Bennett employs the phrase it equally describes *The Old Wives' Tale* itself. And never have the tens of thousands of acts which make a lifetime of daily life been more cunningly disposed.

However much Bennett might try to emulate Maupassant, *The Old Wives' Tale* has a quite un-Naturalistic warmth. It is much less objective than it seems at first glance. And this is shown by a comparison between the Paris section, where Bennett is objective, and the rest of the novel. Brilliant as it is, the account of life during the siege is something "got up," a tour de force. But it is not sufficiently woven into the texture of the work as a whole, and indeed it was scarcely possible that it could have been. At the time of writing the novel, Bennett had lived eight years in Paris, but he had spent the twenty most formative years of his life in the Potteries, some of them in the very draper's shop of which he was writing. The Bainses, the Poveys, Mr. Critchlow, Maggie, must have been as familiar to him as his childhood, for they were part of it. Writing the novel and preparing to do so must have meant a reliving of his childhood, and it is impossible to relive one's childhood without experiencing acute emotion. The emotion may be hatred, as with Samuel Butler. With Bennett it was plainly warm affection, even love, though tinged with exasperation. At rare moments, as in the description of the death of Samuel Povey, the affection breaks through so strongly as to destroy altogether the pretense of objectivity. Elsewhere Bennett protects himself, as it were, by means of the facetious irony of his style.

What he kept of the Naturalists in *The Old Wives' Tale* was their concern for form, and little else. He has become an English humorist, though rather more disciplined than English humorists generally are. His affinities are obvious and unexpected; had the restraint slackened, Mr. Critchlow would have been a Dickens character, while Mr. Povey, in the toothache scene especially, might appear in early Wells. The restraint with which he holds his characters in check is remarkable; without the sense of form they might easily have spilled over and swamped the book. For what in the end characterizes *The Old Wives' Tale* is richness in order. Reading, one is aware all the time of the brilliance of character creation and of invention; a whole world and epoch are brought to life. Yet everything has been sternly subordinated to Bennett's overriding conception, and one is left with the feeling that never has the rhythm of ordinary life, life in time, been so faithfully, so surely transcribed. The novel ranges from the trivial, the farcical, and the grotesque to the most gravely serious, from the recording of a shop assistant's toothache and the adventures of souvenir hunters round the corpse of a circus elephant to the hazards and endurances of the siege of Paris and the reflections of an old woman in the presence of death. Within the limits Bennett set himself—the limits are those of life conceived as being wholly in time—*The Old Wives' Tale* is almost unassailable.

In the *Clayhanger* novels Bennett was attempting something of a lower order of creation and on a smaller scale, yet they make a very considerable achievement. In *Clayhanger* Bennett was much closer to his subject. Edwin Clayhanger is not Bennett's exact contemporary, but he is only eleven years older, and while the novels are not autobiographical, Edwin represents a perfectly conceivable development of the young Bennett. He is without his creator's talent and ambition; he has his sensitiveness and shyness without the aggressive assertion that compensated for them; he has his neurotic mania for tidiness; he has his humanitarian, liberal sympathies, his generosity of mind; unlike Bennett, he has no panache. He is one of the most attractive heroes in twentieth-century fiction. Bennett, who believed inordinately in the "interestingness" of ordinary things and ordinary people, was never more successful in revealing the "interestingness" of an apparently ordinary man than in Edwin Clayhanger.

D. H. Lawrence once criticized Bennett's characters for their acceptance of, their acquiescence in, the frustrations of existence. Actually, it is from this that a very considerable part of Bennett's strength as a novelist comes. Clayhanger does not kick against the pricks. But this does not mean he is a passive character. One sees him as a natural growth, shaped by innumerable pressures of circumstance into his own individuality as a tree is shaped to its own form by wind, rain, the hazards of climate, and the nature of its species. There is in *Clayhanger*, apparently, a complete absence of contrivance on the part of the author; Bennett follows the grain of life.

Clayhanger lives, as it were, by a series of continual small revelations, discoveries about life, human nature, and relationships to which, though they may be ordinary enough in themselves, part of common experience, Edwin responds with such open-mindedness as to make them completely fresh; he has the capacity to be continually surprised into ever-widening mental and emotional horizons, and it is this that gives him his vividness, his life, and the pathos that always attends him.

From its very nature the chronicle novel must lack an overriding conception, a Commanding Center. The beauties, to use the eighteenth-century word, of *The Old Wives' Tale* are not detachable. Those of the *Clayhanger* books are. But, though episodic, they are genuine beauties—the renderings of Shushions and of Big James, the descriptions of the clog dance, the glee party, and the Sunday school centenary, the struggle between Edwin and Darius, Darius's death and Edwin's triumph, the creation of Aunt Hamp, surely one of the great achievements in the comic during this century, and the beautifully accurate representation of the birth of love between Edwin and Hilda Lessways.

During the first half of the century, the name of John Galsworthy (1867-1933) was inevitably associated with those of Wells and Bennett. Now, Galsworthy appears beside his contemporaries as a very shadowy third, and of the *Forsyte Saga* itself the first novel alone, *The Man of Property* (1906), has much interest today. It shows him in his strength and weakness and in the confusion which seems to be at the heart of his work. The Forsytes, it might be said, are the spiritual descendants of the Osbornes of *Vanity Fair*; they represent the apotheosis of the British merchant. As we first meet them in *The Man of Property* they are on top of the world, secure in their self-regard, encased in their possessions. They live entirely in terms of property; money conditions them completely. It takes the place of family affection, but as a link binding them together it is no less strong. Their sense of property is so powerful and all-pervasive as to have ossified their vital feelings and produced in them sclerosis of the imagination. For Forsytes what cannot be bought does not exist; art and the things of the spirit are objects to be collected, but not for their own sake, rather as manifestations of their success in life. They are so encrusted with property that they are only half alive; they are pathetic though they do not know it; the life of the emotions, the "holiness of the heart's affections," are as closed to them as the life of pure thought. The standards they uphold are standards that lead in the end to death.

This side of the Forsytes is very well done; as we see in the dinner at Swithin's, or the description of the "at home" to celebrate June Forsyte's engagement to Bosinney, Galsworthy is very successful in his attempt to present satire through Naturalism. His failure is somewhat akin to Butler's in *The Way of All Flesh*; it is the failure to establish an adequate compensating principle for what is being satirized. In his preface to the *Forsyte Saga* Galsworthy wrote:

This long tale is no scientific study of the period; it is rather an intimate incarnation of the disturbances that Beauty effects in the lives of men. The figure of Irene, never present except through the sense of the other characters, is a concretion of disturbing beauty impinging on a possessive world.

But as a symbol of beauty and its disturbing influence Irene, whom Soames Forsyte marries as he might buy a piece of bric-à-brac, never comes alive; it is scarcely possible that she should, presented as she is through the minds of the Forsytes, since they are, by definition, characters which do not possess the kind of mind through which beauty can be vividly realized. Irene exists as a thin sentimentality, as does the notion of art which Galsworthy also opposes to the standards of the Forsytes. It is as though he is much more convinced by the Forsytes and what they stand for than he is of the strength of beauty and art.

His defense against the Forsytes is in fact sentimentality, into which he constantly retreats. Old Jolyon, for example, the head of the family, is a wholly sentimental conception; and it comes as no surprise that, in the Forsyte novels following the Saga proper, the novels grouped together as *A Modern Comedy,* Soames Forsyte, who has been throughout the Saga the arch-Forsyte, the epitome of pride of possession and the property instinct, becomes the persona of Galsworthy himself.

Of the other novelists who came to maturity in the Edwardian period three only seem to me now to merit serious consideration: Maugham, Ford Madox Ford, and E. M. Forster. At the time it doubtless looked rather different. William de Morgan (1839-1917), whose first novel *Joseph Vance* was published in 1906, was seen as the heir both of Dickens and of Thackeray. Today, though it is possible to see why he was praised, he is unreadable in his archness and prolixity and the implausibility of his stories; he appears now as a belated echo of the mid-nineteenth century, as a very minor Trollope. May Sinclair

(?1870-1946) stands rereading more successfully, yet she doesn't seem more now than a pioneer in a kind of psychological fiction later women novelists were to do better. Then there is F. W. Rolfe, "Baron Corvo" (1860-1913). Fascinating no doubt as a psychopath, Rolfe possessed almost none of the attributes of a novelist. His best book is *Hadrian the Seventh* (1904), which is certainly one of the most striking examples of the wish-fulfillment dream in literature: Rolfe, who in life was never allowed to become the Roman Catholic priest he believed he ought to be, here has his own back on his Church by imagining himself suddenly elevated to the papacy. But what is interesting here, apart from the light the character of George Arthur Rose throws on Rolfe's pitiably obsessed mind, is the knowledge shown of the organization of the Roman Church. Once Rose is elected Pope the novel becomes nonsense. The attention paid to Rolfe in recent years is a tribute not to his own writings but to the spell exercised by A. J. A. Symons's biography of him, *The Quest for Corvo*.

These writers, it seems to me, stand far less chance of being read in any foreseeable future than such avowedly frivolous novelists as "Saki" (H. H. Munro) (1870-1916) in his *The Unbearable Bassington* (1912), and the Irish ladies Edith Somerville and "Martin Ross" with their *The Real Charlotte* (1895) and *Some Experiences of an Irish R. M.* (1899).

Maugham throughout his life has been an admirably professional writer whose strength, whether as novelist, short-story writer, or playwright, has come from his knowing perfectly his own limits. Too much self-knowledge is probably not good for an artist, and for the most part Maugham has been content to work in a very narrow range of subject and character, without any compensating quality of style to make up for it. In three novels, however, he does rise above the civilized entertainment which

has generally been the end he has proposed for himself.
These are his first novels, *Liza of Lambeth* (1897), *Of Human Bondage* (1915), and *Cakes and Ale* (1930). With the
early work of Moore, *Liza of Lambeth* is the completest
specimen of the Naturalistic novel in English. It was written, as Maugham has said, with Maupassant as its model.
He has also said that it is a picture "of a life that has long
since ceased to be." This is true; in sixty years the East
End has changed almost out of recognition, and the account here is of the London slums as we see them in Gissing and Morrison. Yet the novel remains remarkably
fresh, and Liza still has her unquenchable vitality.
Maugham is as detached as ever he has been, but the novel
vibrates still with the passion of deeply felt observation.

Maugham's has always been the role of the impartial
spectator who watches but does not judge. In *Of Human Bondage* he is the spectator of himself as a boy and young
man, for we know that the Philip Carey of that novel is at
any rate a version of himself; *Of Human Bondage*, he
has said, "is not an autobiography, but an autobiographical novel." Although very considerably too long, it is a
work of real distinction the total impact of which more
closely resembles that of Theodore Dreiser's *An American Tragedy* than any English novel. This is not accidental.
Maugham and Dreiser were writing from a similar view
of life. Philip reflects:

> Life had no meaning. On the earth, satellite of a star speeding through space, living things had arisen under the influence of conditions which were part of the planet's history;
> and as there had been a beginning of life upon it, so, under
> the influence of other conditions, there would be an end;
> man, no more significant than other forms of life, had come
> not as the climax of creation but as a physical reaction to
> the environment. . . . There was no meaning in life, and
> man by living served no end. It was immaterial whether he
> was born or not born, whether he lived or ceased to live.
> Life was insignificant and death without consequence.

It is a view of life less commonly held now than at the time the novel was written, for we no longer share the view of science on which the belief was based. And the character of Philip, and Maugham's interpretation of him, are so thoroughly impregnated by the belief that for most readers the novel will always seem an inadequate rendering of life. This obviously limits the value of the novel; it makes it very much less than universal, even by comparison with Bennett's *Clayhanger*. Yet *Of Human Bondage* has its value, and it comes precisely from Maugham's honesty, his unflinching acceptance of his belief in the meaninglessness of life. He is not, nor is Philip, to be comforted, and the novel gains in poignancy from the condition of Philip, the isolated man, the man cut off from his fellows by the sense of an unbridgeable difference of which his clubfoot is the symbol.

Of Human Bondage is one of the most moving accounts of loneliness in our language, and in a curious way this effect of loneliness is increased by what seems to me Maugham's failure quite to persuade us of the fact of Philip's continued dominance by the dreadful, anemic, vulgar Cockney waitress Mildred, one of the most unpleasant women in fiction. The fault of the novel does not lie here, but in the ending. Maugham was caught in the trap that no writer of the autobiographical novel in chronicle form can escape. A story can end; when we close *David Copperfield* or *Middlemarch* we do so with the feeling that something has been completed, an action is over. But life—and the flow of a personal life is the autobiographical novelist's theme—goes on, and any point the novelist chooses to end his novel must be arbitrary unless he ends with his character's death. This means that the chronicle autobiographical novel is almost bound to conclude on a note of artificial resolution which must appear faked; the end of *Sons and Lovers* is an instance. *Of Human Bondage* ends in a fake idyll; Sally, the girl with the placidity and acceptance of an earthgoddess, never becomes credible, nor does her father, Athelny. The Athelny family, which seems carefully planted where it is in the novel to make a happy ending possible, and the values they stand for seem to me devices out of Samuel Butler, and their appearance flaws the novel as nothing else does.

Maugham's third outstanding novel is *Cakes and Ale*. As a wittily malicious satirical comedy it is bound to survive as a most entertaining footnote to twentieth-century literary history; but the characters—the old novelist Driffield, his wife Rosie, and the absurdly engaging careerist novelist Alroy Kear—are splendidly realized.

Writing novels was only one of the literary activities of Ford Madox Ford (1873-1939)—he changed his surname from Hueffer to Ford in 1919. His career as a novelist falls into two parts, divided by the war of 1914-18. At the beginning of the century he had collaborated with Conrad in *The Inheritors* and *Romance,* and throughout his life his attitude towards fiction was very close to Conrad's. In the first part of his career his aims were limited to the writing of light novels, of little interest now, and historical fiction; his *Fifth Queen* trilogy, on Katherine Howard and Henry VIII, remains a very fine set of historical novels. Ford liberates his characters—Henry, Katherine, Cranmer, the Princess Mary, Cromwell, Throckmorton, and the rest—from the associations encrusting them from four centuries of bitter sectarian history, so that they live as human beings. But the great achievement of this first part of his career is *The Good Soldier* (1915). Like the Tietjens novels that were to follow after the war, it springs out of his own sufferings, so that in it the whole man is engaged. By religion, Ford was a Roman Catholic, but one cannot call him a Catholic novelist as Mauriac or Bernanos is. Human life, as Ford reveals it in his novels, is meaningless, and his values are purely stoic. Dowell, in *The Good Soldier,* asks:

Are all men's lives like the lives of us good people—like the lives of the Ashburnhams, of the Dowells, of the Ruffords— broken, tumultuous, agonized, and unromantic lives, periods punctuated by screams, by imbecilities, by deaths, by agonies? Who the devil knows?

In the midst of tribulation Ford can only put forward a code of conduct: the façade of civilized life must be preserved at all costs; husband and wife, no matter how unhappy their marriage, do not make scenes before servants; and so on. As he remarks in *The Good Soldier*:

> Pride and reserve are not the only things in life; perhaps they are not even the best things. But if they happen to be your particular virtues you will go all to pieces if you let them go.

Judged as a technical feat alone *The Good Soldier* is dazzling, as near perfection as a novel can be. It is amazingly subtle, this account, by one of them, of the lives of four people who appear to have lived in harmony and friendship for more than ten years:

> Our intimacy was like a minuet, simply because on every possible occasion and in every available circumstance we knew where to go, where to sit, which table we should unanimously choose; and we could rise and go, all four together, without a signal from any one of us, always to the music of the Kur orchestra, always in the temperate sunshine, or, if it rained, in discreet shelters.

So Dowell, the narrator of the novel, saw the relationship while it existed; but Dowell is a deceived man, deceived at every turn of the action; his wife and the Ashburnhams have united to keep him in ignorance of the relationship between them. Yet, what is the truth? What is the truth about Ashburnham, the gallant, stupid Tory gentleman whose code is *noblesse oblige* and who cannot resist pretty women? What is the truth about Leonora Ashburnham, the narrow Irish Catholic who loves him, protects him, keeps up the appearance of a happy marriage in public and does not speak to him in private, who acts as procuress for him and in the last analysis is responsible, through defects in upbringing and perhaps in character, for his deterioration? What is the truth about Dowell himself, whose life is one long meaningless self-sacrifice? We do not know the answers, do not attain to full knowledge of the characters and the pattern they make between them, until the last pages of the book. Ford's technique resembles a kaleidoscope; with each chapter the kaleidoscope is shaken anew to reveal fresh and unexpected aspects of the Dowell-Ashburnham relationship.

But dazzling as it is, the technique is a means to an end, the exposure of the characters in all the poignancy of their intolerable situation; and at the end the pattern is restored, the partners have changed, but the figure is the same: they are still dancing their pathetic minuet.

Ford was a man the conduct of whose life was marked by great unwisdom. One consequence of this has been that his novels have never received anything like the general recognition their merits deserve. Whatever the truth about his unwisdom and his appalling run of bad luck, which was perhaps an aspect of the unwisdom. it seems pretty safe to say that he saw himself not as the world did but as he saw Tie⁺jens in the four books dealing with that character. He wrote, of the genesis of the Tietjens books: "I needed someone, some character, in lasting tribulation —with a permanent shackle and ball on his leg. . . . A physical defect it could not be, for if I wrote about that character he would have to go into the trenches. It would be something of a moral order, and something inscrutable." He had in fact been rendering such a character on and off ever since he wrote *The Benefactor* in 1905, where it appears as George Moffat. In *The Good Soldier* it appears as Ashburnham. Together with Tietjens they define the essential Ford character and also, one suspects

from the evidence of his nonfictional works, his own conception of himself: the English gentleman—Ford sometimes calls him the Tory—for whom money exists only in
order that others may be helped, who neither explains his
actions nor apologizes for them, who follows his code
without question and in full knowledge of the consequences, which are inevitably that his motives will be misunderstood and that he will be betrayed by those whom
he has befriended. He suffers, but he suffers in silence.

I do not mean that *The Good Soldier* and the Tietjens
novels are autobiographical fiction or contain self-por-
traits. They are objective correlatives of Ford's own emotional situations. By pushing, as it were, his personal problem out of arm's reach and staging it in terms of characters
other than himself and those closely associated with him,
he depersonalized it, raised it to the level of the material
of art. We do not, in fact, dream of referring these novels
to the private life of their creator until we know something of his private life, for they are models of objectivity.
As a novelist, Ford is always and completely outside his
subject matter.

The four novels that make up the Tietjens series, *Some
Do Not, No More Parades, A Man Could Stand Up*, and
Last Post—the last, the weakest, being in the nature of an
afterthought—appeared between 1924 and 1928. "The
two young men—they were of the English public official
class—sat in the perfectly appointed railway carriage."
This first sentence of *Some Do Not* indicates the world
Ford is re-creating, that of the ruling class of Edwardian
England. It is a world already breaking up; one of the
young men in the railway carriage is there through brains
not family, a lower-middle-class careerist from Leith. But
for the most part, Ford's characters are of that world by
birth, cabinet ministers, permanent undersecretaries, gen-
erals, right-wing journalists; and they are these not out of

interest, inclination, or the desire for fame or money, but simply from duty. Some, like the novelist Mrs. Wannup, are very poor; others, like Tietjens, very rich; it makes no difference: they are members of an elite so well established that it does not even have to think of itself as an elite. So one of the themes of these novels is duty, the observance of the code that says without argument, "It isn't done."

The title of the first book, *Some Do Not,* is significant. Tietjens's lasting tribulation, his shackle and ball, is his wife, a wanton, whose child may not be his, who deserts him, whom he takes back, who throughout his life does her best to ruin him and indeed does so in the eyes of the world. He will not divorce her because a gentleman does not divorce his wife; she cannot divorce him because she is a Catholic. He is in love with Valentine Wannup, the daughter of his father's oldest friend; he will not tell her so because he is married. But loving him, she becomes yet another means by which his wife Sylvia can persecute him, for Sylvia is possessed by a lust to ruin him. Tietjens suffers all her attempts passively, with a sort of Christian stoicism. Partly through her intrigues, partly through his integrity, which will not permit him to depart from his code and, for example, fake statistics in the Government interest, his career as a civil servant comes to an early end. In the war he is no more successful as a soldier: beloved of his men, he suffers the final ignominy of being put in charge of prisoners behind the line.

Tietjens is Ford's presentation of the Christian Gentleman, which is one reason why his wife persecutes him; he is, maddeningly, too good for her, and bitterly she realizes it.

To depict a positively good character is the most difficult problem a novelist can set himself. Does Ford succeed with Tietjens? I think not wholly. The tribulations are piled on too heavily. So many make us suspicious, just as the psychologist raises his eyebrows in the presence of a man who is accidentally knocked down by motorcars too often. Tietjens's role in the four novels is always that of the victim of the booby traps set by his wife or by fate. He is, and has to be, a static character, ending as he began, the Tory Christian. A satirist might have made him a sort of Don Quixote, a good simpleton. But Tietjens is not a simpleton; he is, specifically, a man of great learning, and, much more important, he is quite without illusions about human nature. Yet in the end one is forced to see him as a sentimental creation; perhaps too much of Ford crept into him.

He is a fixed character, but Ford's marvelous technical adroitness helps to blind us to this. In the four books he is examined and exposed from every possible angle, through the eyes of his wife, of his careerist friend Macmaster, his brother the permanent undersecretary, his godfather and commanding officer, General Campion, the woman who loves him, his fellow officers, and the men under him. And the whole is presented in terms of the utmost compression. Ford rarely indulges in direct narration; everything is allusive, elliptical, for the story progresses always through the thoughts of the character who is engrossing his attention at the moment. As he claimed himself, Ford was a master of the "time switch."

Yet despite the suspicion we may have that Tietjens is a character too good to be true, such a figure was essential to the work Ford was aiming at, the subject of which was to be no less than "the public events of a decade." Tietjens is the fixed point round which the flux eddies, his integrity the measuring rod of that of the other characters and of the decade itself. When Tietjens is driven out of public life the bankruptcy of a ruling class is exposed. Whether such a ruling class existed outside Ford's imagination scarcely matters; he imposes his own belief in it upon the reader.

8

E. M. Forster's most recent novel, *A Passage to India,* was published in 1924; his other four novels appeared between 1905 and 1910. As a novelist he is often delightful and always baffling and ambiguous; and he has always stood apart from his contemporaries. Virginia Woolf, in *Mr. Bennett and Mrs. Brown,* associated him with herself, Lawrence, and Joyce as one of the novelists writing in reaction against the novel as understood by the Edwardians. This is true neither as fact nor in implication; Forster was the strict contemporary of the Edwardians, and the bulk of his fiction was written before Mrs. Woolf and Lawrence were writing at all. Yet though there are moments when one sees affinities between him and Mrs. Woolf in some respects and Lawrence in others, he cannot be regarded as a pioneer, as a John the Baptist going before them. Technically, he is a sport, a throwback; so far as his novels are concerned, neither James nor the French Naturalists might have written them; he is there, a man telling a story in his own voice, in the older English tradition which, beginning with Fielding, ends, we normally assume, with Meredith. His plots are as improbable —at any rate in the four novels before *A Passage to India,* which on the surface is much more realistic than the earlier books—as any in Victorian fiction, as melodramatic and as far-fetched. In his own person of the omniscient narrator, he comments on his characters, interprets their motives and actions, moralizes on them, bids us admire or detest. As with Fielding and Thackeray, his novels at their best are triumphs of a personal attitude expressed in a special tone of voice. His is the most personal style in modern fiction, the most personal style since Meredith's, to whom he owes much, and it is the style, the tone of voice, which gives his novels their unity and which almost persuades us to ignore the improbable violence and the discontinuities of his attitude.

But what is his attitude? Outside his fiction, he has been a great spokesman of the liberal tradition, agnostic, anti-imperialist, antiauthoritarian, concerned with social justice. "My motto," he has written, "is—Lord, I disbelieve, Help thou my unbelief." Fundamental to his public attitude has been his faith in the holiness of the heart's affections; and perhaps his conception of the good life comes from his experiences as a young man at Cambridge with its emphasis on personal relations, rational discourse, and disinterestedness.

Yet though this public attitude of Forster's is expressed in his novels, it appears there as part of something much more complex and much less clear-cut; something that cannot be expressed in simple statements but only, and therefore darkly, through symbols. These at their most convincing appear as perceptions of the nature of reality, as in Helen Schlegel's experience of Beethoven's Fifth Symphony, in *Howard's End* (1910): the passage is quintessentially Forster, and in a sense the whole of him is there:

> . . . the music started with a goblin walking quietly over the universe, from end to end. Others followed him. They were not aggressive creatures; it was that that made them so terrible to Helen. They merely observed in passing that there was no such thing as splendour or heroism in the world. After the interlude of elephants dancing, they returned and made the observation for the second time. Helen could not contradict them, for, once at all events, she had felt the same, and had seen the reliable walls of youth collapse. Panic and emptiness! Panic and emptiness! The goblins were right.
>
> Her brother raised his finger: it was the transitional passage on the drum.
>
> For, as if things were going too far, Beethoven took hold of the goblins and made them do what he wanted. He appeared in person. He gave them a little push, and they began to walk in major key instead of in a minor, and then

—he blew with his mouth and they were scattered! Gusts of splendour, gods and demi-gods contending with vast swords, colour and fragrance broadcast on the field of battle, magnificent victory, magnificent death! Oh, it all burst before the girl, and she even stretched out her gloved hands as if it was tangible. Any fate was titanic: any contest desirable; conqueror and conquered would alike be applauded by the angels of the utmost stars.

And the goblins—they had not really been there at all? They were only the phantoms of cowardice and unbelief? One healthy human impulse would dispel them? Men like the Wilcoxes, or President Roosevelt, would say yes. Beethoven knew better. The goblins really had been there. They might return—and they did. It was as if the splendour of life might boil over and waste to steam and froth. In its dissolution one heard the terrible, ominous note, and a goblin, with increased malignity, walked quietly over the universe from end to end. Panic and emptiness! Panic and emptiness! Even the flaming ramparts of the world might fall.

Beethoven chose to make all right in the end. He built the ramparts up. He blew with his mouth for the second time, and again the goblins were scattered. He brought back the gusts of splendour, the heroism, the youth, the magnificence of life and of death, and, amid the vast roaring of a super-human joy, he led his Fifth Symphony to its conclusion. But the goblins were there. They could return. He had said so bravely, and that is why one can trust Beethoven when he says other things.

This perception into the nature of things Forster calls, in *The Longest Journey* (1907), "the knowledge of good-and-evil," and he describes it there as "the primal curse." When allowance is made for its comparative lightness and whimsicality of expression, Helen Schlegel's intuition anticipates Mrs. Moore's in Marabar Caves, in *A Passage to India,* when the echo murmurs to her:

"Pathos, piety, courage—they exist, but are identical, and so is filth. Everything exists, nothing has value." If one had spoken vileness in that place, or quoted lofty poetry, the comment would have been the same—"ou-boum."

Beneath the surface of things for Forster, then, is a nullity, a void. Fundamentally, Forster is a tragic humanist for whom man is justified by his self-awareness and by the fruits of his imagination, by the arts and, especially perhaps, by music. He is the advocate of balance, of the whole man; but man is rarely balanced and few can be said to be whole. The criticism of lack of balance, of lack of wholeness, is the impulse behind his first four novels, *Where Angels Fear to Tread*, *The Longest Journey*, *A Room with a View*, and *Howard's End*.

The target of Forster's satirical analysis in these novels is "the undeveloped heart." The fate of those who suffer from this condition is suggested in this passage from *A Room with a View* (1908):

> She gave up trying to understand herself, and joined the vast armies of the benighted, who follow neither the heart nor the brain, but march to their destiny by catch-words. The armies are full of pleasant and pious folk. But they have yielded to the only enemy that matters—the enemy within. They have sinned against passion and truth, and vain will be their strife after virtue. As the years pass, they are censured. Their pleasantry and their piety show cracks, their wit becomes cynicism, their unselfishness hypocrisy; they feel and produce discomfort wherever they go . . .

In the earlier novels, then, there is usually a young person impressed as it were into the army of the benighted and striving to break free from it. Forster's villains are those who refuse to recognize, or betray, the holiness of the heart's affections. They are, generally, the emotionally immature; and in Forster's world they may be equated with that aspect of English upper-middle-class values which can be summed up in the words public school and established church. Against these values is set the symbol of a different way of life. In Forster's short stories the symbol is often Greece, in the early novels Italy. These symbols are not sentimentalized, for Greece contains Pan, and Forster's symbol always includes the life of impulse, of impulse even to brutishness and cruelty. We see this in his first novel, *Where Angels Fear to Tread* (1905), a book which in some respects strikingly anticipates Lawrence's *Lost Girl*, though in it what is being rebelled against is not the industrial Midlands but the conventional Home Counties of the middle class.

The plots of these early novels are very complicated; for Forster, plot is a sort of obstacle race which his characters must undergo, a series of tests which serve to expose them. To synopsize them is fatally to distort them. But the two crises in the plot of *Where Angels Fear to Tread* are Lilia Herriton's sudden marriage to Gino, the son of a small-town Italian dentist, and her family's outraged efforts to prevent it and buy Gino off; and, after Lilia's death, the Herritons', attempt to "rescue" her baby from its father. The two characters who are, so to speak, changed by Italy are Philip Herriton, Lilia's brother-in-law, and Caroline Abbott, who was her ineffective chaperon when she fell in love with Gino. The Herritons, the whole Sawston circle, are brilliantly well done; as the satirical scrutineer of the heart Forster is the peer almost of Jane Austen herself, and his values, the bases of his judgments of them, are as precise as hers. With Gino, however, we realize that something has gone wrong; Forster is at pains to make him a "real" Italian, as opposed to the romantic tourist's notion of one; it is not beside the point that he is the son of a dentist, the least romantic of professions. He is presented as unsentimentally as possible, but he fails in the part he must play in the scheme of the novel because he has to stand for too much. He is the symbol of "good-and-evil," and the symbolism creaks. It does so particularly in the scene in which Gino tortures Philip Herriton by twisting his broken arm. Forster is saying in effect that the reality we must accept is essentially Janus-faced, unpredictable in evil as in good. But the detail invented to represent this is insufficient; Gino is made to appear nothing more than an unschooled little boy, nasty and nice by turns.

This failure in the symbol which is Forster's measuring rod of his upper-class, public school, Anglo-Saxon characters is still more evident in *The Longest Journey* (1907), in many ways the most delightful of his novels. Its theme is reality and its nature, as is made plain in the first chapter, in which the hero Rickie, then an undergraduate, is discussing with his friends the metaphysical problem, Does a cow exist when there is no one there to see it? Rickie is in quest of reality; the glimpses he catches of it he expresses in little mythological stories obviously akin to his creator's own short stories in *The Celestial Omnibus*. All the same, through his wife Agnes and his brother-in-law he is seduced into joining the army of the benighted. He becomes a master at a public school, where his brother-in-law Pembroke teaches. He drifts further and further away from reality until in the end he is brought back to it by contact with his illegitimate half-brother Stephen Wonham. Wonham is the Gino of *The Longest Journey*. He is even less adequate and, as Gino is not, a sentimentalization.

Forster has often been attacked for the implausibility of his plots and the reckless unreality of some of his most important scenes. When Rickie's philosopher friend Ansell suddenly breaks into Sawston School and denounces Rickie before the assembled boys we are in the presence of something we know is inconceivable. But this does not seem to me greatly to matter; the passage has a truth which could be expressed in scarcely any other way. The great weakness in Forster is simply and all the time the inadequacy of his symbolism; his novels are a mingling of social comedy and poetry; the social comedy, even remembering Meredith, is the best we have had since Jane Austen, but the poetry doesn't work.

This is strikingly apparent in *Howard's End,* his most ambitious novel, and the most explicit as a statement of his values. "Only connect" is the motto of the book: "Only connect the passion and the prose." The novel is an attempt at reconciliation, as though Forster has realized that his own liberal, humanitarian position is not enough. On the one side are the representatives of that position, Margaret and Helen Schlegel, on the other the Wilcoxes, a middle-class family that stands for what is called in the novel "the outer world of telegram and anger," the world of action. One might say that the portrayal of the Wilcoxes shows Forster in a determined effort to be fair to the Forsytes.

Neither Schlegels nor Wilcoxes, however, are big enough for the parts they must play. For, in some sense at least, *Howard's End* is a symbolical novel about the state of England at the time of writing. Yet, if there is virtue in action at all—and this is certainly Margaret Schlegel's belief, since, defending the Wilcoxes against her sister Helen, she tells her, "They made us possible"—then the Wilcoxes are certainly not fitting representatives of it, any more than the Schlegels, for all their liberal-mindedness and culture, can really stand for the life of the spirit; they seem now to express little more than ghastly good taste and the luxury of combining advanced opinions with a private income. Nor is Leonard Bast, the representative of the working class, any more satisfactory; indeed, he is less so, since it is hard to see that any observation of working men went into his creation.

The characters are too small for the general thesis of the novel. This in turn makes the plot obtrusive and in the end absurd, a fabrication; we are aware in reading that something devised and not wholly corresponding to life as we know it is being forced upon us. Then, too, since it is Margaret Schlegel who is at the center of the novel, the representative of her creator's awareness and judgments, something else creeps into the book: a curious nagging note of governessy priggishness.

"Only connect," though what must be connected is something rather different, might be the motto also of *A Passage to India* (1924), a much more successful novel. Why more successful it is easy to see. His very subject of India, with its clashes of race, religion, and color, compelled Forster to interpret his values in terms of a concrete situation taken from contemporary history. The complicated plot had to disappear. Instead, within the brilliantly described world of conventional Anglo-Indian relations, we have the attempts, fumbling yet moving, of English and Indian —Mrs. Moore, Adela Quested, Fielding on the one hand, Dr. Aziz on the other—to make contact as human beings. They fail—the mysterious event in the Marabar Caves seems to represent a perverseness in the very nature of things. In one way, the attempts at contact have merely exacerbated the Anglo-Indian situation. And yet . . .

The "and yet" indicates the ambiguity at the heart not only of the novel but of Forster's attitude to life. India, he has written, is not a mystery, it is a muddle; and herein it is very much like life itself as Forster sees it. The novel exists on two planes and has a different meaning according to the plane we choose to concentrate on. There is the plane of realism, and here Forster's great gifts of satire and of sympathy, his humor and understanding, are seen to their fullest advantage. All his previous criticisms of the "undeveloped heart" are summed up in his descriptions of the behavior of the English at Chandrapore; all his sympathy with those who seek reality, who feel the necessity to connect, are implicit in his presentation and analysis of Mrs. Moore, Adela, Fielding, and Aziz; while his humor and understanding are wonderfully embodied in the evocations of Hinduism and its ceremonies. On this level, *A Passage to India* is a superb realistic novel, and its conclusion, with Aziz and Fielding meeting on horseback in a native state years after Aziz's trial, is what the facts of the novel dictate:

> "Why can't we be friends now?" said the other, holding him affectionately. "It's what I want. It's what you want."
> But the horses didn't want it—they swerved apart; the earth didn't want it, sending up rocks through which riders must pass single file; the temples, the tank, the jail, the palace, the birds, the carrion, the Guest House, that came into view as they issued from the gap and saw Mau beneath: they didn't want it, they said in their hundred voices: "No, not yet," and the sky said: "No, not there."

But on the other plane on which *A Passage to India* exists this conclusion is contradicted. Reconciliation *is* possible, and it comes about through the figure of Mrs. Moore, the old English lady on whom India has such a strange effect and who becomes, after she leaves India to die on the voyage home, almost a local goddess. She is not presented as an especially remarkable old lady, but she has her moments of perception; she expresses Forster's own awareness of the nature of things; and when Adela at the trial suddenly perceives reality and knows that whatever did happen in the Caves—and that we never know— certainly Aziz didn't assault her, it is, as it were, through Mrs. Moore's eyes that she sees. And it is significant that when Fielding appears in the last part of the novel it is as the husband of her daughter.

Mrs. Moore seems to me a wholly successful symbol. What she means cannot be paraphrased, though one might make many guesses about her significance. She is among other things obviously a Magna Mater figure, older than English and Indian and the strife between them. When Forster attempted through a cognate figure, Mrs. Wilcox, a similar reconciliation in *Howard's End,* he failed completely. With Mrs. Moore he succeeds. The symbol *works*; the figure of Mrs. Moore broods over the novel, not benignly, anything but that, but as a symbol of acceptance.

of unconscious life going on heedless of the disputes of the passing moment. Mrs. Moore, one feels, will be there when England and India alike have been forgotten.

Forster is a novelist difficult to assess; he can be as easily overestimated as underestimated. As the moralist expressing himself through the novel of social comedy, he seems to me fully the equal of Meredith, which means that here he is surpassed by no English novelist since Jane Austen. As a poetic novelist, a symbolist, he fails, except in *A passage to India,* whether we compare him either with Hawthorne or with D. H. Lawrence. Yet it is impossible to regret the symbolism or to regret that he did not confine himself wholly to social comedy. Had he done so he would not have been Forster.

1914 AND AFTER

"ON OR ABOUT December 1910 human nature changed."
When Virginia Woolf made this pronouncement at Cambridge in 1924 to the undergraduate audience of her lec-
ture *Mr. Bennett and Mrs. Brown,* she was not being
whimsical; she was violently overstating a fact in order to
shock her listeners into recognition of it. The fact is this:
that though human nature may not change, men's notions
of their nature do, and one such change occurred roughly
during the first decade of the twentieth century. Professor
Isaacs has pointed out, in his *An Assessment of Twentieth-
Century Literature,* that Virginia Woolf's choice of date
was not arbitrary: December 1910 was the date of the first
London exhibition of Post-Impressionist paintings, organized by her friends Roger Fry and Desmond MacCarthy.
For most English people interested in art this exhibition
was their first glimpse of the work of Cézanne, Van Gogh,
Picasso, and Matisse. It proclaimed that Impressionism
was dead and that a well-established movement in vigorous
reaction against it was in existence, rescuing the object
from the circumambient air and light into which the Impressionists had all but dissolved it. And here the kinship
of the theories of Impressionism in painting and Naturalism in fiction should be remembered.

Virginia Woolf herself quotes as the first signs of this
change in man's idea of himself Butler's *The Way of All*

Flesh and the plays of Bernard Shaw. There were others as significant. Chekhov's short stories appeared in English in 1909; Dostoevski's novels did not begin to appear in Constance Garnett's influential translations until 1912, but there had been earlier English versions, and the great Russian was also known here through French renderings. In Vienna, Freud had already laid the foundations of psychoanalysis, and though he was not yet published in England he and Jung had lectured, in 1909, in the United States. At least one can say that his theories were in the air.

All these instances have one thing in common: they emphasize the individual human being, the individual sensibility, the individual reaction. There is a complete shift from the Naturalistic point of view of man, as we find it in Moore and Bennett, in which the great shaping force on the individual is environment, and the related Socialist point of view, which dominated Wells, that a change in the ordering of society would of itself change the men and women who live in it. The shift was strengthened by the results of the 1914-18 war, which discredited so many institutions, and it goes far to explain a curious fact about our fiction at this time. In 1914, the most promising young English novelists appeared to be Hugh Walpole, Compton Mackenzie, J. D. Beresford, Gilbert Cannan, W. L. George, and D. H. Lawrence. Of these only Lawrence appeared in the postwar period as a significant novelist, a literary force. The others went on writing—except George, who died, and Cannan—often with distinction and certainly as professional novelists of great skill; they achieved wide public fame but added nothing of more than passing interest to the novel. Walpole's best novel, *Mr. Perrin and Mr. Traill,* which is still worth reading, the novel from which stems most of the fiction and drama dealing with its subject of schoolmasters, was written when he was twenty-seven, in 1911. Similarly, Compton

Mackenzie's best novel, *Sinister Street,* which expressed the feelings of a whole generation of young men about Oxford, appeared in 1913-14, and Beresford's finest work, *The History of Jacob Stahl,* an autobiographical novel in the direct line from Samuel Butler, in 1911. These novelists survived, but survived into a changed world in which the novelists whose works were the growing points of the future in fiction bore very different names, those of D. H. Lawrence (1885-1930), Dorothy Richardson (*b*. 1882), Virginia Woolf (1882-1941), and James Joyce (1882-1941), novelists with an entirely different and new approach to the art of fiction.

It is still too early to assess either the total achievement or the total significance of these novelists, for two of them, Joyce and Lawrence, violently unlike though they are, were writers of very formidable original genius. It sometimes seems that no literary form can afford genius of extreme revolutionary talent too often, for the consequence may easily be a temporary shattering of it. Something like this seems to have happened in the novel in our time. None of the best living novelists has escaped, in one way or another, the influence of at least one of the four, yet it is plain that after thirty years Lawrence and Joyce are still well ahead of any English novelist writing today. They are as advanced now as they were then. For novelists today they pose a problem the solution to which is probably vital to the future of the novel as a serious literary form. Their technical innovations, which were a result of their view of man's nature, were such that they wrecked the whole structure of the novel as we have normally conceived it. Yet if the novel is to fulfill its purpose as the agent, in Trilling's phrase, of the moral imagination, structure is as necessary as ever it was. At the same time, no later writers can afford to neglect the discoveries of these novelists. The problem is how to marry these discoveries to an adequate conception of structure. No one has yet succeeded in solving the problem on a large scale, but it is because they have solved it, or partly solved it, within the limits they have set themselves that we can consider Graham Greene, Joyce Cary, Elizabeth Bowen, Henry Green, Anthony Powell, L. P. Hartley, James Hanley, and P. H. Newby as among the most significant English novelists at present writing.

Since the time has not yet come for a full judgment of the achievement of Joyce, Lawrence, Virginia Woolf, and Dorothy Richardson, though the two latter have probably already fallen into perspective as the smallest talents of the four, all one can do here is briefly to indicate their aims and attempt a purely personal assessment. They were not, of course, anything like a school; they were as various as four contemporaries could be; the one thing that unites them is their common reaction, its intensity differing with each, against the Naturalist tradition, in which each in some measure began writing.

Their quarrel with their Naturalist forbears, which for them meant Bennett, Wells, and Galsworthy, turned, as quarrels between literary generations so often do, on the meaning of reality and the real. Virginia Woolf took it upon herself to speak for her fellows in *Mr. Bennett and Mrs. Brown*. The distinctive quality of the novelist, she says, is a permanent interest in "character in itself." Bennett, she admits, would agree with this: "He says that it is only if the characters are real that the novel has any chance of surviving." She turns the tables on him by suggesting that his characters, and those of Wells and Galsworthy, are not real. "They have laid an enormous stress upon the fabric of things. They have given us a house in the hope that we may be able to deduce the human beings who live there." She states her whole point rather more carefully in a famous passage in her essay "The Modern Novel," in *The Common Reader*:

Admitting the vagueness which afflicts all criticism of novels, let us hazard the opinion that for us at this moment the form of fiction most in vogue more often misses than secures the thing we seek. Whether we call it life or spirit, truth or reality, this, the essential thing, has moved off, or on, and refuses to be contained any longer in such ill-fitting vestments as we provide. Nevertheless, we go on perseveringly, conscientiously, constructing our two and thirty chapters after a design which more and more ceases to resemble the vision in our minds. So much of the enormous labour of proving the solidity, the likeness to life, of the story is not merely labour thrown away but labour misplaced to the extent of obscuring and blotting out the light of the conception. The writer seems constrained, not by his own free will but by some powerful and unscrupulous tyrant who has him in thrall, to provide a plot, to provide comedy, tragedy, love interest, and an air of probability embalming the whole so impeccable that if all his figures were to come to life they would find themselves dressed down to the last button of their coats in the fashion of the hour. The tyrant is obeyed; the novel is done to a turn. But sometimes, more and more often as time goes by, we suspect a momentary doubt, a spasm of rebellion, as the pages fill themselves in the customary way. Is life like this? Must novels be like this?

Look within and life, it seems, is very far from being "like this." Examine for a moment an ordinary mind on an ordinary day. The mind receives a myriad impressions—trivial, fantastic, evanescent, or engraved with the sharpness of steel. From all sides they come, an incessant shower of innumerable atoms; and as they fall, as they shape themselves into the life of Monday or Tuesday, the accent falls differently from of old; the moment of importance came not here but there; so that, if a writer were a free man and not a slave, if he could write what he chose, not what he must, if he could base his work upon his own feeling and not upon convention, there would be no plot, no comedy, no tragedy, no love interest or catastrophe in the accepted sense, and perhaps not a single button sewn on as the Bond Street tailors would have it. Life is not a series of gig-lamps symmetrically arranged; life is a luminous halo, a semi-transparent envelope surrounding us from the beginning of consciousness to the end. Is it not the task of the novelist to convey this varying, this unknown and uncircumscribed spirit, whatever aberration or complexity it may display, with as little mixture of the alien and external as possible?

Professor Isaacs, in *An Assessment of Twentieth-Century Literature,* has provided us with a valuable gloss on the passage by setting beside it a quotation from William James's *Principles of Psychology,* published in 1890, which Virginia Woolf seems to have had in mind:

> Every definite image in the mind is steeped and dyed in the free water that flows round it. The significance, the value of the image is all in this halo or penumbra that surrounds and escorts it.

The quotation continues:

> Consciousness does not appear to itself chopped up in bits. ... It is nothing jointed; it flows. ... Let us call it the stream of thought, of consciousness, or of subjective life.

The phrase "stream of consciousness" was taken over—first, it seems, by May Sinclair, in 1918, reviewing Dorothy Richardson's novels—to denote the new method of rendering consciousness in itself as it flows from moment to moment, a method used with varying degrees of intensity by Dorothy Richardon, Joyce, and Virginia Woolf, though never by Lawrence. A simple modification of the technique is this passage from Joyce's *Ulysses;* Mr. Bloom is seated in a carriage on his way to a funeral:

> As they turned into Berkeley Street a street organ near the Basin sent over and after them a rollicking rattling song of the halls. Has anybody here seen Kelly? Kay ee double ell wy. Dead march from *Saul.* He's as bad as old Antonio. He left me on my ownio. Pirouette! The *Mater Misericordiae.* Eccles Street. My house down there. Big place. Ward for incurables there. Very encouraging. Our Lady's Hospice for the dying. Deadhouse handy underneath. Where old Mrs. Riordan died. They look terrible the women. Her feeding cup and rubbing her mouth with the spoon. Then the screen round her bed for her to die. Nice young student that was dressed that bite the bee gave me. He's gone over

to the lying-in hospital they told me. From one extreme to the other.

There we are inside Bloom's mind. The old barriers between the reader and the novelist's characters are down. The novelist as mediator has almost disappeared. In the past, even in James and Conrad, the novelist figured as reporter or historian, recounting a sequence of actions ended before the reader takes up the novel to read. But with Joyce and Dorothy Richardson and Virginia Woolf, we, as readers, are as it were at the cutting edge of the characters' minds; we share the continuous present of their consciousness. There is, obviously, an immense gain in intimacy and immediacy. We know Bloom and Dorothy Richardson's Miriam in a way we know no characters in fiction before them. Whether we know them more truly than we do Fielding's Booth, Jane Austen's Emma, or George Eliot's Dorothea Brooke is another question.

Who first invented the stream-of-consciousness technique and what were its sources are questions more interesting than important. Something like it occurs intermittently in many novelists of the past when dealing with characters whose mental control is lax; there are obvious instances in Richardson, Smollett, Maria Edgeworth, and of course Dickens. Something like it, too, often occurs when characters surrender themselves to impassioned self-scrutiny: Professor Isaacs quotes *Emma* here. *Tristram Shandy* may be taken as a stream-of-consciousness novel in its own right now; after Joyce and Virginia Woolf it no longer looks the sport in our fiction that it did. No doubt as a conscious technique the stream of consciousness derives from what in the first decade of the century was the new science of psychology, at first from William James, though Joyce, who pushed the method to its furthest, in *Ulysses* (1922), certainly knew all about Jung's invention of free-association tests as a tool in psychotherapy; these had been devised in Zurich, the city in which Joyce was living. Given the scientific authority, along with some hints from the past, and the technique was born; translate the first pages of James's *The Wings of the Dove,* in which Kate Croy's thoughts and sense impressions are reported in *oratio obliqua,* into *oratio recta* and you have the stream of consciousness.

But the first novelist deliberately to employ the technique was Dorothy Richardson, whose novel *Pointed Roofs* (1915) was the beginning of a dozen novels which together compose the single work *Pilgrimage,* completed in 1935. *Pilgrimage* satisfies Virginia Woolf's requirements in that it contains in the accepted sense no plot, no comedy, no tragedy, no love interest or catastrophe; there is only Miriam Henderson, living from day to day, experiencing, feeling, reacting to the stimuli of the outside world of people and things: life for Miriam is precisely "an incessant shower of innumerable atoms," and reading, we live within her in an eternal present.

Pilgrimage is a remarkable achievement, and yet, having read it once, it is not, I think, a novel one wishes to return to. In the end, one is bored, bored by Miriam and by the method of rendering her. This is not so at first. The first volumes, recounting Miriam's life as a governess in a school in Germany, are remarkable in their freshness; the day-to-day flux of the very intelligent girl's moods and sensibility to the world outside her and the people who dwell in it, is enchantingly caught. We experience Miriam's own individual re-creation of her world from moment to moment. But when she returns to England, falls in love and is disappointed, against a background of advanced thought, it is another matter. Miriam's momentary perceptions are often delightful; her aspirations are not; they are dull even in their worthiness. And at the end we are left wondering what is the significance of it all, what has it all amounted to. One feels, indeed, that for Dorothy Richardson, as sometimes for Virginia Woolf, the world exists only to provide fodder, as it were, for the voracious sensibility of her character. Of *Pilgrimage* it might be said that if one robbed Miriam of her sensibility there would be not only no novel and no Miriam but also no world at all.

But *Pilgrimage* raises another problem: how, if the novelist's material is to be extreme subjectivity, the movement of the mind from moment to moment, with the phenomena of the external world merely reflected in it or picked out sporadically as the headlamps of a motorcar briefly illuminate objects within their range, how is structure to be retained at all? How are limits to be set? On what principle is the selection of thoughts, sense impressions, and associations that must stand for the whole flow of mental activity, to be made? It is impossible, with *Pilgrimage,* to speak of structure or form at all. There is selection, but it is largely the selection of censorship in the Freudian sense, which is very much a negative form of selection: there are whole areas of a woman's experience Miriam is never allowed to be conscious of; she might still be living in a nineteenth-century novel. And we are the more keenly aware of this because of the stream-of-consciousness technique.

How impose significance on the flux? In a sense, the whole subject of Virginia Woolf's novels is this very question; when one thinks in the abstract of a typical Virginia Woolf character one seems to see a tiny figure on tiptoe eagerly grasping a butterfly net alert to snare the significant, the transcending moment as it flies. Mrs. Woolf's characters are always in search of a pattern in the flux that shall give meaning to the whole, and Mrs. Woolf herself is as it were seeking a pattern of meaning through them. One feels all the time in her work an intuition akin to Pater's belief: "Every moment some form grows more perfect in hand or face; some tone on the hills or the sea is choicer than the rest; some mood of passion or insight or intellectual excitement is irresistibly real and attractive for—for that moment only." It comes out in such a passage as this from *Mrs. Dalloway* (1925):

> "What are they looking at?" said Clarissa Dalloway to the maid who opened her door.
>
> The hall of the house was cool as a vault. Mrs. Dalloway raised her hand to her eyes, and, as the maid shut the door to, and she heard the swish of Lucy's skirts, she felt like a nun who has left the world and feels fold round her the familiar veils and the response to old devotions. The cook was whistling in the kitchen. She heard the click of the typewriter. It was her life, and, bending her head over the hall table, she bowed beneath the influence, felt blessed and purified, saying to herself, as she took the pad with the telephone message on it, how moments like these are buds on the tree of life, flowers of darkness they are, she thought (as if some lovely rose had blossomed for her eyes alone); not for a moment did she believe in God; but all the more, she thought, taking up the pad, must one repay in daily life to servants, yes, to dogs and canaries, above all to Richard her husband, who was the foundation of it—of the gay sounds, of the green lights, of the cook even whistling, for Mrs. Walker was Irish and whistled all day long—one must pay back from this secret deposit of exquisite moments, she thought, lifting the pad, while Lucy stood by her, trying to explain how . . .

Like Pater's, her attitude to experience is aesthetic. Transience is the very stuff of her material. In a novel like *Mrs. Dalloway* one sees life as in a state of constant creation, changing endlessly from moment to moment, like a fountain, the moment being the individual drop of water of the fountain. Mrs. Woolf's characters are abnormally aware of the moment as it passes, and this very awareness gives it a remarkable complexity, for it is compounded not only of the character's thought, feeling, mood at the instant of apprehension but also of a most delicate sensuous though perhaps not more than half-conscious apprehension of the physical world in which the character moves; and at the same time the moment experienced is bound to and recapitulates moments of similar experience in the past through the links of association. Here Virginia Woolf is constantly doing on a small scale what Proust did in *A la Recherche du Temps Perdu*.

What happens in a Virginia Woolf novel is on the face of it unimportant. In *Mrs. Dalloway* a fashionable lady gives a party, a man who has been in love with her comes back from India, a young man suffering from war neurosis commits suicide. In *To the Lighthouse* the issue is simply whether or not a family on holiday in the Hebrides will be able to row out to the lighthouse. In *The Waves* action in any normal sense is dispensed with altogether. Yet even so slight as action is in her novels, it is enough for Virginia Woolf's purposes. Her art has a bubblelike iridescence, and part of its end is simply to convey a bubblelike evanescence; but this does not mean the world created in it is anything but solid: in *Mrs. Dalloway,* for instance, one aspect of the London scene is rendered as perfectly and as vividly as anywhere in fiction; London is as much "there" as in the novels of Dickens or in *The Princess Casamassima* for all that it is not in any sense a detachable background but caught, reflected, and refracted through the consciousness of the characters moving through it.

But how does Virginia Woolf manage to give significance to her characters' moments of perception out of which her novels are made? She does so in a number of ways. First, the succession of moments can be enough, as with Clarissa Dalloway and Peter Walsh, to recapitulate the lives of the characters apprehending them. Then, again as in *Mrs. Dalloway*, individual characters are brought into relationship with a number of others of whose existence they may be quite ignorant, brought into relationship by shared experience, of watching a motorcar in which the Queen may be sitting on its progress through the West End, of gazing at an airplane sky-writing, even of being vaguely aware of the chimes of Big Ben striking through the day. These together, in *Mrs. Dalloway,* create the illusion of many lives lived simultaneously, of a specific place and a sense of community.

In her last novel, in some respects her most successful, *Between the Acts* (1941), she sets the action, which is played out in a country house in whose grounds a pageant is to be held, against the whole background of the history of life. She presents, as it were in capsule form, in the setting of a summer day in the English countryside just before the war, the whole epic of the human story, racial as well as national.

In *To the Lighthouse,* apart from the beautifully suggested relationship between Mrs. Ramsay and her husband and children, a powerful unifying factor is the lighthouse itself, which becomes a symbol carrying many meanings. In *The Lighthouse* too, in the second part of the novel, which is an interlude between the two periods of the action, time itself is evoked; rather as in *The Waves* the soliloquies of the characters are set in the context of nine passages descriptive of the sun's progress over the sea from first light to night.

Some of these devices making for unity seem to me much more successful than others and to be successful, indeed, almost in inverse ratio to their ambition. It has become customary to write of Virginia Woolf as though she were essentially a poet who happened to use the medium of prose. But she is at her weakest when she is most consciously the poet, and the interludes in *The Waves* and the celebration of time in *To the Lighthouse* suffer from the usual faults of prose-poetry; they appear overwritten and pretentious and, in my view, can stand very little close examination. And to put character in juxtaposition with descriptions of the sea or of the ravages of time is not necessarily to integrate them. The unity and significance are factitious, imposed from without. These are much more satisfactorily realized when, at the end of *To the Light-*

house, Lily Briscoe suddenly completes the painting she
has been working on for years. Almost by chance, her vision, which among other things is her vision of Mrs. Ramsay and everything that has happened in the Ramsays'
house, is set down. For Virginia Woolf art alone can impose
order on the flux of lives lived in time; art is her substitute for religion, and the artist's act of creation an equivalent of the mystic's intuition.

It is not quite accurate to speak of the stream of consciousness in relation to Virginia Woolf's rendering of
character, at any rate as we know it in Dorothy Richardson's and Joyce's fiction. What she uses is a very deft adaptation of it, which suggests rather than ever quite follows
it. The nature of her characters alone made the use of the
full stream of consciousness impossible. Her characters
are highly articulate and quite abnormally self-aware,
watching their thoughts and feelings the whole time as
Leopold and Marion Bloom never do. Indeed, the movement of the mind as Virginia Woolf describes it is closely
akin to the nature of the self as seen by Peter Walsh in
Mrs. Dalloway:

> For this is the truth about our soul, he thought, or self,
> who fish-like inhabits deep seas and plies between obscurities
> threading her way between the boles of giant weeds over sun-
> flickered spaces and on and on into gloom, cold, deep, in-
> scrutable; suddenly she shoots to the surface and sports on
> the wind-wrinkled waves; that is, has a positive need to
> brush, scrape, kindle herself, gossiping. What did the Gov-
> ernment mean—Richard Dalloway would know—to do about
> India?

There is in her work a rendering, vivid almost to the point
of the hallucinatory, of the scene and bustle of everyday
living refracted through the consciousness of the character, together with the very strong sense, below it, of a
mind engaged in perpetual soliloquy, obsessed with a question that is always the same. We deduce the continuous

existence of the soliloquy from the moments when suddenly it breaks through the surface of everyday living; indeed, in *The Waves* soliloquy breaks clean through altogether, and we are presented with characters, taken up at selected points in their lives, whose sole end is to soliloquize; the actions they perform in everyday life have to be inferred from their soliloquies.

Virginia Woolf is a novelist of very narrow limits. It is absurd to say she could not create character; her characters are thoroughly convincing. But the range of those she creates is very small. They belong not only to a certain class, the upper-middle-class intelligentsia, but also to a certain temperament. They tend to think and feel alike, to be the aesthetes of one set of sensations; they think and feel and express their thoughts and feelings, in fact, exactly as Virginia Woolf herself does in such nonfiction works as *Mr. Bennett and Mrs. Brown* and *A Room of One's Own*. They are distinguished by a discriminating intelligence and an acute self-consciousness which weave a close sieve through which the greater part of the common experiences of life will not pass.

At present, the reaction against her work is probably at its greatest, and I must admit to sharing in it. Much of her fiction seems to me marred by portentousness, and I cannot escape the feeling that from time to time the exercise of sensibility has become an end in itself. Nor do the moments of revelation and illumination always seem illuminative in any very real sense, but rather a succession of short, sharp female gasps of ecstasy; an impression intensified by Mrs. Woolf's use of the semicolon where the comma is ordinarily enough. All the same, it is difficult not to believe that the future will see her as an indubitable minor master in the novel, who expressed with lyrical intensity her apprehension of the beauty and terror of life.

James Joyce, whose talents were so much greater, will be regarded as much more than this. It is the very magnitude of his talents and ambitions that makes him so difficult to assess now. We are altogether too near to him. For my own part, to limit the discussion to *Ulysses,* after repeated readings I am still unable to see the novel as a whole. Whether it is a whole or a magnificent ruin I do not yet know, but it seems important to note that the more arduous one's attempts to come to a decision the greater the novel appears. The difficulty lies in its complexity. It is a bewildering network of associations and cross references, or rather, it consists of layer upon layer of such networks, and the problem is to decide which of the layers are truly significant and which merely pedantic elaborations, for it has, I think, to be admitted that among other things Joyce was a pedant on the most formidable scale, with a quite obsessive sense of relationships and correspondences. The problem has not been made the easier for the layman by the vast literature that now accretes round Joyce's work. Twelve years after his death one has already to talk about the layman where Joyce is concerned, for the compiling of works of exegesis of *Ulysses* and *Finnegans Wake* has become a major academic industry, especially in the United States. I write on Joyce as a layman.

The first thing that needs stressing, it seems to me, is that, whatever else he is not, Joyce is a very great comic writer, a comic writer of the quality of Rabelais and Sterne. In my view this is the most useful point of departure from which to approach him. In *Ulysses* Joyce, more than Fielding ever did, is writing the comic epic, and the epic basis is even more essential to him than it was to Fielding. It was essential, in the beginning, because it provided him with a structure for his novel. It does something else, too, though how far successfully is still a question.

The action of *Ulysses* covers one specific day—rather less than the whole twenty-four hours—in Dublin in 1904. The Ulysses of the title is the Jewish advertisement space salesman Leopold Bloom; the Telemachus is Stephen Dedalus, a young poet whom we may take as Joyce himself as a young man—he has already appeared as the central character of Joyce's autobiographical novel *A Portrait of the Artist as a Young Man* (1916); Penelope is Bloom's wife, Marion. Nothing extraordinary happens. Bloom and Dedalus wander about the city, their paths cross, towards the end of the novel they come together in a brothel, and Bloom takes Dedalus home with him. During the course of the day Bloom goes to the butcher's to buy a kidney for breakfast, visits a newspaper office, calls in at the National Library, attends a funeral, has an erotic daydream about a young girl, drops in at the students' common room of a maternity hospital. During the day, too, his wife is unfaithful to him. Dedalus quarrels with the young men he lives with, teaches in a school, propounds his theory of *Hamlet* at the National Library, goes to the brothel, and is rescued by Bloom.

Each episode in the novel is made to correspond with an episode in the *Odyssey,* and one can see the virtue of this for Joyce, however strained the parallels may sometimes appear. The separate episodes in Homer's story were, so to speak, the coordinates by which Joyce could plot his own vision of life during one Dublin day. Incidentally, he produced a parody of Homer which could also be taken as a criticism of twentieth-century life, a representation of what the heroic shrinks to in an age of *muflisme.* But by basing his story in Homer, Joyce does something more than that. He expresses the universal in the particular; Bloom, Dedalus, and Marion Bloom become modern versions of archetypal figures, and we are to feel the presence of the archetypes behind them.

That at least is the theory. Whether it works I am not sure. *Ulysses* does not seem to me to throw light on Homer's epic, and I doubt if, apart from the matter of structure, the *Odyssey* notably illuminates Joyce's novel.

I think it is more fruitful to regard the parallel with Homer as a means towards a severely practical purpose rather than as an end. And in a way Joyce himself seems to have felt this. For Dedalus is not only Telemachus, he is Hamlet, or at any rate an aspect of Hamlet, and it is out of this that the organic structure of the novel arises. Dedalus, having spurned his mother and renounced his father, is in search of a father figure, a spiritual father; Bloom, whose only son has died in infancy, is looking for a son; and in a shadowy way Dedalus and Bloom find what they want in each other.

But all this merely touches the fringe of *Ulysses.* What Joyce is out to show is nothing less than all life, all history, contained in a single day in Dublin in 1904. He is writing Virginia Woolf's *Between the Acts* on a gargantuan scale, though *Ulysses* preceded that novel by almost twenty years. It attempts to encompass the whole of life; it takes in birth and death; and whatever it deals with is done in terms of astonishing virtuosity. When, for instance, Bloom is with the medical students at the maternity hospital, the episode is related in a series of parodies of the English language from its earliest forms to its manifestations in modern newspaper journalism. This is one of the most wonderful feats of literary virtuosity ever performed, and it is also a wonderful piece of comic writing. But it is not gratuitous virtuosity. The students are waiting for a child to be born, and the parodies of the successive stages in the development of language are Joyce's way of mirroring the development of the embryo in the womb. "Ontogenesis repeats phylogenesis." But even that does not represent the whole of Joyce's intention, which is to give yet another instance of how a single event contains all the events of its kind, how all history is recapitulated in the happenings of one day.

There is no real analogy to *Ulysses,* though a rough comparison would be with a much-scored palimpsest, or one of those archeological sites that reveal, the deeper the excavators dig, layer after layer of successive civilizations. Presumably, the day will come when the scholiasts have laid bare all the possible meanings, references, parallels, correspondences so artfully embedded in the text. Will interest in the novel then be exhausted? If it is, *Ulysses* will have been proved a gigantic stillbirth. But it may be that the real fructifying interest in the novel will begin to operate only after the scholiasts have finished their work. In any case, it is exceedingly unlikely that they would ever have begun it but for *Ulysses'* obvious and immediate virtures as a novel. Beside these, its mythological and cryptographic aspects seem to me of secondary interest, important only for the light they throw on the work as a novel.

Ulysses must be the most thoroughly documented novel in the language. Where the background of Dublin is concerned, it would be possible almost to use it as a guide-book to the city; no place in fiction has ever been re-created in such detail, and it is re-created in the detail of one particular day in history. But the re-creation is not that of a museum piece. Part of Joyce's triumph is the intensely living quality he gives to his Dublin; it is like an element in which the characters live. Indeed, it pervades them, flows through them, all the time, for it is through them, as they walk its streets and are aware of its impinging on the periphery of their consciousnesses, that we principally know it. *Ulysses* is, and had to be for Joyce's purposes, an intensely local novel.

The three main characters we know almost wholly from the inside, but Joyce's way of rendering their inner lives differs with each. The characters in Virginia Woolf's novels tend to think and experience the moment as Virginia Woolf herself does; they share her sensibility and her mode of apprehension. But it is impossible from *Ulysses* to say what Joyce's sensibility is like or what his mode of apprehension is. Stephen Dedalus says, in *A Portrait of the Artist*:

> The artist, like the God of creation, remains within or behind or beyond or above his handiwork, invisible, refined out of existence, indifferent, paring his finger-nails.

Joyce himself is refined out of existence in *Ulysses*; as much as Flaubert, his chief literary ancestor, he is outside his creation—or almost. Bloom, Marion, and Dedalus think, feel, and speak in utterly different ways; Joyce perfects a separate style for each of them, as contrasted as the characters.

Joyce uses the stream-of-consciousness method most thoroughly in his treatment of Marion Bloom. She enters the novel as a character in her own right only at the end; her thoughts, poured out pell-mell, form its tremendous climax. She is in bed at night, relaxed, drowsy after love, isolated from any contact with the world outside, so that the flow of her thoughts, her erotic reverie, her memories of love, and her speculations about Bloom and Dedalus, can proceed in spate, unchecked, uninhibited, unpunctuated—and here it may be remarked that Dorothy Richardson said that "fe.ninine prose . . . should properly be unpunctuated, moving from point to point without formal obstructions." But the justification of a method is in what it produces, and in his rendering of Marion Bloom Joyce creates an image of femaleness that can be compared only with Chaucer's Wife of Bath. Marion Bloom has the fullness, the rankness, the sensuality, the wholehearted acceptance of life of a Magna Mater, an earth goddess.

With Bloom, Joyce suggests rather than fully records the stream of consciousness. As Bloom walks through Dublin, stray thoughts flicker through his mind like fishes, thoughts suggested by whatever business he is about, by things that catch his eye in the streets, by smells that assail his nostrils;

and all the time, coming sometimes to consciousness through association with these sense impressions, below the surface froth of thought are certain permanent preoccupations: the void in his life because of his child's death, his father's suicide, his humiliation as a cuckold, his feeling of being, as a Jew, an outsider. Again the justification of the method is in the results. We know Bloom better than any other character in modern fiction. He is *l'homme moyen sensuel* and also the "little man," vulgar, unfailingly curious, half educated, nursing his "dirty little secret" of sex, essentially unheroic, indeed the antihero; but he is also kind, and in his naivety there is even a sort of innocence. He is a figure of great pathos, and comic at the same time. He seems to me to be, as he was meant to be, the most universal character in modern fiction, a creation of Shakespearean amplitude comparable in achievement with Falstaff.

I am less sure of Joyce's Hamlet, Stephen Dedalus. In my view he is much more a special case; he is a projection of the author himself as a young man, arrogant, tortured by a vast ambition not yet realized, struck with remorse for his behavior towards his mother, the repudiator of his family, his religion, and his country. "Oh, an impossible person," is Buck Mulligan's comment on him in the first pages of the novel; and so he is, drawn with unsparing detachment. One can't say he is not successfully rendered, but simply because he is the representation of a special case he lacks the universality of Bloom and his wife, and his problems remain by comparison local and personal.

For his rendering of Stephen Joyce uses a device which cannot quite be called the stream-of-consciousness technique. Stephen's mode of thought is absolutely distinct from Bloom's; when we are taken into his mind we are aware of a much greater degree of awareness, control, and purpose. Stephen thinks in highly intellectual terms, in learned, latinate words, the language of the schoolmen;

but "thinks" is not quite the right word; the language Joyce puts into his mind is much more a notation of the way in which Stephen thinks than an attempt literally to transcribe his thoughts.

One of the astonishing qualities of *Ulysses* is the variety of ways in which Joyce renders his characters and his scene. One instance of this is the series of parodies of the growth of the language in the episode of the lying-in hospital. Another is the episode of Gerty MacDowell, the young girl whose display of exhibitionism moves Bloom to self-abuse; her fantasy of love is presented not directly, in any form of stream of consciousness, but as pastiche of cheap romantic fiction, with whose heroines she identifies herself. Another is the Nighttown episode, which is cast in the form of an Expressionist play, reasonably, since here Joyce is dealing with his characters in a state of drunkenness; their conscious control of their minds has relaxed so that the fantasia of the unconscious is released and comes to the surface.

This extreme variety of methods is one reason for the difficulty of seeing *Ulysses* as a whole, but it makes for continuous interest in the work. Among other things, it gives to *Ulysses* beyond any other novel the quality Flaubert sought when he wrote of his desire "to give verse-rhythm to prose, yet to leave it prose and very much prose, and to write about ordinary life as histories and epics are written." Joyce is Flaubert's true successor, both in this and in the related ambition to make language new. As a poet in the usual sense, that is, when writing in verse, Joyce is surprisingly banal and sentimental, a minor member of the school of the nineties and the Celtic Twilight. But in his prose he is a very great poet who renders superbly the very feel and texture of specific scenes and atmospheres, as for example, at the very beginning of the novel, the evocation of early morning. And every sentence of description in the novel is as right in its order of words, as inevitable, as a line of classical poetry. It is in these sentences, so wonderfully modulated and musical, sentences that seem almost to *imitate* what is being described, that we feel ourselves in Joyce's mind. We never identify ourselves with his characters; they exist in their own profoundly felt world, a world of great density and solidity, that of Dublin on that June day of 1904. It is this world that gives *Ulysses* its real unity, over and above the factitious one of the bases in Homer, for it links organically through the shared experiences of the scene character with character.

Joyce was the most highly conscious artist in the novel of our time, and if we were to take him as the only kind of artist we should have to deny altogether the title of D. H. Lawrence. Lawrence exists at the opposite pole of the creative impulse to Joyce; he is a great romantic poet who used the form of the novel, short stories, verse, travel books, and essays to express his criticism of modern civilization and his vision of the good life. Of his contemporaries, Joyce, it seems to me, is the only writer who is his peer, though they are so removed from each other that comparison is impossible.

A common view of Lawrence is that he was a great novelist *manqué* who, after *Sons and Lovers,* fell deeper and deeper into hysteria and the preaching of a bastard mysticism. *Sons and Lovers* is a great novel, but not in my opinion his greatest; and all his later work is implicit in his first three novels and his first books of poems. He was against his age; he loathed it, and if he had lived beyond his forty-fourth year no doubt his loathing would have increased.

Lawrence's was a very English genius, partly because he had been brought up in the tradition of religious dissent, as a nonconformist. He was fully conscious of the strength of the nonconformist tradition within him—see his essay "Hymns in a Man's Life"—and in *The Plumed Serpent* he was to write his own hymns. At his shrillest, he often reminds one of a nonconformist local preacher. Then, he came from the working class, and almost inevitably he was class conscious. It is the rancor of his class consciousness—in his novels working men and aristocrats may be praised, but never the bourgeoisie—which is responsible for so much of the unpleasant side of his genius, the hectoring, jeering, bullying note he drops into when imagination flags. We are told he confuted Aldous Huxley's arguments for Darwinism by pressing his two hands on his solar plexus and saying, "I don't feel it *here*." All nonconformity begins with "I don't feel it *here*," and this is no criticism of nonconformity. But the nonconformist attitude, combined with a rancorous class feeling, does give rise to a nagging, intolerable tone of moral superiority which makes him appear at times a latter-day Carlyle.

More important is the clash within him symbolized by the conflict between his parents. His father was a miner, practically illiterate, nonintellectual, often drunk, but possessed of an extraordinarily vivid apprehension of natural life and living; his mother was of a somewhat higher social class, spiritual, intellectual, refined, high-minded, "cut out," as he was to write towards the end of his life, "to play a superior role in the god-damned bourgeoisie." The meeting between them is most beautifully described in the first chapter of *Sons and Lovers*:

> . . . the dusky, golden softness of this man's sensuous flame of life, that flowed off his flesh like the flame from a candle, not baffled and gripped into incandescence by thought and spirit as her life was, seemed to her something wonderful, beyond her.

But their marriage was unhappy, and something was killed in the father. The children were caught up in the clash, and in *Sons and Lovers*, try to be fair as he may, Lawrence is on his mother's side.

In form, *Sons and Lovers* is the conventional autobiographical novel of its date—1913. The obvious comparison is with Bennett's *Clayhanger*. *Clayhanger* is a fine novel, but there can be no question which of the two books has the greater impact. Bennett is detached; he contemplates his characters from a height; he records a completed action. Lawrence is much closer to his characters, and we are brought into immediate, intimate relation with them through the sheer urgency of his writing; the words seem hot and quivering on the page. It is not an experimental novel, and indeed Lawrence never used any techniques like that of stream of consciousness, but he takes us right inside his characters; we apprehend them instantaneously through the force of his intuition. He captures, it seems, the moment of life itself, both in men and women and in the physical world of nature. There is a delighted, immediate, nonintellectual response to everything alive. It was precisely this quality that distinguished Lawrence's father. Unlike him, Lawrence was never a miner, but he had what one feels is essentially a miner's response to the world of nature; it is as though he has emerged daily from the darkness of the pit and daily seen the world newborn. His novels are full of this delighted, naive, lyrical vision, *Lady Chatterley's Lover* as much as *Sons and Lovers*.

But after *Sons and Lovers* the vision deepens and extends, though the first indication of that deeper vision is apparent even in his first novel, *The White Peacock* (1911). On the face of it, Lawrence in that novel, which is the work of a brilliantly clever young man steeped in George Eliot and Meredith, circumvents the problem of his father by practically omitting him. Lawrence's spokesman, the narrator, Cyril, is a young man of middle-class family, and the father is scarcely present at all; he dies halfway through the book, a bad lot who has deserted his wife and children. Even so, it was not so easy for Lawrence to kill his father, for before the end of the novel Cyril is standing almost in the relation of a son to Annable, the gamekeeper, "a man of one idea—that all civilization was the painted fungus of rottenness. He hated any sign of culture." Annable has been a clergyman married to a peer's daughter who went "souly" on him. And the white peacock of the title, fouling the tombstones in the abandoned churchyard, is, for Annable, "the very soul of a lady . . . a woman to the end, I tell you, all vanity and screech and defilement"; in other words, the agent of destruction, as she was to remain for Lawrence for many years. In *The White Peacock* Annable has been defeated by the highborn lady; nearly twenty years later he was to get his own back on her, as Mellors, the gamekeeper of *Lady Chatterley's Lover,* which is, incidentally, a far better novel than it is normally given credit for being. The situation—the destruction of the instinctive man by the spiritual woman —is fundamental to Lawrence, and Annable's peeress-wife becomes Miriam in *Sons and Lovers,* Hermione Roddice in *Women in Love,* and Aaron's wife in *Aaron's Rod.*

Annable is, of course, a highly sophisticated version of Lawrence's father, a Morel of *Sons and Lovers* who has become articulate. Lawrence was anti-intellectual, but if he was to communicate his vision at all he had to intellectualize his anti-intellectuality. For it *was* a vision. He expressed it negatively in his essay on Poe in *Studies in Classic North American Literature*: "These terribly conscious birds, like Poe and his Ligeia, deny the very life that is in them; they want to turn it all into talk, into knowing. And so life, which will *not* be known, leaves them." Life, which will *not* be known: the concept goes to the heart of Lawrence. L. H. Myers, one of the best English novelists writing between the wars, makes his mystic Wentworth, in *Strange Glory,* describe the mystical experience in these words: "There is no illusory sense of understanding—only the profound realization that Mystery *is.*" For Lawrence too the great fact of existence was that mystery *is.* The mystery was not to be apprehended or explained in terms of reason and logic—that was the way to kill it. It could be experienced only by direct intuition, transmitted only by touch. The value of people, for Lawrence, consisted in how far mystery resided in them, how far they were conscious of mystery. And since the analyzing, scientific intellect killed the mystery, it obviously flourished most powerfully where the analyzing scientific intellect was least powerful, on the instinctual level, in sexual relationships, in the experience of death, in the impulsive life of animals and nature.

The vision explains Lawrence's peculiar methods of character creation. He was a man of great intellectual capacity, but he also had to an extraordinary degree the faculty Jung calls primitive thinking and feeling. "The ancients," Jung has said, "had, if one may so express it, an almost exclusively biological appreciation of their fellow men"; it is much the same sort of appreciation Lawrence was continually seeking. This primitivism enabled him to explore, as no one else has done in modern literature, what are still relatively "unknown modes of being," though they have to some extent been charted scientifically and are the basis of much in religion.

To express these unknown—better, unconscious—modes of being in fiction Lawrence had to dispense with character as it is generally conceived. Any method of character creation is a convention. The majority of novelists tend to draw characters from the outside, almost as though describing the behavior of actors on a stage; even Henry James, with all his minute analysis and the analysis he puts into his characters' minds, is in a sense only translating in the fullest possible terms what an infinitely subtle actor, an ideal actor, might make us feel about the figure represented on the stage. We deduce emotion from gesture. But Lawrence's problem was to express emotions, feelings, as they exist far beneath the surface of gesture. He cannot do without gesture altogether, of course, but a simple instance of his method may be seen in his description of the pocket picking in *Aaron's Rod*:

> As he was going home, suddenly, just as he was passing the Bargello, he stopped. He stopped, and put his hand to his breast-pocket. His letter-case was gone. He had been robbed. It was as if lightning ran through him at that moment, as if a fluid electricity rushed down his limbs, through he sluice of his knees, and out of his feet, leaving him standing there almost unconscious. For a moment unconscious and superconscious he stood there. He had been robbed. They had put their hand to his breast and robbed him.

Lawrence could create character in the normal convention perfectly well when he wanted to, but after *Sons and Lovers* such characters, except for Hermione Roddice in *Women in Love,* tend to be minor. He was early attacked for his departure from the convention, and he defended himself at length—he was writing *The Rainbow* at the time—in a letter to Edward Garnett:

> I have a different attitude to my characters . . . I don't care so much what the woman feels. . . . That presumes an ego to feel with. I only care for what the woman *is*. . . . You mustn't look in my novel for the old stable ego of character. There is another ego, according to whose action the individual is unrecognizable, and passes through, as it were, allotropic states which it needs a deeper sense than any we've been used to exercise, to discover—states of the same single radically unchanged element. (Like as diamond and coal are the same pure single element of carbon. The ordinary novelist would trace the history of the diamond—but I say, "Diamond, what! This is carbon!" And my diamond might be coal or soot, and my theme is carbon.)

What interests him, then, in his characters is not so much the social man, though he is interested in him, as the seven eighths of the iceberg of personality submerged and never seen, the unconscious mind, to which he preaches something like passivity on the part of the conscious. This accounts for so much of the difficulty experienced when first reading Lawrence. His convention must be accepted, as the conventions of any artist must be, if he is to be read with pleasure and profit. It accounts, too, for mannerisms of style that are usually considered blemishes: a Lawrence character "dies," "swoons," is "fused into a hard bead," "lacerated," "made perfect," time and time again. He is, if you like, fumbling for words, words with which to describe the strictly indescribable.

Because he is describing character at the unconscious level, at the depths and in the darkness, it is often extraordinarily difficult to say what isolated passages of his novels, *The Rainbow,* for instance, or *Women in Love,* are about in detail. Thus two of his best critics, Stephen Potter and Horace Gregory, have produced entirely opposed accounts of the character of Ursula, in *The Rainbow.* The difficulty is, of course, that we know, or think we know, so much about the psychology of men and women; we make no such claims where animals are concerned, and so Lawrence often appears to be much more successful—at any rate acceptable—when he is re-creating the lives of birds, beasts, and flowers. But if there is anything to the findings of depth psychology, we must accept as legitimate the territory Lawrence chose for himself and expect future novelists to explore it further. Any such exploration must be through the symbol, since the unconscious, as unconscious, is by definition unknowable, or rather, is knowable only through the symbol. Lawrence is a master of the symbol in the psychological sense, as Jung has described it:

> In so far as a symbol is a living thing, it is the expression of a thing not to be characterized in any other or better way. The symbol is alive in so far as it is pregnant with meaning.

An example of Lawrence's use of the symbol is the scene in the final chapter of *The Rainbow,* in which Ursula encounters the horses on the common. Have the horses an

objective existence? Are they a projection of her unconscious? The passage cannot be reduced to any one prose
meaning; it is "the formulation of a relatively unknown
thing." Another example is the scene in *Women in Love*
in which Birkin throws stones into the pool to shatter the
image of the moon. Symbolism of this kind cannot be paraphrased; it can only be experienced. It is probably the
rarest kind of artistic creation, and it is everywhere in
Lawrence.

Lawrence's use of the symbol explains also his failures,
as for instance *The Plumed Serpent*, which is a brilliant
fabrication, as may be seen when the figure of the god
Quetzalcoatl is compared with the African carving described in *Women in Love* of "a woman sitting naked in
a strange posture, and looking tortured, her abdomen
stuck out," a true symbol for a way of life which can never
be completely apprehended.

But if Lawrence's characters are not always easy to explain, at least they always triumphantly *are*. Formally, his
novels are probably as defective as any written, which is
why he is at his best artistically in his short stories. All the
same, to get his full effect he needed length; and what
should be stressed is the intense and complex reality of
the world he describes, whether it is the changing life over
three generations in the Erewash Valley in *The Rainbow*,
a small town in the north midlands in *The Lost Girl*, a
mining village at the end of the 1914-18 war in *Aaron's
Rod*, the Australian scene in *Kangaroo*, or Mexico City in
The Plumed Serpent. Lawrence could reproduce the natural world with a Van Goghlike intensity, but he had
too an unfailing eye for what was significant in the social
worlds in which the actions of his novels are set. He was,
as one of his best critics, Father William Tiverton, has
said, "an astonishing diagnostician of life. His sensitive
nose could smell death a mile away." For ultimately—and
it is this as much as anything that marks him out from the

other novelists of his time—his attitude to life was sacra-mental, religious.

Joyce and Lawrence: in the history of the English novel they stand in curious and uneasy juxtaposition. We know what Lawrence thought of Joyce's work: he did not like it; and it is not probable that Joyce liked his. As artists they are eternal opposites. But in their opposed ways they took the English novel as far as it has yet gone, and none of their younger contemporaries, except Wyndham Lewis, in a way totally different from either, has come near catching up with them. They are still the advance guard.

INDEX